A Handbook for Women Mentors

A Handbook for Women Mentors

Transcending Barriers of Stereotype, Race, and Ethnicity

Carole A. Rayburn, Florence L. Denmark, Mary E. Reuder, and Asuncion Miteria Austria, Editors

Foreword by Bonnie R. Strickland, PhD, ABPP
Michele A. Paludi, Series Editor

 PRAEGER

AN IMPRINT OF ABC-CLIO, LLC
Santa Barbara, California • Denver, Colorado • Oxford, England

Library of Congress Cataloging-in-Publication Data
A handbook for women mentors : transcending barriers of stereotype, race, and ethnicity / Carole A. Rayburn . . . [et al.], editors ; foreword by Bonnie R. Strickland.
    p. cm.
  Includes bibliographical references and index.
  ISBN 978-0-313-36625-3 (print : alk. paper) — ISBN 978-0-313-36626-0 (ebook : alk. paper) 1. Mentoring. 2. Women—Counseling of.
I. Rayburn, Carole A.
  BF637.M45H36   2010
  158'.3082—dc22   2009044671

14 13 12 11 10   1 2 3 4 5

This book is also available on the World Wide Web as an eBook.
Visit www.abc-clio.com for details.

ABC-CLIO, LLC
130 Cremona Drive, P.O. Box 1911
Santa Barbara, California 93116-1911

This book is printed on acid-free paper ∞

Manufactured in the United States of America

We dedicate this handbook to our mentors and mentees. You enriched our lives and showed us the prize of work well done and achievements well earned. We thank you for your skills, talents, knowledge, wisdom, encouragement, enthusiasm, sensitivity, and caring and for sticking with challenging tasks to realize successful outcomes. We are all winners because of you.

Contents

Foreword, *Bonnie R. Strickland*   xi

Introduction, *Carole A. Rayburn, Florence L. Denmark,*
Mary E. Reuder, and Asuncion Miteria Austria   xiii

PART I: HISTORY OF WOMEN MENTORS

1. Women Mentors and Their Effect on Educational and
   Professional Career Development   3
   Florence L. Denmark and Maria D. Klara

PART II: WOMEN IN NONTRADITIONAL CAREERS, ACADEME, AND BUSINESS

2. Gender Issues in Academic Mentoring:
   Personal Experiences Set in a Theoretical Framework   23
   Judith Waters

3. Mentoring Women in Science, Technology, Engineering,
   and Mathematics Fields   43
   Bianca L. Bernstein, Ryan Jacobson, and Nancy Felipe Russo

4. Mentoring Undergraduate Women   65
   Joan C. Chrisler and Jennifer Gorman Rose

5. Promises and Pitfalls of Mentoring Women in Business and Academia   79
Michele Paludi, Jennifer Martin, Tina Stern, and Darlene C. DeFour

6. Service Learning as a Model for Mentoring Women   109
Arvilla Payne-Jackson, Kathleen Scott, Ajeenah Haynes, and Germon Miller

PART III: FOCUS ON WOMEN OF COLOR

7. Enhancing Capabilities of Women and Ethnic Minorities   129
Asuncion Miteria Austria and A. Marie M. Austria

8. Mentoring Asian American Women   149
Reiko Homma-True

9. *Madrinas, Comadres,* and *Luminarias:* Latina Mentors in Action   161
Lillian Comas-Diaz

10. Women of Color as Mentors   173
Melba J. T. Vasquez and Jessica Henderson Daniel

PART IV: MENTORING FOR ALL WOMEN

11. A Mentor—A Friend in Deed   189
Mary E. Reuder

12. Mentoring Needs of EVERYWOMAN: The Accidental Mentor and Beyond   197
Carole A. Rayburn

13. Perspectives from a Nontraditional Mentor   223
Helen D. Pratt

14. Beyond Mentoring: Opening Doors and Systems   233
Shari E. Miles-Cohen, Gwendolyn Puryear Keita, Gabriel H. J. Twose, and Susan J. Houston

PART V: MENTORING FROM THE PERSPECTIVE OF MENTAL HEALTH

15. The Road to Leadership Roles   251
Jean Lau Chin

16. A Social Psychological Approach to Mentoring 261
Janet Sigal and Katharine L. Loeb

PART VI: CONCLUSION

17. Conclusion 275
Carole A. Rayburn, Florence L. Denmark,
Mary E. Reuder, and Asuncion Miteria Austria

Index 279

About the Volume Editors and Series Editor 283

About the Contributors 287

Foreword

Mentoring has a long history but has been generally male oriented. Yet within the last few decades, we have witnessed an extraordinary upturn in the number of women pursuing higher education, engaging in the workplace, entering new careers, and taking on nontraditional roles. This suggests a need for a new and more affirming sensitivity to the interests of women in regard to mentoring. These chapters meet this need by providing new understandings of the process of mentoring as it relates specifically to women.

This book is written by women who bring insights about both the theoretical and practical, hands-on aspects of mentoring. They delve into history and note the changing social scene with a special concern for the culture the mentors and their mentees occupy. Their writings cover a spectrum of ethnocultural backgrounds and experiences that are usually not considered. Although each mentoring event is unique, they note the importance of mentors being aware of the differing backgrounds and experiences of their mentees and vice versa. They write about the ways stereotypes and perceptions, or misperceptions, influence the mentor–mentee relationship.

The authors cover the various forms of mentoring, ranging from the traditional one-on-one process to peer to community situations. A particular focus of some of the chapters is proposing new models of mentoring, including a feminist approach that is relational, supportive, and interactive in contrast to a usual linear, hierarchical model.

The chapters are innovative and comprehensive, covering all aspects of mentoring for women. Some of the information will be well known to some. But, no matter how well informed, the reader will, in all likelihood, find new understandings and insights about the role of mentoring for women.

Bonnie R. Strickland

Introduction

Mentoring is the helping hand of an expert in some enterprise, usually one who has had experience in some field or activity for quite some time, offered to a less knowledgeable or experienced individual. The many functions of a mentor include being a person who guides, teaches, coaches, advises, sponsors, counsels, challenges, accepts, confirms, serves as a role model for, protects, and exposes a protégé or mentee to other helpful individuals, often also enabling her to be part of a network and to navigate the system of academe, career, job, or any other endeavor. The contributors to this book have all been fortunate enough to have had mentors at one time in their lives, and they have, in turn, provided mentoring to others to help them along their paths in life. Mentoring has held a very vital and viable place in their lives, professions, and careers.

In the past, women were able to find only men mentors, because women available as role models and mentors were scarce. The few who were available were usually so overloaded with fulfilling service tasks that they had little time or energy to also serve in mentoring relationships. Even more rare were women mentors of color and of diverse cultures. Many barriers of stereotype, gender, race, and ethnicity had to be overcome to have the women mentors that now serve in various departments in academe, in professions, in job markets, and in other places of interest to the world of women. The goal of maximal opportunity for good mentoring relationships is to have the broadest availability of women mentors for the myriad needs of protégés and mentees who want, need, and seek them. This handbook will aid mentors and mentees in planning programs for their progress, analyzing themselves and their needs, projecting ahead for their most important goals and achievements, and living as successful, self-actualized, fulfilled, and contented lives as possible. The contributors have shared their personal experiences of mentoring relationships, providing a road map that serves more as a treasure map to find the prized gold of life, profession, and career fulfillment more easily and readily. We, the co-editors, are grateful to Michele A. Paludi, Women's Psychology Series Editor, for including this handbook in her Praeger series.

In "Women Mentors and Their Effect on Educational and Professional Career Development," Florence Denmark and Maria Klara give a history of mentoring (from Greek mythology to the present day) and of women mentors from roles as wise guides or sages to teachers, sponsors, guides, counselors, and role models. They discuss the needs for and the scarcity of women and diverse women to serve as role models and mentors, the functions of women mentors (sponsorship, exposure and visibility, coaching, challenging assignments, protecting, role modeling, acceptance and confirmation, counseling, and friendship mutuality). Denmark and Klara examine the importance of networking, analyzing good versus bad potential mentoring relationships, gender considerations, and they offer personal reflections on their own mentoring and mentors.

Reflecting upon women in nontraditional careers and in academic and business settings, Judith Waters, in "Gender Issues in Academic Mentoring: Personal Experiences Set in a Theoretical Framework," explores the benefits of good mentoring and the pitfalls of destructive mentoring relationships. Some of the very useful information in her chapter pertains to tailoring mentoring to meet students' needs, overcoming gender hurdles such as attitudes toward authority figures, finding a good mentor, and mentoring children and returning and special needs students.

Bianca L. Bernstein, Ryan Jacobson, and Nancy Felipe Russo, in "Mentoring Women in Science, Technology, Engineering, and Mathematics Fields," write about the lag of women at the graduate level in computer sciences and engineering. This, they hold, could be much improved by skilled and effective women mentors becoming a powerful force to change the culture and climate of their institutions and maybe even their disciplines. High value is placed on a multifaceted, context-based perspective in academic mentoring, along with feminist mentoring models of shared power, collaboration, relational sharing, and commitment to diversity.

Joan Chrisler and Jennifer Gorman Rose, in "Mentoring Undergraduate Women," write of mentor strategies for opening doors and minds. Without undergraduate mentoring, students may not be accepted to graduate programs. Those undergraduates who do come to graduate schools experience more success in their programs, aim higher to accomplish their goals, and are more satisfied with graduate school. Students often need to overcome a poor self-image (feeling unworthy) and being overly shy, modest, fearful, and perfectionistic (all-or-none thinking).

In "Promises and Pitfalls of Mentoring Women in Business and Academia," Michele Paludi, Jennifer Martin, Tina Stern, and Darlene DeFour stress that women mentors need to transform patriarchal practices, penetrate the old boys' network that has prevented women from participating in informal networks necessary for career advancement, and widen their power base. They discuss counseling for returning students, life–work integration (home/education/career), intersectionality in women of color mentoring (identity, power, control issues), mentoring as feminist praxis (promoting less favorable women and women of color), womentoring (sharing of power and competence), and peer and Web-based mentoring.

In "Service Learning as a Model for Mentoring Women," Arvilla Payne-Jackson, Kathleen Scott, Ajeenah Haynes, and Germon Miller look at mentoring women through the perspective of special projects: Youth Summit and Reaching Out to Others Together. In their "learning to do for others" mentoring model, students are drawn out to venture in the lesser known, unfamiliar community outside Howard University (Washington, DC) and are inculcated into the harsher daily problems faced by those outside academe. Thus, they mentor the students by preparing them for challenges in working in the new environment and for the world beyond college.

Asuncion Miteria Austria and A. Marie M. Austria (a mother–daughter collaboration, as well as a mother professionally mentoring her daughter), in "Enhancing Capabilities of Women and Ethnic Minorities," discuss the underrepresentation of ethnic minority women, especially in the field of psychology at the doctoral level. For not only women but even more for ethnic minority women, there are barriers to advancement in the forms of tokenism, professional isolation, criticism and devaluation of research projects, and decreased networking and collaborative opportunities. Discussing Asian American, Latina American, and African American students and the role that cultural differences can play in mentoring and advancement, they point out the difficulty in initiating the mentoring relationship and the benefits of positive psychology in students' building better self-esteem and seeing the worth of their personal values.

Reiko Homma-True, in "Mentoring Asian American Women," writes of the wide diversity of ethnicity and culture among Asian Americans. Subjected to grave stereotyping and discrimination, from images of China doll, Madame Butterfly, and Suzy Wong—sex objects to be toyed with and not taken seriously—to images of being aggressive or too assertive, cunning and devious "dragon ladies," Asian American women have been quite maligned. Even their cultural image of efficient, loyal, hardworking, subservient handmaidens to their men is debilitating to their self-actualization and accomplishments. Asian American women benefit from multiple mentors of both ethnic majority and minority identity and from having role models—particularly "women warriors" (Asian American leaders well recognized in their fields)—advise them on speaking out and being assertive in a positive fashion.

Using parables to explain the plight of two Latinas who were "psychological twins," Lillian Comas-Diaz, in *"Madrinas, Comadres, and Luminarias:* Latina Mentors in Action,*"* demonstrates the vast advantages of Latinas having mentors in their college programs and careers. *Madrinas* (godmothers) can team with their godchild's mother to form a *comadre* (co-mother) to mentor the girl or woman. They emphasize also *luminarias*—historical, religious, spiritual, literary, or political figures—who also serve as role models. Effective mentoring includes mentors dealing with "soul wounds," acknowledging the effects of historical sexism, racism, and xenophobia on Latinas.

Melba Vasquez and Jessica Henderson Daniel, in "Women of Color as Mentors," write of race ethnicity being more important than gender concerning workplace training and advancement. While most women report being socially excluded from men's networks, women of color experience more discrimination than white women and both men of color and white men, and U.S.-born women of color receive more prejudice than non-U.S.-born women of color. Women of color superstars do not shatter the glass ceiling for all women of color. Subtle, "aversive" racism may put some at the "outer edge of the inner circle," with stereotype threat or the threat of knowing one is stereotyped often leading to anxiety and underperformance. Acknowledging painful, hurt feelings and events by transforming them into constructive anger and rage can lead to empowerment and refusing to be discounted. Women of color mentors seek to prevent or mediate sex and racial bias in the workplace; suggest paths to healthy personal and racial group identities; and help transform social justice commitments to theory, practice, and research.

Mary Reuder, in "A Mentor—A Friend in Deed," sees mentoring as looking out for, being sensitive to, and taking care of the needs of others. Appreciation of others' achievements and letting them know that their accomplishments are appreciated, whether by a friendly note or a phone call, is very important in mentoring. Performing acts of thoughtfulness in preparing others for leadership positions—such as giving them information about job opportunities, helping them prepare their vita, sharing skills and talents, reworking resumes, giving reassurance and building up mentees' confidence to meet challenges—is truly being a friend in action and being a caring friend when needed. A good mentor takes seriously, "need a mentor, be a mentor: Develop the habit of becoming a friend in deed." Rewards for a good mentor are the pleasure and delight in seeing the successful outcome of the mentee's achievements: Mentoring is fun!

In "Mentoring Needs of EVERYWOMAN: The Accidental Mentor and Beyond," Carole Rayburn describes her lifelong experiences with being mentored and having role models, from family members, friends, school peers, teachers, colleagues, and coworkers, all forming a chain of mentors who helped her through rough spots to achieve important goals. Diversity in mentorship is enriching, educative, and inspiring. Her recipe for good mentoring is having strong beliefs in the skills, talents, and potential of the mentee; a huge portion of enthusiasm and encouragement; and gentle stirring for the sensitive caring of the needs and goals of the mentee. Every woman, in all walks of life, needs a mentor to smooth the way. She discusses the importance of women mentors, diverse mentors, critical thinking versus one size fits all, and guidelines for women mentors and mentees.

Helen Pratt, in "Mentoring: Perspectives from a Nontraditional Mentor," describes a mentor who will work with anyone who is willing to meet the constraints of her schedule and other criteria to gain the benefit of her skills and talents. She recommends an inclusionary net in mentoring as an example for diversity. Pointing out the dearth of women mentors and women of color mentors, she counsels that mentors who work with women and people of color must be committed to developing a mentoring style that promotes confidence and trust, acknowledging the traumatic results that discrimination and bias have had on women and people of color. Mentors of color usually are more understanding of the personal, cultural, and ethnic needs of mentees of color. She discusses the crucial role that family and peers have in shaping mentoring style.

In "Beyond Mentoring: Opening Doors and Systems," Shari Miles-Cohen, Gwendolyn Puryer Keita, Gabriel Twose, and Susan J. Houston relate the commitment of the American Psychological Association's (APA) Committee on Women in Psychology (CWP) to work to ensure equal opportunity for women, including making changes in existing structures and policies to promote positive opportunities for women's achievements and advancements. The five categories of mentoring at structural and individual levels are discussed: macro-mentoring initiatives (creating overarching initiatives transcending extant systems, targeting structural barriers, addressing sexist recruitment and retention by employers, ruling out sexist language in publications, and ensuring diverse representation at the governance level of organizations); mentoring by community activities (with a nontraditional, nondyadic model for CWP serving as a sponsor, being involved in nominations processes, fellow status considerations, and leadership awards); resources of CWP and the APA Women's Program Office (providing women the needed authoritative information, moral support, and resources to self-mentor for individual empowerment); virtual mentoring activities (development of alternate delivery methods, such as Web-based resources); and the Leadership Institute for Women in Psychology (preparation, support, and empowerment of women psychologists to promote positive changes in organizational and institutional structures, in numbers of women, effectiveness of women, and increases in diversity of women in psychology as leaders.

In "The Road to Leadership Roles," Jean Lau Chin analyzes who is a leader, self-described versus ascribed leaders, what is leadership, modern views on leadership, and transformation/visionary/inspiring and motivating leadership. For the best mentoring of women and people of color and diversity, it is essential that the mentor become culturally literate and transculturally competent. Transformational leadership within a multicultural and feminist framework involves commitment to change and upholding basic values. It is vital that perceptions of diverse women be taken into account in mentoring women to be leaders and counseling them in how they can transcend barriers of gender, stereotype, race, and ethnicity.

Regarding mentoring from the perspective of mental health, Janet Sigal and Katharine Loeb, in "A Social Psychological Approach to Mentoring," proffer social psychology as a good model for defining the process of mentoring as the effect or influence of some people on the behavior of other people. They discuss the mentor's need to have communicator credibility and expertness, including honesty, truthfulness, trustworthiness, warmth, and caring. Leadership may be transactional (task centered, stressing critical guidance) or transformational (collaborative, stressing encouragement). They compare egoistic and altruistic mentoring as well as mentoring three types of faculty hires (early career, midcareer, and senior-level career individuals). Mentoring at the United Nations, with APA's nongovernmental organization team, is also analyzed.

It is our hope and desire that readers will benefit from the guidance, advice, coaching, teaching, challenging, and concern and caring of all of our contributors. For mentors, we desire that you experience personal pleasure, delight, and satisfaction in helping others; the stimulation of new and challenging ideas; and increased professional visibility. We wish for protégés and potential mentees the very best in seeking a good mentor and finding the most satisfactory, fulfilling, and sustaining path to your success.

Carole A. Rayburn, Florence L. Denmark
Mary E. Reuder, and
Asuncion Miteria Austria

Part I

History of Women Mentors

Chapter 1

Women Mentors and Their Effect on Educational and Professional Career Development

Florence L. Denmark and Maria D. Klara

The emphasis on this chapter is on the dynamics of mentoring students in psychology—specifically, the role of women mentors in the field, although women mentors are important in other disciplines as well. We have found that having a woman mentor can be a positive experience for women in higher education as well as a critical factor in women's professional career development. Getting mentored is important not only for women but for minority students and men as well. This chapter also includes research on mentoring as well as individual reports of positive and negative experiences of mentoring for women and the effect this had on their development and aspirations.

THE POLITICS OF MENTORING: PROFESSIONAL NETWORKS

Mentoring: what is it? The term itself dates back to ancient Greek mythology and is known as "a relationship between a younger adult and an older, more experienced adult [who] helps the younger individual learn to navigate the adult world" (Kram, 1988, p. 2). There are many definitions of mentoring, including an extreme classical view which sees mentor relationships as intense, emotional interactions between an older person and a younger person. This view stresses the part of the older persons as a wise guide or sage to the younger person. A more modern view of mentoring includes such labels as teacher, sponsor, guide, counselor, and role model, where one holds expertise in an area but the two engage in a more shared relationship (Gilbert, 1985).

Bogat and Redner (1985) offer the following principles that are crucial to the mentoring process: (a) The mentor provides opportunities for the protégé to observe and participate in her work by inviting the protégé to work with her and (b) teaches his protégé the politics of getting ahead in the organization. They also state that a mentor is usually a person of high organizational or specific career status who by mutual consent takes an active interest in the career development of another person. Therefore, a mentor is someone who, through personal experience, can impart knowledge, advice, and encouragement to someone who is beginning in her prospective field.

In the process of growing and learning, young and inexperienced persons, or even older persons who need to continue their learning and acquisition of new skills, will look to someone who is more experienced than themselves for guidance, nurturance, and training. People who act as mentors play an important role in the development of their protégés by helping them to develop themselves to their full potential.

Mentoring is an enriching experience that enhances the lives of both the mentor and the protégé. The mentor opens new doors for the protégé and teaches him all that she can, connects him to people in their field, and helps him to become more visible to their peers. The mentor also gains personal satisfaction as well as having a growing support group to whom she too can look for assistance when needed.

FUNCTIONS OF MENTORS

Inherent in the definition of a mentor are numerous ways in which a mentor can positively affect her protégé. Johnson and Huwe (2003) discuss these as nine career and psychosocial mentor functions: sponsorship; exposure and visibility; coaching; protection; challenging assignments; role modeling; acceptance and confirmation; counseling; and friendship/mutuality. These are broken into two main categories: benefits toward someone's career and benefits on a more personal level.

Sponsorship

One primary benefit of having a mentor can result from the mentor nominating the protégé for awards or recommending the protégé for certain assignments or publications. The mentor, having gone through many of these experiences herself, is more knowledgeable about the best way to navigate the field.

Exposure and Visibility

Another benefit of mentoring is that, presumably, the mentor has developed a network of connections and colleagues in the field who can be introduced to the protégé. This association can be greatly beneficial since the protégé already has a reference for his ability and work ethic. The mentor can draw attention to the protégé's accomplishments in college and therefore start a positive reputation for the protégé among more accomplished professionals.

Coaching

Mentors can also aid their mentees in decision making and determining the best options when choices arise. From determining what classes to take to what internship to accept to learning how to talk to other professors, the mentor can be invaluable in giving advice about how to proceed in many important circumstances.

Challenging Assignments

By proximity to their mentors, protégés are exposed to a greater variety and scope of assignments than they would be without the association with the mentor. The mentor can invite the protégé to work together on specific projects from research to publication. This increases the protégé's skill level and competence.

Acceptance and Confirmation

Beginning graduate school can be a difficult transition, one that can cause insecurity about one's abilities and skills. Having a mentor who instills confidence and provides support can be a powerful source of encouragement to continue and to succeed.

Counseling

Although counseling per se does not occur in the mentor relationship, what does occur frequently is advice, discussion, and the development of the protégé's goals. Through this communication, the protégé can exchange ideas and flesh out the visions for the future. In turn, the mentor can offer opinions about what would be the best way to proceed.

Friendship/Mutuality

With so much time being spent with each other, friendship and trust are likely to develop. This can be extremely rewarding for both parties, and it is one of the benefits that the mentor experiences from the relationship. Mutuality can be a very empowering force, for a graduate student to feel valued and trusted by an older colleague and vice versa.

MENTORING IN BUSINESS AND ACADEMIA

Some of the effects of mentoring have been explored in studies in business. Roche (1979) surveyed 4,000 executives about whether they had been mentored; 1,250 executives responded, but less than 1 percent of them were women. Two-thirds said that they had had mentors, and one-third said that they had had at least two mentors. Roche reported that those who had mentors earned more income at an earlier age, were better educated, and in general were more satisfied with their work.

Mentoring for groups of people within companies has been very successful in recent years. It is usually included as part of career development programs and uses specific guidelines that both mentors and protégés follow. One such program, the Merrill Lynch Management Readiness Program, has had excellent results. Gerstein (1985) reports that this program can develop employees with high potential, pass on the corporate patterns and culture, and increase company loyalty. Gerstein also reports that benefits accrue to the mentors as well as the protégés. Such benefits include job advancement, creating supportive systems, more accessibility to system resources, and greater overall personal satisfaction.

Neither of these studies presents any quantitative data. They report findings in a general and nonspecific manner, and neither breaks down its sample of executives or protégés into men and women. Because these studies were done in private industry, it is fairly safe to assume that the executives, at least, would be primarily men.

In a study carried out in the retailing industry (where women are found in greater numbers), Keele and DeLaMare-Schaefer (1984) surveyed and interviewed 65 women and 35 men and found that, regardless of whether a person has had a mentor, career benefits can come to them from serving as a mentor and building a work team. This work team suggests a support system whereby mentors can rely on others for help and support in their work, thus increasing efficiency and networking on the job.

MENTORING IN PSYCHOLOGY DEPARTMENTS

In academia, three studies of psychology doctoral students (Cronan-Hillix, Gensheimer, Cronan-Hillix, & Davidson, 1986; Kirchner, 1969; Mintz, Bartels, & Rideout, 1995) found that about half of students surveyed reported having a mentor. In a more recent study, Clark, Harden, and Johnson (2000) reported that 66 percent were mentored, indicating that there might be a rise of the number of psychology graduate students being mentored. There also seems to be a relationship between the size of the program and the number of students within the program who are mentored (Johnson & Huwe, 2003). For instance, graduates of PsyD programs were significantly less likely to be mentored than students in smaller and more traditionally research-focused PhD programs (Clark, Harden, & Johnson, 2000).

Some studies stress the importance of graduate students having a mentoring relationship with faculty. The faculty mentor can facilitate the student's success by performing certain tasks that help the student's transition and performance in the program. Bogat and Redner (1985) reported that faculty mentors (sex unspecified) may expedite the student's progress and development through graduate program requirements, instill confidence in the student, and promote the student's welfare as well as visibility within the department. This mentor also may help the student define career goals. In addition, it has been found that having been mentored highly correlated with success and satisfaction in academia (Sanders & Wong, 1985). Additionally, Kinnier, Metha, Buki, and Rawa (1994) discovered, after reviewing the obituaries of 161 psychologists, that being mentored was the fourth most common value detected in the themes.

Clearly, the active participation of a mentor must benefit the student in numerous ways. The benefits of having a mentor can be twofold. Mentors can assist students with early career development, form and establish their identity both in a personal and professional sense, and help them to network within the profession (Wright & Wright, 1987). This includes career objectives such as increased opportunities for research, higher salary once the student begins to work, and so on. Second, mentors can be a great source of personal strength and responsibility. They can help advance a protégé's sense of personal power and intrinsic rewards such as generativity, personal fulfillment, happiness and contentment in the work as well as substantiation that they are doing well (Levinson, 1978; Newby & Heide, 1992; Phillips-Jones, 1982; Wright & Wright, 1987).

Why does mentoring work? There are numerous reasons that make mentoring advantageous to both the mentor and mentee. The first is that mentoring serves as a mechanism for information exchange and knowledge acquisition (Mullen, 1994). With more years of experience, mentors can help mentees reap the benefits of their established network of connections, which includes a great deal of information. This also includes social networks where the mentee can go with the mentor and meet people personally. Entry into this social sphere also allows the mentee an opportunity to display talent and interests to this wider group directly (Allen, Eby, Poteet, Lentz, & Lima, 2004). A second hypothesized reason surrounds social learning theory (Bandura, 1977). Social learning describes the process by which people vicariously learn through those whom they are surrounded by or by the environment in which they find themselves. If a protégé is spending a substantial amount of time with a mentor, she will begin to learn the ins and outs in various situations (Allen et al., 2004). To test this hypothesis, Allen et al. (2004) conducted a meta-analysis and found that mentored individuals were more satisfied with their career, were more likely to believe that they would advance in their career, and were more likely to be committed to their career than nonmentored individuals. Additionally, they discovered that greater career mentoring related to greater compensation.

Mentoring has also been linked to the personal characteristics of the mentor, and literature has supported that these were very important to prospective protégés in choosing who would be an ideal mentor (Cronan-Hillix et al., 1986). It is possible for a mentor to have technical expertise without having the appropriate character traits; having one without the other will not necessarily lead to a successful mentoring relationship (Wilson & Johnson, 2001). Wilson and Johnson (2001) found that personality characteristics have been largely ignored in professional literature, although this is clearly not the case when a mentee chooses a mentor. Given that graduate students rate mutual support and comprehensive relationships that extend beyond graduate school as two of the most important factors in successful mentoring (Wilde & Schau, 1991), it is easy to see how personality variables coincide with the success of these factors. Bell (1998) identified balance, trust, generosity, passion, and courage as the characteristics of mentors that most often led to successful relationships. Wilson and Johnson (2001) postulate that integrity, courage, and care are three virtues that set the basis for a strong mentoring foundation.

Although the benefits of having a mentor are clear, it is unfortunately not the standard in psychology departments. Cronan-Hillix et al. (1986) discovered that only 53 percent of the 90 psychology doctoral students who were interviewed had a mentor, and, among clinical psychology graduate students, the numbers dropped to 43 percent. However, graduate students readily agree that mentoring is important, and they rate mutual support and comprehensiveness of relationship as two of the most critical factors in successful mentoring (Wilde & Schau, 1991).

A lack of adequate mentors for women in graduate school compounds the problems that they face while in graduate school and later on when seeking employment. Bogat and Redner (1985) cite several reasons why women in psychology are more likely to suffer from lack of mentoring benefits: Women receive a smaller share than do men of financial support such as institutional support and nonfederal aid, and mentors provide their students with opportunities for professional socialization. Because women are lacking in mentor relationships, they are also lacking in the benefits that result from these relationships, such as networking experiences, publications, and professional socialization. In addition, Solomon (1978) reported that in all disciplines women are less likely than men to receive financial support, which could include a student working with a faculty member on research. This in itself may reduce the opportunities for women to develop meaningful contacts with potential mentors. Another reason that there is a lack of mentors for women is because women are underrepresented on most faculties. Russo, Olmedo, Strapp, and Fulcher (1981) reported that women students are finding it difficult to secure a woman faculty mentor; therefore, women will not only face the problems of finding a mentor but finding a woman mentor as well.

Dohm and Cummings (2002) found that research mentoring is positively related to a woman in clinical psychology doing research and whether she also becomes a research mentor for others.

Lack of mentoring for women in graduate school can also have an effect on employment status. Women graduate students who have had a mentor have already begun to establish a professional networking system with their peers and members of the faculty. Without this networking system, one can imagine how much more difficult it could be to establish ties that would help one to get a decent job. Lack of mentoring means that there is a lack in professional visibility. Bogat and Redner (1985) also state that most information concerning potential jobs is obtained via networks, including ones that mentors have made available to the protégé. A communication network study reported by Denmark (1986) is relevant here.

CONCERNS ABOUT MENTORING

The literature points to some potential problems or unforeseen issues that are likely to arise within the context of a mentoring relationship. First, mentoring relationships many times are not smooth and consistent but rather transverse through many phases (Kram, 1988). Given that a mentoring relationship can be full of emotional give and take, there is potential for disappointment as well as for pride.

The quality of the mentoring received by the protégé depends on a few factors. Mentoring may not always be beneficial to the protégé, possibly because the mentor is too isolated from other colleagues, as Denmark (1986) points out. If the mentor is relatively isolated and not well connected, then this may not have a positive trickle-down effect on the protégé. Also, as Merriam (1983) reports, the protégé could become too attached to the mentor, or the protégé can be limited by having only one other person's perspective. It could prove beneficial to have multiple sources of influence instead of just one. However, most of the time the mentor–protégé relationship has positive outcomes for both parties, and in most cases it is a rewarding growth experience for both.

Additionally, there are a number of ethical concerns that must be addressed. Mentors have long been one manner in which ethical values have been corresponded to students. However, with the decline in the number of mentors in psychology programs and the corresponding lack of modeling, students perhaps are learning less about ethics and what to do in ambiguous situations (Folse, 1991). Although students have mandatory ethics classes, it is also helpful to hear another opinion from a mentor who might have encountered a similar situation. If a mentor is not available, then the student may lack guidance on a particularly critical point. Additionally, mentors must be competent, know the boundaries and nature of a mentoring relationship, and must give equal opportunities to all students (Johnson & Nelson, 1999).

THE INFLUENCE OF SEX ON THE MENTORING RELATIONSHIP

Women are just as likely as men to get mentored in psychology doctoral programs (Clark et al., 2000). However, although research indicates that women have the same access to mentors as do men, this may not be the case in other disciplines (Johnson & Huwe, 2003).

So far we have seen that mentors are helpful to women in academia and business, but do women need or benefit more soundly from having a woman mentor? Research on the possible benefits to women of having a woman as compared to a man mentor or role model is scarce and often contradictory. Women have been encouraged to seek out mentors who embody certain characteristics such as those who can balance career and personal life expectations and who embody feminist ideals of equity, reciprocity, and cooperation (Gilbert, 1985; Richey, Gabrill, & Blythe, 1988).

A study of PhD psychologists by Goldstein (1979) found that, while men and women published equally during their first four years following degree conferment, both men and women who have same-sex dissertation advisors published significantly more than did graduates who had advisors of the opposite sex. As pointed out by Goldstein, however, these results must be interpreted with caution, because no information is available that allows us to infer any causal relationship. While it may be the case that the higher rate of publication among the same-sex group is a result of the factors directly attributable to the mentor–protégé relationship, no information is present that indicates what those factors, if they exist, may be. Further, as suggested by Goldstein, it is equally possible that the results obtained were due to self-selection; in this case, that the more ambitious or intelligent graduate students seek out, for whatever reason, same-sex mentors. If this is the case, the question of why more successful students seek out mentors of same sex needs to be answered.

Although the results of Goldstein's study indicate that there may be some valid basis for concluding that women who have had women advisors are subsequently more professionally successful than their peers who chose men advisors, as least during the first few years of graduation, the generalizability of the findings are limited by a number of factors. First, the research sample consisted solely of recipients of doctoral degrees in psychology from three New York City institutions. Second, scholars were sampled between 1965 and 1973. Clearly, a study of individuals in other disciplines from a broader range of geographic areas and covering different time periods would greatly enhance the generalizability of the results.

In direct contrast to the findings of Goldstein (1979) are the results of a more recent study of PhD recipients in psychology and biology (author unknown), which found that, for four years following degree conferment in 1980 or 1981, there were no statistically significant differences in the frequency of publication between graduate students who had dissertation advisors of the same sex and those who had advisors of the opposite sex. These results were true for both psychologists and biologists included in the study. Similarly, this study found neither sex of the degree recipient nor sex of the faculty advisor to be significantly related in the number of publications produced. Also, it is interesting to note that scholars in this study were sampled from colleges and universities covering a much larger geographical area (29 states and Canada for biologists, 28 states and Canada for the psychologists), thus lending support to the argument that the results of the Goldstein study may be somewhat out of date.

It is important to note that, in both of these studies, the relationship examined was that between graduate student and dissertation advisor, and information was obtained solely from a review of dissertation abstracts. Therefore, no information is available about whether the advisor also served as a mentor or role model to the student while in graduate school or the extent to which the student, now a professional, perceived herself as having been influenced professionally by the advisor. Given the lack of empirical data, such a relationship cannot be presumed to exist, and the interpretation of results of both studies must be confined to the student–advisor relationship.

Denmark, in several studies carried out with Carey and McKenna, (1980, 1986), noted that, in attempting to reach high-status targets in psychology in a network chain, significantly more male-targeted chains reached completion than did high-status female-targeted chains. In addition, chains to women targets were longer than men targets. Low-status women are harder to reach, especially for other women. Chains composed of all men participants were more likely to reach their targets than chains which were all women. However, chains with the highest completion rates included both men and women participants. Women contacted other women twice as often as would be expected; men were more likely to reach another man. Do men see women as not being well connected? Do women choose other women because they lack the ties to those with "better communications"? Student–teacher ties occurred twice as often when the chains were male targeted compared with female-targeted chains, and men were more likely to use first names, which expedites contacts and the ability to deal with other people. These results may put women at a disadvantage where teacher–student relationships are concerned.

Trow (1977) initiated a large faculty survey where it was found that faculty perceived men graduate students as having more drive than women graduate students. This suggests the possibility that, in the case of women, male faculty may believe their mentoring efforts will not produce a favorable result which would justify the amount of time that they dedicated to the mentoring process. Although women and men have the services of mentors equally, it could be the case that the men enjoy the first pick or selection of mentors and are more readily accepted than women.

Additionally, because women are often underrepresented on many faculties, there may be a lack of women mentors available to women entering graduate programs (Bogat & Redner, 1985). This is coupled by the fact that many more women than men are applying and being accepted to psychology programs. In 1981, 44 percent of the new doctorates in psychology were women (Syverson, 1982). Today, nearly 72% of new PhD's and PsyD's entering psychology are women (Cynkar, 2007). A cyclical pattern may be developing where there are few women mentors and many women graduate students, creating a competitive scenario where mentors are a scarce commodity. Bogat and Redner (1985) suggest that if women graduate students lack mentors, then years later these same women who become academics will be less likely to become mentors.

Other research has attempted to study the effects of same-sex versus opposite-sex mentor–protégé relationships more directly; for example, Gilbert, Gallessich, and Evans (1983) assessed 80 women and 77 men graduate psychology students on self-evaluations of competency, stress, and satisfaction in regard to their student and intended professional roles. Students were asked to identify by gender and academic rank a particular faculty member whom they felt to be a professional role model. Results indicated that, at least in some areas, same-sex role models do have a certain positive influence on the graduate student's professional development. Those women graduate students who identified women role models viewed themselves as more career oriented, more confident, and more instrumental than did women students identifying men role models. Further, women students with women role models reported higher satisfaction with their student role than did men or women students with a man role model. However, no significant interactions for sex of student and sex of role model were found on measures of overall stress, role conflict, assimilation into or satisfaction with graduate department, or perceived competence, thus indicating that any potential benefits of choosing a role model of the same sex for women are limited to certain dimensions. Also, because the study was confined to individuals currently enrolled in graduate school, no generalization can be made regarding potential benefits to the student once she enters the professional realm.

Further, in a study of mentoring relationships among college students, Ekrut and Mokros (1984) found many more similarities than differences among same-sex versus opposite-sex mentor–student pairs. For both men and women students, same-sex mentors were equally as likely to give academic assistance and encouragement and career assistance, coach for graduate school application, offer the student the opportunity to work on his own research project, and provide moral support as were opposite-sex mentors. Similarly, there were no differences in students' perceptions of the amount of influence from the role model on their decisions about college major, scholarly interests, postcollege career or educational plans, and personal lifestyle. Women with women mentors who attended a single-sex college were significantly likely to claim that they learned greater self-confidence from the mentor than were men, women at single-sex colleges with men mentors, and women at coed colleges with mentors of either sex.

The greatest difference was found in the area of students' plans after graduation. Women with men mentors who attended single-sex colleges were academically most successful, felt more successful relative to their male and female peers, and were significantly more likely to have plans to attend graduate or professional school than any other group.

One of the more interesting findings of the study is that the activities of the mentor or role model seemed to be mainly confined to academic areas directly related to the college experience. For both men and women, mentors were not likely to engage in such activities as providing information on careers, helping to establish connections, and influencing the students' decisions about graduate schools. These findings indicate that the role of mentor for undergraduate college students may be very different than that of serving as a mentor to graduate students.

Due to the limited number of studies regarding same-sex versus cross-sex mentoring, firm conclusions cannot be drawn about the benefits or deficits of each. Kahn (1987), completed in her doctoral research, proposed that doctoral student mothers may benefit from having role models and mentors who are both professionals and mothers. She felt it may be important for this group of students to see firsthand that role integration is possible. Another issue that needs to be investigated is whether it is good to choose as a mentor one professional woman. Is she too isolated from others? Long-term follow up of the careers of women and men mentored by women and men is also needed. Women may offer protégés warmth and caring; men may offer them contacts and network know-how. Perhaps one could best benefit with two mentors. Research by Farylo and Paludi (1985) and Paludi and Fahey (1986) lends support to this suggestion. Paludi et al. reported that graduate women would select a man over a woman mentor because of his connection power, competency, independence, and scholarship. Graduate women further reported that they would select a woman over a man mentor when men were sexist; when the woman had children and/or was in a relationship; and when the woman had expressive personality characteristics of nurturance, warmth, and understanding. Thus, the mentoring relationship may need to go beyond the academic advising role to include social and confidant relationships. To the extent that men mentors may be relatively unable to share personal as well as professional experiences with women protégés in a collegial and not a dating relationship, women protégés may benefit from a woman mentor. And it is true that many women mentors have a networking system as well as power in their discipline. Their power, however, may not be perceived and labeled as such by their men colleagues and protégés. Research into the attributional analysis of mentoring functions would also greatly increase our understanding of same-sex and cross-sex mentor–protégé pairs.

Hammer (2006), in a survey of women students, discovered that themes of empowerment, connection, and career advising arose. Mentors were considered to be role models for the women students. Students recognized the role strain that professional women experienced and sought guidance about how to successfully navigate both areas of their lives: personal and professional. Additionally, many mentees spoke of the personal connection they felt with their mentors and viewed the personal connection as important and felt that it, in turn, increased the value of the mentor's opinions and advice. Last, many of the women students took pride in the confidence that the mentors had in them, and this was experienced as "a very powerful, empowering and affirming tool" (Hammer, 2006, p. 159).

RACE AND GENDER

Race, gender, and class add complexity to a developing mentoring relationship (Parker, 2003). Atkinson, Casas, and Neville (1994) found that 51 percent of ethnic minority psychologists had been mentored in graduate school. Like any human interaction, issues of race and class are not silent presences but contribute to the interactions between two people. Mentoring can be particularly important for women and minority women, because they are a group that has typically had less access to mentoring structures (Johnston, 1987). Therefore, underrepresented groups may use the mentoring relationship as a way to rebalance (or attempt to rebalance) power structures in their favor and to gain advantages that are most likely difficult for them to ascertain as easily as those in the majority group (Wilson & Johnson, 2001). Issues of diversity within the mentoring relationship must be examined and explored. In fact, the Wisconsin Mentoring Seminar that began at the University of Wisconsin–Madison includes diversity as one of the main tenets of the seminar. The objectives of the seminar are to train mentors to communicate effectively, consider issues of diversity, discuss mentoring approaches, and apply a scientific teaching technique to mentoring. Results of an investigation to determine the effectiveness of this program found the largest increase in the consideration of diversity, with those attending the seminar to be significantly more aware of diversity and its place in the mentoring relationship than those who did not attend (Plund, Pribbenow, Branchaw, Lauffer, & Handelsman, 2006). This indicates that diversity is an entity that must be included in the discussion regarding mentoring.

Within a cross-race relationship, it may be difficult for a trusted mentoring arrangement to begin. Thomas (1993) interviewed 22 individual in cross-race (African American and white) pairs of juniors and seniors to examine how a relationship develops. His interviews showed that only when the two parties involved preferred the same strategy (either both openly discussing or ignoring the issue of race) did a more supportive mentoring relationship emerge between them.

Blake (1999) interviewed 11 African American women and found a lack of African American role models and a sense of mistrust in using white women mentors. This is also supported by Bell and Nkomo's (1992, 2001) studies that revealed that gender and race were critical issues involved in a mentoring relationship. African American women in these studies reported having fewer positive relationships with their white male bosses than did white women, due to the fact that both race and gender discrimination could be working against these women. Therefore, in these professional atmospheres, African American women would find it more difficult to find a mentor who could help them negotiate their professional development.

PERSONAL REFLECTIONS ON MENTORING

Florence L. Denmark

As an academic, one of the greatest satisfactions I get is mentoring students and new faculty members and other newcomers to the field of psychology. My academic mentor was Albert Pepitone, who was a great influence on my decision to become a social psychologist. However, I have had wonderful women mentors, including Mary Reuder, whom I knew briefly at the University of Pennsylvania, since she entered the doctoral program several years before I did. When I moved to New York, after I got my doctoral degree, Mary hired me as an adjunct faculty member at Queens College of the City University of New York (CUNY). Mary was in charge of the evening session undergraduate program at Queens College. She showed me the ropes on how to be a good faculty member and instructor and being available to students. Mary set an example that influenced me throughout my career.

Another woman who played a great role in my career was Virginia Staudt Sexton, who was on the committee that hired me at Hunter College CUNY.

Mary Reuder had wanted to offer me a full-time position at Queens College, but no faculty lines were available and it was Mary who suggested that I apply to Hunter College. I was assigned to Hunter College in the Bronx (now Lehman College), and it was Virginia who promoted my organizational activity. Virginia would ask, "Are you a member of the New York State Psychological Association [NYSPA] or the New York Academy of Sciences?" As a Philadelphian, I wasn't aware of these organizations, but thanks to Virginia, I joined them. At the time I joined NYSPA, Virginia was president of the academic division, and she appointed me as newsletter editor. In the New York Academy of Sciences, it was Virginia who appointed me to the advisory committee and in a few years nominated me as fellow of the academy. Later, she encouraged me to obtain a New York State license in psychology.

Both Mary Reuder and Virginia Sexton made me realize how important mentoring is. As a feminist, I feel it is particularly important to mentor young women entering the field, who are often unaware of how to maneuver through the politically charged atmosphere of graduate-level psychology departments, as well as how to succeed in the job market once they complete their degrees. Undergraduates often needed mentoring in how to make the best presentation for admission to graduate programs and what they should do to become desirable candidates for admission. I have also mentored those who were interested in how to get their papers published and those who wished to be involved in organizations. The importance of collaboration, whether in publishing papers or protesting against social injustice, cannot be overstated.

Maria Klara

Mentoring is an important reciprocal relationship, and both halves of the dyad must be examined. Many of my classmates over the years have found it valuable to have someone to turn to for help and guidance. Although mentoring is important at any age, students who enter graduate schools are increasingly younger. They have less life experience and thus find it helpful for someone to show them the ropes and the unwritten rules of the department. Graduate programs may be very different from the academic environment of their undergraduate experience and may approach this new, more stressful and intense experience with anxiety and trepidation. Having someone to help them can be very valuable in an academic and an emotional manner.

Mentors also help students develop particular areas of interest. Some students enter programs with particular subject areas that they would like to pursue, and others have more vague interests. Mentors are in the unique position of either cultivating already-formed interests or bringing new ones to fruition.

Being mentored has had a great impact not only in my academic progression in my doctoral program but has also had a personal, positive benefit as well. Entering a doctoral program was laden with obvious anxieties and doubt regarding the next five years of my life. Although I anticipated it being challenging, I was not totally prepared for the ups and downs. Having a mentor allowed me to have someone who could answer any question, someone who I knew would have my best interests in mind. The advice I received on how to approach certain situations, what classes to take, and which doctoral projects to undertake was invaluable. Having a mentor also made the psychology department more accessible to me. I spent a great deal of time there, and this allowed me to get to know staff, professors, and other students. Therefore, when I needed help, I had an established network that was available to me.

This connection went a long way in terms of calming my anxiety and making the academic sphere one where I was confident. Florence Denmark was encouraging and provided me with a great deal of support that I could do the work and do it successfully,

Additionally, Florence invited me to conferences and workshops, which provided important academic and factual knowledge about psychology but also had the added benefit that I could meet other, established professionals in the field. In meeting other professionals, I felt as though there was an invisible layer of approval placed on me since I was connected to her. People were most gracious to me, and I believe that this warm reception was due to the high esteem in which they held Florence Denmark.

CONCLUSION

There is a great deal we have learned and also a large amount we still need to learn about mentoring and professional networks. Perhaps those of us who do mentor and are considered good role models can stimulate our protégés to carry out some of the needed research in this area.

REFERENCES

Allen, T. D., Eby, L. T., Poteet, M. L., Lentz, E., & Lima, L. (2004). Career benefits associated with mentoring protégés: A meta-analysis. *Journal of Applied Psychology, 89,* 127–136.

Atkinson, D. R., Casas, A., & Neville, H. (1994). Ethnic minority psychologists: Whom they mentor and benefits they derive from the process. *Journal of Multicultural Counseling and Development, 22,* 37–48.

Bandura, A. (1977). *Social learning theory.* Englewood Cliffs, NJ: Prentice: Hall.

Bell, C. R. (1998). *Managers as mentors.* San Francisco: Berrett Kochler.

Bell, E. L., & Nkomo, S. (1992). *The glass ceiling vs. the concrete wall: Career perceptions of white and African American women managers.* Working paper no. 3470–92. Cambridge: Massachusetts Institute of Technology.

Bell, E. L., & Nkomo, S. (2001). *Our separate ways: Black and white women and the struggle for professional identity.* Boston: Harvard Business School Press.

Blake, S. (1999). At the crossroads of race and gender: Lessons from the mentoring experiences of professional black women. In A. Murrell & F. Crosby (Eds.), *Mentoring dilemmas: Developmental relationships within multicultural organizations* (pp. 83–104). Mahwah, NJ: Erlbaum.

Bogat, A., & Redner, R. (1985). How mentoring affects the professional development of women in psychology. *Professional Psychology: Research and Practice, 16,* 851–859.

Clark, R. A., Harden, S. L., & Johnson, W. B. (2000). Mentor relationships in clinical psychology doctoral training: Results of a national survey. *Teaching of Psychology, 27,* 22–31.

Cronan-Hillix, T., Gensheimer, L. K., Cronan-Hillix, W. A., & Davidson, W. S. (1986). Student's views of mentors in psychology graduate training. *Teaching of Psychology, 13,* 123–127.

Cynkar, A. (2007). The changing gender coposition of psychology. *Monitor on Psychology, 38,* 46.

Denmark, F. L. (1980). Psyche: From rocking the cradle to rocking the boat. *American Psychologist, 35,* 1057–1065.

Denmark, F. (1986, April). *Evaluation of gender effects on access to communication networks.* Presidential address to the Eastern Psychological Association, New York, NY.

Dohm, F. A., & Cummings, W. (2002). Research mentoring and women in clinical psychology. *Psychology of Women Quarterly, 26,* 163–167.

Ekrut, S., & Mokros, J. R. (1984). Professors as models and mentors for college students. *American Educational Research Journal, 21,* 399–417.

Farylo, B., & Pauldi, M. A. (1985). Developmental discontinuities in mentor choice by male students. *Journal of Social Psychology, 125,* 521–522.

Folse, K. A. (1991). Ethics and the profession: Graduate school training. *Teaching Sociology, 19,* 344–350.

Gerstein, M. (1985). Mentoring: An age old practice in a knowledge-based society. *Journal of Counseling and Development, 64,* 156–157.

Gilbert, L. A. (1985). Dimensions of same-gender student-faculty role model relationships. *Sex Roles, 12,* 111–123.

Gilbert, L. A., Gallessich, J. M., & Evans, S. L. (1983). Sex of faculty role model and students' self-perceptions of competency. *Sex Roles, 9,* 597–606.

Goldstein, E. (1979). Effect of same-sex and cross-sex role models on the subsequent academic productivity of scholars. *American Psychologist, 34,* 407–410.

Hammer, E. Y. (2006). Mentoring female students. In William Buskist and Stephen F. Davis (Eds.), *Handbook of the teaching of psychology* (pp. 159–163). Malden, MA: Blackwell.

Johnson, W. B., & Huwe, J. M. (2003). *Getting mentored in graduate school.* Washington, DC: American Psychological Association.

Johnson, W. G., & Nelson, N. (1999). Mentor-protégé relationships in graduate training: Some ethical concerns. *Ethics & Behavior, 9,* 189–210.

Johnston, W. B. (1987). *Workforce 2000: Work and workers for the twenty-first century.* Indianapolis, IN: Hudson Institute.

Kahn, S. (1987). Socialization, solidarity or sheer stamina: The effects of departmental role models and family status on the future psychologists. Unpublished manuscript: Graduate Center, City University of New York.

Keele, R. L., & DeLaMare-Schaefer, M. (1984). So what do you do now that you didn't have a mentor? *Journal of the National Association for Women Deans, Administrators and Counselors, 47,* 36–40.

Kinnier, R. T., Metha, A. T., Buki, L. P., & Rawa, P.M. (1994). Manifest values of eminent psychologists: A content analysis of their obituaries. *Current Psychology, 13,* 88–94.

Kirchner, E. P. (1969). Graduate education in psychology: Retrospective views of advanced degree recipients. *Journal of Clinical Psychology, 25,* 207–213.

Kram. K. E. (1988). *Mentoring at work: Developmental relationships in organizational life.* New York: University Press of America.

Levinson, D. J. (1978). *The seasons of a man's life.* New York: Ballantine.

Merriam, S. (1983). Mentors and protégées: A critical review of the literature. *Adult Education, 33,* 161–173.

Mintz, L. B., Bartels, K. M., & Rideout, C. A. (1995). Training in counseling ethnic minorities and race-based availability of graduate school resources. *Professional Psychology: Research and Practice, 26,* 316–321.

Mullen, E. (1994). Framing the mentoring relationship in an information exchange. *Human Resource Management Review, 4,* 257–281.

Newby, T. J., & Heide, A. (1992). The value of mentoring. *Performance Improvement Quarterly, 5,* 2–15.

Paludi, M. A., & Fahey, M. (1986, November). *Women and the mentor-protégée relationship: Perceptions of competency, aspirations, and self worth.* Paper presented at the Research on Women and Education Conference, Washington, DC.

Parker, P. (2003). Control, resistance, and empowerment in raced, gendered and classed work contexts—The case of African American women. *Communication Yearbook, 27,* 257–291.

Philips-Jones, L. (1982). *Mentors & protégés.* New York: Arbor House.

Plund, C., Pribbenow, C. M., Branchaw, J., Lauffer, S. M., & Handelsman, J. (2006). The merits of training mentors. *Science, 311,* 473–474.

Richey, C. A., Gabrill, E. D., & Blythe, B. J. (1988). Mentor relationships among women in academia. *Affilia, 3,* 34–47.

Roche, G. (1979). Much ado about mentors. *Harvard Business Review, 20,* 14–16, 20, 24, 26–28.

Russo, N. F., Olmedo, E. L, Strapp, J., & Fulcher, R. (1981). Women and minorities in psychology. *American Psychologist, 36,* 1315–1363.

Sanders, J. M., & Wong, H. Y. (1985). Graduate training and initial job placement. *Sociological Inquiry, 55,* 154–169.

Solomon, L. C. (1978). Attracting women to psychology: Effects of university behavior and the labor market. *American Psychologist, 33,* 990–999.

Syverson, P. D. (1982). Two decades of doctorates in psychology: A comparison with national trends. *American Psychologist, 37,* 1203–1212.

Thomas, D. A. (1993). Racial dynamics in cross-race developmental relationships. *Administrative Science Quarterly, 38,* 169–194.

Trow, M. (1977). *Aspects of American higher education, 1969–1975.* Berkeley, CA: Carnegie Council on Policy Studies in Higher Education.

Wilde, J. B., & Schau, C. G. (1991). Mentoring in graduate schools of education: Mentee's perceptions. *Journal of Experimental Education, 59,* 165–179.

Wilson, P. E., & Johnson, W. B. (2001). Core virtues for the practice of mentoring. *Journal of Psychology and Theology, 29,* 121–130.

Wright, C. A., & Wright, S. D. (1987). The role of mentors in the career development of young professionals. *Family Relations, 36,* 204–208.

Part II

Women in Nontraditional Careers, Academe, and Business

Chapter 2

Gender Issues in Academic Mentoring: Personal Experiences Set in a Theoretical Framework

Judith Waters

This chapter is dedicated to all the important mentors with whom I have worked over the years. In alphabetical order, they are Florence L. Denmark, the late Barbara Dohrenwend, the late Stanley Milgram, the late Harold Proshansky, Mary Reuder, and the late Bernard Seidenberg. Many other wonderful individuals influenced my life choices for a short period of time but are too numerous to mention here. I have been very fortunate.

THEORIES ABOUT MENTORSHIP RELATIONSHIPS

According to Homer, Mentor was the wise and faithful advisor as well as tutor to Telemachus, the son of Odysseus. Several terms are related to the mentoring process. A *mentor* is an authority figure with the expertise in a particular field to support facts, opinions, and/or actions. *Masters* are the people who possess the highest levels of knowledge or skills in a discipline, while *apprentices* are the learners. Formally, an apprentice is often bound by legal documents to learn some art, trade, or profession. Clearly, the implication is that an apprentice is a youth, or one not yet well versed in a subject. As a verb, *to mentor* means to be put under the care of a skilled master for the purpose of learning a trade or profession. Another term for apprentice is *novice,* a person who is not yet familiar with the requirements of his field (e.g., any profession or business). For example, with the goal of becoming nuns, novices spend probationary time in religious orders. Novices are thus socialized to be fit for a life in the companionship of specific others in the religious community. A *protégé* is someone under the care and protection of a master who shows a personal interest in the protégé's career or future. *Sages* transmit knowledge from one generation to another. *Heroes* have counselors and tutors (e.g., Alexander the Great was advised by Aristotle, and the young Arthur was guided by Merlin). Among Jung's archetypes are heroes and wise old men and wise old women (Jung et al., 1964). One of the major critical thinking strategies in philosophy is the concept of "appeal to authority" both for information and for solutions to problems. We ask physicians, lawyers, and architects for their opinions, and, if we respect and trust them, we act on their advice

I recently received a gift from one of my graduate assistants, a popular book about the mentorship relationship between a former student and his terminally ill professor. In *Tuesdays with Morrie,* Albom (1997) discusses his relationship with Morrie Schwartz, his college professor of some 20 years prior to their discussions published in the book. He describes the relationship on the cover of the book:

> Maybe it was a grandparent, or a teacher or a colleague. Someone older, patient and wise, who understood you when you were young and searching, helped you see the world as a more profound place, gave you sound advice to help you make your way through it.

Despite very early references to wise men and wise women (Jung et al., 1964) and the story of Mentor's education of Telemachus, the current focus on the value of mentorship relationships began in the mid-1970s (Tenner, 2004). Tenner cited Daniel Levinson, who described the relationship between an older man and a younger man. The mentor takes the young man under his wing by sharing wisdom, caring, sponsoring, and, of course, criticizing the protégé. The role of the mentor has become a significant subject in the career development literature and includes the most recent concept of a coach or a facilitator. Counselors work with clients as life coaches rather than therapists (Maples, 2008). Although most life coaches are women, the relationship is usually discussed in terms of men participants. In the corporate world, most managers were once men. Despite the increase in the proportion of women at the upper levels of the corporate hierarchy, many men are concerned about the potential for sex harassment charges, real or imagined, and tend to avoid mentoring women.

McCluskey, Noller, Lamoureux, and McCluskey (2004) discuss the origin of the mentoring concept in Homer's epic *The Odyssey*. They have identified three important aspects concerning Mentor's guidance of Telemachus:

1. Mentor had other duties in addition to his role of wise advisor to a youth. Consequently, he did not spend all his time with Telemachus.
2. Mentor provided information from many sources, not just his own opinions, to Telemachus.
3. Mentor and Telemachus developed a long-term relationship.

It is the mentor's role to "provide support through listening, advocacy, sharing of self, establishing structure, highlighting strengths, and making the experience unique and positive" (Daley, 1986, cited in McCluskey et al., 2004).

THE RESPONSIBILITIES OF THE MENTOR

Lindner, Dooley, and Williams (2003) stated that teachers must develop student-centered learning strategies that incorporate each student's "unique background, experiences, knowledge, skills, abilities, personality type, social style, and/or personal styles and values" (p. 26). If we fail to gear the material for the individual needs and resources of the student, we are frequently accused of teaching to the middle and losing both ends of the continuum. Thus, Lindner and his colleagues expect faculty to individualize the educational process. When reading the article by Lindner et al., I began to think seriously of a career change. In a one-semester content-based graduate course, there is little time to formulate individualized learning plans for 30 or more students. Even if there were only 10 students in the class, it is not always possible to address individual needs for other reasons. For example, a class of students may feel that individualized plans are unfair. Furthermore, it is expected that, by graduate school, the students have acquired the necessary skills to initiate their own projects and carry them through to completion with minimal supervision by faculty. The authors suggest that students must pass through a hierarchical set of learning stages that eventually lead to the student's ability to take responsibility for her own achievement. The process begins with dependent students in need of authoritative teachers who engage in activities that facilitate learning. Eventually, students must become self-motivated and capable of completing a project with as little external guidance as possible. The learning style utilized may also depend upon the complexity of the subject matter. For example, introducing the concepts of profile analysis even to graduate students may require more intensive coaching in the beginning than other topics. Increased self-direction develops late in the semester.

Most successful individuals (researchers, faculty members, corporate executives, police officers, and mental health workers, among others) would affirm that a mentor, or more probably mentors, played important roles in shaping their career goals and achievements. Most professions require a period of time when the individual functions as an apprentice under the tutelage of an expert professional just as physicians fulfill the roles of intern and resident before becoming independent practitioners. Their supervisors engage in coaching the novice and also evaluate their performances. Mentorship relationships may not extend beyond the walls of the institution, or they may involve a strong social component. The mentor serves as a role model as well as a guide and a coach. If the employee, assistant, or doctoral candidate is more than a mere student, the mentor may enjoy opening doors and providing unique opportunities for him to meet important people in the field.

There are guidelines that govern a successful mentoring relationship. However, the ways in which these guidelines are utilized may be more a reflection of the mentor's personality than a job description.

COMMON CHARACTERISTICS OF A MENTORING RELATIONSHIP

1. The mentor establishes her own rules or follows established standards. Apprentices are evaluated according to these standards.
2. The mentor provides direct assistance on an as-needed basis or engages in prevention activities to ward off disasters.
3. The mentor oversees the development of a knowledge base and of relevant skills.
4. Included in the knowledge base is an understanding of overall organizational structure as well as particular informal rules and practices.
5. The mentor provides career guidance and opportunities for the protégé.
6. The mentorship relationship can be mutually rewarding or one fraught with conflict and disagreements. Most commonly, both deference and defiance exist simultaneously in the same relationship.
7. Sometimes, it is necessary to seek mentoring outside of the organization due to internecine conflict among senior advisors.
8. Mentors can be depicted as treating some students unfairly when they are only attempting to individualize plans for the specific needs of the students.
9. The best mentors are portrayed as wise, caring sponsors who criticize while at the same time bestowing their blessings on their protégés.

My own guidelines for mentoring were derived from my experiences first with Mary Reuder and later with Florence Denmark. They both fostered independence and productivity in all their students, not just the women. Moreover, they modeled and continue to model exactly what they expected from us. While both are retired now, they lead very active lives participating in American Psychological Association (APA) programs. Denmark is one of the APA representatives to the United Nations and spends several days a week at her office at Pace University, where she still mentors students. Mary Reuder is still very involved with APA committees.

Sometimes, mentoring can be an informal and spontaneous process that happens when an individual gives both support and direction to recipients such as juveniles in correctional institutions and drug treatment facilities. Mentorship relationships may be institutionalized in organizations where mentors are formally assigned to apprentices and the nature of their contact is shaped by well-established guidelines. Such formal internship programs frequently include training manuals and evaluation forms.

The role of the mentor goes beyond that of teacher in terms of providing additional guidance and socialization into one's chosen milieu, such as medical school. According to Beresin (2004), "Having a mentor is critical to a successful career in academic medicine" (p. 60). Although there are critiques that delineate the potential disadvantages of a mentorship relationship, most individuals do report positive experiences. In a review article, Johnson (2002) discusses the basic premises of mentoring, the frequency with which mentoring occurs in the field of psychology, the barriers to successful mentoring relationships, ethical issues, and guidelines to improve the mentoring experience. Johnson cites Levinson, Darrow, Klein, Levinson, and McKee (1978), who stated that, despite the mandate of higher education to enhance the professional and personal development of students, mentoring relationships are both infrequent and inadequate. They question whether psychologists are properly prepared to mentor graduate students. Being a professor of psychology, a broad and diverse discipline, with expertise in a particular area of study, does not equate to having counseling skills. Levinson et al. also point out that the competing demands on faculty time such as research requirements, teaching, and committee work can easily interfere with the commitment to mentoring. The university milieu must be conducive to fostering mentorship relationships, especially because the products of these relationships are difficult to measure, especially in the short term. The academic culture must accept the concept that criticism is normal. For example, when we are strict with our protégés, the recipients may not appreciate our efforts and complain to deans and other senior administrators. Many students evaluate criticism as a completely hostile act. Anything short of constant applause seems to be perceived as insulting and disrespectful. While we all desire unconditional positive regard, the process of education demands that there be a realistic relationship between the quality of the students' work and our feedback.

THE ROLE OF THE INSTITUTION AS MENTOR

The culture of an academic—or, for that matter, a corporate—institution helps to shape the career choices of students or employees, faculty or managers, and new hires. Sometimes, the message given to recently hired faculty members is very clear; sometimes it is ambiguous. For example, new assistant professors are usually given course reductions to enable them to prepare their dissertations for publication or to initiate new programs of research. The granting of automatic release time ensures that the criteria for tenure and promotion will be met. Occasionally, a senior faculty member or the department chair assumes the responsibility for coaching new hires. In all cases, the department chairs are responsible for overseeing the activities that will lead to renewal and eventually to tenure. However, in some schools, the needs of the department (e.g., a heavy teaching load and a demanding advising schedule) do not match the rules of the discipline and the external academic world. The goals of our field favor contributions to the body of knowledge in the discipline. Thus, subscribing to the objectives of the field may, in fact, jeopardize the chances that new assistant professors will remain in the same university or college where they began their careers. What is even more challenging to novice faculty is the fact that institutional missions may change with each new administration.

GENDER AS A HURDLE

As Tenner (2004) points out, men have long enjoyed the benefits of close professional relationships with teachers and senior colleagues. Those benefits need to be extended to women and to members of diverse cultural groups. Because being a role model is also a component of the mentor's identity, we need to increase the number of women faculty and members of those diverse cultural groups available as mentors.

In corporate America, both new hires and experienced employees are generally perceived as needing the support and counsel of an individual who can supply perspectives on the processes of acculturation and appraisal (Kram, 1983). However, Kram suggests that,

> while the mentor relationship has the great potential to facilitate career advancement and psychosocial development in both early and middle adulthood . . . the potential value of a mentor relationship is limited and that, indeed, a relationship of this kind can become destructive. (p. 608)

A hostile relationship can interfere with independent thinking and creativity. The mentor's personality and standing in the field can and sometimes does inhibit individuality.

Whether we are discussing early childhood education, secondary education, college, postgraduate degrees, or initiation into a workforce where the domains are business, professions, or academic communities, the developmental tasks usually require the guidance of a person with the requisite technical, social, and political skills. A mentor can shape our philosophy of life and provide pragmatic advice on the rules of the game. However, attitudes toward authority figures are frequently ambivalent, sometimes ending in battles reminiscent of an adolescent's fight for independence from his parents. Of course, not every mentor and protégé relationship is doomed to conflict and termination. Many individuals form lifelong friendships that include continuing professional as well as social contacts.

In her research on corporate mentor relationships, Kram (1983) found two major mentoring categories: career functions and psychosocial functions. The major career functions include sponsorship, exposure and visibility, coaching, protection, and challenging assignments; the psychosocial category is composed of role modeling, acceptance and confirmation, counseling, and friendship. She also found that mentor relationships vary in length and proceed through four predictable and somewhat overlapping phases. The first phase is labeled *initiation,* which is essentially an orientation stage. The second phase is *cultivation,* a time when the relationship reaches its pinnacle. The third phase can be *separation,* when the basic nature of the relationship is altered due to organizational structure or psychological changes in the players. The last phase is called the *redefinition,* when the relationship may undergo a metamorphosis into a different entity or may terminate permanently. My relationships with Mary Reuder and Florence Denmark as well as the late Stanley Milgram turned into friendship and collegial experiences.

The National Institutes of Health (NIH) provides guidelines for mentors in its internship program. There are 10 roles that mentors can assume depending on the situation and the needs of the students. The roles include those of teacher, guide, counselor, motivator, sponsor, coach, advisor, role model, referral agent, and door opener.

The teacher needs to transmit the skills and knowledge of each discipline, including past mistakes. The guide assists the student in learning the idiosyncratic and often unwritten rules of the game. These rules include hidden agendas and the "around-here-isms" of every institution, academic as well as corporate. The counselor creates a trusting atmosphere that emphasizes the importance of confidentiality. Respect is also an essential component of the counselor role. The counselor facilitates the development of independent problem-solving skills. The mentor, in the role of motivator, is usually working with already highly motivated protégés who basically need only small incentives or encouragement to complete a specific difficult task (e.g., one's dissertation). The mentor as sponsor provides opportunities for the mentee. As always, the role of the coach can be difficult to perform. Coaches use feedback to reinforce desirable behaviors and to eliminate less desirable behaviors. The coach must try to avoid being judgmental and provide frequent guidance based on direct personal observation rather than as the result of information gathered from hearsay sources. The advisor's role is also to assist the student in setting goals and making good professional choices. As a role model, a mentor must exemplify the values and ethical and professional practices of the organization. As a referral agent, the mentor facilitates the development of an action plan for the mentee that will help achieve her career goals. Finally, as a door opener, the mentor also provides entrée to the sources of information that the protégé needs.

Despite the external pressures on faculty achievement, many professors remembering their own mentors—or perhaps lack of mentors—commit themselves to meeting the needs of as many students as is realistic, given the usual time constraints. Some faculty members have a mentoring style that is essentially the same for everyone. In fact, they may consciously or unconsciously select students who work best with their own particular mentoring style of guidance. Others tailor their styles to work with each student individually according to the student's needs. The goal, however, remains the same. In each case, it should be to facilitate the development of independent, productive students who are capable of identifying problems and issues and formulating potential solutions.

The process of mentoring progresses in stages from compliance to conformity to internalization of values. In the initial period, even graduate assistants must follow instructions, only later being given the opportunity to suggest their own ideas. The relationship is often authoritarian with the expectation of deference. Of course, overt deference often masks the duality of defiance and deference. Eventually, the novice will establish his own rules in order to pass on the traditions of the field. It is interesting to see three generations of students at conferences.

CHILDREN

When mentoring is discussed, most people think of adult relationships in college, graduate school, and professional situations. We also conceptualize the mentor relationship as a long-term experience in a formal setting. However, mentorship relationships can have an impact on our lives beginning at an early age and progressing through the educational system to midcareer changes and all the way to the point where we become mentors while still receiving the benefit of advice on our own endeavors. Sometimes, although important influences may come from strangers and only last a moment or two, they also have a strong impact on the decisions that we make.

Consequently, it is important to begin mentoring children early. I once taught a class of elementary school teachers from Newark in the Thistle Program at Montclair State University in New Jersey. They contributed stories about their students who are starving for guidance and approval. For example, they told us about seven-year-old children who could be found sitting outside elementary schools at seven o'clock in the morning in the dead of winter, waiting for beloved teachers to arrive. Children have also been known to misbehave in class so that they would be kept in at lunchtime with the teacher and thus have an opportunity to talk to a rational authority figure, perhaps the only such adult role model in their lives. These early relationships facilitate the development of self-efficacy and self-esteem. Most of these important authority figures are women.

We have, as a discipline, planned and implemented formal interventions designed to overcome the dysfunctional backgrounds of children raised in decaying inner cities. Although not all children rise above the challenges they have encountered (e.g., early childhood physical and sexual abuse), many of them are survivors who will outlive the consequences of harsh experiences, especially if they have the support and guidance of a mentor who is able and willing to facilitate the growth of the hardiness factor. A significant number of children have the ability to become healthy, self-protective, and productive independent individuals instead of vulnerable youth and adults at the mercy of environmental pressures. Brown (2004) was a former at-risk youth who met three mentors who each had a major impact on his life, one of whom he did not appreciate at the time. Eventually, he was able to earn a doctoral degree from an Ivy League school and go on with his life.

PROBLEMS IN MENTORING

Not all influences in mentorship relationships are positive. As Johnson (2002) suggests, economic exigencies at institutions of higher learning can negatively influence the number of mentor relationships as well as the quality of those relationships. The increase in part-time faculty and the overwhelming workloads for full-time faculty severely reduce the time left for mentoring. Due to the fact that most of us would like to spend enough time with a student to have an impact on his career, we are forced to turn away many students interested in working with us. On the student's side, it becomes increasingly difficult to find a mentor, any mentor. Furthermore, if the student wants to have a same-gender mentor and a racial match plus a mentor who has some interest in the student's area of research, we have an impossible situation. Moreover, students do not understand that we cannot always supervise research on completely new topics outside of our own areas of expertise.

Tenner (2004) includes many examples of mentors who always require first authorship or a contributing authorship even if they have not written a word. Although the excuse may be the pressure that universities exert for faculty to publish or indeed perish, faculty members still have choices. Wundt demonstrated that it is possible to be a mentor and to produce one's own research (Thorne & Henley, 2004).

There are, of course, some disadvantages to mentoring that are not inherent in the relationship. They depend on the character traits of the individuals involved. Tenner (2004) suggests that, apparently, many faculty fail to give credit to students for their contributions to the faculty member's research. In such situations, mentors are only as good as the ethics that they model. Some mentors have been sued for not giving credit when it was due.

Another problem is associated with seeking advice from a faculty member other than one's own mentor. A sponsored protégé may find it difficult to approach someone else in the department with a question or an issue. If a student remains dependent on a single mentor, there is the danger of developing a narrow perspective and losing the advantages of alternative viewpoints.

A basic problem involves finding a dissertation mentor. As previously noted, many senior faculty members will not supervise dissertations on topics outside their own domains of expertise and interest. I was fortunate to have Florence Denmark as my dissertation chair and the late Barbara Dohrenwend, the late Bernie Seidenberg, and the late Robert Buckhout as committee members. The title of my 1977 dissertation was "The Image of the President: A Study of the 1972 Election." None of the committee members was engaged in any projects related to political psychology. Nor was anyone else in the Social/Personality Psychology Department at the Graduate Center or the other senior colleges considered an expert on political psychology. It was a miracle that these faculty members agreed to serve on my committee. In addition, since I utilized the semantic differential as my primary instrument, the late Sam Messick, well known for his work with the semantic differential, had to serve as an outside consultant for some of the technical issues. Given the increased pressure on faculty to publish, I am not sure how many mentors would be willing or able to devote so much time and effort to a single student nowadays. Even at that time, many of my fellow students could not find dissertation chairs easily and had to rewrite their proposals to fit the changes mandated by the chairs they did find. I did not want to change my topic since it was a study of voter attitudes toward the two candidates with data collected immediately prior to and just following the 1972 election and the events of the Watergate scandal. I now know how generous my committee was with their time and how atypical that was.

The recent focus on the importance of mentorship has led to the belief that careers without the benefit of a mentor are doomed to failure as the worst scenario and to mediocrity as the best situation. It is true that mentors, as the gatekeepers to the field, once held the keys to professional opportunities. However, now that the number of academic jobs has decreased, even the input of a renowned professor may have less influence than it once did.

On the other hand, I disagree with Tenner (2004), who wrote that students have succeeded without mentors. It may be that the students queried did not have a strong relationship with a single specific individual or that they are not giving credit where it is due. Every student in a graduate program has had the guidance of a mentor or a role model somewhere in her career path. I agree with Tenner when he writes, however, that all mentoring is essentially self-mentoring. We always need to choose from among the alternative directions ourselves.

THE MENTORING OF RETURNING AND SPECIAL NEEDS STUDENTS

In addition to the recent trend for many mature adults (most of whom are women) to attend college for the first time or to return to the academic world following absences of as long as 20 or 30 years, there are individual disciplines such as addictions counseling that are particularly attractive to people who have been working in the field for many years with little or no formal education beyond high school. Many of these individuals have already achieved positions of responsibility at work, but possess only high school general education diplomas and the experience of having successfully "graduated" from a drug treatment program themselves. They usually begin their educational journey with two years at a community college and then look for a combined bachelor's- and master's-level program to accelerate the academic process. Because they are already functioning as professionals in the field without necessarily having a strong commitment to the academic world, they are often nervous about meeting the standards of a discipline such as psychology. The formal requirements, including writing papers according to APA publication style, may appear to be unnecessarily rigid to them. They only want to study coursework that relates directly to the practice of counseling (e.g., family therapy). They would like to avoid even the components that are essential for licensure or certification (e.g., psychometrics, psychopharmacology, and research design). Because a significant proportion of the applicants do not have a strong academic background, the faculty and graduate assistants must engage in more tutoring and career guidance than would otherwise be the case. Sometimes returning students have to rewrite papers three or four times before the quality reaches an acceptable standard. Time spent tutoring in basic academic skills is costly for any university and detracts from efforts to mentor talented graduate students who want to apply for doctoral programs. It has been my experience that many of the women returning to school have not been socialized into the academic community well enough to function without considerable guidance.

AND THE PROCESS CONTINUES

Over the years, I have attended regional and national conferences where I was pleased to see new faculty who were once my students engaged in helping their own students become acculturated into the profession. The best gift that they can give us is to share what they have learned from us with their own apprentices and to avoid stereotyping and discriminating against students by gender, age, and race or any other unrealistic criterion.

PERSONAL EXPERIENCES

When I first contemplated the focus of this book on gender issues with respect to mentoring, I was not sure that I had anything to contribute. I did not immediately discern any distinct gender-related behavioral patterns among my mentors when I was in college or graduate school. Nor could I see any aspect of my own behavior that was an obvious reflection of early gender influences. However, after some serious reflection, I started to remember incidents that occurred when I was a student and, in all probability, still affect students today.

Most of the time, it was difficult to discern differential treatment or identify such treatment as gender discrimination. For example, when I taught at Brooklyn College as an instructor (a graduate student's line), there was a class action lawsuit against the City University of New York (CUNY) claiming a pattern of discrimination against the women faculty with respect to rank and salary. To this day, I think that I was treated with respect and did not see a pattern of discrimination against the women in the Brooklyn College Psychology Department. Of course, instructors are not privy to all the workings of the department or the university. However, when the suit was settled in favor of the claimants, and the damages were assessed, I did receive a check that I promptly cashed.

Each of my college and graduate school mentors is or was a unique individual. How many students have the privilege of working with a person who was to become president of the American Psychological Association and one of the founders of Division 35, The Psychology of Women (Florence Denmark) or the most controversial and well-known social psychologist of his day (Stanley Milgram) or the president of the Graduate School and University Center at CUNY and one of the founders of the subdiscipline of environmental psychology (Harold Proshansky)? I do believe that the women faculty, as a category, recognized the nature of the uphill battle that we all faced in building careers in the academic world better than the men and were as concerned with our personal progress as they were with our research projects. None of the women, for example, would ever have written a letter of recommendation that was penned by a male faculty member and began with statements such as, "Despite his strange appearance, X is quite brilliant," or "Despite the fact that she returned to school very late in life, Y is the best graduate student I've had."

The examples of concerned advice by the women faculty are numerous. Without the guidance of Mary Reuder, my undergraduate mentor, I never would have applied for graduate school. Later, as a doctoral student, I instinctively knew that if Florence Denmark were to be my dissertation chair, I would finish my dissertation, publish my research, and get a job.

Besides the sincere concern with our careers, there were other aspects of the mentorship relationship that seem to be associated with gender. If our chairs were women, we were more likely to be encouraged to strike out on our own research paths rather than be clones of our mentors. Generally, if our topics did not fit the theme of one of the male faculty, we were told to go elsewhere. After Dr. Denmark agreed to be my chair, I asked one of the men to be on my committee. He said that he would be more than happy to work with me, but only under the condition that he be the chair and that I change my topic to one that suited him better. After that incident, Professor Denmark asked if I would like her to put together the committee. Needless to say, I happily agreed.

As discussed earlier in the chapter, there are many realistic constraints on the time and commitments of doctoral faculty. Political psychology, my area—specifically the image of the president of the United States—was not at that time considered to be a mainstream interest in the field. While it was certainly not Professor Denmark's main focus, the question of changing the topic was never raised. That meant that she needed to do reading outside of her areas of interest.

During the time that I was an undergraduate at Queens College (at CUNY), a doctoral student at the Graduate Center, and an instructor at Brooklyn College, there were few women faculty at any of these institutions of higher learning. At the Graduate Center in the social personality program, I only remember the late Barbara Dohenwend actually having a Graduate Center line. The other women faculty such as Professor Denmark were on loan from their colleges. In over 20 doctoral classes, my courses were taught by a woman only once, and that was Barbara Dohrenwend for field research. With the exception of the graduate students who were full-time instructors or part-time adjunct faculty, I remember very few women at Brooklyn College. What was even more surprising was the fact that I did not even think about the imbalance; I just took it for granted. When I became a faculty member at Fairleigh Dickinson University, there was only one woman in the department, and she had a half-time appointment shared with the recreation and leisure program. Today, 30 years later, all of the university senior academic administrators are men (e.g., the university president, the vice president for academic affairs, the provosts, and the college deans). In my department, however, the chair is a woman, and more than half of the faculty members are women.

I would like to describe a few of my personal experiences with some of my long-term mentors and with other faculty and even neighbors who have been most generous with sound advice, sometimes in very brief encounters.

In addition to my mentors, many faculty members served as role models, despite the fact that they probably did not know that I even existed. For example, the only way that any of my undergraduate classmates or I would have been noticed in some of the large lecture halls would have been to change our seats from the prescribed seating plan. To support graduate education and small, specialized classes for juniors and seniors at the undergraduate level, most universities resort to balancing their budgets by the use of large auditoriums designed to hold hundreds of anonymous students. My daughter was fortunate enough to have Martin Seligman in her first psychology course at the University of Pennsylvania. However, there were over 400 students in her class.

CHRONOLOGY

Family influences can have an enormous impact on the direction that our professional lives take with respect to career and marriage. In an article in the *New York Times,* Maureen Dowd (2005) clearly delineates the influences of culture and gender on choices. For example, she points out that women with advanced degrees are choosing traditional roles over careers in the law. She adds that women who are independent and accomplished are at a distinct disadvantage in dating and the marriage market. The implication is that you cannot have it all. My mother wanted to see me marry well. I once asked my father what his aspirations for me had been when I was a child. He replied that he never even thought about my future. He assumed that I would get married. And I did at the age of 18.

When I decided to apply to graduate school, my mother predicted that my children would suffer and that I was jeopardizing my marriage. She also stated that she would not be a party to the disaster and would not baby-sit or come to my graduation. Fortunately for me and for other women, there have been faculty role models and mentors who guided us along the way.

My original undergraduate major at Queens College was education, because I thought, as did many women in the 1960s, that the best way to raise a family, earn a living, and contribute to society at same time was to teach on the elementary or secondary school system level. In that era, as the parent of three children, I was certainly not a traditional student. While times have since changed, the composition of urban commuter campus populations in the 1960s and 1970s had not yet begun to include the large number of women who would soon start college or return to school. As a full-time parent (also with a part-time job), I was only able to attend college at night. That was when I met Mary Reuder, chair of the psychology evening session at Queens College, CUNY. She could inspire a research class to work from six o'clock in the evening to one o'clock in the morning (technically, the class ended at 10 P.M.). Moreover, once she set her expectations for us, she did not even have to be in the room to oversee our progress. On the first night of the class, she showed us the required course texts that included Woodworth and Schlossberg's 1954 classic experimental tome and announced that we would be responsible for the entire book and two smaller books and that we would be tested in three weeks. We were also assigned five experiments for the semester to be designed ourselves based on a review of the literature (no replications were allowed) and conducted with the data analyzed and papers written using American Psychological Association publication style. The first night of the course, there were 11 students in the room. The second night, there were 6. In the end, the survivors all produced projects that were either published or delivered at regional or national conferences. Dr. Reuder did not add her name to any of the papers, although she clearly contributed substantially to each one. I will never forget that class and the time that each of us spent in her office developing our projects. At that point in my life, although I was a junior, I had not contemplated going to graduate school. Without her guidance, I would not have applied to doctoral programs; taken the Graduate Record Examinations; won a National Institute of Mental Health Predoctoral Fellowship and a New York State Regents College Teaching Fellowship; ended up at the Graduate Center of the City University of New York as Stanley Milgram's graduate assistant; or met Florence Denmark, Harold Proshansky, Bernard Seidenberg, Barbara Dohrenwend, and the other mentors who played strong roles in my life.

My first conference paper was sent to the Eastern Psychological Association (EPA) when I was an undergraduate (Waters, 1969). I truly believed, even before it was submitted, that it would be accepted because it was much more difficult to have a project approved by Dr. Reuder than by any external reviewer. Dr. Reuder also requested applications for graduate fellowships in my name and reminded me that I had to take the Graduate Record Examinations by October of the year in which I would apply for doctoral programs and fellowships. I applied for two fellowships and won two, probably because, under her tutelage, I had already finished the research for the EPA paper. When we went to the EPA conference, Dr. Reuder introduced me to Dr. Denmark from CUNY; the executive director of EPA, Dr. Murray Beninoff; and the executive director of Psi Chi, Ruth Cousins. I was later to become involved with both organizations. Mary Reuder opened the doors to a graduate education that I had never considered. At that point, no one in my family, male or female, had applied to a doctoral program or medical school or law school, and only a few of my cousins went to college. My father had an eighth-grade education, and my mother had two years of a vocational high school.

With Dr. Reuder's assistance, I chose the Graduate Center of CUNY for two reasons. One reason was, of course, the excellent faculty that rivals any Ivy League school, and the other reason was a personal commitment to demonstrate that public education could be just as rigorous as a private university curriculum. My entire educational history has been in the New York City system. In elementary school, I was enrolled in the demonstration class in the Bronx that was followed by four years at Hunter College High School (an excellent college prep school), one year at City College followed by a 10-year hiatus when I was raising a family, and then Queens College at night. Finally, I was accepted at the Graduate Center in the Social/Personality Program. Because I had won a National Institute of Mental Health Predoctoral Fellowship, I was introduced to Stanley Milgram, who was to become my fellowship sponsor. At every step along the way, I had the benefit of guidance by dedicated teachers who exposed me to the *New York Times* in the second grade and to professional organizations in graduate school. Since I came from a generation and a family that focused on marriage and parenthood as the goals for young women, it was my teachers from the second grade forward who presented me with new alternatives. In high school, we were all expected to go to college. With few exceptions, we all did. The culture of each of these institutions was almost as important to my career as the influence of each individual mentor. The early teachers were all women.

While there were many wonderful faculty members at the Graduate Center, one's dissertation sponsor can have an important influence on one's career goals. Among my memories of working with Dr. Denmark are hours spent collaborating on projects and working together anywhere that we could find space, which sometimes included the beauty parlor. Multitasking is not a new concept to any doctoral student. The wonderful aspect of working with Florence Denmark is that ideas really do turn into projects. The most casual remark becomes a study or a book and does get published.

In graduate school, you are a graduate student. Unless there is an emergency, you keep your priorities straight. Both Mary Reuder and Florence Denmark knew that I was married with children, just as I knew something about their private worlds, but we never discussed our families outside of the school. First of all, who had the luxury of time spent discussing anything but work? The Graduate Center was only three blocks from Lord and Taylor's department store. In all the years that I was a student, I never saw the inside of that store.

PSI CHI

From the time that I was a graduate student, I was involved with Psi Chi, the national honor society in psychology, and its programs at the American Psychological Association national conferences and regional meetings. These programs are particularly important to women who may have difficulty finding a mentor at their own academic institutions.

The first session in which I participated concerned graduate school admissions procedures. The faculty officers of Psi Chi led by Florence Denmark thought that some mentoring could take place in group settings. Business organizations already provided networking sessions with outside speakers to guide employees at all levels of skill and experience, so why not the academic world? For over 30 years, Psi Chi has allocated time at regional and national conferences to address the needs of students applying to doctoral programs. At the end of these sessions, the speakers on the panel respond to individual questions from the audience. The topics range from the choice of degrees to the content of personal statements, letters of reference and who should serve as a reference, regular and stress interviews, and research requirements. The Psi Chi panels about admission procedures for doctoral programs included experienced faculty and recent graduates as well as graduate students making presentations to ensure the relevance of the material to current practices. Over the years, the Psi Chi panels have tried to be honest and helped even students with poor academic credentials to make realistic choices that utilize their skills.

Psi Chi's efforts can only address the questions of a few students. Therefore, large numbers of students are still in need of advice, if not complex career management. In business, there are publications to which people can submit questions anonymously that will be answered in a column. In order to cover a broad spectrum of inquiries, the column might simply be called "Professional Development." The American Psychological Association also has publications designed to guide students and faculty. Some years ago, another conference session, also sponsored by Psi Chi, was designed to cover the issues surrounding career changes from traditional academic positions to jobs in business, law enforcement, government, advertising, and politics. These sessions were planned as a substitute for advice from one's own faculty and have become extremely popular.

ADVICE FROM A NEIGHBOR

I mentioned that I have received important advice even from strangers. An example of such counsel came from someone living in my own neighborhood when I was an undergraduate. During the fall semester of my senior undergraduate year, I casually mentioned to a neighbor that I might want to apply for a doctoral program. Since the local communication network was operating at its usual peak efficiency, it took less than a day for the information to travel several blocks and for my doorbell to ring. My visitor was another neighbor and comparative stranger. She simply said, "You don't really know me, but I'd like to talk to you." She was correct; I didn't even know her name. I'd only seen her once or twice in the supermarket. We sat down and she proceeded to tell me that she had once started a master's program in social work but had never finished. She said that if I listened to her, my future would be different. She advised me about how to set my priorities and how to avoid deviating from them. With the exception of a sick child or husband, she said, everything else should be considered trivial. Meals can be ordered, and silverware doesn't really need to be polished. Although this was not yet the era of takeout food that we have today, when I graduated, I made a very short speech. I said, "This degree is courtesy of Chung King Chow Mein, Swanson's TV dinners, and Rex's Pizza Palace that Delivers." I did stay focused.

BROOKLYN COLLEGE

As graduate students, we were treated quite well. My first teaching position was as a graduate student instructor in the Psychology Department at Brooklyn College, one of the 22 units of the City University of New York. The department employed approximately 70 full-time tenured or tenure track faculty, 110 adjuncts, and several advising staff members, most of whom were doctoral students from Brooklyn College or one of the other senior CUNY units such as the Graduate Center. With the exception of the graduate students, most of the full-time faculty members were men. In the years that I worked at Brooklyn College, I was reminded of my lowly status as a graduate student only once, and I believe that the comment was really more of a warning to finish my dissertation than an insult. In fact, life was so good at Brooklyn College that none of us wanted to finish. Our jobs were contingent on our being students, so we remained students too long. During my time at Brooklyn College, I wrote several articles with my mentors and alone but avoided my dissertation completely. Thus, the delay was not due to laziness or lack of time. As a group, we just didn't want to leave. Finally, someone at CUNY figured out what we were all doing and raised the fee for "maintenance of matriculation" tenfold. After that, I finished my dissertation in four months. What was it about the Brooklyn College Psychology Department—and, indeed, the entire college—at that time that was so nurturing that none of us wanted to leave? Our teaching load and class sizes were reasonable, we had large offices and secretarial support, we attended and participated fully in faculty meetings, and we were immersed in a pattern of professional behavior that was exhilarating. It seemed to me that almost everyone was actively engaged in research, the animal laboratories were working on fascinating projects, and we read and discussed each others' work with enthusiasm. We were invited to dinners with the president of Brooklyn College and the rest of the faculty to honor such distinguished speakers as the historian Henry Steele Commager and the linguist Noam Chomsky. At the Graduate Center, during the same period of time, we were exposed to all the academic pressures that graduate students encounter in most other doctoral and research institutions. Thus, the stress and tension that we faced in our other existence made the camaraderie of Brooklyn College all the more attractive. The support of the Psychology Department also lasted long after we had left for other jobs. When I graduated and was ready to leave the college, the late Bernie Seidenberg gave me some advice. He said, "Tread softly and if you get into trouble, call. Don't try to solve every problem yourself." And I did call when I needed help. However, the people I called were usually Dr. Denmark and Dr. Reuder.

REFERENCES

Albom, M. (1997). *Tuesdays with Morrie.* New York: Doubleday.

Beresin, E. V. (2004, September). Experiences as protégé and mentor. *Psychiatric Times, 59*–64.

Brown, W. K. (2004). Resiliency and the mentoring factor. *Reclaiming Children and Youth, 13*(2), 75–79.

Dowd, M. (2005, October 30). What's a modern girl to do? *New York Times.* Retrieved from http://www.nytimes.com/2005/10/30/magazine/30feminism.html.

Johnson, W. B. (2002). The intentional mentor: Strategies and guidelines for the practice of mentoring. *Professional Psychology: Research and Practice, 33*(1), 88–96.

Jung, C. G., von Franz, M., Henderson, J. L., Jacobi, J., & Jaffee, A. (1964). *Man and his symbols.* Garden City, NY: Doubleday.

Kram, K. E. (1983). Phases of the mentor relationship. *Academy of Management Journal, 26*(4), 608–625.

Levinson, D. J., Darrow, C. N., Klein, E. B., Levinson, M. H., & McKee, B. (1978). *The seasons in a man's life.* New York: Knopf.

Lindner, J. R., Dooley, K. E., & Williams, J. R. (2003). Teaching, coaching, mentoring, facilitating, motivating, directing. What is a teacher to do? *Agricultural Education Magazine, 76*(2), 26–27.

Maples, M. F. (2008). *Counseling and life coaching: Complementary or competitive? (ACAPCD-21).* Alexandria, VA: American Counseling Association.

McCluskey, K. W., Noller, R. B., Lamoureux, K., & McCluskey, A.L.A. (2004). Unlocking hidden potential through mentoring. *Reclaiming Children and Youth, 13,* 85–93.

National Institutes of Health. (n.d.). Mentor roles and responsibilities. Retrieved November 22, 2004 from http://internships.info.nih.gov/mentor.html.

Tenner, E. (2004). The pitfalls of academic mentorships. *Chronicle of Higher Education, 50*(49), B7.

Thorne, B. M. & Henley, T. B. (2004). *Connections in the history and systems of psychology* (3rd edition). Boston: Houghton Mifflin.

Waters, J. (1969, March). *Test taking format and locus-of-control.* Paper presented at the Eastern Psychological Association Conference, Boston, MA.

Chapter 3

Mentoring Women in Science, Technology, Engineering, and Mathematics Fields

Bianca L. Bernstein, Ryan Jacobson,
and Nancy Felipe Russo

Acknowledgements. We would like to thank Kendra Michael for her assistance in obtaining reference materials.

Although women continue to be underrepresented in some science, technology, engineering, and mathematics (STEM) fields, National Science Foundation (NSF) data show that, overall, the picture in the last decade has been improving; since 2000, bachelor's degrees have been awarded to women and men in approximately equal numbers. Indeed, women earned 50.5 percent of STEM degrees in 2006. Further, the proportion of minorities has increased; in 2006, 17 percent of bachelor's STEM degrees went to underrepresented minorities (defined by the NSF as blacks, Hispanics, and American Indians/Alaska Natives), up from 10 percent in 1989. Progress, however, lags at the graduate level and continues to be uneven across the disciplines. Proportions of graduate women have increased overall (from 39% in 1966 to 43% in 2006) (NSF, 2009).

Whether these numbers signify a glass half full or half empty depends on one's focus. The large proportions of graduate women in psychology (76%), biological sciences (56%), and social sciences (54%) are occasions for optimism. However, the numbers in engineering and computer sciences (23% and 25% in 2006, respectively), when compared to healthier proportions (ranging from 30% to 45%) in other fields, continue to be occasions for concern. The status and outlook depend on the perceiver's standpoint.

With regard to full-time employment in universities and four-year colleges, the settings where the bulk of the mentoring of future generations of STEM aspirants takes place, women were 33 percent of the 269,400 STEM doctoral holders employed full-time (all occupations) in 2006 (again, with proportions varying by subfield). White women were the largest group (24.9% of STEM faculty and staff), followed by Asian (4.5%), black (1.7%), Hispanic (1.3%), and American Indian/Alaska Native (0.2%) women (NSF, 2009).

Good data on attrition in STEM fields are sparse, but results from the most comprehensive study to date have been recently released. The Council of Graduate Schools (CGS) found that men had higher cumulative doctoral completion rates than women at 10 years from first enrollment in engineering, life sciences, and mathematical and physical sciences, with nine, eight, and seven percentage point gaps, respectively (CGS, 2008).

There are several lessons in these figures for mentors in STEM fields. First, the proportions of graduate women in STEM fields means that understanding their needs and equipping them to thrive in STEM educational and workplace contexts is a mandated necessity, not a luxury. This mandate applies to all disciplines—and even the lowest figure of 23 percent translates into one in four graduate students in that field. Second, the gap between the number of women students who graduate with undergraduate STEM degrees and the number of women students who complete their PhD and pursue STEM-related careers means that understanding and addressing issues related to what has been known as the leaky pipeline problem stands out as a priority for those who seek to be effective mentors of women in the sciences. It is important to note as well that the pipeline metaphor has been replaced with the notion of career pathways— a more accurate way of portraying the choices women make about how to apply their knowledge, experience, and values to the career alternatives available to them. Third, the variation in progress across the disciplines means that interventions must be context based. They must also be tailored to counter the effects of complex interactions among unexamined cultural beliefs, norms, and expectations characteristic of both individual disciplines and particular institutional contexts. Fourth, the fact that one out of three STEM doctorate holders employed in universities and four-year colleges (all occupations) are women means that skilled and effective women mentors are potentially a powerful force for changing the climate and culture of their institutions, if not their disciplines. Fifth, the underrepresentation of ethnic minority women as mentors is of particular concern and emphasizes the need for all faculty, regardless of gender or ethnicity, to understand the dynamics involved in negotiating multiple social identities.

The first step in being an effective STEM mentor is to understand the factors that foster as well as undermine educational and career development in STEM careers. Such factors include the nature of doctoral education; lack of access to effective role models; lack of support for women with family commitments; the atmosphere of the work environment, sexual harassment, and targeted microaggressions; and subtle stereotyped beliefs, attitudes, and cultural biases that operate beyond conscious awareness and that are often discipline- and department-specific (Bernstein & Russo, 2007, 2008; National Academy of Sciences [NAS], 2007, 2009; National Research Council [NRC], 2001;). The culture of science has been shaped by the masculine ideal of 17th-century England and has yet to fully adapt to contemporary realities (Ferreira, 2003).

This androcentric perspective is reflected in the gendered nature of academic disciplines and institutions. As Lotte Bailyn (2003) eloquently observed, "the academy is anchored in assumptions about competence and success that have led to practices and norms constructed around the life experiences of men, and around a vision of masculinity as the normal universal requirement of university life" (p. 143). In this chapter, we consider some of what mentors in STEM fields need to know to broaden their vision of mentoring; to better understand the gendered nature of disciplines, institutions, and careers; and to become effective mentors in today's diverse and changing world. We consider the origins and limitations of traditional mentoring models, highlight some of the things that mentors and protégés need to know to have mutually satisfying and effective mentoring relationships in today's academic context, and identify mentoring resources tailored to STEM fields.

MENTORING: TOWARD A BROADER VISION

Scholars have often emphasized the ancient Greek origins of mentoring (Armstrong, Allinson, & Hayes, 2002; Bushardt, Fretwell, & Holdnak, 1991; Cunningham & Eberle, 1993; Hunt & Michael, 1983; Johnson, 2002; NAS, 1997). In 2003, the American Association for the Advancement of Science, in collaboration with the National Science Foundation, convened an interdisciplinary study group to assess what was known about mentoring in STEM fields and the structure and functioning of mentoring in STEM educational and workforce sectors (George & Neale, 2006). In a report commissioned for the study group (Packard, 2006), mentoring was described as

> a term generally used to describe a relationship between a less-experienced individual, called a mentee or protégé, and a more-experienced individual known as a mentor. It is important to acknowledge that the term 'mentor' is borrowed from the male guide, Mentor, in Greek mythology, and this historical context has informed traditional manifestations of mentoring. (p. 39)

As noted by these authors, the term *mentor* can be traced to the character Mentor in Homer's *The Odyssey*. In the story, Odysseus must leave Greece to fight in the distant Trojan War and so charges his wise and trusted friend Mentor with the responsibility of guiding, educating, and protecting his infant son Telemachus. Thus, at least superficially, Mentor and Telemachus would seem to provide a paragon for modern-day mentoring relationships. In the classic version of this often-emulated model, an older and more experienced individual takes primary responsibility for nurturing the educational, professional, and, to some extent, personal development of a promising young novice. However, as Koocher (2002) points out, the vision drawn from this portrait of mentoring's origins neglects an important subtext to Homer's story. A closer reading reveals that Mentor's guidance is often inadequate and that the goddess Athena must impersonate him on several occasions to provide the wise guidance that Telemachus needs. Further, Athena must impersonate Mentor rather than appearing in her true form because the norms of Greek culture of the period would have prevented a woman from providing such counsel.

In recounting this neglected feminist element to the origin story of mentoring, Koocher (2002) emphasizes the importance of transcending stereotypes that unnecessarily limit available sources of wisdom. In addition to this important point, we suggest two additional morals of Mentor's story that have particular implications for envisioning the present and future of mentoring women in STEM fields.

First, Mentor's story highlights the potential limitations of envisioning mentoring solely in terms of top-down, dyadic relationships cast in the images of Mentor and Telemachus. Based on existing mentoring literature, there are several reasons to believe that a rigid reliance on this form of relationship is unlikely to meet the increasingly diverse needs of academic protégés. Indeed, as Packard's (2006) briefing report pointed out, this model is one of many possible models that can be structured in diverse ways in addition to dyadic relationships, including multiple mentoring, peer group mentoring, electronic mentoring (e.g., MentorNet at www.MentorNet.net), and cascade mentoring (a system often found in academic research laboratories whereby the professor may supervise graduate or advanced undergraduate students, and they in turn supervise lower division or more inexperienced students).

Second, Mentor's story reminds us that cultural beliefs, norms, and expectations can create artificial barriers that restrict mentoring opportunities to a limited range of acceptable outlets. As is illustrated by the necessity of a covert role for Athena, cultural norms of academe in general, and in differing disciplines in particular, may obscure the presence of helpful alternative resources as well as introduce unintended barriers to protégé development.

We argue for a broader, multifaceted, and context-based perspective on academic mentoring—one that acknowledges the diverse needs of protégés, emphasizes the value of a multifaceted approach, and is tailored to specific disciplinary and institutional context of the student.

TRADITIONAL MENTORING: BENEFITS AND LIMITATIONS

The importance of role models and mentors in STEM fields has been well established (Fort, 2005; Nettles & Millett, 2006). Research suggests that traditional hierarchical dyadic mentoring can have substantial benefits. First, it focuses on the student's immediate context—both the mentor and the student are in the same institutional and disciplinary context and have direct interpersonal contact. A major limitation of this model is that when something goes wrong in the relationship, the student has few resources to buffer negative outcomes. This is particularly true in fields where the mentor is all powerful—that is, where educational admission and advancement, as well as job placement and opportunities for professional networking, all depend on the mentor's opinion of the student.

When the mentor is knowledgeable, supportive, and respected in her field, students can thrive with this model. Indeed, this model of mentoring has been linked to scholarly productivity and satisfaction with the doctoral program among predoctoral students (Clark, Harden, & Johnson, 2000; Johnson, Koch, Fallow, & Huwe, 2000; Mellott, Arden, & Cho, 1997; Nettles & Millett, 2006) and has been associated with higher incomes and increased career satisfaction among former protégés in a variety of settings (Fagenson-Eland, Marks, & Amendola, 1997; Roche, 1979; Russell & Adams, 1997). A recent quantitative review of mentoring research in general concluded that mentoring has strong effects on job and career satisfaction when demographics, human capital, and core self-evaluations are controlled, but it is only one, and not necessarily the strongest, predictor of career outcomes (Kammeyer-Mueller & Judge, 2007).

The extent to which this research can be applied to the diverse population of STEM graduate students that has emerged in the last decade has yet to be determined. Also, there may be context-specific effects that differ depending on the activity. For example, a recent study pointed to the remarkable difference a mentor can make in the probability of STEM women assistant professors receiving grants: Over six fields, the probability of receiving a grant (critical for STEM faculty) was 68 percent for women and 86 percent for men without mentors and 93 percent for women and 83 percent for men with mentors (NRC, 2009).

Another limitation on generalization from mentoring research in non-STEM contexts is that the model of mentoring assessed in such research is typically limited to a traditional vision of mentoring. For example, respondents are often given a definition of mentoring that envisions mentors as "persons usually considered as more experienced, who support, train, 'teach the ropes to' or sponsor others as they pursue their career goals" (Allen, Poteet, Russell, & Dobbins, 1997, p. 9). The extent to which the findings of such research can be generalized to alternative visions of mentoring is unknown. In academic settings, peer mentors and organizations such as faculty women's associations may provide networking and mentoring opportunities that do not fit the traditional model.

A critical limitation of the traditional form of top-down, dyadic mentoring associated with STEM fields emanates from the complex needs of protégés with increasingly diverse backgrounds. The growing presence in graduate programs of individuals who are unlike their professors on one or more aspects of social differences—such as gender, ethnicity, sexual orientation, religion, and nationality, among others—presents a significant challenge for this form of mentoring. These diverse individuals may have needs and goals that differ from those of the typical traditional STEM students who have historically been predominately white and male. Such needs may not be met if their available mentors are also those white men and others who have neither the training nor the personal experiences to understand the student's situation.

That is not to imply in any way that all white men lack the knowledge needed for effective mentoring of women and ethnic minorities. Mentor-Net (2007) analyzed four years of evaluation data for effects of mentor gender on mentoring relationships among STEM women protégés. In some years, the women protégés paired with women mentors had significantly higher satisfaction with the program than women protégés with men mentors. But in other years, women protégés with men and women mentors reported comparable satisfaction.

Similarly, ethnic minority protégés who had mentors of the same race/ethnicity reported comparable satisfaction as those in a cross-race pair. Higher proportions of Hispanic (79%) and African American (76%) were satisfied overall with their mentoring relationships than were Asian American (69%) and white (72%) protégés. Of course, mentors willing to participate in a national e-mentoring program that provides mentoring support and guidance may be more dedicated, committed, flexible, and knowledgeable than the mentors who do not participate, so generalization should be made with caution. The effect of communicating via e-mail, which strips visual and auditory cues that cue stereotypes and can affect the emotional tone of the interaction, may also benefit protégés who are women or ethnic minority. Generalization is further limited by the fact that 71 percent of the mentors came from industry; only 11 percent came from academic institutions.

In academic institutions, gender and ethnic diversity in STEM fields has increased more slowly among faculty than student populations (NSF, 2009). Thus, women, particularly ethnic minority women, may have limited access to mentors who share these social identities. Given the potential benefits of such pairings in an academic context, underrepresented students may be at a disadvantage in disciplines and in academic institutions that rely almost exclusively on a traditional model of dyadic faculty-to-student mentoring. In addition to presenting a challenge for existing academic departments with low faculty diversity, it is also important to note that reliance on traditional dyadic mentor pairings in these contexts may have the unintended consequence of discouraging future growth in student diversity. In academic programs that rely on dyadic faculty pairings, research suggests that students often prefer gender- and ethnicity-congruent mentors (Santos & Reigadas, 2002; Scandura & Williams, 2001). The lack of availability of such matches may deter otherwise qualified individuals from pursuing careers in these areas.

So the ideal situation of a knowledgeable and supportive mentor may be a far cry from the reality experienced by STEM graduate students even today. Even when mentors are well intentioned and want to be supportive, they are also very busy people and may not have to time to equip themselves with what they need to know to understand and communicate with diverse graduate students. Strategies for overcoming these problems include providing both mentors and mentees ready access to information that will enhance their knowledge and communication skills and establishing multiple mentoring opportunities so that students will not have to rely solely on one source of mentoring support. Professional development initiatives such as the Preparing Future Faculty program have further encouraged the practice of multiple mentors for different roles of the aspiring faculty member; good research mentors may differ from faculty members who are most effective in mentoring for teaching, community outreach, or careers in industry, government, or nonprofits.

Given the array of mentor and protégé characteristics that can affect the success of mentoring relationships and given the unique distributions of those characteristics in individual mentors and protégés, it is simply not reasonable to expect that any one mentoring relationship, even if matched based on gender and ethnicity, could adequately fulfill all (or perhaps even the majority) of a protégé's needs. There are a variety of personal qualities (e.g., cognitive or work style) that can determine the success of the mentoring relationship (Armstrong et al., 2002; Ensher, Grant-Vallone, & Marelich, 2002). There is evidence that women tend to be more dissatisfied than men with the quality of their mentoring relationships with senior faculty, and this is linked to perceptions that their departments are "uninviting, unappealing, and unaccommodating" (Trower & Chait, 2002, p. 34). It appears that relying exclusively on one dyadic mentoring relationship virtually ensures that some of the needs of protégés will remain unfulfilled.

An alternative is to re-envision mentoring from a dyadic to a multiple mentorship model. The traditional model of focusing on one dyadic relationship limits exposure to diverse perspectives. Thus, although cross-gender or cross-ethnic pairings have potential disadvantages, particularly if the mentor is unskilled, such pairings have potential advantages as well. Cultural diversity has often been championed as a means to stimulate creative ideas and solutions, and its value in this regard has been supported by research that demonstrates greater work efficiency and creativity among diverse as opposed to homogeneous work teams. Just as Telemachus's development would have been limited by a system in which Athena was unable to collaborate in his guidance, modern academic mentoring arrangements that rely rigidly on dyadic relationships may prevent protégés from obtaining valuable alternate perspectives and insights. Indeed, there is increasing evidence that women disproportionately benefit from participating in collaborative groups and professional or women's networks (NAS, 2007; NRC, 2009).

Finally, a top-down, dyadic approach to mentoring may be incongruent with other cultural traditions of guidance, and this may lead to two somewhat different sets of limitations. Individuals from other cultural traditions may be more familiar with somewhat more communal forms of mentoring that involve multiple mentors or forms that involve a lower (or higher) degree of power differential between mentor and protégé. In a multicultural academic context, these differences in traditions may present problems as the protégé struggles to understand the role expectations and norms of a different mentoring model. To the extent that the mentoring model is inflexible, the burden for overcoming these challenges is shifted disproportionately to the individual whose values and background are not consistent with the dominant paradigm. In addition, a rigid reliance on one form of mentoring model means that individuals cannot benefit from other, potentially valuable approaches. For example, Fassinger and Hensler-McGinnis (2005) describe a feminist alternative to traditional mentoring that emphasizes, among other concepts, shared power, relational sharing, collaboration, and a commitment to diversity. The use of alternative mentoring models (or select elements of those models) based on different cultural traditions could be quite useful, especially in increasingly diverse contexts. Multicultural feminist models of mentoring may offer particularly effective approaches for mentoring ethnic minority women (Benishek, Bieschke, Park, & Slattery, 2004).

THE NEED FOR INSTITUTIONAL CHANGE

The model of top-down dyadic mentoring is embedded in an institutional culture that has implicit as well as explicit expectations for the process. As noted, this may create unrealistic expectations for what mentoring can be expected to provide. Especially as demographic conditions change, these assumptions can lead to a series of missed opportunities and unintended barriers to graduate student success. Addressing the ways in which mentoring is influenced by this larger institutional culture is therefore essential for change to occur.

Institutional policies that recognize contributions of graduate committee chairs but not committee members, promote competition among students, do not recognize peer mentoring efforts, and discourage students from communicating and establishing relationships with faculty beyond their primary mentor foster a rigidity in approach that can create obstacles to student development. Keyser et al. (2008) exemplify an effort to enhance institutional support for research mentorships. They describe how institutions affect mentoring by influencing (a) criteria for selecting mentors, (b) incentives for motivating faculty to serve effectively as mentors, (c) factors that facilitate the mentor-mentee relationship, (d) factors that strengthen a mentee's ability to conduct research responsibly, and (e) factors that contribute to the professional development of both mentees and mentors. Although based on experiences in academic medicine, the framework has potential for application to other disciplines.

Other effects of sole reliance on the traditional form of mentoring can obscure the presence of other forms of valuable mentoring resources. For example, research suggests that peer support is often nearly as strongly related as mentor support to outcomes like career commitment, satisfaction, and success (Gram, 1992; Grant-Vallone & Ensher, 2000; Ulku-Steiner, Kurtz-Costes, & Kinlaw, 2000). Peers often serve as valuable mentors, yet their role in student development is often overlooked and left uncultivated and unrewarded. Little is known about mentoring relationships among peers in STEM fields, and perhaps the concept of protégé, which implies a subordinate power relationship among the parties, contributes to neglect of this important area of research. Similarly, the development of coaching programs in addition to mentoring programs, signifies efforts to distinguish between hierarchical models that vest the power to determine outcomes in the mentor versus efforts to vest that power in the mentee (Law, Ireland, & Hussain, 2007). Because the research has focused on mentor–protégé relationships, we continue to use that language here, with the caveat to be mindful that we are talking about one type of mentor–mentee relationship when using that language.

The traditional approach to mentoring can also undermine opportunities by discouraging individual mentors and protégés from taking fresh perspectives and openly discussing alternative mentoring approaches. This unquestioned reliance on traditional mentoring creates the illusion of rigidity and permanence that may prevent individuals from identifying unique solutions to problems.

An inflexible culture of mentoring can also create a series of unintended barriers for individuals seeking alternative forms of guidance. For example, in an environment where the mentoring relationship is viewed as an exclusive and permanent pairing between two individuals, protégés may be discouraged from seeking potentially helpful advice from other faculty. Similarly, potential mentors may be discouraged from offering useful guidance to students for fear of negative feedback from primary mentors.

In this kind of environment, the lack of rewards for creative approaches to mentoring can also be expected to inhibit an active, problem-solving approach to mentoring challenges. Further, the potentially unrealistic expectations for this form of mentoring (i.e., that protégé needs should be fully met by a dyadic mentoring relationship) may lead to an inevitable sense of failure for both mentor and protégé. Finally, in this system there is no protection from the toxic or antimentor who provides a hostile, demeaning, or otherwise negative graduate experience.

In sum, we live in a time of societal change that is occurring at all levels of society. Historically, one acquired mentoring skills by informal observation and personal experience. But the qualities and skills needed to mentor today's younger generation are not the same as those required in previous generations. Not only are members of the current generation more socially and culturally diverse, they are pursuing their education and careers during a time of social and economic change.

WHAT DO MENTORS NEED TO KNOW?

The two most essential things mentors should keep in mind is that what they need to know constantly evolves, and it depends on disciplinary and institutional contexts as well as mentee stages of education and career development. Thus, mentors need to be informed about what is happening in their disciplines and maintain an open and flexible stance regarding what may be needed for particular students to achieve their educational and career goals. One size will not fit all. As the National Academy of Science's Committee on Science, Engineering, and Public Policy (1997) observed, "As the employment environment and the conduct of science and engineering change continuously, *it is wise to view the career as an evolutionary process*" (p. 43). The book *Advisor, Teacher, Role Model, Friend: On Being a Mentor to Students in Science and Engineering* (NAS, 1997) provides a mentoring guide that articulates the steps faculty members can take to increase their mentoring effectiveness and encompasses a variety of roles that mentors may play for STEM students, including faculty advisor, career advisor, skills consultant, and role model.

In previous work (Bernstein & Russo, 2007, 2008), we have reviewed the literature on the progress and challenges facing women in STEM fields and have emphasized that understanding STEM women's progress begins with the view that careers are constructed by each individual in dynamic, nonlinear, and unique ways (Bernstein & Russo, 2008). From this perspective, mentors need to understand that women's lives and circumstances do not conform to the masculine script in which a successful life is envisioned as linear, singularly purposeful, and narrowly focused on career advancement. Protégés are active agents who assess their options, weigh alternatives, and make choices in keeping with their values and priorities.

As aspiring students pursue their education and careers, they begin to consider multiple priorities in their lives and must consider the extent to which they will balance their continuing passion for science and meaningful work with their commitment to other priorities. For women, in particular, this consideration becomes more salient in graduate school (Bernstein & Russo, 2007). Mentors have key roles to play in helping their women students resolve perceived incompatibilities between meeting the demands of academic culture with fulfilling other life goals (such as family formation or community service). Interestingly, in *Athena Unbound*, Etzkowitz, Kemelgor, and Uzzi (2000) point out that Athena has strong female and male elements in her identity and thus personifies the dilemma of the contemporary woman scientist who expects herself (and is expected to) combine a demanding personal and professional life without diminishing either.

Men mentors may have difficulty fully understanding the issues of work–family balance faced by their women protégés (Gilbert & Rossman, 1992). This point is supported by research demonstrating the potentially beneficial effects of matching mentor and protégé on key demographic characteristics. For example, undergraduate Latino students matched with same-ethnic faculty mentors of the same ethnicity perceived them to be more supportive in promoting career and personal advancement than those in cross-ethnic mentor pairs (Santos & Reigadas, 2002), and gender-matched men and women reported more positive effects from role modeling than those in cross-gender mentoring relationships (Scandura & Williams, 2001).

Mentors who understand the processes women use to make career choices should be better able to provide the information and support that is needed to keep them on track in their careers. The issues may differ depending on mentor and protégé ethnicity (e.g., Crawford & Smith, 2005; Gonzáles-Figueroa & Young, 2005). Mentors also may not recognize that problems that contribute to withdrawal from graduate school may not arise in graduate school. Individuals make choices in the context of their imagined "possible selves" (Markus & Nurius, 1986), which may encompasses future selves they want to become as well as those they want to avoid. Women aspiring to STEM careers find themselves in highly competitive, male-dominated environments, with few women role models, mentors, or guidance for how to negotiate their ideals for their careers and personal lives (Bernstein & Russo, 2008).

Mentors can play key roles in helping women, particularly ethnic minority women, overcome difficulties they may have in imagining their future selves in STEM careers, clarifying unrecognized options and opportunities to consider, and helping them find exemplars of the possibilities they seek to explore (Gibson & Cordova, 1999). In doing so, it is important to recognize how elements of the situational context can create barriers that undermine women's choices, including ambiguous and gendered expectations, lack of access to resources, and discriminatory practices—subtle and not so subtle (Sonnert & Holton, 1995, 1996).

Ambiguous and shifting evaluation criteria combined with a competitive environment create an extremely stressful context. Mentors can help young STEM graduate students and faculty learn to assess their environments, identify hidden or implicit weights among evaluation criteria, and evaluate and negotiate the balance among expectations and demands at work and at home as they construct their career paths. The gendered nature of these expectations and demands in the context of a hierarchical work environment means that women in STEM fields have a more complex task, which contributes to avoidance and attrition of women in the sciences (Corley, 2005; Fox, 2001).

Productivity is essential for educational and career success, but what defines productivity may be implicit and unclear. Women graduate students, particularly women who are ethnic minority students, may be asked to spend time in service roles or helping with departmental activities, and then may be devalued for not spending as many hours in the lab as male peers who do not contribute in such ways. Mentors are the translators of the criteria that define productivity so that the student understands what does and does not count. However, performing some service can provide worthwhile experiences for students, regardless of gender. Mentors have a role to play in helping students set and enforce boundaries on teaching and service activities. Advanced graduate students may be asked to take on large undergraduate courses to free up faculty time to focus on research or teach smaller graduate courses. Because women who refuse requests for help are often viewed as violating female gender stereotypes, the ability for a woman to say something like "my mentor advises me to turn down this request so that I can focus on publishing my research findings" can be helpful in impression management.

Mentors also play a major role in ensuring that their protégés' products (ideas, presentations, publications) are recognized as achievement. Praising students to others, articulating the importance of their contributions, and providing opportunities for the students to increase their visibility can determine whether a student's activities become recognized as achievements. These principles also apply to mentoring young faculty members.

Mentors need to understand the subtleties, range, and impact of the various forms of sexism and racism that women and minorities continue to encounter in the 21st century. The more blatant and egregious forms of discrimination that were visible and documentable have been replaced by more subtle forms of marginalization and discouragement of women in the sciences. These forms of "modern" or "subtle" sexism (Benokraitis, 1997) are rooted in gendered stereotypes, perceptions, and assumptions (Bernstein & Russo, 2007, 2008; National Academy of Sciences, 2007; Rapoport, Bailyn,

Fletcher, & Pruitt, 2002). Gender stereotypes differ among subcategories of women (e.g., stereotypes of white, black, and Hispanic women differ; they also differ for women physicists and women artists). In particular, stereotypes of women change when they become mothers such that they are both more liked but also seen as less competent (Biernat, Crosby, & Williams, 2004; Cuddy, Fiske, & Glick, 2004).

Mentors must also understand how the well-documented and pervasive effect of in-group favoritism, when examined in STEM contexts, becomes reflected in more positive evaluations of in-group members. Further, people make more positive attributions for the behavior of in-group members, allocate more rewards to them, and find them more persuasive than out-group members (Brewer & Brown, 1998). Thus, as eloquently put by Faye Crosby (2007),

> Often, those in positions of power (men) may not be as interested in keeping women out of good jobs as they are in bringing other men into their in-group. Discrimination in favor of men has the same effect as discrimination against women. (p. 50)

Psychologists have identified a number of intrapersonal mechanisms by which subtle sexism and unconscious bias can create stress and interfere with productivity. In addition to the normal stress of graduate school, diverse students may face issues of discrimination or more subtle forms of prejudice such that they may battle against a persistent "stereotype threat" (e.g., Steele & Aronson, 1995) that interferes with academic performance. It may be difficult for mentors unfamiliar with diverse student backgrounds to adequately attend to these needs.

These are but a few selected issues that mentors need to understand. We point to other sources (Bernstein & Russo, 2008; NAS, 2007) for a more detailed discussion of the variety of ways modern forms of sexism can affect educational and career experiences of women in STEM fields. Bernstein and Russo (2007) discuss how gendered stereotypes related to motherhood shape perceptions of women's competence and provide information on other issues, particularly those related to negotiating work and family goals and priorities.

WHAT DO PROTÉGÉS NEED TO KNOW?

Research on predictors of mentoring supports a less hierarchical view of mentoring, one that recognizes protégés as playing a critical role in the success of mentoring relationships. In a general review of the mentoring literature, Kammeyer-Mueller and Judge (2007) concluded that women and ethnic minorities report more barriers to obtaining a mentor, but whether they ultimately fail to find mentors or obtain less mentoring or poorer mentoring is not clear. In any case, mentees are selected based on their anticipated productivity and ability to provide information and to enhance the mentor's status in the organization. A protégé's self-image has a strong relationship to motivation, job performance, and job satisfaction, and motivation and job performance are qualities sought by mentors. Thus, the most important thing for protégés to know is that they need to learn how to present themselves and be prepared to identify and solve a variety of problems as they arise.

There are resources for protégés as well as mentors that can be of assistance in acquiring the knowledge and skills needed to attract and maintain a positive mentoring relationship. In particular, the on-line *Career*WISE project is designed to equip STEM graduate women with skills that will help them find well-suited mentors and more generally deal with a variety of problems that can be encountered in STEM educational and occupational contexts, including problems in the mentor–advisor relationship. The project is described below in more detail.

MENTORING: CONTEXT AND RESOURCES

The National Academy of Science's Committee on Science, Engineering, and Public Policy (1995), in its report on *Reshaping the Graduate Education of Scientists and Engineers,* envisioned a new kind of STEM PhD, one that emphasizes adaptability and versatility along with technical proficiency. Such a reshaping will require substantial institutional and cultural change, including change in conceptions of how graduates are socialized into their disciplines. This context requires a broader and transformative vision of mentoring. In it, mentors continue to teach protégés how to problem solve and overcome obstacles to advancement that arise in educational and work settings, but it is not be seen as inappropriate or illegitimate for protégés to seek help to overcome obstacles that may originate from other sources, such as family and friends. An individual may have multiple mentors, who may be professors or fellow graduate students or individuals in industry, and will not be required or advised to rely on a single person for access to knowledge and support. Further, mentoring goals are not limited to just teaching the mentee how to negotiate the existing system, which continues to have structural elements that are designed in keeping with the developmental life course of the traditional white male. Transformative mentoring includes building skills that enable mentees to act on and change systems they may encounter so that academic and research environments can become more responsive to new developments and foster the well-being of individual members of the institution. Movement toward healthy collaborative (as opposed to exploitive) relationships among research teams is essential for sustained creativity and productivity.

The policy context is currently supportive of change. Today, a broad range of federal laws prohibits discrimination in education, employment, contracting, housing, and other areas. In particular, Title IX of the Education Amendments of 1972—which declares that "No person in the United States shall, on the basis of sex, be excluded from participation in, be denied the benefits of, or be subjected to discrimination under any educational program or activity receiving Federal financial assistance"—has had a revolutionary impact on women's access to higher education.

There have been a host of national policy initiatives aimed at promoting diversity and equity. Major reports and policy statements issued by prestigious groups continue to inform policy and practice despite not being mandated by force of law. In particular, reports by the National Academy of Science, such as *Beyond Bias and Barriers* (NAS, 2007), and by the National Research Council, such as *Gender Differences at Critical Transitions* (CGS, 2009) and *Broadening Participation in Graduate Education* (CGS, 2009), have guided the development of funding priorities and programs. Other important reports that have focused on women in higher education in general and in STEM fields in particular have come from the American Council on Education (2005) and the National Research Council (NRC, 2001), among others. These provide a foundation for the identification and implementation of effective change efforts.

In the United States, targeted funding programs on the part of federal agencies have stimulated projects that are designed to meet particular goals. The ADVANCE program supported by the National Science Foundation targets university projects designed to increase the participation and success of women in STEM fields. Recognizing that more needs to be done than simply "fixing the women," "institutional transformation" projects are specifically designed to foster lasting institutional and cultural change in STEM disciplines (see NSF.gov). Through ADVANCE and other granting mechanisms, NSF supports a variety of studies related to changing the academic climate and culture through enhanced mentoring relationships.

Resources—on the Web and distributed as hard copy materials—have become widely available. ADVANCE programs have developed a host of models and materials that can be used to inform oneself and one's peers and that can be adapted to one's particular mentoring context. The Graduate College at the University of Michigan distributes an online mentoring guide that that is specifically targeted to graduate students (Regents of the University of Michigan, 2007). The National Academy of Sciences' (1997) mentoring guide described above also includes a chapter on resources, including Internet and professional resources.

The Association for Women in Science (AWIS) provides an institutional structure for peer networking and mentoring across scientific fields and access to mentoring resources. A new mentoring handbook written by former AWIS President Donna J. Dean (Dean, 2009) can be ordered from the AWIS Web site www.awis.org/. The AWIS Web site also has a section on useful links to other scientific and professional organizations that have committees or projects related to women and ethnic minorities, as well as to women's policy organizations. The latter section has a list of resources for working mothers. AWIS offers several types of mentoring and networking opportunities, including a coaching program that is available for a relatively low fee.

A variety of opportunities for electronic mentoring exist for mentors as well as protégés. For example, the Society of Women Engineers has a professional development program that includes webinars and podcasts, free to members (low cost to others) and provides links to a variety of resources, including information for addressing work–family balance issues (see www.societyofwomenengineers.swe.org).

MentorNet (www.MentorNet.net) is a nonprofit e-mentoring network that pairs motivated protégés (men and women) in STEM fields with mentors in higher education, government, and industry. In addition to providing opportunities for a one-on-one e-mail-based mentor relationship, MentorNet maintains an e-forum hosting Web-based discussion groups around pressing issues such as work–life balance, job searching, and graduate school, a resume database for students seeking internships or jobs, and links to resources for and about mentoring, diversity, and careers in engineering and science.

The *Career*WISE project (www.asu.edu/careerwise) is a new resource for protégés that seeks to develop and evaluate a Web-based personal resilience development program. With support from the National Science Foundation, the *Career*WISE research program was created in response to the growing numbers of women graduate students in STEM fields who fail to complete their doctoral programs.

The content of the psychoeducational training program is based on a combination of findings from previous researchers and new findings from *Career*WISE research studies. In focus group studies (Anderson-Rowland, Bernstein, & Russo, 2007a, 2007b; Bernstein, McBride, Russo, & Rohlfing, 2007), four domains of concern were identified as particularly discouraging to doctoral student women in STEM fields. In addition to trouble managing the relationship with their dissertation advisor, students reported lack of timely success or progress with dissertation research, difficulty balancing the demands of academic work with a personal life, and coping with an unfriendly professional climate.

*Career*WISE provides an array of original instructional materials, a broad spectrum of information briefs and video clips from interviews with women in science and engineering careers, and links to other resources, all to counter the discouragement that some women experience along the way to a doctoral degree. The beta materials have been tested with STEM women in an extensive series of studies on the usability, applicability, and intention to apply concepts (e.g., Bekki et al., 2008; Rolfing et al., 2009). Based on the encouraging results from these studies and final revisions after the forthcoming clinical trials, the *Career*WISE site is scheduled to be launched publicly in 2010.

CONCLUSION

In conclusion, mentors and protégés in STEM fields have complex relationships that are affected by their personal and social relationships as well as their disciplinary and institutional cultures. It is recognized that the traditional hierarchical dyadic model is insufficient to meet the diverse and changing needs of today's graduate students for multiple reasons, and new visions of mentoring have emerged. In these new visions, mentoring is less hierarchical and more reciprocal; it may involve peers in addition to subordinates, multiple mentors for different professional roles, and forms of communication other than face-to-face and one-on-one interaction. It is shaped not only by the goals and skills of the individuals but by the culture of the discipline and department. The goal of mentoring is not simply to teach the system but also to change the system so that it becomes more flexible and responsive to the needs and pathways of its members—mentors and protégés. Women must deal with issues related to their expected roles in the family and society but have had less access to mentors who have themselves dealt with such issues. Lack of access is particularly severe for ethnic minority women, who may have to deal with additional issues that emerge from the intersection of gender and ethnicity. Barriers to women's career development have multiple roots and must be addressed at multiple levels. Thus, successful mentors will consider the development of a protégé in context and be flexible in developing strategies to meet her mutual needs. Successful protégés will understand that mentoring relationships have mutual rewards and obligations and will take an active role in equipping themselves with the knowledge and skills needed to negotiate them.

REFERENCES

Allen, T. D., Poteet, M. L., Russell, J.E.A., & Dobbins, G. H. (1997). A field study of factors related to willingness to mentor others. *Journal of Vocational Behavior, 50,* 1–22.

American Council on Education, Office of Women in Higher Education. (2005). *An agenda for excellence: Creating flexibility in tenure-track faculty careers.* Washington, DC: Author.

Anderson-Rowland, M. R., Bernstein, B. L., & Russo, N. F. (2007a, June). The doctoral program in engineering and computer science: Is it the same for women and men? *Proceedings of the WEPAN 2007 Conference*, Orlando,

Anderson-Rowland, M. R., Bernstein, B. L., & Russo, N. F. (2007b, June). Encouragers and discouragers for domestic and international women in doctoral programs in engineering and computer science. *Proceedings of the 2007 ASEE Annual Conference and Exposition,* Honolulu, HI.

Armstrong, S. J., Allinson, C. W., & Hayes, J. (2002). Formal mentoring systems: An examination of the effects of mentor/protégé cognitive styles on the mentoring process. *Journal of Management Studies, 39,* 1111–1137.

Bailyn, L. (2003) Academic careers and gender equity: Lessons learned from MIT. *Gender, work and organizations, 10*(2), 137–153.

Bekki, J. M., Bernstein, B. L., Ellison, K., Sridharan, A., Hita, L., & Spadola, Q. (2008, October). Work in progress: Using case studies to increase the retention of female doctoral students in STEM Fields. *Proceedings of the 38th ASEE/IEEE Frontiers in Education Conference,* Saratoga Springs, NY.

Benishek, L. A., Bieschke, K. J., Park, J., & Slattery, S. M. (2004). A multicultural feminist model of mentoring. *Journal of Multicultural Counseling and Development, 32,* 428–442.

Benokraitis, N. V. (Ed.). (1997). *Subtle sexism: Current practice and prospects for change.* Thousand Oaks, CA: Sage.

Bernstein, B. L., McBride, D., Russo, N. F., & Rohlfing, J. (August, 2007). Everyday discouragers and encouragers for women in physical science and engineering Ph.D. programs: Implications for persistence and attrition, B. L. Bernstein (chair), *Predictors of Science and Engineering Involvement: Three NSF Funded Studies.* Symposium conducted at the meeting of the American Psychological Association, San Francisco, CA.

Bernstein, B. L. & Russo, N. F. (2007). Career paths and family in the academy: Progress and challenges. In M. Paludi & P. Neidermeyer (Eds.), *Work, life and family imbalance: How to level the playing field* (pp. 89–119). Westport, CT: Praeger.

Bernstein, B. L., & Russo, N. F. (2008). Explaining too few women in academic science and engineering careers: A psychosocial perspective. In M. Paludi (Ed.), *The psychology of women at work: Challenges and solutions for our female workforce:* Vol. 2. *Obstacles and the identity juggle* (pp. 1–33). Westport, CT: Praeger.

Biernat, M., Crosby, F. J., & Williams, J. C. (2004). The maternal wall: Research and policy perspectives on discrimination against mothers. *Journal of Social Issues, 60*(4).

Brewer, M. B., & Brown, R. J. (1998). Intergroup relations. In D. T. Gilbert, S. T. Fiske, & G. Lindzey (Eds.), *Handbook of social psychology* (4th ed., pp. 554–594). New York: McGraw-Hill.

Bushardt, S. C., Fretwell, C., & Holdnak, B. J. (1991). The mentor/protégé relationship: A biological perspective. *Human Relations, 44*(6), 619–639.

Clark, R. A., Harden, S. L., & Johnson, W. B. (2000). Mentor relationships in clinical psychology doctoral training: Results of a national survey. *Teaching of Psychology, 27,* 262–268.

Committee on Science, Engineering, and Public Policy. (National Academy of Science, National Academy of Engineering, and Institute of Medicine) *Reshaping the graduate education of scientists and engineers.* 1995. Washington, DC: National Academy Press. Retrieved June 4, 2009, from www.nap.edu/readingroom/books/grad

Corley, E. A. (2005). How do career strategies, gender, and work environment affect faculty productivity levels in university-based science centers? *Review of Policy Research, 22,* 637–655.

Council of Graduate Schools. (2008). *Ph.D. completion and attrition: Analysis of baseline demographic data from the Ph.D. Completion Project.* Washington, DC: Author.

Council of Graduate Schools. (2009). *Broadening participation in graduate education.* Washington, DC: CGS 2009. Author. Retrieved October 9, 2009, from http:// grad.arizona.edu/system/files/Broadening%20Participation%20in%20 Grad uate%20Education.pdf

Crawford, K., & Smith, D. (2005). The we and the us: Mentoring African American women. *Journal of Black Studies, 36,* 52–67.

Crosby, F. (2007). Sex discrimination at work. In J. E. Chrisler (Ed.), *Lectures in the psychology of women* (4th ed., pp. 220–235). New York: McGraw-Hill.

Cuddy, A.J.C., Fiske, S. T., & Glick, P. (2004). When professionals become mothers, warmth doesn't cut the ice. *Journal of Social Issues, 60,* 701–718.

Cunningham, J. B., & Eberle, T. (1993). Characteristics of the mentoring experience: A qualitative study. *Personnel Review, 22*(4), 54–66.

Dean, D. J. (2009). *Getting the most out of your mentoring relationships. A handbook for women in STEM.* New York: Springer.

Ensher, E. A., Grant-Vallone, E. J., & Marelich, W. D. (2002). Effects of perceived attitudinal and demographic similarity on protégés' support and satisfaction gained from their mentoring relationships. *Journal of Applied Social Psychology, 32,* 1407–1430.

Etzkowitz, H., Kemelgor, C., & Uzzi, B. (2000). *Athena unbound: The advancement of women in science and technology.* New York: Cambridge University Press.

Fagenson-Eland, E. A., Marks, M. A., & Amendola, K. L. (1997). Perceptions of mentoring relationships. *Journal of Vocational Behaviors, 51,* 29–42.

Fassinger, R., & Hensler-McGinnis, N. (2005). Multicultural feminist mentoring as individual and small-group pedagogy. In C. Ennis & A. Sinacore (Eds), *Teaching and social justice.* Washington, DC: American Psychological Association.

Ferreira, Maria M. (2003). Gender differences in graduate students' perspectives on the culture of science. *Journal of Women and Minorities in Science and Engineering, 9,* 119–135.

Fort, D. C. (Ed.). (2005). *A hand up: Women mentoring women in science.* Washington, DC: Association for Women in Science.

Fox, M. F. (2001). Women, science, and academia: Graduate education and careers. *Gender and Society, 15,* 654–666.

George, Y. S., & Neale, D. (2006). Report from study group meetings to develop a research and action agenda on STEM career and workforce mentoring. Retrieved June 5, [2009], from http://ehrweb.aaas.org/sciMentoring/ MentoringReport.pdf

Gibson, D. E., & Cordova, D. I. (1999). Women's and men's role models: The importance of exemplars. In A. J. Murrell, F. J. Crosby, & R. J. Ely (Eds.), *Mentoring dilemmas: Developmental relationships within multicultural organizations* (pp. 121–141). Mahwah, NJ: Erlbaum.

Gilbert, L. A., & Rossman, K. M. (1992). Gender and the mentoring process for women: Implications for professional development. *Professional Psychology: Research and Practice, 23,* 233–238.

Gonzáles-Figueroa, E., & Young, A. M. (2005). Ethnic identity and mentoring among Latinas in professional roles. *Cultural Diversity and Ethnic Minority Psychology, 11,* 213–226.

Gram, A. M. (1992). Peer relationships among clinicians as an alternative to mentor-protégé relationships in hospital settings. *Professional Psychology: Research and Practice, 23,* 416–417.

Grant-Vallone, E. J., & Ensher, E. A. (2000). Effects of peer mentoring on types of mentor support, program satisfaction and graduate student stress. *Journal of College Student Development, 41,* 637–642.

Hunt, D. M., & Michael, C. (1983). Mentorship: A career training and development tool. *Academy of Management Review, 8,* 475–485.

Johnson, W. B. (2002). The intentional mentor: Strategies and guidelines for the practice of mentoring. *Professional Psychology: Research and Practice, 33,* 88–96.

Johnson, W. B., Koch, C., Fallow, G. O., & Huwe, J. M. (2000). Prevalence of mentoring in clinical versus experimental doctoral programs: Survey findings, implications and recommendations. *Psychotherapy, 37,* 325–334.

Kammeyer-Mueller, J. D., & Judge, T. A. (2007). A quantitative review of mentoring research: Test of a model. *Journal of Vocational Behavior, 72,* 269–283.

Keyser, D. J., Lakoski, J. M., Lara-Cinisomo, S., Schultz, D. J., Williams, V. L., Zellers, D. F., & Pincus, H. A. (2008). Advancing institutional efforts to support research mentorship: A conceptual framework and self-assessment tool. *Academic Medicine, 83,* 217–225.

Koocher, G. P. (2002). Mentor revealed: Masculinization of an early feminist construct. *Professional Psychology: Research and Practice, 33,* 509–510.

Law, H., Ireland, S., & Hussain, Z. (2007). *The psychology of coaching, mentoring and learning.* New York: Wiley.

Markus, H., & Nurius, P. (1986). Possible selves. *American Psychologist, 41,* 954–969.

Mellott, R. N., Arden, I. A., & Cho, M. E. (1997). Preparing for internship: Tips for the prospective applicant. *Professional Psychology: Research and Practice, 28,* 190–196.

MentorNet. (2007). Success sustained by study: A documentation of MentorNet's growth and a summary of research findings—October 2007. Retrieved June 4, 2009, from http:// www.MentorNet.net

National Academy of Sciences, Committee on Maximizing the Potential of Women in Academic Science and Engineering & Committee on Science, Engineering, and Public Policy, National Academy of Sciences, National Academy of Engineering, and Institute of Medicine. (2007). *Beyond bias and barriers: Fulfilling the potential of women in academic science and engineering.* Washington, DC: National Academies Press.

National Academy of Sciences, Committee on Science, Engineering, and Public Policy. (1997). *Advisor, teacher, role model, friend: On being a mentor to students in science and engineering.* Washington, DC: National Academies Press.

National Research Council, Committee on Gender Differences in the Careers of Science, Engineering, and Mathematics Faculty; Committee on Women in Science, Engineering, and Medicine; National Research Council. (2009). *Gender differences at critical transitions in the careers of science, engineering and mathematics faculty.* Washington, DC: National Academies Press.

National Research Council, Committee on Women in Science and Engineering, Panel for the Study of Gender Differences in the Career Outcomes of Science and Engineering Ph.D.s. (2001). *From scarcity to visibility: Gender differences in the careers of doctoral scientists and engineers.* Washington, DC: National Academies Press.

National Science Foundation. (2009). *Women, minorities, and persons with disabilities in science and engineering, 2009.* NSF 09-305. Arlington, VA: National Science Foundation, Division of Science Resources Statistics. Retrieved [2009], from http://www.nsf.gov/statistics/wmpd

Nettles, M. T., & Millett, C. M. (2006). *Three magic letters: Getting to the PhD.* Baltimore: Johns Hopkins University Press.

Packard, B. W. (2006). Definition of mentoring—Appendix B. In Y. S. George & D. Neale (Eds.), *Report from study group meetings to develop a research and action agenda on STEM career and workforce mentoring.* Retrieved June 5, [2009], from http://ehrweb.aaas.org/sciMentoring/MentoringReport.pdf

Rapoport, R. L., Bailyn, L., Fletcher, J. K., & Pruitt, B. H. (2002). *Beyond work-family balance: Achieving gender equity and workplace performance.* San Francisco: Jossey-Bass.

Regents of the University of Michigan. (2007). *How to get the mentoring you want: A guide for graduate students at a diverse university.* Retrieved July 6, 2008, from http://www.rackham.umich.edu/downloads/publications/mentoring.pdf

Roche, G. R. (1979). Much ado about mentors. *Harvard Business Review, 57,* 14–28.

Rohlfing, J. E., Kube, E., Yabko, B. E., Murguia, E., Bekki, J., & Bernstein, B. L. (2009, June). Improving STEM doctoral students' relationships with their advisors: Web-based training in interpersonal problem-solving skills. *Proceedings of the 2009 ASEE Annual Conference and Exposition,* Austin, TX.

Russell, J.E.A., & Adams, D. M. (1997). The changing nature of mentoring in organizations: An introduction to the special issue on mentoring in organizations. *Journal of Vocational Behavior, 51,* 1–14.

Santos, S. J., & Reigadas, E. (2002). Latinos in higher education: An evaluation of a university faculty mentoring program. *Journal of Hispanic Higher Education,* 1(1), 40–50.

Scandura, T. A., & Williams, E. A. (2001). An investigation of the moderating effects of gender on the relationships between mentorship initiation and protégé perceptions of mentoring functions. *Journal of Vocational Behavior,* 59, 342–363.

Sonnert, G., & Holton, G. (1995). *Gender differences in science careers.* New Brunswick, NJ: Rutgers University Press.

Sonnert, G., & Holton, G. (1996). Career patterns of women and men in the sciences. *American Scientist, 84,* 63–71.

Steele, C. M., & Aronson, J. (1995). Stereotype threat and the intellectual test performance of African Americans. *Journal of Personality and Social Psychology,* 69, 797–811.

Trower, C. A., & Chait, R. P. (2002). Faculty diversity: Too little for too long, *Harvard Magazine, 104*(4), pp. 33–37, 98.

Ulku-Steiner, B., Kurtz-Costes, B., & Kinlaw, C. R. (2000). Doctoral student experiences in gender-balanced and male-dominated graduate programs. *Journal of Educational Psychology, 92,* 296–307.

Chapter 4

Mentoring Undergraduate Women

Joan C. Chrisler and Jennifer Gorman Rose

Athena, the Greek goddess of wisdom, warfare, and handicrafts, was known throughout the ancient world for her intellect, "craft, versatility, strength, diplomacy, initiative," and canny guidance (Silverberg, 1998, p. xiii). She is said to have invented weaving, pottery, carpentry, the flute, the chariot, and the Trojan horse. She is associated with success (especially in battle) and is a model of patient teaching and wise counsel. Most prominent among the many heroes whose causes she championed is Odysseus. During his long years at sea, Athena often visited his wife Penelope and his son Telemachus while disguised as an older man named Mentor, who came to be a friend of the family, a tutor to Telemachus, and a source of support and guidance for Penelope. As a result of this story, we call older people who take younger ones under their wings *mentors*. No doubt Athena took the guise of a man because, at that time, no woman would be seen as able to provide the type of guidance and counsel she wished to impart. Today, however, both women and men can engage in mentoring, and women role models and mentors play important roles in encouraging young women to fulfill their potential.

Most of the literature on mentoring is focused on the benefits of mentoring in business and the professions (e.g., Murrell, Crosby, & Ely, 1999; Powell, 1999). It discusses such important mentoring functions as opening doors, explaining aspects of institutional culture, and introducing protégés to "the right people." A subset of this literature is focused specifically on careers in academe. Many women faculty have written about the dearth of mentoring they received early in their careers and the effect it has had on their ability to succeed (e.g., Aisenberg & Harrington, 1988; Caplan, 1993; Clark & Corcoran, 1986). Formal studies have been conducted about experience of and need for mentoring of graduate students (e.g., Hite, 1985; van Anders, 2004), faculty (e.g., Cohen & Gutek, 1991; Kite et al., 2001), and administrators (e.g., Brown, 2005; Moore & Salimbene, 1980). Recent studies (O'Neill, Horton, & Crosby, 1999) suggest that women and men are equally likely to have mentors, which is an important sign that women have arrived as professionals, but it is interesting to note that the evidence is equivocal about whether women prefer other women as mentors (Clark, Harden, & Johnson, 2000; Gilbert, 1985) or have no gender preference (Erkut & Mokros, 1984; Olian, Carroll, Giannantonio, & Feren, 1988). In some academic disciplines and employment fields, there are still too few senior women available for every junior woman who would like the attention of a woman mentor, so it is good to know that many have no gender preference.

Much less has been written about mentoring undergraduate students. Some attention has been paid in the literature to academic advising (e.g., Titley & Titley, 1982; Trombley, 1984), peer mentors (e.g., Young & Cates, 2005), and the importance of role models, especially for women and ethnic minority students (e.g., Karunanayake & Nauta, 2004; Mendoz, 1986). A few feminist professors have reflected on their experiences in trying to mentor both undergraduate and graduate students in new, less masculine or less controlling, ways (e.g., Bona, Rinehart, & Volbrecht, 1995; Cain, 1994). Advice books for new faculty and department chairs tend to either focus on mentoring of graduate students (e.g., Zanna & Darley, 1987), mention working with undergraduates outside the classroom only briefly in relation to service on committees that deal with policy matters (e.g., Schoenfeld & Magnan, 1992), or describe advising as a necessary chore to which most faculty do not pay sufficient attention (e.g., Hecht, Higgerson, Gmelch, & Tucker, 1999). Yet, if undergraduates do not receive the benefits of mentoring, they will not advance to graduate school, where faculty will be more interested in guiding their careers.

Evidence suggests that fewer than one-half of undergraduates have mentors (Baker, Hocevar, & Johnson, 2003; Packard, Walsh, & Seidenberg, 2004), but almost all of them can identify role models (Erkut & Mokros, 1984). Role models are important to students, because their presence indicates that it is possible to succeed in students' careers of interest, they demonstrate the qualities and modes of behavior that exemplify professionalism, they provide evidence that it is possible to balance work and family, and they show students what skills are necessary for particular careers and how to utilize them effectively. However, role models are often more distant from students than mentors are and thus are not as effective as mentors in some areas. Undergraduates with mentors are more satisfied with their academic major departments and their colleges/universities than are those without mentors, and mentored students tend to become loyal alumni (Koch & Johnson, 2000). Those with mentors aim higher, mentor other students, are more likely to graduate, and report greater levels of achievement, personal growth, and well-being during their college years than do those without mentors (Baker et al., 2003; Cannister, 1999; Pascarella, 1980).

Clearly, mentoring is important to the personal and professional development of undergraduates, and it may be particularly important to women students. Jo Freeman (1975) hypothesized that a null environment (i.e., an environment in which students or workers are neither encouraged nor discouraged) would have a greater negative impact on women than on men. This is because many women enter higher education (or the workplace) with a history of belittlement and discouragement, which academe's null environment does nothing to diminish; feeling ignored by one's professors might even reinforce early messages that one is unlikely to achieve very much. Although young women are much less likely today than was the case in the 1970s to hear overt sexist messages telling them that they should not apply to college (in fact, today, women students are the majority of undergraduates in the United States) or should attend college mainly to find a husband, subtle sexism remains in play. Popular culture continues to send the message that girls who are "too smart" and women who are "too successful" are not likable. Our students often speak of having been encouraged to major in women-dominated disciplines and to prepare for feminine careers, especially those that can easily be exited and re-entered or that are amenable to "mother's hours." This experience is especially true of women of color, women from working-class families, and women who are the first in their families to attend college. Without a mentor's encouragement to define and pursue their goals, many of these young women will drift down life paths that they will later find unfulfilling or into jobs that will not pay them enough to enjoy a good standard of living.

Some women students experience the imposter phenomenon (Clance & O'Toole, 1987), an uneasy sense that they are frauds who do not deserve to be in college and a dread that others will discover their low aptitude and advise them to drop out. The imposter phenomenon is most likely to be experienced by students who are unusual in some way that makes them feel as though they are in the spotlight. Women who major in men-dominated disciplines, working-class students on campuses where most students are upper middle class, students of color on campuses where most students are white, and lesbians on heterosexist campuses with no active lesbian/gay/bisexual/ transsexual groups are perhaps more likely than other students to feel like an imposter. Mentors who are sensitive to the notion of being in the spotlight can help to reduce imposter feelings by providing praise and encouragement that is based on the student's own work and abilities. Specific, rather than global, praise is more authentic and easier for insecure students to accept.

Women students crave personal attention from faculty (Warren, Rose, & Barnack, 2005), but they may not feel worthy of the mentor's time. Women students often approach us by saying, "I know that you are very busy . . ." It is sometimes necessary to assure them that answering their questions is part of our job. Furthermore, many women students who would like to seek career advice from their faculty do not know how to ask for it. If they are not from families where college graduation is the norm, they may not have much familiarity with career planning, graduate school, and professional socialization. It is difficult to request mentoring when one does not know what one needs. This is another example of how the null environment hurts women. If faculty say that they are willing to spend time mentoring any student who approaches them, they will most likely spend their time with white, upper-middle-class men, and the students who most need their help will go unaided. Mentors must be proactive; they should seek out talented students and groom them for success. Most students respond to faculty outreach; they are grateful for the attention, and they rise to the occasion and challenge themselves in ways they would not otherwise have done.

Finally, many women students need encouragement to take risks, a strategy necessary for success. Women who identify with the feminine gender role often lack self-confidence and have been taught to play it safe. Modesty is part of femininity, and the first reaction of a woman student to an invitation to join a research team or present her work at a conference might be to say, "Oh, I couldn't do that. I'm not (or my work isn't) good enough." In a null environment, the professor might think, "She doesn't want to do it. I'll ask someone else." Furthermore, high-achieving young women may be perfectionists — that is, people who hold "rigid, unrealistically high standards" and use "all-or-none thinking" to evaluate their performance (Campbell & Di Paula, 2002, p. 182). If anything less than perfection is considered a failure, then perfectionists will avoid trying new activities unless they are sure that they can do well. The possibility of failure and embarrassment (and, perhaps, of being exposed as an imposter) is too anxiety-provoking for the perfectionist. Both the modest and the perfectionist students need an assertive mentor who will not easily let them off the hook, a mentor who will say, "Don't worry. I have confidence in you, and I'll be here to help and to show you what to do."

HOW TO MENTOR UNDERGRADUATES: STRATEGIES FOR OPENING DOORS AND MINDS

The first step to becoming a good mentor is to decide that you want to be a mentor, a role model, and a leader to your students. However, mentoring is more than a state of mind. Mentoring is an active process; it is the establishment and maintenance of a relationship that grows and changes over time. Strategies for cultivating and sustaining mentoring relationships include being accessible and informative, providing opportunities and encouragement, promoting students for awards, and creating networks.

Mentoring can begin at the first introduction between student and professor. Just as children mimic their parents' behaviors, undergraduates look to their faculty to learn about professionalism. Faculty demonstrate professional behavior by the way they dress, carry themselves, and provide constructive criticism. Professional women are role models to other women. Professors' enthusiasm for their careers and excitement about their professional interests can energize students. Students can benefit from hearing about professional women's struggles and successes. Undergraduates often have a difficult time picturing themselves in the professional world, and they often do not know much about different career paths. It is useful to tell students about the processes and interworkings of being successful in academia and in life. It is also important to give students a realistic picture of what academic life entails. For example, the research and publication processes are quite intimidating at first. Professors can help students by breaking down these processes step by step and encouraging students to collaborate with faculty on projects, assist more senior students with their projects, and attend and present at conferences, especially those designed for or otherwise friendly to undergraduates.

Research groups in which faculty and students collaborate on projects can provide a forum for discussions about the research process. Weekly meetings are also a way to motivate students on a regular basis. Students are held accountable for their work and are encouraged by the other group members. In effect, the group atmosphere may inspire them to be better students and people. They can learn time management and life skills from their mentor and their peers. Research groups not only cultivate mentoring relationships among students and faculty, but also mentoring relationships among beginning and advanced students. Such groups provide a venue to teach students how to be good mentors and role models to their classmates. Research groups dedicated to the study of women's issues are also a great place for diverse women to meet and feel comfortable talking about their struggles, conquests, and accomplishments. This type of atmosphere and group cohesion can encourage women to take risks and speak their minds in other settings.

The accessibility of mentors initiates and sustains mentoring relationships. It is important that professors/mentors are available both outside of class and during class. In class, an atmosphere can be created that fosters mentoring. For example, students can be encouraged to participate and share their opinions in class. In response, the professor can give positive feedback and share his or her own experiences or opinions, which may help the students become more confident. Confidence in academic abilities often leads to empowerment that can help students attain their goals. Students can also be encouraged to meet with professors outside of class by stopping by their offices, attending department social and academic events, or joining a research group. A mentor who eats lunch in the student dining hall from time to time can also encourage out-of-class communication among students and faculty. Students enjoy the opportunity to get to know their professors in a less formal environment. They are very curious about their professors' lives and career paths. This combination of formal and informal communication can open the door to lasting mentoring relationships.

Mentors provide encouragement and opportunities for success. They set high expectations and accept nothing less than the best effort and work from their students. Mentors want their students to strive for excellence. We conduct an annual workshop about how to write a curriculum vita (CV), which we have found is a good way to motivate students to achieve. In the workshop, we show students our and other faculty's CVs. By examining them, students gain a deeper respect for their professors, and they learn some important lessons about how academic careers begin and unfold. During the CV workshop, the students are encouraged to join clubs, honor societies, and professional associations; to apply for work-study jobs in the department or with a professor; to do volunteer work with community agencies; to nominate themselves to be student representatives or officers in psychology-related clubs or honor societies; to help with department-sponsored events or socials; to write an honors thesis or conduct an individual study; to attend department colloquia and other events; to apply for summer jobs and internships in their field; to attend conferences; and to embrace academic life in general. These topics are all introduced (or reviewed) in the CV workshop under the guise of showing students what they will need to do in order to construct a professional CV of their own. We point out what our students have already done, and what they could do, to get started on their own career paths.

Mentors also promote their students by nominating them for awards. Faculty are often sent announcements of awards, prizes, scholarships, competitive internships, and other opportunities that might be suitable for their students. Rather than simply posting these opportunities on department bulletin boards (a null environment tactic), mentors think about whether they know a student who would be a good candidate. It is insufficient in most cases just to let the target student know about the opportunity, because many women and students from certain cultural groups will be too modest to apply without encouragement. Mentors might say, "The faculty want to nominate you for this prize. The announcement contains a list of the materials you will need to prepare so that we can submit the nomination by the deadline." An important part of mentoring is cheerleading for protégés so that they receive the acknowledgment and opportunities they deserve.

One way a faculty member can become a mentor to several students at once is by volunteering to be an academic advisor or a faculty advisor to an honor society such as Psi Chi, the national honor society in psychology. Psi Chi provides students with many opportunities. Membership in Psi Chi gives students access to awards, grants, and other national recognition. Psi Chi members can acquire leadership roles within the organization, and, perhaps most important, they often network with Psi Chi members and advisors at other institutions. Networking is essential to attaining success in the professional world.

The development of a professional network is one of the greatest benefits of having a mentor. A mentoring relationship can be likened to a private club. Once people are in the club, they have access to knowledge, advice from experienced others, and hidden opportunities that may not be widely advertised. These clubs or networks consist of the mentor's colleagues, professional friends, former students, and current students. Most of those people are also part of other networks. In effect, a large interconnected network of mentoring professionals and students forms. Students can be introduced to successful alums who may offer career advice or job opportunities. Academics may collaborate on research projects or community action. Professional conferences are a great place to gather socially, expand the network, and solidify the mentoring relationships over time. Mentoring relationships can be long-standing, reciprocal relationships that last for many years. A mentor's students may become colleagues or friends later in life; mentoring does not have to end at graduation.

FROM MENTEE TO MENTOR: JENNY ROSE'S PATH

The best piece of advice I received in life was to chart my own course. As a student, this meant that I should seek opportunities to get involved in academics, community service, and extracurricular activities. As a faculty member, this means that I should seek opportunities to get involved in teaching, scholarship, and service. There are many opportunities in life; however, it usually takes some initiative and networking to take advantage of them. For example, many scholarships and grants go unclaimed each year because students and faculty do not know where to find them or how to apply for them. A mentor can guide students through the winding roads of academe, from start (student) to finish (faculty/professional).

I was fortunate to have parents who pushed and encouraged me, undergraduate professors who recognized and supported me, and graduate professors who inspired and motivated me. As a child, I had mostly positive experiences with teachers. I trusted and respected them. I always imagined myself as a teacher, and thus I enjoyed talking to my teachers outside of class. This probably set the stage for my school-related choices and mentoring experiences later in life. I chose to apply to and attend a small liberal arts college. Based on my personality, I knew that I wanted to go to a school where the classes were small and the professors were accessible to students. In my sophomore year, I devoted much of my classes and time to my major, psychology. I learned that I loved statistics and research methods. Yes, this was an odd realization. My statistics and research methods professors must have noticed and supported my uncanny passion because they offered me a position to work in the psychology computer lab. This was my foot in the door, so to speak.

There are four experiences of mentoring that clearly stick out in my mind as incidents that created the foundation for my academic future. The first was my statistics and research methods professors who not only offered me the opportunity to learn about computers and statistical and presentation software, but also gave me a chance to get to know the other psychology faculty. I worked near the faculty offices, which provided many occasions for informal discussions. My statistics professor was also my major advisor. We immediately established a mentoring relationship that was reinforced when I accepted the job with the department. My position in the department and the discussions with my professors motivated me to be a better student, to be more confident as a researcher, and eventually to pursue graduate study. Through this experience, I also assisted and got to know many psychology majors. As a result, I was elected student representative and Psi Chi co-chair in my senior year. My membership and position in Psi Chi led to my second and third significant mentoring experiences.

The two faculty co-advisors of Psi Chi, Carole Corcoran and Christine McBride, became my mentors. They were always available to answer questions and give advice. In addition to being a resource for Psi Chi, they also helped me personally. They advised me about my courses, graduate school, and volunteer and work opportunities, and they encouraged me to get more involved in research. I took an experimental social psychology course with Carole, who planted the seed of interest about gender roles and the psychology of women. I ended up doing an individual study/research project with Christine, who was interested in the psychology of women's health. My experience working on this project was invaluable. We won a departmental award for it, and we presented our results at our department's Psi Chi conference and our state conference. Attending the state conference was a great way to network with students and faculty at other schools. Our annual department conference also provided opportunities to meet professors at other schools. For example, as Psi Chi officers, we got to choose a speaker for the conference. We invited Joan Chrisler, a friend of Carole's and a women's health researcher who was cited several times in the literature review of our project paper, to give the keynote address. This chance meeting with Joan set the stage for my fourth significant mentoring relationship.

Joan became my mentor the first day that we met. She asked me about graduate school and encouraged me to apply to the graduate program at her college. I attended the program at her school, and she continued to mentor me throughout graduate school and beyond. She helped me get a teaching assistantship to pay for school, advised me about what courses to take, suggested different activities to do on campus, and encouraged me to attend her research group. She invited me to conduct research with her, to do different types of editorial activities, and to attend local and national conferences with her. After graduate school, she even helped me attain a full-time faculty position at the college. I now have a wonderful job, and I get to work with my mentor and friend on a daily basis. Her dedication and commitment to teaching, scholarship, and service to the college and to the field have inspired me to be a better teacher, researcher, and mentor to my own students.

I recognize that I have been very fortunate to have had more than one mentor to guide me through life. I have many friends who have struggled through undergraduate and graduate programs feeling isolated and discouraged. I have always felt supported and encouraged in my academic endeavors. It is because of the dedication of my mentors that I am the person I am today. I try to be a good mentor and role model to my students. I want my enthusiasm for learning and research to infect them. When I talk to my undergraduate advisees or incoming graduate students, the first piece of advice I offer is the same as I received: "Chart your own course." Mentors can set the stage and lay the foundation for mentoring relationships, but the students also have to be open to initiate and sustain the relationships. I encourage incoming students to find a professor who shares similar academic interests or with whom they'd like to work and find a way to connect outside of class. I also encourage them to seek out a broad array of experiences, such as attending talks on campus, joining volunteer activities, or involving themselves in community action. There is so much more to college (and to life) than formal classroom learning.

WITH A LITTLE HELP FROM MY FRIENDS: JOAN CHRISLER'S PATH

My own experience could not be more different from Jenny's. I did not have a mentor during my student days. I attended a large, urban university, where I received an excellent undergraduate education but did not have much contact with my professors outside of class. The doctoral students were the center of the faculty's attention, that much was clear to us undergrads. There was no Psi Chi chapter, and the Psychology Club was disorganized and rarely met. I was too shy to approach faculty for casual conversation, and it never occurred to me that they would be interested in me or even recognize me outside the classroom. When I realized that I would need letters of recommendation for graduate school, I forced myself to go to the offices of the three professors who seemed most approachable. All kindly agreed to write letters for me, but they knew so little about me that creative writing must have been necessary.

I had never met a professor before I took my first college course. I had no idea how one qualified for that job or what professors did when they weren't lecturing or grading papers. My parents were not college graduates, and the only professional women I knew were my teachers, my school and town librarians, and a couple of nurses who were friends of my mother. There were few women on the faculty of my university in the early 1970s, when I was an undergraduate. In four years, I had only two classes with women professors, neither of whom taught psychology. My professional role models were the women graduate students. There were not many of them, but I did have several as lab instructors, and, in my senior year, I took some courses with graduate student classmates. I talked to them a bit, and I paid close attention to how they comported themselves and what they discussed with each other. I suppose I must have decided that they and I were not so dissimilar.

In my junior year, the Psychology Club announced a meeting on the topic "What are the GREs, and why should I take them?" I had never heard of the GREs, so I attended the meeting. When it was over, one of my classmates said, "Let's take the GREs." I said, "Okay." I applied to graduate school with no career plan in mind. I only knew that I enjoyed studying psychology, and I did not want to stop doing so. I applied only to graduate programs in New York City because that is where my boyfriend and I were living. I thought we might get engaged soon, so I did not want to move away. I applied to programs in experimental psychology because I had particularly enjoyed courses with labs. I applied to all of the relevant programs without regard to whether there were faculty there with whom I might like to work, without regard to whether I was a good fit for the program, without regard to whether financial aid was available to me. In other words, I did everything wrong. I was lucky to be accepted anyplace!

There were several women on the psychology faculty at my graduate school; however, they were all in the clinical and school psychology programs. I took courses on gender with two of them, one supervised my master's thesis research, and another served as a reader on my dissertation committee (although she gave me little feedback on my drafts and never met with me privately). My master's thesis supervisor was a good role model for me. In our private meetings, she talked about the way she balanced her home and family life, and, once, when I was late with a draft and tried to get away with saying that "something came up," she lectured me sternly about how things are always "coming up" in professional women's lives, and so we must learn to work ahead of schedule. Her words made an impression on me; since then, I have always tried to work ahead, and I rarely miss a deadline.

My dissertation supervisor was a nice man who encouraged me and com-plimented my work but provided me with little direction. He taught me noth-ing about academic life or about how to publish my work, never asked me what I intended to do after graduation, and did not offer to write letters of recommendation for me. I did not realize until years later that other graduate students went to conferences with their professors, published with them, were coached about preparing for and applying for academic positions, and, of course, had glowing letters of recommendations written for them.

While I was in graduate school, I worked as an administrative assistant in the continuing education program at a nearby college. There I became friendly with the part-time faculty who taught the courses we offered. They told me that I was qualified to be an adjunct instructor, helped me figure out what I could teach, and showed me how to organize a CV and write a letter asking to be considered for part-time work. By the time I finally graduated, I had a solid track record of teaching a variety of courses at a number of colleges and universities in and around New York City. The department chairs who had hired me provided the letters of recommendation I needed for my tenure-track job search. It must have seemed very peculiar to the search committees that I did not provide a letter from my dissertation super-visor (or, indeed, any of my graduate school faculty), and I only attracted interest from small colleges where teaching was the main focus.

Around the same time I started working as an adjunct, I saw a notice on a bulletin board about a meeting of the local chapter of the Association for Women in Psychology (AWP). I went to the meeting, and there I finally found my mentors. Florence Denmark, Ethel Tobach, and Leonore Tiefer were sup-portive and offered me advice about attending and presenting at confer-ences. They became close friends as time went by, and I have always felt I could count on them. Florence, especially, opened doors for me and invited me to collaborate with her. At AWP conferences, I met Rhoda Unger, Irene Hanson Frieze, Nancy Felipe Russo, Carole Rayburn, and other senior women who have been wonderful mentors and friends to me. My AWP net-work also includes a group of friends who were in graduate school about the same time I was, and we have been peer mentors to each other over the years — sharing knowledge, working together on projects, and providing op-portunities to each other. Doris Howard, Maureen McHugh, Suzanna Rose, and Kat Quina have been especially valuable peer mentors and confidantes to me. I cannot imagine where I would be without them — probably not a ten-ured, full professor with an endowed chair, that's for sure.

The reason why my role as a mentor is at the core of my professional life is because I do not want my students to have to struggle to find their way as I did. I learned about how to succeed in my career by reading books about academic life, talking to my friends about their graduate school experiences with their mentors, and benefiting from the generous attention I received from the senior women mentioned above. In watching master mentors like

Florence, Rhoda, and Irene at work, I discovered the impact that a good mentor can have on her protégés. Even as I serve as a mentor to younger generations of women, I continue to turn to my own mentors for advice. Yes, I get by with a little help from my friends.

REFERENCES

Aisenberg, N., & Harrington, M. (1988). *Women of academe: Outsiders in the sacred grove.* Amherst: University of Massachusetts Press.

Baker, B. T., Hocevar, S. P., & Johnson, W. B. (2003). The prevalence and nature of service academy mentoring: A study of navy midshipmen. *Military Psychology, 15,* 273–283.

Bona, M. J., Rinehart, J., & Volbrecht, R. M. (1995). Show me how to do like you: Co-mentoring as feminist pedagogy. *Feminist Teacher, 9*(3), 116–124.

Brown, T. M. (2005). Mentorship and the female college president. *Sex Roles, 52,* 659–666.

Cain, M. A. (1994). Mentoring as identity exchange: Conflicts and connections. *Feminist Teacher, 8*(3), 112–118.

Campbell, J. D., & Di Paula, A. (2002). Perfectionistic self-beliefs: Their relation to personality and goal pursuit. In G. L. Flett & P. L. Hewitt (Eds.), *Perfectionism: Theory, research, and treatment* (pp. 181–198). Washington, DC: American Psychological Association.

Cannister, M. W. (1999). Mentoring and the spiritual well-being of late adolescents. *Adolescence, 34,* 669–779.

Caplan, P. J. (1993). *Lifting a ton of feathers: A woman's guide to surviving in the academic world.* Toronto, Ontario, Canada: University of Toronto Press.

Clance, P. R., & O'Toole, M. A. (1987). The imposter phenomenon: An internal barrier to empowerment and achievement. *Women & Therapy, 6*(3), 51–64.

Clark, R. A., Harden, S. L., & Johnson, W. B. (2000). Mentor relationships in clinical psychology doctoral training: Results of a national survey. *Teaching of Psychology, 27,* 262–268.

Clark, S. M., & Corcoran, M. (1986). Perspectives on the professional socialization of women: A case of accumulative disadvantage? *Journal of Higher Education, 57,* 20–43.

Cohen, A. G., & Gutek, B. A. (1991). Sex differences in the career experiences of members of two APA divisions. *American Psychologist, 46,* 1292–1298.

Erkut, S., & Mokros, J. R. (1984). Professors as models and mentors for college students. *American Educational Research Journal, 21,* 399–417.

Freeman, J. (1975). How to discriminate against women without really trying. In J. Freeman (Ed.), *Women: A feminist perspective* (pp. 194–208). Palo Alto, CA: Mayfield.

Gilbert, L. A. (1985). Dimensions of same-gender student-faculty role-model relationships. *Sex Roles, 12,* 111–123.

Hecht, I.W.D., Higgerson, M. L., Gmelch, W. H., & Tucker, A. (1999). *The department chair as academic leader.* Phoenix, AZ: Oryx Press.

Hite, L. M. (1985). Female doctoral students: Their perceptions and concerns. *Journal of College Student Personnel, 26,* 18–22.

Karunanayake, D., & Nauta, M. M. (2004). The relationship between race and students' identified career role models and perceived role model influence. *Career Development Quarterly, 52,* 225–234.

Kite, M. E., Russo, N. F., Brehm, S. S., Fouad, N. A., Hall, C.C.I., Hyde, J. S., et al. (2001). Women psychologists in academe: Mixed progress, unwarranted complacency. *American Psychologist, 56,* 1080–1098.

Koch, C., & Johnson, W. B. (2000). Documenting the benefits of undergraduate mentoring. *Council on Undergraduate Research Quarterly, 19,* 172–175.

Mendoz, F. S. (1986). Increasing minorities in academia: The faculty role model. *Journal of Medical Education, 61,* 850–851.

Moore, D., & Salimbene, A. (1980). The dynamics of the mentor-protégé relationship in developing women as academic leaders. *Journal of Educational Equity and Leadership, 2,* 51–64.

Murrell, A. J., Crosby, F. J., & Ely, R. J. (Eds.). (1999). *Mentoring dilemmas: Developmental relationships within multicultural organizations.* Mahwah, NJ: Erlbaum.

Olian, J. D., Carroll, S. J., Giannantonio, C. M., & Feren, D. B. (1988). What do protégés look for in a mentor? Results of three experimental studies. *Journal of Vocational Behavior, 33,* 15–37.

O'Neill, R. M., Horton, S., & Crosby, F. J. (1999). Gender issues in developmental relationships. In A. J. Murrell, F. J. Crosby, & R. J. Ely (Eds.), *Mentoring dilemmas: Developmental relationships within multicultural organizations* (pp. 63–80). Mahwah, NJ: Erlbaum.

Packard, B.W.L., Walsh, L., & Seidenberg, S. (2004). Will that be one mentor or two? A cross-sectional study of women's mentoring during college. *Mentoring and Tutoring, 12,* 71–85.

Pascarella, E. T. (1980). Student-faculty informed contact and college outcomes. *Review of Educational Research, 50,* 545–595.

Powell, G. N. (Ed.). (1999). *Handbook of gender and work.* Thousand Oaks, CA: Sage.

Schoenfeld, A. C., & Magnan, R. (1992). *Mentor in a manual: Climbing the academic ladder to tenure.* Madison, WI: Magna.

Silverberg, J. C. (1998). A feminist classicist reflects on Athena. In L. H. Collins, J. C. Chrisler, & K. Quina (Eds.), *Arming Athena: Career strategies for women in academe* (pp. ix–xiv). Thousand Oaks, CA: Sage.

Titley, R. W., & Titley, B. S. (1982). Academic advising: The neglected dimension in designs for undergraduate education. *Teaching of Psychology, 9,* 45–49.

Trombley, T. B. (1984). An analysis of the complexity of academic advising tasks. *Journal of College Student Personnel, 25,* 234–239.

van Anders, S. M. (2004). Why the academic pipeline leaks: Fewer men than women perceive barriers to becoming professors. *Sex Roles, 51,* 511–521.

Warren, E. A., Rose, J. G., & Barnack, J. (2005, August). *"I like teachers who . . ." Qualities that matter most to college students.* Poster presented at the meeting of the American Psychological Association, Washington, DC.

Young, R. W., & Cates, C. M. (2005). Playful communication in mentoring. *College Student Journal, 39,* 692–701.

Zanna, M. P., & Darley, J. M. (1987). *The compleat academic: A practical guide for the beginning social scientist.* New York: Random House.

Chapter 5

Promises and Pitfalls of Mentoring Women in Business and Academia

Michele Paludi, Jennifer Martin, Tina Stern, and Darlene C. DeFour

> White men in our culture typically are reared with feelings of confidence and specialness granted them simply because they are born male. This specialness is an essential aspect of male entitlement, which encourages men to feel that what they do or want should take precedence over the needs of women and that their prerogatives should not be questioned.
> —Albino Gilbert & Rossman, 1992, p. 235

As this quotation by Albino Gilbert and Rossman suggests, male privilege and entitlement do not occur in a vacuum. They affect organizational culture and practices and consequently affect women's lives and career advancement (Werhane et al., 2006). Mentoring relationships can be crucial for women in their achievement of career success, career rejuvenation, organizational recognition, improved job performance, and advancement (Ragins & Cotton, 1993). Engaging in mentoring relationships produces many positive outcomes, including reduction in stress and depression and an increase in self-esteem and self-actualization (Liang, Tracy, Taylor, & Williams, 2002).

However, because of the unique obstacles women face in the academy and workplace, it is often difficult for them to find mentors. Likewise, it is difficult for professional women to find protégés to pass on the knowledge they have accrued over time. Among the reasons for the latter is the belief that women do not possess as much organizational power or access to powerful others within the organization or their discipline as do their men counterparts. Thus, potential protégés may choose mentoring relationships with men colleagues, thereby reducing the chances for women to pass on their knowledge of the organization as well as their expertise.

This chapter discusses these and other issues regarding the traditional concept of mentoring and its effects on women in the academy and business. Recommendations for a feminist restructuring of the traditional mentoring relationship and organizations are provided. We note that mentoring is instrumental for women in the workplace in general and can be crucial for individual women in achieving success in nontraditional workplaces. Mentoring can benefit all women by helping to transform patriarchal practices by educating women on the ins and outs of the organization, how to navigate the old boys' network, and how to transmit this information to other women. These transformative practices can be used to promote women's organizational advancement. When women advance to the higher ranks, they can then work to transform the organization by instituting more egalitarian practices, such as open communication and advancement that is based on merit as opposed to patriarchal privilege.

TRADITIONAL MENTORING DEFINED

> So with that word he sat him down; then in the midst up rose Mentor, the companion of noble Odysseus. He it was to whom Odysseus, as he departed in the fleet, had given the charge over all his house, that it should obey the old man, and that he should keep all things safe.
>
> —Homer, *The Odyssey*

One of the main challenges in the study of mentoring in business and in the academy is the lack of consensus on its definition (Allen, Poteet, Eby, Lentz, & Lima, 2004; Gabriel & Kaufield, 2008; Gardiner, Tiggemann, Kearns, & Marshall, 2007; Gibson, 2004; Hackney & Bock, 2000; Paludi & DeFour, 1992). Mentoring has been traditionally defined as a relationship between a protégé and a senior, higher-ranking, influential individual who possesses experience and knowledge that are crucial to the career advancement of the protégé (Indvik, 2004; Ragins, 1989).

According to Ragins (1989), mentoring can serve three functions: to provide training and insider/political information about the organization, to provide emotional support and bolster the protégé's self-confidence, and to create a buffer between the organization and the protégé such that the protégé is protected from insider politics but granted access to informal networks and resources. Furthermore, according to Ragins and Cotton (1999), "Mentors are individuals with advanced experience and knowledge who are committed to providing upward support and mobility to their protégé's careers" (p. 529).

This definition of a mentor–protégé relationship that has characterized much of the literature in business and academia is based on the belief that men must mentor other men to assume leadership positions and power. This definition stems from Greek mythology, according to which Mentor was a loyal friend and advisor to Odysseus, king of Ithaca. Mentor assisted in raising Odysseus' son, Telemachus, while Odysseus was fighting the Trojan War. In Homer's *The Odyssey*, Mentor guides Telemachus in search of his lost father. He provided guidance in Telemachus's struggle to discover his father and his heritage. Mentor thus became Telemachus's teacher, counselor, coach, and protector in a relationship based on affection and trust.

The first recorded modern usage of the term *mentor* is attributed to *Les Aventures de Telmaque,* by Fenelon in 1699 (see Roberts, 1999). The protagonist in the book is Mentor. Mentor was described as a trusted friend, teacher, a more experienced person who guides a younger individual in life. The word *mentor* means wise counselor. It meant *advisor* in Greek and derives from the Indo-European root *men,* meaning to think.

TRADITIONAL MENTORING RELATIONSHIPS AS EXCLUSIONARY

> I've learned that people will forget what you said, people will forget what you did, but people will never forget how you made them feel.
>
> —Maya Angelou

This traditional mentoring model of men teaching other men has been criticized for its potential for negative outcomes that could inordinately affect women (Albino Gilbert & Rossman, 1992; Keyton & Kalbfleisch, 1993; Shakeshaft, Brown, Irby, Grogan, & Ballenger, 2007; Werhane et al., 2006). For example, women are excluded from informal networks, which are often crucial to career advancement within male organizational culture. Furthermore, women tend to be viewed stereotypically within such organizations, making it difficult for them to obtain important assignments that are required for advancement (Bagilhole & White, 2003). Thus, male managers select men over comparably qualified women for upper-level managerial positions (Hitt & Barr, 1989). According to Keefe (2003) and Shakeshaft et al. (2007), there is disparity about who receives mentoring within the academy; mentors tend to mentor those most like them: "In a department dominated by white males, white men get most of the mentoring. Women and minorities too often fall through the cracks" (Keefe, 2003, p. 34). This reality is similar for women in business.

In both the academy and business, men have a wider power base and thus easier access to resources that make them effective in sponsoring and promoting their protégés (Kanter, 1977; Shakeshaft et al., 2007). There is ample research to support advancement inequity between women and men. Women in the academy and business are underrepresented in senior positions and are promoted and tenured more slowly than men. In the medical field, only 12 percent of women have achieved the rank of full professor; this figure has increased only 2 percent in the last 20 years. The figure for men is 30 percent (Mayer, Files, Ko, & Blair, 2008). In engineering, the figure is even lower: 1 percent. Mayer and colleagues (2008) reported that, according to *Harvard Business Review,* women make up only 6 percent of high-ranking positions in Fortune 500 companies such as chief operating officers, chief executive officers, and presidents.

Edson (1995) noted that, without a mentor, only 17 percent of women whose career goals include being school principals are able to advance. The majority of women who are successful in becoming school administrators had mentors (Shakeshaft, 1985). As Shakeshaft et al. (2007) noted:

> While family support is important for women to be able to gain the time and the approval of those immediately impacted by a decision to work longer hours, professional mentoring is vital to gain the knowledge and political information necessary for a woman to position herself as a viable top-level candidate. (p. 111)

Jandeska and Kraimer (2005) have referred to this condition as the "opportunity gap," the factors that bar women from advancing in their careers at the same rate as men. In short, modern-day mentoring parallels mentoring in *The Odyssey:* men advising other men in order to advance the protégé's career and in turn bring prestige to the mentor. Explanations that have been studied to explain the opportunity gap include evaluations of women's achievement, discrimination in the workplace (e.g., pay inequity), sexual harassment in education and the workplace, the availability of role models and mentors, lack of access to senior professional networks, lack of family-friendly policies (including on-site child care), and an educational and corporate culture that is not welcoming to women (i.e., gatekeeping) (Jandeska & Kraimer, 2005; Martin, 2008; Paludi et al., 2007; Quinlan, 1999; Ragins & Cotton, 1993).

Because of these societal factors with which women still have to cope and the implicit lack of advantage within the organizational structure which still privileges men, mentoring becomes especially important for women. Women report feeling marginalized, experiencing subtle bias, and finding their research devalued (Gibson, 2006; Hackney & Bock, 2000; Moss et al.,

1999; Wasburn, 2007). Women may lack access to senior faculty or professional networks (Casto, Caldwell, & Salazar, 2005; Quinlan, 1999). Traditional mentoring, therefore, becomes exclusionary rather than inclusive.

As Martin (2008) stated:

> It is easier for men, with their informal informational networks, to successfully acclimate themselves. Women often have to compensate simply for being women. . . . Women often face tremendous obstacles to gain acceptance in an organizational culture, especially in non-traditional fields. They must deal with negative expectations, gender-role stereotypes, and doing more than is expected to be seen as competent. They must try to find a mentor or a way into the informal networks that are often closed to them so that they can learn to navigate the hostile waters of organizational culture. (p. 172)

According to Ragins (1989), women are less likely than men to seek mentors; the reason being that women may assert that their abilities and competence will be sufficient to gain career advancement. However, this is often not the case. Women are often kept out of the loop in terms of what it takes to advance within an organization due to tacit rules and traditions that are revealed only through informal networks. Ragins (1989) argues that, although mentoring is important for men, it is *essential* for women, because women are often excluded from the networks through which individuals can gain career advancement. Mentoring can assist women in gaining this "secret" information via other women who have been in the organization over time and gained this collective wisdom; mentoring can also help women gain insight into the politics of the corporation. Mentors can provide feedback on performance that can be beneficial for women's career advancement. Working with a mentor can provide the protégé with on-the-job training that they would not have had the opportunity to experience at all or not until later in their career.

Mentors can gain career boosts from mentoring relationships. Although achievement is frequently portrayed as a solitary enterprise, in academia and business, success is frequently the result of building and working with a team. Building a research or work group consisting of protégés at different stages of their careers can help all reach their aspirations (Albino Gilbert & Rossman, 1992). There are thus many benefits of mentoring relationships for women, including familiarizing themselves with organizational politics, networking, and increasing personal motivation to achieve goals.

RISKS FOR WOMEN MENTORS

In addition to problems for the protégé, researchers have identified potential negative outcomes for women mentors as well. Risks for the mentor can inordinately affect women faculty members and chief executive officers (Quinlan, 1999). Mentoring takes time and commitment; this is often time taken away from activities in which the woman mentor needs to participate in order to advance her own career (Paludi, 2002). Because there are fewer women and women minorities at higher ranks, women are often pressed into institutional service roles where their representation is desired. Excess requests for participation in service behaviors interacts with gender role expectations for women to be helpful and can result in women taking time away from career-advancing activities like conducting research, publishing, and grant writing (Wasburn, 2007).

GENDER POLITICS OF MENTORING: ATTITUDES AND ATTRIBUTIONS ABOUT WOMEN'S ACHIEVEMENT AND CAREERS

Gender stereotypes also contribute to whether women are perceived to be potential protégés and mentors (Young, Cady, & Foxon, 2006). In 2005, Harvard University president Lawrence Summers (2005) argued that innate differences between women and men explain women's inability to succeed in math and science. Stereotypes such as this statement refer to individuals' thoughts and cognitions that typically do not correspond with reality. Stereotypes occur when individuals are classified by others as having something in common because they are members of a particular group or category of people (e.g., women professors, women executives). Psychological research has identified that stereotypes have the following characteristics (Fiske & Stevens, 1993):

a. Groups that are targeted for stereotypes are easily identified and relatively powerless.
b. There is little agreement between the composite picture of the group and the actual characteristics of that group.
c. This misperception is difficult to modify even though individuals who hold stereotypes have interacted with individuals of the group who disconfirm the stereotypes.
d. This misperception is the product of a bias in individuals' information-processing mechanisms.

Gender stereotyping is a psychological process that describes individuals' structured set of beliefs about the personal attributes of men and women. Psychologists have identified an emotional component to stereotypic cognitions: prejudice as well as a behavioral component to individuals' cognitions (i.e., discrimination and harassment). Thus, individuals' statements and nonverbal gestures toward women and men provide insight into their structured set of beliefs about each sex (Paludi, 2002).

Attribution factors affect women in positions of management and the academy as well. According to Young et al. (2006), attributions made by men mentors for women protégés are different from ones they make for their men protégés (also see Fleming, 1996). Men mentors perceive a woman's apprenticing herself to them as requiring help or remedial assistance. Men protégés, however, are perceived by men mentors as individuals whose careers need to be developed. This difference raises a serious paradox, as LaFrance (1987) commented: As women continue to get the mentoring they need, they will be seen as needing the mentoring they get.

The perception of men being more helpful is due to definitions of help in terms of heroic and chivalrous acts (Young, 1988). When men with this perception are mentoring women, each woman is in a culturally defined relationship vis-à-vis the man. Therefore, attributions for the women's success will be external—due to the help of their mentor, a man—not due to their abilities and effort. Thus, women may need to be especially independent in developing their own achievements if they are to attain full professional status in the eyes of colleagues (Betz, 2007) and have their successes be attributed to themselves, not to the senior man who mentored them.

Furthermore, women may find it difficult to secure a man mentor, both because they may find them difficult to approach and because they fear the presumption of a sexual relationship by others in the organization. On the other hand, men may be hesitant to seek out or accept women protégés for a variety of reasons, the fear of a presumption of a sexual relationship existing being one. Some men may feel that women are not equal to them and thus do not want to waste their time mentoring when women are not capable of advancing on par with their men counterparts. If women are, in fact, deemed as capable and worthy of mentoring, men mentors may still choose men to mentor because it is simply more comfortable and easier. More difficulties may ensue when racialized gendered stereotypes interact with race and gender roles and add additional barriers for women of color.

WOMEN'S UNIQUE CAREER PATHS

Another problem with cross-sex mentoring is that men's career patterns often differ from those of women, and the man mentor may not understand or be sympathetic regarding issues that women academics and managers commonly face (Chandler, 1996; Quinlan, 1999). For example, women academics and managers are likely to include parenting and family issues as integral to their career decisions, whereas these considerations are often thought of as separate issues by men (Chandler, 1996; Quinlan, 1999). Bronstein, Black, Pfennig, and White (1986), for example, reported that men mentors, in their letters of recommendations for women protégés for faculty positions, described women's family responsibilities as a burden. Similar results were obtained by Trix and Psenka (2003) in their content analysis of letters of recommendation for applicants for a faculty position at a medical school. As Paludi (2002) noted with respect to this research: "We need to consider the reactions of individuals reading these descriptions—individuals who will consider which applicant would be more willing to relocate and who would make the most promising and productive colleague" (p. 296). Bronstein and colleagues (1986) also noted that none of the women applicants mentioned lifestyle/family status in their resume or cover letters; men mentors, however, mentioned it.

The mentoring relationship becomes very important for women during the college years, because college is a time of transition and stress; it is a time of new beginnings when students may be leaving home for the first time (Liang, Tracy, Kauh, Taylor, & Williams, 2006). Stress from such changes can be assuaged with the help of mentors who can provide emotional support. According to Thomas, Hu, Gewin, Bingham, and Yanchus (2005), women graduate students can benefit from mentoring relationships; they become more involved in their professions and achieve higher rates of research and publications. Allen, Russell, and Maetzke (1997) found that women graduate students were more likely to mentor than were men graduate students. Kelly, Bobo, McLachlan, Avery, and Burge (2006) found that mentoring can be beneficial for both girls and adult women, for it can promote empowerment. As Casto, Caldwell, and Salazar (2005) state, "Female mentors can offer the personalized attention that female students need to deal with the problems specific to them as women that they may encounter in the higher education environment" (p. 331).

RETURNING WOMEN STUDENTS

Stereotypic attributions for women's achievement by men mentors are illustrated by older women's career development (Paludi, 2002; Young, 1988). Mentoring typically occurs during a transitional period in a student's or employee's career life. Some transitions for women and men are similar (e.g., from college to first job); however, some are not. For example, some women make a transition from homemaker and mother to full-time employee or from homemaker to college student. These transitions may negatively affect their mentoring opportunities, because they seem out of step with well-known career transitions for men. As a consequence of the timing of their transitions, women probably have fewer prospects of finding a mentor willing to invest in them and their shortened career in business (Young, 1988).

LIFE–WORK INTEGRATION

Men mentors may treat women and men protégés similarly and fail to take into account the different impacts of educational and organizational practices on their experiences (Albino Gilbert & Roseman, 1992). For example, men mentors may not have had to deal with integrating work and family roles and therefore may lack experience and skills in areas that will impact women protégés more than men protégés (Paludi & Neidermeyer, 2007). There are costs to women who integrate work and family roles. For example, employed women who report experiencing work–life conflict are as much as 30 times more likely to experience a significant mental health problem (e.g., depression or anxiety) than women employees who report no work–life conflict (Gonzalez-Morales, Peiro, & Greenglass, 2006). Because women are integrating work and child care and elder care, they work longer than men. Longer work hours impact emotional and physical well-being (Karsten, 2006). Hewlett and Luce (2006) noted that women indicated their children had the following experiences due to the number of hours they worked each week: watching too much television, acting out/lack of attention, eating too much junk food, having too little adult supervision, and underachieving in school.

Heyman (2000) noted that there is an impact on children's health when parents are not achieving work–life balance. For example, she reported that sick children have shorter recovery periods, better vital signs, and fewer symptoms when their parents participate in their care. In addition, Heyman found that the presence of a parent reduces hospital stays by 31 percent. When parents are involved in a child's care, the child recovers more rapidly from outpatient procedures.

Hewlett and Luce (2006) noted that 57 percent of the women in their survey indicated they do not want to continue working long days for more than a year. They interpreted this result as indicating that women are more in tune than men to the "fallout on their children . . . they see a direct link between their long workweeks and a variety of distressing behaviors in their children" (p. 56). Mentors who do not take these realities of women's lives into account or attribute women's behavior as meaning they are not serious about a career will not effectively counsel and advise them (Quinlan, 1999).

CAREER ADVANCEMENT

Traditional mentoring relationships can jeopardize a protégé's career advancement in that the mentor may function in multiple relationships with the protégé. During mentoring, the protégé is encouraged to ask for help, reveal her concerns, questions, needs, and uncertainties to the mentor who is a senior faculty member. That faculty member may, eventually, serve on a tenure or promotion committee that evaluates the protégé's performance, and some critics express concern that information from the mentoring process could be used for evaluative purposes (Barnett, 2008; Boyle & Boice, 1998; Cawyer, Simonds, & Davis, 2002). The protégé's acknowledgement of her concerns or weaknesses during the mentoring process could be raised later in a context that is evaluative and, in some cases, unfriendly or hostile.

WOMEN, MEN, SEX, AND POWER

According to Mayer et al. (2008):

> Men and women think and behave differently in the workplace. Early socialization and schooling experiences result in different work styles and goals. These socialized differences lead women to place a greater priority on interpersonal satisfaction and integration than men do. . . . In both work and social settings, men quickly and informally establish a hierarchy that governs how they relate. In contrast, women quickly establish equalizing relationships, even with their obvious subordinates. (pp. 204–205)

Some men mentors assume more of a paternal role with a woman protégé than with a man protégé in order to avoid sexual rumors and romantic involvement. This strategy creates a dependent relationship for women, who are typically inhibited by the mentor from growing out of the relationship and into a more egalitarian one (Fleming, 1996).

Furthermore, at least 50 percent of women students and employees will experience sexual harassment, often by a man mentor, that will be related to negative physical and mental health consequences (e.g., anxiety, depression, headaches, eating disorders, gastrointestinal disorders, sleep problems) (Dansky & Kilpatrick, 1997; Lundberg-Love & Marmion, 2003; Rospenda, Richman, Ehmke, & Zlatoper, 2005) and career consequences (e.g., changing careers, dropping out of school, absenteeism from work, termination from employment for complaining about sexual harassment to their employer) (Lundberg-Love & Marmion, 2003; see Paludi & Paludi, 2003, for a review).

Common sexual harassment experiences include: *unwanted sexual attention,* which includes unsolicited verbal comments, gestures, or attempts at physical contact (e.g., a professor attempts to touch or kiss a student or repeatedly asks the student for dates), and *sexual coercion,* which includes job-related and education-related threats or benefits that are contingent upon compliance with sexual demands (e.g., a department chairperson promising to vote to promote a faculty member only if she is sexually cooperative or not support her promotion if she refuses sexual demands) (Fitzgerald, Gelfand, & Drasgow, 1995; Woods & Buchanan, 2008). *Contrapower sexual harassment* involves a subordinate sexually harassing a superior—for example, a man student in a women's studies course sexually harassing the woman professor (DeSouza & Fansler, 2003).

For certain student groups, the incidence of sexual harassment appears to be higher than for others. Graduate students, for example, report more sexual harassment than undergraduates. Other groups reporting higher-than-average experiences of sexual harassment include women of color, especially those with "token" status; students in small colleges or small academic departments, where the number of faculty available to students is quite small; women students in male-populated fields, such as engineering; students who are economically disadvantaged and work part time or full time while attending classes; lesbian women, who may be harassed as part of homophobia; physically or emotionally disabled students; women students who work in dormitories as resident assistants; women who have been sexually abused; inexperienced, unassertive, socially isolated women, who may appear more vulnerable and appealing to those who would intimidate or coerce them into an exploitive relationship (Woods & Buchanan, 2008).

Peer sexual harassment is also common among college students. The main form of peer sexual harassment experienced by women students involves lewd comments or sexual comments from classmates. Peer sexual harassment of Chinese women by men college students occurs twice as frequently as faculty–student sexual harassment (Tang, Yik, Cheung, Choi & Au, 1996).

In addition, the incidence of contrapower sexual harassment in colleges and universities is widespread, especially for women professors who are sexually harassed by men students. Grauerholz (1989) noted that approximately 48 percent of women professors in her research reported contrapower sexual harassment from men students that ranged from sexist comments to sexual assault. Similar findings have been reported by women professors regarding sexual harassment from colleagues and superiors in the academy at several universities.

Furthermore, Keller and Moglen (1987) reported that younger women students seeking career success "were sometimes asked to buy them [mentoring relationships] with their bodies—from the males who agreed to be their mentors" (p. 496). Sexual relationships between mentors and protégés will negatively impact the mentoring process (Haring-Hidore & Paludi, 1988).

INTERSECTIONALITY: WOMEN OF COLOR AND MENTORING

The concept of intersectionality, which explains the oppressions faced by people who are simultaneous members of more than one disenfranchised group (Hill Collins, 2004; Hooks, 2004) provides further evidence that the experiences of white women do not reflect the experiences of all women (Blake-Beard, 1999). Researchers often ignore this fact, and thus do not include reference to the interlocking oppressions of class, race, and gender (and other social categories) in their work. Typically, these forms of oppression are examined individually. Enough attention has not been paid to how these intersections may uniquely affect the mentoring experience. Historically, women of color have been excluded from the mentoring literature (Blake-Beard, 1999). Researchers and theorists have established the importance of mentoring for career advancement, but women of color often lack these relationships (Gonzalez-Figueroa & Young, 2005). They are less likely to be mentored because they are underrepresented within organizations; and, as indicated previously, people tend to mentor those who are "most like themselves." The fewer women of color who receive mentoring the less likely they are to advance to the higher ranks within the organization (for it may take them longer to learn the hidden rules of the organization on their own), and thus to mentor other women of color like themselves. A potential protégé should not allow differences (e.g., race, geography, socioeconomic) to prevent her from establishing a mentoring relationship. According to Gonzalez-Figueroa and Young (2005), "Mentoring may be used as a strategy to promote success among underrepresented individuals in higher ranks" (p. 215).

According to a study conducted by Thomas and colleagues (2005), 90 percent of black students reported having a mentor outside their academic area; thus, the researchers concluded, women and minorities may have trouble gaining access to mentors in their own academic departments. Thomas and Hollenshead (2001) found similar results in their research on women of color faculty. The women of color in their study were more likely to have mentors who were not located in their campus units or departments or their academic institution than were white women, white men, and men of color. In addition, they were more prone to use ethnic minority sections of their professional organizations to obtain career advice.

This, in turn, may limit their access to career advancement and professional development. Maton, Kohout, Wicherski, Leary, and Vinokurov (2006) suggest that having a critical mass of faculty of color in a department may improve retention of graduate and undergraduate students of color. It can also serve to recruit more faculty and students of color. Seeing a diverse faculty can suggest that the department will be a comfortable place to pursue their degree. The institution may be viewed as a place where they can study topics relevant to race/ethnicity.

Racist and sexist beliefs about women's and minorities' lack of abilities and thus advancement may prevent mentors from taking on minority protégés for fear that their predetermined lack of future advancement will be a negative reflection on the mentors. Thus, a negative self-fulfilling prophecy is created and perpetuated that affects choice of protégé within the mentoring relationship (Evans & Cokley, 2008; Thomas et al., 2005). Moreover, according to Liang et al. (2006), at times there are cultural barriers to developing mentoring relationships; that is, potential mentors may have trouble detecting an Asian student's interest in developing a mentoring relationship with them because of cultural differences in the expression of emotion.

Another potential difference involves the notion that "Euro-American mentors expect students to initiate the relationship, Asians expect those in authority to initiate the relationship" (Liang et al., 2006, p. 150). According to Gonzalez-Figueroa and Young (2005), "Latina professional women are a unique population who report feeling marginalized from their professional group as well as their social ethnic group, which leads to feelings of stress and loneliness" (p. 213). In sum, if we desire to promote the mentoring relationship to facilitate the career advancement of women in general, we must understand how culture, ethnicity, and other differences between people can potentially divide us. And, as Gonzalez-Figueroa and Young (2005) state, "it is critical that we understand how ethnic identity (as a cultural construct) influences the mentoring process, willingness to be mentored, and the preference for being mentored by someone of the same ethnicity" (p. 214).

Women in Moses' (1988) research on mentoring indicated:

When I first came to the department, I was the "token" needed for affirmative action purposes. Now I believe that among Whites I am viewed with suspicion. I also feel some sense of competitive concern among minority men. (p. 3)

When we talk about Black issues in class I am called upon, but not at any other time. I am always used as an example. As far as White students go, I am usually ignored if I attend social events. (p. 14)

We have no real faculty mentoring or support programs for Black women faculty. What we need is a program similar to the one created for students. Why not a faculty mentor program for minority faculty? Why not special assistance programs, release time, research grants for minorities and women only? (p. 16)

Similar findings have been reported by Gonzalez-Figueroa and Young (2005) with Latinas. African American women and Latinas lack mentoring relationships because of sexism and racism, further supporting Danksy's (1996) research that indicates that employees who differ demographically from their supervisors receive less mentoring by those supervisors.

Research on women attorneys in private law firms also showed that women of color have unique mentoring experiences (ABA Commission on Women in the Profession, 2006). Having a mentor did not ensure that: they would be included in the internal workings of their firms, their contact with clients would increase, or they obtained more of the coveted high-prestige work assignments. Women of color associates reported that the types of assignments that they had appeared to be tied to their race and gender. For example, they only met with clients when being a woman or a person of color was advantageous to the firm. In addition, the few times that they were invited to meetings with clients, they did not have critical responsibilities. Their role was essentially to enhance the clients' comfort level and not to utilize their skills and talents.

FEMINIST RESTRUCTURING OF THE TRADITIONAL MENTORING RELATIONSHIP

> You really can change the world if you care enough.
> —Marion Wright Edelman

> Do not wait for leaders; do it alone, person to person.
> —Mother Teresa

One response to the difficulties in cross-sex mentoring experiences for women is for them to seek out a woman mentor. Arguments in favor of women mentors for women have stressed the importance of women's identification with other women, the significance of the information provided by the woman mentor's behavior, and the positive incentive through women's illustrative success (Fleming, 1996; Gilbert, Gallessich, & Evans, 1983; Paludi, Waite, Howeing-Roberson, & Jones, 1988; Young, 1988). Gilbert et al. (1983) reported that women graduate students who identified women professors as their mentors viewed themselves as more career oriented, confident, and instrumental than did women who identified with men professors. In addition, women students paired with women also reported higher satisfaction with their student role than women or men students paired with a man. Same-sex mentoring relationships tend to be more effective because of a sense of shared experiences (Allen & Eby, 2003). Young, Cady, and Foxon (2006) indicate that protégés who defined themselves as similar to their mentors reported being happier and more satisfied with the relationship. According to Allen and Eby (2003), individuals who have been previously mentored tend to advance more quickly throughout an organization, earn higher salaries, stay longer in the organization, and express more positive attitudes about work.

Gardiner, Enomoto, and Grogan (2000) discussed what a quality mentoring relationship entails. A quality mentor should practice an open communication style, be reflective about her abilities as a leader, create opportunities for her protégé, encourage the protégé to take risks, and shield the protégé from criticism. Successful mentors teach and lead by presenting their protégés with hands-on learning experiences (as opposed to simply learning through observation). According to Albino Gilbert and Rossman (1992), mentoring has several functions: psychosocial functions, which include role modeling, validation, and friendship (interpersonal); and career functions such as coaching, protecting, and networking (systemic).

An effective mentor possesses the following qualities: is a good listener, is respected in the organization, good communication skills, is flexible, has influence within the organization, encourages the protégé, and believes in the mentoring process in general (Keefe, 2003). According to Curry (2004):

> Mentors have a choice in affecting their protégé's development. They can choose to deal on the emotional level or simply stick with the procedural issues. . . . Using this construct, women should make the best mentors, since their training and socialization is more attuned to emotional and social issues. Men are more apt to want to feel in control or exhibit rescuing behaviors, but not to deal with the details of emotionality in mentoring. (pp. 1–2)

Several studies examined the outcomes of mentoring programs for women faculty, but there are few quantitative, empirical outcome studies (Gardiner et al., 2007). Gardiner and her colleagues (2007) have provided empirical evidence for the value of mentoring to women's objective career success. They conducted a seven-year longitudinal evidence-based study of a mentoring program at an Australian university to evaluate the objective career outcomes for women participants. One of the purposes of the mentoring program was to address the underrepresentation of women in more senior ranks of the institution. Using a control group, they found that the women who had received mentoring were more likely to stay at the university, were more likely to be promoted, received more external research grants, and produced more publications than those who had not been mentored. Regarding subjective career outcomes, while those who had been mentored experienced an increase in their confidence as academics, there was no difference on many other subjective measures such as job satisfaction, career planning, and work-related distress or morale between those who had been mentored and those who had not. In addition, the protégés perceived the mentoring experience positively. The authors concluded that mentoring, as conceived and structured in this study, had positive outcomes not only for the participants, but for the university as well.

Gibson (2004, 2006) conducted a phenomenological study on the characteristics that define the essence of being mentored for women faculty across different types of mentoring relationships. She identified five themes as essential to women faculty of the mentoring experience across mentoring programs using diverse definitions, models, or structures. These themes included: (1) having someone who truly cares and acts in one's best interest, (2) a feeling of connection, (3) being affirmed of one's worth, (4) not being alone, and (5) the recognition that politics are part of one's experience. Further, Gibson (2004) advocated that, because mentoring was perceived as being highly valuable for participants, it should be considered a means to promote career success for women and seen as even more important for women than men because women are more likely to feel isolated in the academy.

Eliasson, Berggren, and Bondestam (2000) studied 14 women participants in a mentoring program in Sweden. They reported that a positive outcome for the participants was the change in perceptions about women's problems in academe. Early in the program, the protégés stated the belief that their academic problems resulted from their own personal inadequacies. As some of these perceptions were tested, they came to recognize the contribution of contextual problems to the challenges they experienced. This study cited other benefits to protégés, including being recognized as a peer, developing a sense of their own knowledge and expertise, and having career interest from a senior colleague.

Holmes, Land, and Hinton-Hudson (2007) cite other benefits for women, including having a role model, gaining a deeper understanding of role expectations, and gaining access to information, including grant funding and research opportunities. For African American women faculty, the literature shows a correlation between having been mentored and success in higher education. Holmes et al. (2007) found that, ideally, mentors would be of the same race/ethnicity; however, cross-cultural and cross-sex relationships can also be beneficial. They conclude that it is more important for minority women to have mentors who are committed to the protégé's professional development than to have a mentor of the same race/ethnicity.

Other studies have also found positive outcomes of mentoring for women in academe and business. Favorable outcomes cited in the literature include career enhancement through research collaboration, job placement, networking, as well as gains in feelings of competence and self-esteem (Chandler, 1996).

MENTORING AS FEMINIST PRAXIS

> There's a special place in Hell for women who don't help other women.
>
> —Madeleine Albright

Moss and colleagues (1999) urge that mentoring become part of a general feminist practice and approach within the academy. "Mentoring as feminist praxis means promoting women, people of colour and others who are less favourably positioned within the academy and assisting them in negotiating the relations within the academy" (p. 414). Although their focus is primarily on the mentoring of undergraduate and graduate students, there is application to the mentoring of women faculty and managers/executives for both the protégé and the mentor. Because there are fewer women and other marginalized people in positions of authority within the academy, mentoring for these groups suffers; there are fewer women to turn to for guidance, fewer role models, and increased workloads for the small number of women and minority faculty members who have made it to senior rank. They urge the integration of feminist values into the mentoring process. Such values include working from a woman-centered approach, forming alliances with marginalized groups, making intellectual resources available to everyone equally, engaging in collective decision-making processes, and dismantling academic structures of oppressive power relations. They present feminist guidelines for choosing a mentor in both supportive and hostile environments, for graduate and undergraduate students, and for mentors providing feminist mentorship. The recommendations for mentors include recognizing multiple roles and responsibilities, being aware of possible tension, respecting the other person's autonomy, being aware of the needs of the other person, and guarding one's own energy. Finally, while they recognize the necessity of input from experienced guides, they also emphasize the importance of being one's own mentor by reflecting on our own experiences, thinking for ourselves, and serving as our own guide and counsel.

Paludi and colleagues (1988) asked women students the following question: "Describe a situation in which you would choose a female over a male role model." Examples from this research are the following:

A woman who has experienced the casualties of womanhood, who knows discrimination, harassment, fear of violence, and who overcomes through her action and spirit would be a much more likely role model than a man.

I have a very strong resentment for males who are not willing to admit that females are equal intellectually and in most other ways. If I had to choose between a male role model who wanted to keep women in the home where they belong and a female role model, I would definitely choose the female.

It takes a wise woman to impress me—wise being a great deal more than smarts. I like a mix of warmth, firmness, compassion without sentimentality, humor, wisdom, and competence. Such a woman, in a leadership role, I prefer to a male as a role model because I can learn so much more so much faster. (p. 24)

The Office for Women's Affairs at Indiana University (1995, p. 2) noted women's concerns related to women mentors. For example:

As a woman aspiring to participate in a male-dominated, intellectually-driven field, there is nothing like the reassurance one gathers from simply watching other women succeed in academic positions. Mentoring takes that reassurance to new heights.

I agree that have a female advisor/mentor is very important. I feel comfortable discussing with her concerns about childcare, family obligations, etc. that I might not talk about with male profs because I don't want to reinforce any existing stereotypes. On the other hand, the value of female mentors for future job prospects is not as good. Female faculty are fewer in number and (generally) have lower status positions. If they don't have much pull, they might not be able to give their students the extra boost into the job market that male colleagues might have.

As discussed earlier in this chapter, statistics bear out this student's perceptions concerning the relatively lower status of women faculty member mentors. In addition, students who are being mentored by women faculty who themselves have to struggle with sex and race discrimination and/or sexual harassment, pregnancy discrimination, and so on may feel they too will experience retaliatory behavior on the part of their department for associating with a whistle blower.

It is interesting to note that in Greek mythology, the Goddess Athena assumed the shape of Mentor to guide Telemachus and give him prudent counsel. This notion of women having to take the shape of or adopt masculine mentoring functions has dominated the training seminars and articles that provide information for women mentors. A feminist perspective on mentoring stresses the reciprocal nature of mentoring relationships (Albino Glibert & Rossman, 1992; Keyton & Kalbfleisch, 1993; Lash, 2000).

WOMENTORING AND GROUP MENTORING

Moore (1984) identified *womentoring* — a sharing of power, competence, self, and differences. Clifford (2003) identified a group mentoring model. In this approach, mentoring is defined as a process that facilitates a range of experimentation, learning, and development. In the group mentoring approach, "everyone in the group is a mentor and a mentee" (Clifford, 2003, p. 6).

NETWORKING MENTORING

Swoboda and Millar (1986) advocated *networking mentoring,* in which two or more women fulfill the roles of mentor and protégé to each other at different times in the relationship. Both approaches are egalitarian rather than hierarchical and are based on a belief in mutual enhancement. The advantages of networking mentoring include the fact that it is open to all, not just a select few who find an individual to mentor them. In addition, it is not one-to-one mentoring that reinforces and reproduces a hierarchical power relationship (Angelique, Kyle, & Taylor, 2002). These mentoring styles are also more relevant to women's career paths. Such linear career models do not provide time away from the paid workforce for child rearing or elder care, part-time employment, or job-sharing practices. Both womentoring and networking mentoring approaches place value on women's unique career paths. Finally, these formats provide an opportunity to learn how to mentor (Young, 1988).

PEER MENTORING

In the absence of mentors, women may turn to peer relationships as a substitute; these, too, can be beneficial in advancing the careers of women in organizations, for it is a system of support and mutual professional growth. Because of women's historical exclusion from informal power networks, they have often had to work harder and longer than their men counterparts to achieve career advancement. Thus, they may not have the time available to mentor other women without experiencing some negative consequences to their own careers. Informal mentoring relationships can assist in such cases.

Peer and group mentoring as well as networking models all attempt to address problems of the traditional mentoring model (Packard, 2003). They are intended to be nonhierarchical and reciprocal in nature and to expand the availability of mentoring to a greater number of faculty members. They intend to be inclusive rather than exclusionary. Because participants are roughly equal in terms of rank or position, mutuality is emphasized, sharing and feedback are explicitly encouraged, and there may be fewer constraints than when senior faculty members are present.

Peer and network mentoring models involve multiple, but less close, relationships among a larger group of equals (Packard, 2003). Both have the advantage of requiring less commitment of time from the mentor, and protégés are free to choose different mentors for a specific task or aspect of mentoring, thereby getting various points of view. Because the relationships between mentor and protégé are less intense than in traditional mentoring, compatibility issues are less of an obstacle. In addition, participants can benefit from colleagues of diverse backgrounds, strengths, and viewpoints. This model expands the mentoring resources because groups and organizations as well as individuals are seen as potential sources of mentoring (Angelique et al., 2002; Gibson, 2006; Packard, 2003; Quinlan, 1999). Peer relationships also provide opportunities for sharing a wide range of information and overcoming loneliness, isolation, and lack of collegiality, which is particularly important in men-dominated workplaces (Quinlan, 1999).

Peer mentors tend to be more available than traditional mentors; because of this, there are benefits to organizations expanding their definitions of mentoring to include peer mentoring. According to Thomas and colleagues (2005), peer relationships can benefit graduate students greatly, encompassing the benefits of many mentoring relationships (such as providing information, support, career strategies, and feedback) but with the additional benefit of equality within the relationship.

Although peer mentoring programs resolve some of the problems of traditional mentoring, they do not eliminate all difficulties. They are often institution-sponsored programs with institutionally established goals. They generally involve a formal arrangement between two or three peers, and, in some work environments, peer mentoring relationships may become competitive and even hierarchical. Like traditional mentoring programs, peer mentoring programs promote homogeneity within the institution (Angelique et al., 2002). Finally, peer mentoring programs can miss some of the career-enhancing functions of traditional mentoring, such as sponsorship, exposure, protection, and coaching (Quinlan, 1999).

According to Mayer et al. (2008), there are three main types of mentoring: traditional one-on-one mentoring; the multiple mentoring model, where protégés are encouraged to create a community of mentors; and peer mentoring, which encourages equality in relationships as opposed to hierarchy and seniority: "Peer mentoring benefits participants by providing mutual support, facilitating mutual learning, allowing different perspectives, and developing friendships" (p. 205).

Angelique and colleagues (2002) described the New Scholars Network, an alternative mentoring approach that evolved to address the insufficiency of appropriate mentors at a small institution. A group of untenured faculty members came together to begin a peer mentoring support group. The group was open to all new and untenured faculty members and met twice a month. The group provided a wide array of professional development support, engaged in collaborative efforts, and deliberately structured itself on a feminist basis. It was flexible enough to meet member needs, and the authors emphasized the importance of the program's independence from the institution and institutionally established goals. Over time, they modified the group's identification from one of peer mentoring to that of a collective, the goal of which emphasizes the connections among naturally (vs. formally) developing relationships, interdisciplinarity, opportunities for social activities, collaboration, and shared power. Professional development and social support continued to be the ongoing goals for the collective.

STRATEGIC COLLABORATION MENTORING

The strategic collaboration model (Wasburn, 2007) is another alternative program that matches three to five assistant or associate professors with two full professors to form a supportive structure for advancement through the promotion and tenure process. This model extends the reach of a small number of senior professors, and the teams commit to meet monthly for at least a year. Participation requires advanced training in which roles and expectations are specified. The advantage of this model is that its intended focus is on participants' strengths and the creation of a team to replace the role of the individual mentor. Participation is open to any interested faculty member, there is less risk of gossip, fewer problems related to personality differences, greater exposure to multiple perspectives, and reduced impact if one of the mentors withdraws from the project than with traditional mentoring.

WEB-BASED MENTORING

Web-based mentoring programs are another alternative to traditional mentoring, and their advocates propose that they address some of the problems of traditional mentoring (Packard, 2003). They increase the availability of mentors, reduce the time demands of mentoring placed on faculty members, provide multiple role models, and increase flexibility with regard to time and place of mentoring contacts (Packard, 2003). And while they cannot replicate every advantage of traditional mentoring, they are seen as complementary to it.

Packard (2003) proposed that Web-based mentoring utilizes the framework of the networking model of mentoring in that this approach utilizes a large network. The benefits of face-to-face mentoring can be provided by online mentors through e-mail, electronic mailing lists, virtual consulting rooms, bulletin boards, Web sites, Web cams, chat rooms, data bases of mentors for different topics, as well as other online resources. Further, Packard (2003) contends that Web-based networking is absolutely necessary for women in the sciences and other nontraditional areas where there are few senior women faculty members. She proposed shifting the emphasis of mentoring programs from the mentoring relationship to mentoring functions. This change in focus justifies conceptualizing online networking alternatives as mentoring. Online mentoring opportunities are being used by the Department of Labor to promote interest in science, technology, and the health sciences to girls and by the University of Michigan to create an electronic mentoring project in Nursing (U.S. Department of Labor, 2008). An e-mentoring Web site is dedicated to electronic mentoring for teachers' online professional development and includes a review of literature in this area (Bartosciewicz, 2004).

Gabriel and Kaufield (2008) described a reciprocal mentoring model that also utilizes technology as an alternative to traditional mentoring. This model has the goal of helping both protégés and mentors establish a collaborative learning relationship related to teaching online courses with benefits accruing to both partners. Reciprocal mentoring has also been described as collaborative mentoring and co-mentoring. This study paired a mentor, who was not necessarily senior in status or rank but was experienced in online course delivery and pedagogy, with six online instructors. The mentoring occurred initially with a face-to-face meeting and was followed with subsequent weekly contacts via e-mail, group electronic mailing list, dissemination of articles, or less frequent face-to-face meetings. Although an important goal of the program was to develop a community of practice among the online instructors, the participants concluded that the electronic mailing list did not result in a true learning community. Instead, the participants proposed that monthly face-to-face workshops, lunches, and social events would facilitate the development of a community of practice. The face-to-face monthly meetings would be supplemented by online contact.

STRATEGIES TO PROMOTE INSTITUTIONALIZING MENTORING: SOLUTIONS FOR WOMEN

> A lot of people have gone further than they thought they could because someone else thought they could.
>
> —Unknown

> A vision is not just a picture of what could be; it is an appeal to our better selves, a call to become something more.
>
> —Rosabeth Moss Kanter

Similar to most early research on the psychology of women, the focus of lack of mentoring is on identifying pathology in an individual—for example, unassertive women, fear of success, and fear of failure. Advice for women to find a mentor thus takes into account this interpretation of women's behavior (Allen, Eby, & Lentz, 2006; Dessler, 2009). Examples of this type of advice include, "Make it easier for a potential mentor to agree to your request by clarifying what you expect in terms of time and advice," "Have an agenda. Bring an agenda to your first mentoring meeting that lays out key issues and topics for discussion." Trunk's (2004) advice to finding a mentor includes this step:

> Be a good listener. This person is not your therapist. You ask a question, and then listen. If the mentor needs to know more, he'll ask. Do not tell your life story. It is not interesting. If it were, you'd be writing a book or doing standup, right? If you find yourself talking more than the mentor, then get a therapist before you scare your mentor away.

Such advice places the onus for change on women themselves.

Our perspective in this chapter is that change must occur at the institutional or organizational level, not at the personal level. While Hackney and Bock (2000) recognize that traditional mentoring for women is inadequate, they also find alternative forms of mentoring insufficient to offset the barriers academic women face. They make the case that, while women are being hired more readily than in the past, their acceptance and rates of promotion and tenure continue to be problematic. They locate the problem in the patriarchal nature of institutional academic and business culture. They propose that the prevailing culture is a powerful and negative force that cannot be ignored in the development of women's professional identity. From this perspective, regardless of the type of mentoring that is provided, women and other marginalized groups will continue to be disadvantaged until the academic and business culture changes.

Organizations can do much to support and promote the mentoring dynamic by providing training for mentors and protégés, recognizing mentoring activities, and rewarding the relationship (Ragins & Cotton, 1993). These actions all serve to legitimize the mentoring relationship. Organizational support plays a part in the nature of mentoring relationships. According to Jandeska and Kraimer (2005), most organizations are structured by traditional and stereotypical masculine culture, which, in turn, values and rewards men who exhibit these stereotypical traits more so than women. Women often struggle to find their place within such an organization. As Jandeska and Kraimer (2005) argue:

> This "code of conduct" in masculine cultures, while recognizable to males, can be completely alien to females and thus would be considered less hospitable towards women's careers. For example, an "old-boy network" excludes women from centers of influence and valuable sources of information, often trivializing or ignoring their contributions. (p. 465)

According to Jandeska and Kraimer (2005), collective organizational cultures also exist that reward more stereotypical feminine behaviors. The collectivistic culture focuses on cooperation. As such, women will be more satisfied with their careers and more committed to the organization if the organization is more geared to collectivistic goals:

> Even women in senior roles in large corporations find themselves "on the outside looking in" when it comes to information sharing and access to the inner circle, where decisions are made. . . . Women characterize such a culture as exclusionary and claim that upper management often lacks awareness of the barriers it creates to women's assimilation and advancement. (Jandeska & Kraimer, 2005, p. 465)

In general, mentoring in higher education and business has addressed the general goals of helping and supporting novice colleagues with socialization to a new role and institution and career development. Mentoring programs that focus on women may have additional goals of addressing the underrepresentation of women in senior positions (Gardiner et al., 2007). Such goals include reducing women's isolation in men-dominated departments or institutions, addressing women's experience as outsiders or being marginalized (Gibson, 2006), and providing support for challenges particular to women's career development and advancement (Chandler, 1996; Quinlan, 1999; Wasburn, 2007).

One such avenue of support is the provision of flexible job arrangements for women who are integrating life and work roles, including flex time, telecommuting, job sharing, desk sharing, career break/time off, and compressed work week policies. Organizations that implement such policies report positive ramifications for the business as well as employees, including lower absenteeism, less stress, higher morale, improved work satisfaction, lower turnover rate, staffing over a wide range of hours, child care hours that conform to work hours, and access to quality infant and child care (Frone & Yardley, 1996; Paludi et al., 2007).

Such programs are necessary in order to deal with the incompatibility between family and work roles in the United States, as is reflected in the following research findings (Heymann, 2000; Peeters, Montgomery, Bakker, & Schaufeli, 2005; Strassel, Colgan, & Goodman, 2006):

Women carry more of the workload at home.

Salary inequities exist, especially for women of color.

Employed women do substantially more caregiving to children and elder parents than do men.

Implementing sexual harassment, race discrimination, and sex discrimination policies are also required in order to establish and maintain healthy educational and workplace environments for women. Mandatory training programs on diversity and discrimination for faculty and administrators will ensure all individuals can reach their full potential. No longer should sexual harassment and sex and race discrimination be hidden gender equity problems for women in academia and in business that prevent them from being protégés and mentors.

Finally, Luna and Cullen's (1990) research suggests that mentors be trained to focus on individuals' professional and personal development. They interviewed 14 women in administrative or executive positions in the academy and business about their mentoring experience. Luna and Cullen found that women in the academy were more sensitive to protégés' personal development than were women mentors in business. Luna and Cullen described the women mentors from business as taking on qualities of men mentors and not using caretaking or nurturing qualities. Furthermore, Luna and Cullen reported that mentors in both the academy and business did not protect their protégés, did not act as buffers for them, nor did they take responsibility for errors not under their protégés' control. To fully remove the barriers to women and minorities, the academic and business cultures must become collaborative, inclusive, altruistic and value relationships, multiple perspectives, diversity, and different ways of knowing. At that time, mentoring may become "a thing of the past"; an antiquated model incompatible with an inclusive and egalitarian organization (Hackney & Bock, 2000, p. 5).

REFERENCES

ABA Commission on Women in the Profession. (2006). *Visible invisibility: Women of color in law firms.* Retrieved October 1, 2007, from http://www.abanet.org/women/VisibleInvisibility-ExecSummary.pdf

Albino Gilbert, L., & Rossman, K. M. (1992). Gender and the mentoring process for women: Implications for professional development. *Professional Psychology: Research and Practice, 23*(3), 233–238.

Allen, T., Eby, L., & Lentz, E. (2006). The relationship between formal mentoring program characteristics and perceived program effectiveness. *Personnel Psychology, 59,* 125–153.

Allen, T. D., Russell, J.E.A., & Maetzke, S. B. (1997). Formal peer mentoring: Factors related to protégés' satisfaction and willingness to mentor others. *Group & Organization Management, 22,* 488–507.

Allen, T., & Eby, L. (2003). Relationship effectiveness for mentors: Factors associated with learning and quality. *Journal of Management, 29,* 469–486.

Allen, T., Poteet, M. L., Eby, L., Lentz, E., & Lima, L. (2004). Career benefits associated with mentoring for protégés: A meta-analysis. *Journal of Applied Psychology, 89,* 127–136.

Angelique, H., Kyle, K., & Taylor, E. (2002). Mentors and muses: New strategies for academic success. *Innovative Higher Education, 26,* 195–209.

Bagihole, B., & White, K. (2003). Created in their image: An analysis of male cultural hegemony in higher education in Australia and the United Kingdom. In B. Groombridge & V. Mackie (Eds.), *Re-searching research agendas: Women, research and publication in higher education: Proceedings of the Australian Technology Network-Women's Executive Development* (pp. 1–12). Perth, Western Australia: Learning Support Network, Curtin University of Technology.

Barnett, J. E. (2008). Mentoring, boundaries, and multiple relationships: Opportunities and challenges. *Mentoring and Tutoring: Partnership in Learning, 16,* 3–16.

Bartosiewicz, P. (2004). *E-mentoring literature review.* Retrieved September 13, 2008, from http://my-ecoach.com/online/webresourcelist

Betz, N. (2007). Career development. In F. Denmark & M. Paludi (Eds.), *Psychology of women: A handbook of issues and theories* (2nd ed., pp. 717–752). Westport, CT: Greenwood Press.

Blake-Beard, S. D. (1999). The costs of living as an outsider within: An analysis of the mentoring relationships and career success of black and white women in the corporate sector. *Journal of Career Development, 26,* 21–36.

Boyle, P., & Boice, B. (1998). Systematic mentoring for new faculty teachers and graduate teaching assistants. *Innovative Higher Education, 22,* 157–179.

Bronstein, P., Black, L., Pfennig, J., & White, A. (1986). Getting academic jobs: Are women equally qualified and equally successful? *American Psychologist, 41,* 318–322.

Casto, C., Caldwell, C., & Salazar, C. F. (2005). Creating mentoring relationships between female faculty and students in counselor education: Guidelines for potential mentees and mentors. *Journal of Counseling & Development, 83,* 331–336.

Cawyer, C. S., Simonds, C., & Davis, S. (2002). Mentoring to facilitate socialization: The case of the new faculty member. *Qualitative Studies in Education, 15,* 225–242.

Chandler, C. (1996). Mentoring and women in academia: Reevaluating the traditional model. *NWSA Journal, 8,* 79–100.

Clifford, V. (2003, May). *Group mentoring: An alternative way of working.* Paper presented at the Second National Conference on Women in Science, Technology, and Engineering, Sydney, Australia.

Curry, B. (2004). How can lifelong mentoring help to develop leaders? *Women in Higher Education, 13,* 1–2.

Dansky, B., & Kilpatrick, D. (1997). Effects of sexual harassment. In W. O'Donohue (Ed.), *Sexual harassment: Theory, research and practice* (pp. 151–174). Boston: Allyn & Bacon.

Dansky, K. (1996). The effect of group mentoring on career outcomes. *Group and Organizational Management, 21,* 5–21.

DeSouza, E., & Fansler, A. G. (2003). Contrapower sexual harassment: A survey of students and faculty members. *Sex Roles, 48,* 529–542.

Dessler, G. (2009). *Fundamentals of human resource management.* Upper Saddle River, NJ: Prentice Hall.

Edson, S. (1995). Ten years later: Too little, too late? In D. Dunlap & P. Schmuck (Eds.), *Women leading education* (pp. 36–48). Albany: State University of New York Press.

Eliasson, M., Berggren, H., & Bondestam, F. (2000). Mentor programmes—A shortcut for women's academic careers? *Higher Education in Europe, 25,* 173–179.

Evans, G., & Cokley, K. (2008). African American women and the academy: Using career mentoring to increase research productivity. *Training and Education in Professional Psychology, 2,* 50–57.

Fiske, S., & Stevens, L. (1993). What's so special about sex? Gender stereotyping and discrimination. In S. Oskamp & M. Costanzo (Eds.), *Gender issues in contemporary society* (pp. 173–196). Newbury Park, CA: Sage.

Fitzgerald, L., Gelfand, M., & Drasgow, F. (1995). Measuring sexual harassment: Theoretical and psychometric advances. *Basic and Applied Social Psychology, 17,* 425–427.

Fleming, J. (1996). *Who are the protégés? The relationship between mentoring experiences, self-efficacy, career salience, attachment style, and Eriksonian life stage.* Doctoral dissertation, School of Arts and Sciences, Columbia University.

Frone, M., & Yardley, J. (1996). Workplace family-supportive programmes: Predictors of employed parents' importance ratings. *Journal of Occupational and Organizational Psychology, 69,* 351–366.

Gabriel, M. A., & Kaufield, K. J. (2008). Reciprocal mentorship: An effective support for online instructors. *Mentoring & Tutoring: Partnership in Learning, 16,* 311–327.

Gardiner, M. E., Enomoto, E., & Grogan, M. (2000). *Coloring outside the lines: Mentoring women into school leadership.* Albany: State University of New York Press.

Gardiner, M., Tiggemann, M., Kearns, H., & Marshall, K. (2007). Show me the money! An empirical analysis of mentoring outcomes for women in academia. *Higher Education Research & Development, 26,* 425–442.

Gibson, S. K. (2004). Being mentored: The experience of women faculty. *Journal of Career Development, 30,* 173–188.

Gibson, S. K. (2006). Mentoring of women faculty: The role of organizational politics and culture. *Innovative Higher Education, 31,* 63–79.

Gilbert, L., Gallessich, J., & Evans, S. (1983). Sex of faculty role model and students' self-perceptions of competency. *Sex Roles, 9,* 597–607.

Gonzalez-Figueroa, E., & Young, A. M. (2005). Ethnic identity and mentoring among Latinas in professional roles. *Cultural Diversity and Ethnic Minority Psychology, 11*(3), 213–226.

Gonzales-Morales, M., Peiro, J., & Greenglass, E. (2006). Coping and distress in organizations: The role of gender in work stress. *International Journal of Stress Management, 13,* 228–248.

Grauerholz, E. (1989). Sexual harassment of women professors by students: Exploring the dynamics of power, authority and gender in a university setting. *Sex Roles, 21,* 789–801.

Hackney, C. E., & Bock, M. (2000). Beyond mentoring: Toward an invitational academe. *Advancing Women in Leadership Journal, 3.* Retrieved August 8, 2008, from http://www.advancingwomen.com/awl/winter2000/hackney-bock.html

Haring-Hidore, M., & Paludi, M. A. (1988). Sexuality and sex in mentoring and tutoring: Implications for women's opportunities and achievement. *Peabody Journal of Education, 67,* 164–172.

Hewlett, S., & Luce, C. (2006, December). Extreme jobs: The dangerous allure of the 70-hour workweek. *Harvard Business Review,* 45–49.

Heymann, J. (Ed.). (2000). *The widening gap: Why American working families are in jeopardy and what can be done about it.* New York: Basic Books.

Hill Collins, P. (2004). Learning from the outsider within: The sociological significance of black feminist thought. In S. Harding (Ed.), *The feminist standpoint theory reader: Intellectual & political controversies* (pp. 103–126). New York: Routledge.

Holmes, S., Land, L., & Hinton-Hudson, V. (2007). Race still matters: Considerations for mentoring black women in academe. *Negro Educational Review, 58,* 105–129.

hooks, b. (2004). Choosing the margin as a space of radical openness. In S. Harding (Ed.), *The feminist standpoint theory reader: Intellectual & political controversies* (pp. 153–159). New York: Routledge.

Indvik, J. (2004). Women and leadership. In P. Northouse (Ed.), *Leadership theory and practice* (3rd ed.). Thousand Oaks, CA: Sage.

Jandeska, K. E., & Kraimer, M. L. (2005). Women's perceptions of organizational culture, work attitudes, and role-modeling behaviors. *Journal of Managerial Issues, 18,* 461–478.

Kanter, R. M. (1977). *Work and family in the United States: A critical review and agenda for research and policy.* New York: Russell Sage Foundation.

Karsten, M. (2006). Managerial women, minorities, and stress: Causes and consequences. In M. Karsten (Ed.), *Gender, race and ethnicity in the workplace* (pp. 238–272). Westport, CT: Praeger.

Keefe, R. (2003). Practical tips for effective faculty mentoring. *Women in Higher Education, 34.*

Keller, E. F., & Moglen, H. (1987). Competition and feminism: Conflicts for academic women. *Signs, 12,* 493–511.

Kelly, P. J., Bobo, T. J., McLachlan, K., Avery, S., & Burge, S. L. (2006). Girl world: A primary prevention program for Mexican American girls. *Health Promotion Practice, 7,* 174–179.

Keyton, J., & Kalbfleisch, P. (1993, April). *Building a normative model of women's mentoring relationships.* Paper presented at the Joint Meeting of the Southern States Communication Association and the Central States Communication Association, Lexington, KY.

LaFrance, M. (1987, July). *Paradoxes in mentoring.* Paper presented at the International Interdisciplinary Congress on Women, Dublin, Ireland.

Lash, C. (2000). *Athena's daughters: Women's perceptions of mentoring and the workplace.* Doctoral dissertation, Arizona State University, Tempe.

Liang, B., Tracy, A., Kauh, T., Taylor, C., & Williams, L. M. (2006). Mentoring Asian and Euro-American college women. *Multicultural Counseling and Development, 34,* 143–154.

Liang, B., Tracy, A. J., Taylor, C. A., & Williams, L. M. (2002). Mentoring college-age women: A relational approach. *American Journal of Community Psychology, 30,* 271–288.

Luna, G., & Cullen, D. (1990, April). *An ethnographic comparison of mentoring functions for women in academe and business.* Paper presented at the American Educational Research Association Meeting, Boston, MA.

Lundberg-Love, P., & Marmion, S. (2003). Sexual harassment in the private section. In M. Paludi & C. Paludi (Eds.), *Academic and workplace sexual harassment: A handbook of cultural, social science, management and legal perspectives* (pp. 77–101). Westport, CT: Praeger.

Martin, J. (2008). Shifting the load: Personality factors and women in the workplace. In M. Paludi (Ed.), *The psychology of women at work: Challenges and solutions for our female workforce* (pp. 153–200). Westport, CT: Praeger.

Maton, K. I., Kohout, J. L., Wicherski, M., Leary, G. E., & Vinokurov, A. (2006). Minority students of color and the graduate pipeline in psychology—Disquieting and encouraging trends, 1989–2003. *American Psychologist, 61,* 117–131.

Mayer, A. P., Files, J. A., Ko, M. G., & Blair, J. E. (2008). Academic advancement of women in medicine: Do socialized gender differences have a role in mentoring? *Mayo Clinic Proceedings, 82,* 204–207.

Moore, K. (1984). Careers in college and university administration: How are women affected? In A. Tinsley, C. Secord, & S. Kaplan (Eds.), *Women in higher education administration.* San Francisco: Jossey-Bass.

Moses, Y. (1988). *Black women in the academy.* Washington, DC: Project on the Status and Education of Women.

Moss, P., Debres, K. J., Cravey, A., Hyndman, J., Hirschboeck, K. K., & Masucci, M. (1999). Toward mentoring as feminist praxis: Strategies for ourselves and others. *Journal of Geography in Higher Education, 23,* 413–427.

Office for Women's Affairs, Indiana University. (1995). The gender politics of mentoring. *Majority Report Newsletter, 9*(1).

Packard, B. W. (2003). Web-based mentoring: Challenging traditional models to increase women's access. *Mentoring & Tutoring, 11,* 53–65.

Paludi, M. A. (2002). *The psychology of women* (2nd ed.). Upper Saddle River, NJ: Prentice Hall.

Paludi, M. A., & DeFour, D. C. (1992). The mentoring experiences questionnaire. *Mentoring International, 6,* 19–23.

Paludi, M., & Neidermeyer, P. (Eds.). (2007). *Work, life and family imbalance: How to level the playing field.* Westport, CT: Praeger.

Paludi, M., & Paludi, C. (Eds.). (2003). *Academic and workplace sexual harassment: A handbook of legal, social science, cultural, and management perspectives.* Westport, CT: Praeger.

Paludi, M., Vaccariello, R., Graham, T., Smith, M., Allen-Dicker, K., Kasprzak, & White, C. (2007). Work/life integration: Impact on women's careers, employment, and family. In M. A Paludi & P. E. Neidermeyer (Eds.), *Work, life and family imbalance: How to level the playing field* (pp. 21–36). Westport, CT: Praeger.

Paludi, M. A., Waite, B., Hoewing-Roberson, R., & Jones, L. (1988). Mentors vs. role models: A clarification of terms. *International Journal of Mentoring, 2,* 20–25.

Peeters, M., Montgomery, A., Bakker, A., & Schaufeli, W. (2005). Balancing work and home: How jobs and home demands are related to burnout. *International Journal of Stress Management, 12,* 43–61.

Quinlan, K. M. (1999). Enhancing mentoring and networking of junior academic women: What, why, and how? *Journal of Higher Education Policy and Management, 21,* 31–42.

Ragins, B. R. (1989). Barriers to mentoring: The female manager's dilemma. *Human Relations, 42,* 1–22.

Ragins, B. R., & Cotton, J. L. (1993). Gender and willingness to mentor in organizations. *Journal of Management, 19,* 97–111.

Ragins, B. R., & Cotton, J. L. (1999). Mentor functions and outcomes: A comparison of men and women in formal and informal relationships. *Journal of Applied Psychology, 84,* 529–550.

Rospenda, K., Richman, J., Ehmke, J., & Zlatoper, K. (2005). Is workplace harassment hazardous to your health? *Journal of Business and Psychology, 20,* 95–110.

Shakeshaft, C. (1985). *The new scholarship on women in education. Handbook for achieving sex equity in education.* Baltimore: Johns Hopkins University Press.

Shakeshaft, C., Brown, G., Irby, B., Grogan, M., & Ballenger, J. (2007). Increasing gender equity in educational leadership. In S. Klein (Ed.), *Handbook for achieving gender equity through education* (2nd ed., pp. 103–129). Mahwah, NJ: Erlbaum.

Strassel, K., Colgan, C., & Goodman, J. (2006). *Leaving women behind: Modern families, outdated laws.* New York: Rowman & Littlefield.

Swoboda, M., & Millar, S. (1986). Networking mentoring: Career strategy of women in academic administration. *Journal of the NAWDAC, 49,* 8–13.

Tang, C., Yik, M., Cheung, F., Choi, P., & Au, K. (1996). Sexual harassment of Chinese college students. *Archives of Sexual Behavior, 25,* 201–215.

Thomas, G. D., & Hollenshead, C. (2001). Resisting from the margins: The coping strategies of black women and other women of color faculty members at a research university. *Journal of Negro Education, 70,* 166–176.

Thomas, K. M., Hu, C., Gewin, A. G., Bingham, K., & Yanchus, N. (2005). The roles of protégé: Race, gender, and proactive socialization attempts on peer mentoring. *Advances in Developing Human Resources, 7,* 540–555.

Trix, F., & Psenka, C. (2003). Exploring the color of glass: Letters of recommendation for female and male faculty. *Discourse and Society, 14,* 191–220.

Trunk, P. (2004). *7 steps to finding and keeping a mentor.* Retrieved October 31, 2008, from http://blog.penelopetrunk.com

U.S. Department of Labor Women's Bureau. (2008). *E-mentoring.* Retrieved September 13, 2008, from http://www.dol.gov/wb/media/newsletter/e-news 8artl-03.htm

Wasburn, M. H. (2007). Mentoring women faculty: An instrumental case study of strategic collaboration. *Mentoring & Tutoring, 15,* 57–72.

Werhane, P., Posig, M., Gundry, L., Powell, E., Carlson, J., & Ofstein, L. (2006). Women leaders in corporate America: A study of leadership values and methods. In M. F. Karsten (Ed.), *Gender, race and ethnicity in the workplace: Issues and challenges for today's organizations* (pp. 1–29). Westport, CT: Praeger.

Woods, K., & Buchanan, N. (2008). Sexual harassment in the workplace. In M. Paludi (Ed.), *The psychology of women at work: Challenges and solutions for our female workforce* (pp. 119–132). Westport, CT: Praeger.

Young, A. M., Cady, S., & Foxon, M. J. (2006). Demystifying gender differences in mentoring: Theoretical perspectives and challenges for future research on gender and mentoring. *Human Resource Development Review, 5,* 148.

Young, S. (1988). Mentoring of female graduate students by male faculty. *Dissertation Abstracts International, 58,* 3029.

Chapter 6

Service Learning as a Model for Mentoring Women

Arvilla Payne-Jackson, Kathleen Scott,
Ajeenah Haynes, and Germon Miller

Students at Howard University seldom venture beyond the confines of their campus except to go out to eat, for entertainment, and to shop. Consequently, they are virtually unaware of the problems and harsh everyday realities faced by persons living in the surrounding communities. Similarly, academicians tend to stay within the confines of the campus, as are the projects they assign to students. Class lectures, readings from textbooks, and research conducted in the library, the laboratory, or from a database constitute the major part of students' learning activities. The question then becomes how to link classrooms and communities—exposing students to the outside world and preparing them for challenges they will encounter once they have graduated from college. Specifically, how do we mentor and engage our students to invest in building social capital? The answer may lie in the capacity of students and educators working together to build social capital through "the informal and formal networks of community citizens who work to 'make community' and increase the well-being of all residents as well as the community as a whole" (Camino & Payne-Jackson, 2004, p. 15; see also Coleman 1987; Putnam, 1995).

Over the past decade, students in anthropology classes at Howard have been mentored through service learning projects to create awareness of major issues in communities and help students to grasp the roles they can play in addressing community and national issues; for example, alcoholism, literacy, displacement, health issues, ex-offender re-entry, and gun violence, among others (see Green, Payne-Jackson, & Bonthron, 2005; Hayden and Payne-Jackson, 2004).

In this chapter, we focus on one recent service learning project used to mentor students at Howard University—the First National Community in Action Youth Summit, which addressed the causes and solutions for youth violence. Howard participants included a group of mostly women anthropology students (92 percent women).

SERVICE LEARNING

Service learning as a teaching method helps bring positive change to both students and communities by integrating meaningful student community service with curriculum-based or community-based learning and providing opportunities for mentorship through the transmission of knowledge and experience in building social capital. Community service and service learning represent a major pathway for engaging youth in civic service (Camino & Zeldin, 2002). It provides an avenue by which professors can mentor both graduate and undergraduate students in confronting their misconceptions about the reality of life outside the campus and the fears and stereotypes of people they have only studied or heard about.

The focus of this chapter is on the role of mentoring through service learning. Bozeman and Feeney (2007) define mentoring as

a process for the informal transmission of knowledge, social capital, and the psychosocial support perceived by the recipient as relevant to work, career, or professional development; mentoring entails informal communication, usually face-to-face and during a sustained period of time, between a person who is perceived to have greater relevant knowledge, wisdom, or experience (the mentor) and a person who is perceived to have less (the protégé).

Mentoring can be both value and social oriented. At the college level, it provides a way to help students achieve graduation while building their confidence and skills for their entry into the workforce or to further their education. The goals of the Youth Summit were to help Howard students become aware of how they could use their skills and talents to engage in civic issues and to help make a difference. The knowledge gained from the process would help develop their portfolios for future education and careers. As mentors, we found the young women involved to be very energized by their participation in an effort that could be translated into a larger

Figure 1
Venn Model of Academic Service Learning

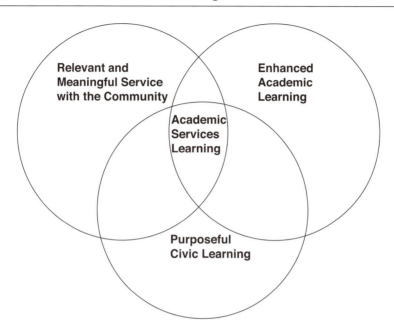

purpose of not only providing them hands-on experience in their major area of study or career interest, but also provide an avenue in which they could add to our understanding of youth violence in the district.

Three key ingredients of academic service learning as an instructional method are: "relevant and meaningful service with the community, enhanced academic learning, and purposeful civic learning" (Porter & Monard, 2001, p. 12). Academic service learning is intentional and purposeful in terms of student community engagement, civic learning, and enhancement of the overall academic learning process. All of these elements overlap and create a reciprocal effect of sharing and learning by all members involved, as seen in the Venn model in Figure 1 (Porter & Monard, 2001, p. 12).

The Venn model provides a good framework in which to mentor, because service learning lends itself to the exchange and sharing of knowledge and the active use of that knowledge in the real world. As mentors, we found that students were apt to keep their enthusiasm throughout the project the more we were able to relate the study issue to their particular majors or career interests. Dividing the students into groups such as marketing, research, fundraising, and so on capitalized on their many talents and kept the students engaged. Also, sharing our knowledge and experiences of the work we had completed with students who worked on previous projects shed light on the work that needed to be accomplished and encouraged the students to complete the established goals of the current project.

Students benefited from their interaction and work with community activists involved in grassroots efforts to address violence in the communities surrounding Howard's campus. They learned of the challenges and hardships nonprofits face while struggling to make a difference. The research that the young women completed and their direct contact with community members and business owners exposed them to an entirely different understanding of the Shaw, Logan Circle, and Howard communities. This form of mentoring enhanced their academic and civic learning and reinforced engagement in meaningful community service by incorporating the classroom curriculum with the goals of the service learning Youth Summit project.

BENEFITS OF SERVICE LEARNING AS A METHOD OF MENTORING

Service learning–based projects provide mentors a threefold method by which to add to the body of *knowledge,* change *attitudes,* and develop *skills* students need to become active community citizens engaged in building social capital. Inherent to service learning is the gaining of academic and civic-based knowledge. Service learning projects are designed to help students gain awareness of the complexity of communities and learn how the important skills and talents they have can help communities make changes. Through mentoring, they learn to communicate more effectively and transfer information in a professional manner. The awareness and knowledge they gain extends to a better understanding of broader domestic as well as world events and issues. Students translate academic skills learned in the classroom to conduct work for the service learning project, such as using various qualitative research approaches learned in the classroom to map the assets and resources of a neighborhood or using the skills of conducting a literature review to discover various perspectives on a specific social issue. We found that the young women involved in the service learning projects enjoyed being able to link what they learned in the classroom to work conducted outside of the school walls.

Mentoring students through service learning develops openness to learning and a positive orientation to new experiences and opportunities. It creates awareness of social problems, develops sociocultural sensitivity, and overcomes prejudices and stereotypes by working directly with community residents and groups and organizations working on problems that affect society as a whole. The result is a greater sense of self, awareness of self-empowerment, a tolerance for the unfamiliar, and an overall better attitude toward civic engagement. When the young women were able to meet women from the community who were on government assistance and members of the community whose family members had been murdered, the social issues they had been researching and learning about in the classroom became real, and their attitudes toward making a difference became more urgent.

Projects allow us to teach students how to conduct both exploratory and explanatory research and conduct comparative analysis. The projects provide mentoring opportunities to students by which they develop leadership skills, personal skills, organizational skills, and team-building skills. They learn to use the latest software and technology in data analysis and develop critical and comparative thinking and thoughtful communication. We found that the women involved learned the skills of ongoing reflection and evaluation of a project from beginning to end. As a result, they improved their knowledge of cultures and historical forces that shaped the current problem that they were working to change.

The project undertaken by students clearly demonstrates that service learning is *"learning by doing* for others" (Dubinsky, 2002, p. 64) as well as learning from others through mentoring.

YOUTH SUMMIT

The Youth Summit grew out of partnerships with Reaching Out to Others Together, Inc. (ROOT)—a grassroots organization building awareness and assistance to families victimized by homicide—and the Ozziddi Project—a grassroots interactive theater group working toward making healthy communities—to address the root causes of and solutions to youth violence.

The partnership with ROOT began in 2004, when students in an ethnography class undertook a project to determine the perceived causes of violence and ways to prevent violence from the perspective of local merchants. In 2006, based in part on the findings of this field work, professors in the Department of Sociology and Anthropology at Howard University in conjunction with ROOT, the University of the District of Columbia, the University of Maryland, the Boston Police Department, and the Ozziddi Project, submitted a proposal to the Centers for Disease Control titled *Community in Action for Community Level Change.* Although the proposal was not funded, the plan put forth in the proposal led to the district's mayor, Adrian Fenty, providing the seed money to ROOT, Inc., in 2007 for the first pilot Community in Action Project for the Shaw/Logan Circle community in the District of Columbia.

The spring semester of 2007, students in Arvilla Payne-Jackson's ethnography class laid the foundation for the Howard University and ROOT—First National Community in Action Youth Summit. In fall 2007, the students in Payne-Jackson's Introduction to Cultural Anthropology class planned, coordinated, and conducted the Youth Summit in conjunction with ROOT,

Inc., and the Ozziddi Project. The Youth Summit incorporated the vision of the original *Communities in Action* proposal. The next two sections examine the mentoring that took place during the planning process and the summit itself. Not only did mentoring take place from the professor and graduate assistant to the students in the class but also from the students in the class to each other, as the skills and experiences of the students brought valuable insight and information to the project and the process.

Phase One—Planning Process

The mentoring process began the first week of class. Students were given the history behind the current project. The proposal submitted to the Centers for Disease Control was loaded on Blackboard for students to read and review. The second week of class, students brainstormed with Payne-Jackson; Germon Miller, a gang mediator and liaison to ROOT; and Kathleen Scott, the graduate assistant, to establish the vision, mission, and goals for the summit. Payne-Jackson and Miller shared with the class their experiences of working with youth who had suffered loss of family and friends through gun violence. Two students from the class grew up in neighborhoods plagued by violence. They shared their experiences with the class, which helped create a better understanding of the dangers and fears that youth in communities face every day and what was needed to help make the summit meaningful. Most of the students in the class were stunned by the intensity of the environment that so many young people are living in.

The service learning project planning model consisted of seven steps: (1) identifying an issue; (2) developing a strategic action plan (vision/mission, victory, resources, tasks, timeline, reflection); (3) building partnerships; (4) conducting research and fieldwork; (5) collecting and analyzing data and writing reports; (6) distributing results and evaluation; and (7) reflection (see Innovation Center for Community and Youth Development and National 4-H Council, 2001). The service learning projects provide multiple opportunities for mentoring.

Once the committees were decided, each student submitted a list of her choice of the three committees she would like to work on in order of preference and where she thought her skills and knowledge would be most useful. When possible, students were given their first choice to maximize the use of their skills. Once a week, committees met during the class period for a half hour to discuss their progress, make or modify plans, and get help and advice from other students, the professor, graduate student, or Miller.

The executive committee, which was formed of the chairs of each of the committees, met once a week outside of class with the graduate assistant and/or Miller to discuss any problems they were encountering and to find solutions and additional ideas. All committees held meetings outside of class time as needed throughout the semester. If students encountered roadblocks, mentors would help students determine the underlying causes for the problems and how best to resolve the problems and come up with creative ways to get results. As mentors, we relayed to our mentees that, without a plan, no mission can be accomplished. Most of all, we learned that when a plan is successfully executed, we can claim victory and celebrate.

Students worked in teams of two or more when going out into the community to do fundraising. Depending on the nature of the project, students were accompanied by the professor, a graduate student, and/or members of the community, who were well known and respected. Specific instructions were given on how to be safe—for example, always work in teams, have maps to know for sure where they were going, have bus and train schedules, be observant of parking signs, know who to ask for help if lost, know how to dress and how to walk, look for a local mom-and-pop store, and become known.

While students began gaining a better understanding of the impact of violence on communities, the two partners in planning the summit and Miller shared their personal experiences. Kenny Barnes, chief executive officer of ROOT, Inc., visited the class and shared his story of the loss of his son to gun violence, how ROOT began, and why it was an important project for the students to participate in. This was followed with a visit from Archie Childs, chief executive officer of Ozziddi, who shared his story of the death of his son to gun violence, his personal experience as a prisoner in Lorton Prison, and how theater can help bring awareness to the urgency of changing society. Germon Miller shared her personal experiences with the students and helped them to more fully understand the impact of violence on the lives of youth and society as a whole. This was an important transfer of knowledge from grassroots activists and mentors to the students/mentees. The young women were able to confront their misconceptions about the reality of life outside the campus and overcome their personal biases and stereotypical views of people they had only studied or heard about.

Fundraising was accomplished in small groups. Miller worked with the students to design the forms to be given out to donors who purchased ads to go in the resource booklet. Students were uncertain about how to approach businesses to ask for money. To help students overcome their fears and apprehension of going out into the community and engaging merchants, Miller spent time in several class periods to do role playing with the students. The women learned how to make the initial presentation on the purpose of the project, ask for a donation, and provide potential donors with a preliminary program and receipt for their donations. Through the role playing, students learned how to deal with the full range of possible reactions of donors—from the amiable to the obstinate to the hostile. They learned the importance of being familiar with the purpose and goals of a project in order to make an effective presentation. Here, the mentoring aspect of gaining skills in terms of personal skills, communication skills, and organizational skills was instilled.

Each student was assigned the task of developing a logo for the project and selecting pictures or drawings that they wanted to be used in the pamphlet and in the resource book being developed by the program committee. Each picture and drawing was shown to the class, and they voted on which one they wanted to represent the logo and which ones would go in the resource book that would best convey the message of the summit. The pamphlet for potential donors was then fine tuned by the fundraising committee with Miller's help. Overall, students were able to raise several thousand dollars from the university and from private and public sectors. The committee members were able to take the knowledge gained in the classroom about fundraising and utilize this material in real-world situations. In addition, students were able to excel in something that they had an interest in doing and accomplishing.

If committee chairs had problems getting cooperation from one or more team members, the graduate assistant or professor met with the chair and student(s) of concern to determine what the problems were and what could be done to resolve any barriers to performance and participation. This helped students learn better mediating and communication skills. In cases where the problems were highly personal, students would talk with the professor, who would work with the student on an individual basis as needed. One important outcome was that students learned how to listen to each other and not jump to conclusions about an individual's willingness, or lack thereof, to participate without knowing all the facts. Students learned the importance of cooperation and communication to achieve their end goals.

Archie Childs of Ozziddi recruited six students from the class to perform Miller's play *The X Factor*. The students were joined by members of the surrounding communities to put on the production. Students learned about commitment and the passion for making change from the members of the community they worked with on the play.

Phase Two—The Summit

The summit provided opportunities for Howard students to mentor the youth and adults who attended and for the youth to reverse the mentoring by sharing their experiences with the Howard students. Creating an awareness of the impact of gun and youth violence on the psychological well-being of youth and public safety was the underlying theme of the summit. The morning session consisted of keynote speakers addressing various aspects of the impact of violence. The afternoon session focused on youth identifying causes of and solutions for violence.

Approximately 100 middle and high school students from Dunbar Senior High School, Anacostia Senior High School, Shaw Junior High School, Sunrise Academy, Booker T. Washington Public Charter School for Technical Arts, Charles Hart Middle School, Cardoza High School, and Terrell, and half a dozen students from M. C. Terrell/McGogney Elementary School attended the Youth Summit. In addition, approximately 50 adults and 55 Howard University students attended the summit.

As the invited youth filtered in, they were given an opportunity to place anonymous comments on "View Board" or "Parking Lot" questions on various aspects of violence (e.g., definition of, blame, solution, victims, etc.) developed by the program committee and designed to stimulate conversation at the tables. View board or parking lot questions are questions that are placed on poster paper and put on a wall. The students go up anonymously to write their comments in response to the questions. These are then collected and discussed later in the meeting and analyzed for the report. Two Howard students were assigned to each table in an effort to provide mentoring, promote conversation on the issue, and establish one-on-one contact with the youth. The questions were considered by participants to be "One of the most effective parts of the conference," because they caused the participants to "think critically about things that were out of the norm. It allowed students the opportunity to answer questions without fear of criticism or ridicule by peers." [Note: all quotes in this and the following sections are those of students' reflections on the project.]

After the speakers in the morning session, students were given the opportunity to place leaves on two fern plants in memory of family and friends lost to violence. A total of 148 leaves were hung on the two fern plants with the names of 35 females and 205 males. Some leaves had up to 13 names on them. During this part of the summit, the mentoring relationship was reversed, with the youth becoming the mentors to the Howard students. The Howard students were overwhelmed by the devastation the young people had experienced in their lives. It brought a new awareness to how privileged their own lives had been and how important it was for them to continue working in their communities to bring about change and to reach out to other youth.

To close the morning session, Germon Miller performed the *Signifying Monkey*, a story about a monkey, a lion, and an elephant. The thrust of the story was how the monkey, looking to cause trouble, incited the lion into attacking the elephant based on "he say—she say" gossip. The lion gets beaten to a pulp by the elephant. The Howard students noted that Miller was "genuinely connected with youth, who recognized her passion to help their community. They paid attention. Her animated monologue was comical, entertaining, captivating, and relatable but portrayed a powerful message to the audience."

One student observed that "the way that Mama G [Miller] presented things showed how some students actually provoke others to start violence. It sparked conversation about non-violent solutions." The Howard students learned the importance of keeping an eye on the goal and engaging young people by talking *with* them and not *at* them. Most importantly, they learned the importance of listening to what the youth had to say. The youth, on the other hand, felt encouraged to find that there were others who were listening to them and who genuinely wanted to make a difference in what was happening in their communities and families. Many felt a sense of safety and opened up to the Howard students, sharing their fears, concerns, and hopes.

After lunch, Ozziddi performed the play *The X Factor.* The play

> portrayed how violence has the capability to destroy our lives and those around us. It was well organized and portrayed the characters and the message well. The play reflected knowledge in performance and entertained the youth with a useful and important take home message—each person has a choice as to whether she will resist or not resist the temptations to go down the path of violence. It gave students first-hand experience in what they could really do to make a difference.

The audience "understood the message being conveyed, the response was positive and they [the youth] were totally engaged."

This was followed by an impromptu appearance by C-Webb, a well-known local community member who "students respect and look up to because he is in their communities." C-Webb showed a documentary on the impact of violence on the district communities. His documentary

> was extremely powerful. It hit home the most because youth saw what violence is really doing to their community. The video was harsh, but it was a serious reality check that the students needed. . . . It brought many students to tears as they recognized the victims shown in the documentary.

At a couple of tables, adults and Howard students gathered around the youth who were struggling with the memories of the lost friends and family shown in the video to bring comfort and support. The reality of the impact of the loss of life on these young people brought a greater sense of urgency to the Howard students to do more to help communities in the district and back in their home states to make a difference and help stop the loss of life— both physical and spiritual—that so many of the youth were experiencing.

David Osher from the American Research Institute led the two afternoon sessions, in which students identified the causes of and solutions to the violence in their communities. The afternoon workshops were very successful. The Howard students assigned to each table led the conversation on the topics. The first topic was to identify causes of violence in their community and schools. The second topic was to identify solutions to the causes identified. The youth identified 110 causes of violence and documented 92 solutions. The Howard students learned how to help the youth to open up about how they saw the causes of and solutions to violence from their own perspective and experience. At the end of the first and second sessions, a youth representative from each table presented the findings for his or her table. This gave the youth a greater sense of ownership in addressing the problems and proposing solutions.

REFLECTIONS

Eyler and Giles (1999) point out the importance of reflection in service learning:

> service-learning is a form of experiential education where learning occurs through a cycle of action and reflection as students work with others through a process of applying what they are learning to community problems and, at the same time, reflecting upon their experience as they seek to achieve real objectives for the community and deeper understanding and skills for themselves. . . . In the process, students link personal and social development with academic and cognitive development.

Reflections of the young women about their experiences at a personal level, the interactional level, and the process level also provide mentors with a way to gauge our success in the transmission of knowledge (both formal and informal), social capital, and psychosocial support they received as a result of working on the summit that will enhance their future educational and career goals as well as their perceptions of their success in mentoring others.

Personal

The Howard students noted that many of the preconceptions that they had formed about the youth, who live in neighborhoods where violence takes place, were dispelled.

> I had a picture of meeting rough kids, who didn't care one way or another, and I was totally proven wrong. They were well dressed, very up kept. These students were just that, kids; kids who are a product of their societies, and are hurting. They live the nightmare everyday of watching their loved ones die, and never knowing if they will be next.

Contrary to anticipated behavior problems, students found the youth were attentive and focused on the goals of the summit.

They followed directions, listened, and displayed good behavior. They were still enthusiastic and full of life. They were young and impressionable in spite of the outer shell. They were responsive and had a lot to say about violence in the community. Most participated in answering questions, but had never felt confident enough before to go and express themselves. Some said they were afraid, and one said he was afraid of being called a snitcher and feared for his life.

As the Howard students were mentored through the service learning process, they also became mentors to the youth who attended the summit, which allowed the Howard students to better understand the problems and challenges youth face. "Youth lack self-esteem, conflict management skills, confidence in themselves, optimism, and a positive outlook on life." The women mentees also learned that they are in a unique position to be mentors to the youth because they can better communicate with them. They can be role models, helping youth to look at different options to violence and set goals that will bring positive change in their lives and in society. They learned the importance of being proactive.

The mentees remarked that the summit "opened my eyes to how overly exposed these youth are at such a premature age." Most commented on "realizing how blessed" they were to have not suffered what these youth had gone and were going through. They learned the importance of "keeping a work ethic" and of "hard work, dedication and time to ensure success."

The importance of the students' work and mentoring with the youth was summarized by one student, who observed,

The presence of the Howard University students was the simplest way to reach youth. The best way to influence a teenage is through the life and voice of another teenager or young adult who can display a certain level of relevancy. One of the most effective and most heard voices is the voice of cultural relevancy.

Interaction

The young women reported that,

through interaction with and by mentoring the youth we helped give youth . . . their voices back. Youth could express very personal, everyday issues involving gun violence and crime in their communities with government officials, professors, police officers, etc. They shared about their lives and why they were so angry.

The downtime and conversation allowed Howard students to bond with the youth and encourage openness. This was considered to be the most important part of the interaction, because it gave the youth a chance to express themselves in a more comfortable and more casual setting. It was a good way to converse with them and allow them to let us "in." Once they "let us in" we were able to address some of the issues they were currently having whether related or not-related to violence. It gave us a chance to offer them solutions that they could possibly take heed of.

Reverse mentoring occurred as well. The Howard students gained insight from the youth into how the impact of violence and loss through violence affected every aspect of the youths' lives. "Everything youth see and hear is negative and it translates into how they interact with each other." The mentoring by the youth helped Howard students to know what the issues are, what resources are needed, what they saw as possible solutions to the violence, and how the Howard students could contribute to the solution.

The impact of violence on the youth became evident to Howard students by observing how they treated each other.

I could see just with their interactions with one another that violence seemed like an effortless endeavor. The way they talked to one another and treated one another when they felt threatened or they weren't being listened to, was filled with violent behavior. The youth see violence as normal and not a problem. It showed me the effect that violence has taken on our children and that we have such a far way to go.

One student related how she

tried to get students to pay attention and stop gossiping and falling into the he say/she say syndrome. I tried to get them to stop listening to the monkeys so the lion didn't go to the elephant. Some of the young men seemed too aggressive and were easily offended. One child said he didn't like how another child was staring at him and said, "I should've stole him." Another child accidentally bumped into the back of one of my students' chairs and got upset even though the young man said "Excuse me." It seemed as though they were trying to create issues out of nothing.

The memorial trees gave the "youth an opportunity to remember a family member or a friend who had been a victim of gun violence or just violence in general." For Howard students, it was a graphic realization of the loss and pain the youth were coping with. Conversations following the activity led to the youth sharing what they wanted in their lives. "The youth want to live peaceful and prosperous lives. They know what the problems are and how to solve them. They can best offer us insight; however, it has to start with *US*."

The Process

At the macro level, the summit was seen as

a success and beneficial to the University, the community, the youth and all who attended the Summit. It addressed the root causes of gun violence and other forms of violence and contributed to finding solutions to the serious threats to public safety. The Summit opened a dialogue and bridged the gap between adults and the youth. The interactive activities encouraged youth to critically think about the possible causes of gun violence and effective solutions to the problems. It gave everyone an opportunity to hear first-hand the experiences that our youth face and what they think can be done to make positive changes.

Students' reactions to the planning process for the summit were the importance of hearing firsthand what people are doing to help bring change to their communities. Barnes and Childs sharing the story of the emotional grief, stress, and shock of the loss of their sons inspired and motivated students to actively participate in the project and take on leadership roles.

Lessons learned from the planning process were summarized by students. First, "we learned the steps on how to put on a function like a Summit. We saw the class unite and every group do a great job." Second, "we had a genuine feeling of ownership," and the process provided us a "good opportunity to incorporate a number of skills gained from previous experiences." Third, and perhaps most importantly, "we learned that *hard work pays off.*"

Students also realized that "We had to become educated about youth gun violence." This part of the process was perceived as both "positive and enlightening."

We learned to see reality through the eyes of the young people invited to the Summit. We learned that violence thrives on ignorance, hypocrisy and the failure of society to accept accountability in this genocidal war. We must remember they [the youth] are watching us practice what we preach.

The Summit gave voice to the voiceless and also gave Howard students a new awareness of their own strengths, skills, and abilities to make a difference.

Two very important outcomes for students were, first, "Realizing I don't have to change the entire world to make a difference. If I reach *one person*

I have achieved something great because in turn it may create a rippling effect that reaches others," and, second, "I can encourage people in the community, at home, and in my school environment to think before they act and always think positive about the situations that life may bring."

The summit also allowed students to network with people in authority positions who can help bring about the desired changes. They learned that they can make a difference in history. Several Howard students commented that they were "inspired to continue work towards saving the youth—to help those who will one day be the future." Others noted that they were "honored and proud to take part in ROOT and Summit."

The overall consensus among the students was that "A great seed was planted and that the Summit was monumental, powerful and incredibly productive. It was a fantastic experience and a great program." Additional comments were that the summit was a "great idea," "very necessary," "uplifting," "inspirational," "innovative," "informative," "brought out the best," and "educational."

For the professor, the summit became another building block for preparing students for future projects and work in their communities. Lessons learned from the planning process and the summit itself will help make future projects even more meaningful to the students, community youth and adults, grassroots organizations, and government and university officials who participate in and sponsor the events. They will also help in establishing more significant dialogue and building stronger bridges between Howard University and communities in the metropolitan area to find solutions to the plague of violence that now exists.

CONCLUSION

Students' reflections confirmed our success in mentoring to increase knowledge and experience. The summit allowed students to bridge the gap between academia and their communities. They gained practical experience and learned how to apply to the real world what they learned in the classroom (see also Willis, Persie, Waldref, & Stockman, 2003). Through this process, Howard University students learned to lessen their fear and other negative emotions of working in any potentially violent environment. They gained better perceptions of themselves as persons of strength and fortitude as they saw the immediate impact and importance of their mentoring younger students. At same time, the format of the Youth Summit allowed the Howard students the necessary environment in which "to bridge the gap between the academic world and surrounding communities."

All the students expressed the importance of being able to make a difference and to be part of a community working for change, which confirmed the goal of civic engagement. As stated by Dubinsky (2002), service learning enables students to boost critical thinking skills and improve the integration of theory and practice. They learn to do for others and themselves by working with others in a reciprocal relationship, thus preparing themselves for the workplace and for their place as citizens in their communities. (p. 72)

Students confirmed Strand's (2000) observation that, "When students must actually do what they have read about . . . select a sample, develop a questionnaire, conduct an interview . . . they are inclined to approach their work with extra amounts of care and enthusiasm." Students who participate in service learning are involved in more than community service; they gain enhanced academic learning, purposeful civic learning, and participate in relevant and meaningful service in the community. Through the partnerships with ROOT, Ozziddi, Miller, the public schools, government agencies, nonprofit organizations, and students, Howard students contributed to addressing the roots causes of youth violence.

The seed planted at the Youth Summit has already begun to take root. The report from the Youth Summit was included in the presentation by ROOT, Inc., to Representative Bobby Rush, who has subsequently presented to Congress Bill HR1303, the Community in Action Neighborhood and Opportunity Bill. This is the first bill to address gun violence from a public health perspective and incorporates the voices of the youth from the Youth Summit.

REFERENCES

Bozeman, B., & Feeney, M. K. (2007). Toward a useful theory of mentoring: A conceptual analysis and critique. *Administrative and Society, 39*(6), 719–739.

Camino, L., & Payne-Jackson, A. (2004). Fostering social capital and community capacity for change: Strategies and impacts of two service learning teams. *The Bridge,* 1–15.

Camino, L., & Zeldin, S. (2002). From periphery to center: Pathways for youth civic engagement in the day-to-day life of communities. *Applied Developmental Science, 6*(4), 221.

Coleman, J. (1987). Families and schools. *Educational Researcher, 16,* 32–38.

Dubinsky, J. (2002). Service learning as a path to virtue: The ideal orator in professional communication. *Michigan Journal of Community Service Learning, 8*(2), 61.

Eyler, J., & Giles, D. E. Jr. (1999). *Where's the learning in service-learning?* San Francisco: Jossey-Bass.

Green, R., Payne-Jackson, A., & Bonthron, S. (2005). Evaluation as learning experience at Howard University. *Community Works Journal, 7*(2), 8.

Hayden, J., & Payne-Jackson, A. (2004, Winter). Graffiti as a sense of place: Lorton Prison Virginia. *Reflections: Special Edition Prison Literacy.*

Innovation Center for Community and Youth Development and National 4-H Council. (2001). *Building community: A tool kit for youth and adults in charting assets and creating change.* Chevy Chase, MD: Author.

Porter, M., & Monard, K. (2001, Fall). *Ayni* in the global village: Building relationships of reciprocity through international service learning. *Michigan Journal of Community Service Learning,* 10–12.

Putnam, R. (1995). Bowling alone: Americans' declining social capital. *Journal of Democracy, 6,* 65–78.

Strand, K. (2000). Community-based research as pedagogy. *Michigan Journal of Community Service, 7,* 85.

Willis, J., Persie, J., Waldref, V., & Stockman, D. (2003). The undergraduate perspective on community-based research. *Michigan Journal of Community Service Learning, 9*(3), 36.

Part III

Focus on Women of Color

Chapter 7

Enhancing Capabilities of Women and Ethnic Minorities

Asuncion Miteria Austria and A. Marie M. Austria

The results of the 2000 census (2002a) indicate that the United States is becoming a diverse nation much faster than anticipated. In the first decade of the 21st century, the ethnic minority population increased by 35 percent compared to just 3.4 percent for the white non-Hispanic population. According to census projections, by 2030, over one-third of the U.S. population will comprise people from minority groups. And by 2050, minority groups are projected to become the majority population. In other words, the future of U.S. society will rely increasingly on people of color.

At present however, college enrollment, graduation, and the pursuit of advanced study are all points where students of color and of low-income backgrounds drop out in disproportionate numbers (Thayer, 2000). The rate at which minority groups are pursuing undergraduate education and advanced study persistently lags behind the rates for white non-Hispanics. According to the 2000 census (2002b), for example, white non-Hispanics earn bachelor's degrees at twice the rate of underrepresented minority groups. Although African American students account for 9 percent of the undergraduate student population, they earn only 55 percent of the bachelor's degrees and less than 2 percent of the doctorates in science and engineering fields. Further, although women earn 56 percent of the baccalaureate degrees in all fields, they account for only 14 percent of the bachelor's degrees in physical sciences. The representation of both minority groups and women in the sciences and engineering is even lower at the doctoral level.

Recent reviews of minority pipeline trends in psychology have consistently demonstrated underrepresentation of minorities at all levels, with underrepresentation increasing as one moves up the pipeline from college entrance to receipt of the doctorate degree. Maton, Kahout, Wicherski, Leary, and Vinokurov (2006) found an encouraging development in the steady increase in the percentage of minority students receiving bachelor's degrees from 1989 to 2000, with minority representation nearly 25 percent of degree recipients in 2000, 2001, and 2002. There also has been a steady increase in the number of ethnic minority students entering master's-granting departments and receiving master's degrees. Ethnic minorities represented more than 20 percent of master's degree recipients for 2000, 2001, and 2002 (Maton et al., 2006).

What is disquieting, however, is that, at the upper end of the pipeline, there has been no growth in the percentage of minority students receiving doctoral degrees since 1999. The percentage of African American and Latino students entering PhD-granting departments has shown no growth either. A comprehensive systematic approach to enhancing minority representation in psychology, such as mentoring, may be one way to enhance minority representation in the field. Increasing the representation of ethnic minorities in psychology has the potential to benefit society by shedding light on unmet needs, contributing new knowledge, and keeping up with the increased demand of psychologists as service providers, scientists, and educators (Jones, Castellanos, & Cole, 2002; Maton & Hrabowski, 2004).

NATURE OF MENTORING

Mentoring is an age-old phenomenon dating back to Greek mythology. It was said that Ulysses placed much importance on the education of his son, Telemachus, so he entrusted his care, education, and protection to Mentor, his wise counselor and friend. According to Homer's tale, it was actually the Greek goddess of wisdom, Athena, who was responsible for mentoring Telemachus while his seafaring father was away. Disguised as Mentor, Athena aided and guided the young man and acted as the trusted friend and counselor in all aspects of the boy's life (Enomoto, Gardiner, & Grogan, 2000). Since then, the term *mentor* has been applied to individuals in a number of different roles, including those of teacher, advisor, supervisor, and employer.

There is no definitional clarity surrounding mentorship, and the lack of consensus has been cited as a deterrent in understanding the impact of mentoring (Crosby, 1999; Jacobi, 1991), but most writers agree that the term mentor indicates teacher, advisor, sponsor, counselor, and role model with a desire to help a student (Jacobi, 1991; Levinson, Darrow, Klein, Levinson, & McKee, 1978). Mentoring is described as a "relationship between a younger adult and an older, more experienced adult who helps the younger individual learn to navigate the adult world and the world of work" (Kram, 1985, p. 2).

Modern writers also note that mentoring connotes a unique and distinctive personal relationship and may incorporate a wide variety of roles, including teaching, advising, supervising, and counseling, with a view to integrate the protégé into the profession. Indeed, mentoring is a multidimensional, dynamic, reciprocal relationship between a more advanced person and a novice. It is a relationship that may also endure for several years.

Although the value of mentoring has been discussed in the literature since the early 1970s, empirical studies have been reported only since the mid-1980s (Crosby, 1999). Most of these empirical studies have addressed mentoring relationships in the corporate or private sector. Only a few empirical studies have been conducted in academic settings.

FUNCTIONS OF THE MENTOR

Kram (1985) noted that the many functions of a mentor can be clustered into two primary domains. The first is career-related support functions, which are typically focused on the career development and preparation for career advancement of the protégé. Career-related functions include sponsorship, coaching, and challenging assignments. The second is psychosocial functions, which include role modeling, counseling, acceptance and confirmation to enhance the protégé's sense of competence and identity. Subsequent studies supported Kram's (1985) two-mentor functions (Clark, Harden, & Johnson, 2000; Wilde & Schau, 1991). Several authors have proposed that academic mentoring includes at least three elements: emotional and psychosocial support, role modeling, and career development (Davidson & Foster-Johnson, 2001; Ragins & Cotton, 1999). Scandura and Viator (1994) identified three overarching mentor functions: career-related, psychosocial support, and role modeling. These distinctions in mentor functions have received considerable theoretical and empirical support. Skillful mentors seamlessly blend these functions in working with their protégés (Clark et al., 2000; Wilde & Schau, 1991).

TYPES OF MENTORING RELATIONSHIPS

Mentoring can be planned and organized, or it can evolve spontaneously or naturally. In formal, planned programs, mentors and protégés are generally matched or assigned by a third party (Johnson, 2002). Such mentoring relationships tend to last between six months and one year, with infrequent or sporadic contacts based on a contractual agreement. The focus of this mentoring relationship is on, for example, new employee orientation or short-term career goals applicable only to the protégé's current position. At my (the senior author's) institution, a private university, we have a formal program of mentoring designed for new full-time and adjunct faculty, where a senior faculty member provides support and guidance to the new faculty. Communication between the mentor and the mentee is held confidential.

Informal or spontaneous mentoring relationships are often unstructured. The relationship develops between two people drawn together by shared interests, assumptions, and developmental needs (Kram, 1988). The two people meet as often as necessary over the course of the relationship, which can take place over a relatively short period of time or can endure for a lifetime. Both mentors and protégés evaluate informal mentoring as being more effective and meaningful than formal or assigned mentoring. Mentees in informal relationships receive more career and psychosocial functions from mentors.

During the time that a spontaneous relationship is taking place, the people involved usually do not recognize its impact. The relationship is only recognized in hindsight as the mentee realizes the great influence the mentor has had on the mentee (Girves, Zepeda, & Gwathmey, 2005; Ragins & Cotton, 1999).

EFFECTIVE MENTORS

The success of a mentoring relationship may hinge on the characteristics of the mentor. Effective mentors are those who provide a climate of respect for their protégés. They provide emotional support and high expectations to their protégés. They are usually described as intelligent, caring, committed, practical, generous, honest, empathic, and patient and have vision for the mentees' future (Clark et al., 2000; Gilbert, 1985). They are also experienced and confident. They also possess nonjudgmental attitudes, which are effective in sustaining positive relationships (Grantham, 2004). A frequently overlooked attribute of communication competence is a good sense of humor (Young & Cates, 2005). Individuals with a good sense of humor are well suited for mentoring, because humor creates a supportive atmosphere.

Interpersonally effective mentors provide support and encouragement to mentees at crisis periods or at turning points in the mentee's career life. They create opportunities for the mentees, allow their work to be unimpeded, and set high performance standards. They encourage mentees to strive for excellence, but not perfection (Clark et al., 2000; Johnson, 2002). Effective mentors are ethical and exhibit professionally valued behaviors, attitudes, and skills to help their protégés achieve competence, confidence, and clear professional identity (Kitchener, 1992). They are honest and forthright with high integrity. They are attentive to performance problems, provide honest feedback, and recommend corrective measures, including termination of the relationship if necessary.

Mentors provide networking opportunities, introducing mentees to top individuals in the profession, and facilitate mentee's entry into committees and other valued activities.

In effect, mentors pass on their professional legacy through fine judgment and knowledge they have accumulated over the years (Healy, 1997).

BENEFITS OF MENTORING

Most of the mentoring outcome research has been conducted in business and industry rather than in education. The general findings are that protégés with a mentor working on their behalf are happier in their work, are more productive in their career, are rated highly by their supervisors, earn higher salaries, and are promoted more quickly (Brinson & Kottler, 1993; Busch, 1985). Students who have been mentored had higher rates of research productivity and publications than students who did not have a faculty mentor (Ragins, Cotton, & Miller, 2000). Mentors provide emotional support and encouragement during the protégé's stressful times. The protégé benefits from the mentor's knowledge and expertise and has help in adapting to the political environment within the industry, university, or academic setting. The protégé also has an advocate who is willing to speak on her behalf and has opportunities for collaborating on research projects. And importantly, the protégé has a successful model to emulate. A mentor's career may also be enhanced by the mentoring process through personal satisfaction obtained from helping another individual and increased professional visibility (Clark et al., 2000; Ragins & Scandura, 1997).

RACE AND GENDER MATTERS: CONCERNS AND BARRIERS

While mentoring is considered a process beneficial for students and professionals in general, it is considered especially important for women and ethnic minorities because of the challenges women face in predominantly male academic cultures and those that ethnic minorities face in predominantly white academic cultures. One of the most challenging barriers facing African American women students and academicians is the perception that there is a racialized and sex-biased environment in their academic department (Evans & Cokley, 2008). There is a perceived exclusion they are not receiving opportunities to participate on research teams and publishing with senior faculty members. This perceived exclusion by people of color represents a significant barrier in the success of their academic career. The formation and effectiveness of mentoring relationships are influenced by sociocultural factors such as gender and race (Evans & Cokley, 2008).

Most mentoring relationships develop from mutual attraction and interpersonal chemistry. Individuals of the same gender and racial background may be more likely to develop the chemistry necessary to form close relationships (Dreher & Cox, 1996). Because white men dominate the power structure of large organizations, they offer protégés more advantages than women mentors and mentors of other racial groups in supporting their career. Further, women and ethnic minorities have been underrepresented in the mentoring process (Blackwell, 1989). According to Blackwell, "mentors tend to select as protégés persons who are of the same gender and who share with themselves a number of social and cultural attributes or background characteristics such as race, ethnicity, religion and social class" (p. 11). Studies in social psychology show that individuals similar to one another on a number of attributes are more likely to perceive one another as attractive, predictable, and as individuals who would enjoy working together (Berscheid, 1985). The tendency of mentors to select protégés of the same gender and ethnicity is problematic because women and ethnic minorities are so underrepresented in professional psychology, especially among university faculty (Dreher & Cox, 1996).

Hetherington and Barcelo (1985) lamented the fact that there is only a small number of senior minority faculty who can act as mentors for younger minority scholars. They further stated that, not only do mentors often choose and assist protégés who are similar to themselves, they also tend to be those who had mentors themselves. In addition, minorities and women are not sought out as often as their white men counterparts for professional opportunities by those in positions of power (Dreher & Cox, 1996).

White men mentors have also been found to be particularly influential in affecting career outcomes among protégés. Difficulties with developing a successful research program are the primary reasons many are denied promotions and tenure. Women and ethnic minorities continue to earn less than men on average and are still underrepresented in most academic departments. Women and ethnic minorities disproportionately hold joint or part-time appointments, have lower academic ranks, and are less likely to be tenured (American Psychological Association [APA], Task Force on Women in Academe, 2000). Women face instances of sex discrimination that affect research productivity. For example, they receive greater requests for participation in non–research-oriented, but job- related activities such as teaching more classes, advising more students, and serving on more departmental and institutional committees than men (Cohen, Morgan, DiLillio, & Flores, 2003; Park, 2000). These duties may count toward fulfilling the teaching and service components of tenure evaluation criteria but decrease much-needed time for research and scholarship responsibilities.

Ethnic minority women experience sex-related issues as do their white women colleagues, as well as additional race-related barriers related to tokenism, professional isolation, decreased networking and collaborative opportunities, and criticism and devaluation of research interests (Turner, 2002). Erut and Mokros (1984) found that men students avoided selecting women faculty members as mentors because they were viewed as less powerful and of lower status. Indeed, women and ethnic minorities are faced with racialized and gender-biased environments.

Many students of color do not have mentoring relationships. In one study, one-third of the African American graduate students surveyed reported that they had received no mentoring support or guidance in their programs (Smith & Davidson, 1992). In a review of a mentoring program for underrepresented students, Haring (1997) found only a small number of mentoring programs for minorities were reported in the higher education literature. She suggested that most of these mentoring programs do not persist over time, and the design of these programs is notably similar, suggesting programmatic weaknesses.

Feminist critiques of traditional men's mentoring suggest that the model's very nature—its hierarchical, dyadic, and unidirectional structure—is limiting. Sullivan (1996) viewed the traditional dyadic model as problematic, with emphasis on the deficiencies of the mentee and positioning the mentor as a teacher or a father substitute. The traditional mentoring is criticized for its Eurocentricity. Feminist scholars reject the linear, one-way socialization model where senior men faculty mentors transform their mentees into copies of themselves (Packard, 2003). Women, in contrast, were left out of this historical mentoring landscape (Noe, 1988). Moreover, contemporary feminist scholars of women's mentoring have criticized the traditional dyadic model, calling it male "grooming" designed to clone mentees and replicate the existing culture, leaving little room for women to create new images in their desired field (Powell, 1999; Swoboda & Millar, 1986). Viewing mentoring from the mentee's standpoint, these scholars caution women against relying on a solitary mentor due to the risks of becoming overly dependent on one mentor, the potential weakening of one's professional training due to the lack of exposure to multiple viewpoints, and disappointments in the mentor's inability to be all things to the student (Kram, 1983, Noelinski, 1995; Swoboda & Millar, 1986).

Compared with men, women tend to seek support more frequently, and their relationships are self-disclosing and intimate (Miller & Stiver, 1997). The traditional hierarchical paradigm for mentoring (i.e., passing advice, role modeling, and socialization) may not necessarily fit women's needs. Women, in contrast, may find more beneficial a paradigm that also recognizes their psychological needs and resources. Literature on women's development identifies relational qualities that women consider growth fostering and that satisfy their desire for connection. Likewise, relational mentoring characterized by growth-producing characteristics is found to be associated with various benefits for women (Liang, Tracy, Kauh, Taylor, & Williams, 2006).

In a study of top business schools, only 18 percent of the women respondents indicated that finding mentors was easy for them while they were pursuing their MBA degrees. In addition, having the opportunity to work with same-race professors appeared to be difficult for persons of color. Only 7 percent of the African American men and women either agreed or strongly agreed that they had adequate opportunities to work with professors of color. In contrast, 17 percent of the white women and 23 percent of the white men felt they had sufficient opportunities to interact with professors of color (Bruce, 1995).

Research shows that cultural factors play an even greater role in mentoring processes. Grant-Thompson & Atkinson (1987) found that black mentors compared with white mentors more often initiated connections with black protégés to play a role in their personal and professional development and to foster perceived credibility and cultural competence. Similarly, Latino students who were matched with mentors of the same race perceived them to be more helpful in their career and personal development, and they were more satisfied with their mentors than those who had mentors of a different race (Santos & Reigadas, 2005). There are data that show that some Latina women have been mentored at varying levels of their careers by mentors of different ethnicities. They, however, found mentors that are of similar ethnicity preferable. Mentoring people of different backgrounds may create confusion and discomfort between protégé and mentor, making the formation of the relationship difficult (Gonzalez-Figueroa & Young, 2005). Results further showed that there was a significant and positive correlation between mentor preference for similar ethnicity and ethnic identity. This is consistent with the literature that people of color would rather be mentored by someone of the same ethnicity (Thomas, 2001). Gonzalez-Figueroa and Young (2005) argued that finding mentors of similar ethnicity helps in preserving the cultural and ethnic identity and the unspoken understanding of similarities in the challenges encountered by Latina women in the workforce.

Meanwhile, there is a dearth of literature on mentoring relationships of Asian Americans. Little is known about the effects of cross-ethnic mentoring among Asian Americans, although cross-ethnic mentoring is often the rule in U.S. colleges, given the limited number of Asian American mentors. In a study by Liang and colleagues (2006) Asian students were found to be less likely than European American students to report a current mentor relationship, and were less likely to report they had a mentor of the same race than were the European American students. European Americans were more likely to report no obstacles in the formation of mentor relationships. Asian students were considerably more likely to say they found no faculty member to whom they could relate (Atkinson, Lowe, & Matthews, 1995; Liang et al., 2006).

CULTURAL VARIABLES TO CONSIDER

Liang and colleagues' study (2006) examined the ways in which culture might affect the development and quality of mentoring. Findings show that, compared with European American students, Asian American students were no less likely to value the notion of having a mentor relationship, but they were less hopeful or satisfied with opportunities to form them. Asian Americans were no more successful in forming relationships regardless of how hopeful they were about forming them. It is possible the European American mentors expect students to initiate the relationships; Asian Americans expect those in authority to initiate the relationships. This shows the importance of culture in forming mentoring relationships. Whereas Western values encourage autonomy-seeking behaviors, Eastern values foster more interdependent relationships between young people and attachment figures (Liang et al., 2006).

The combined characteristics of Asian culture (e.g., status hierarchy, emotional/verbal restriction, and interdependence) may pose for Asian American students a barrier in establishing mentor relationships with authority figures. Whereas European American students are socialized to express themselves openly and initiate relationships with authority figures, Asians are socialized to be more restrictive and deferential to authority figures. Rather than freely voicing their needs or desires, Asians learn to wait until they are acknowledged and invited into a relationship by an authority figure (Austria, 2003).This behavior may be misinterpreted as a student's lack of interest in forming a mentoring relationship (Liang et al., 2006).

Mentors assume similarity between their own experiences and those of their mentees of color. The mentor's approaches to career development and support are largely based on their own training and personal work experiences, which may be different from those encountered by their protégés from various racial and cultural backgrounds.

Traditional counselors do not acknowledge the cultural differences of students of color and the impact that these differences may have on student performances and expectations. The traditional model of mentoring ignores differences between racial and ethnic groups. All graduate students are treated the same with little regard for strengths or differences that might be due to race and culture. There is also an unspoken expectation that graduate students conform to the dominant behavioral norm and assimilate into the graduate school culture (Davidson & Foster-Johnson, 2001).

Research also shows that students who are of European or Anglo descent have little difficulty in approaching their professors on an equal basis, expressing their opinions or disagreements openly, which defines the mentoring relationship as equal. Meanwhile, Latinos and Asian Americans place a relatively high premium on respect for people with authority and status and may be less willing to participate in discussions or debates that might suggest they are questioning the authority of the mentor (Oyserman & Sakamoto, 1997).

Another cultural characteristic that is often overlooked is the individualistic versus collectivist viewpoint. Asian Americans, Latinos, and African Americans tend to display cooperative behavior and are comfortable with teamwork. Asians and Latinos consider self-promotion in poor taste. They rely on friends and superiors to offer praise for their work, because self-promotion is viewed as a sign of inappropriate boasting. Reluctance to draw attention to one's self is often interpreted by white managers and supervisors as an unwillingness to take on a role of authority or to be a strong leader (Carnevale & Stone, 1985).

RECOMMENDATIONS

In light of the barriers and concerns of women and ethnic minorities, mentoring issues with respect to these two groups need to be addressed. The need for mentoring is even more crucial for women and minorities who tend to be more isolated and have less contact with faculty and academic role models. One recommendation is to train mentors in general mentoring skills (Evans & Cokley, 2008; Johnson, 2002), including the importance of mentoring, mentor functions, and how to be an effective mentor (Girves et al., 2005). To be an effective mentor, for example, a faculty member must cultivate understanding of the experiences of students from various cultural backgrounds (Davidson & Foster-Johnson, 2001). Other educational components may include acquisition of knowledge and critical skills development and use of proven methods to enhance a protégé's confidence and success.

Johnson (2002) recommended the need to attend to issues of gender. Some studies (Gilbert, 1985; Gilbert & Rosssman, 1992) show that women may prefer a more psychosocial/relational focus and a mentor who models egalitarianism/inclusiveness and a blending of personal and professional roles. Johnson also recommended attending to issues of race and culture. Mentors should have culturally responsive attitudes and competencies in mentoring ethnic minority students. They must have genuine concern for the experiences and welfare of minority students.

In their discussion of issues on mentor–mentee relationships, Davidson and Foster-Johnson (2001) stated the need to acknowledge cultural differences and the impact that these differences may have on student performance and expectations. One cultural difference is in the area of communication. There are communication difficulties experienced by those for whom English is a second language. There are semantic difficulties and differences in nonverbal cues. Thus, a cautionary style of interpersonal relations of an ethnic minority may be perceived as introversion, aloofness, or disinterest. On the other hand, a confident assertive style by an ethnic minority member may be interpreted as aggressive (Brinson & Kottler, 1993).

Women and ethnic minorities face unique challenges in securing mentorships, because both are underrepresented in academia and in the corporate world. Because of this, women and ethnic minorities have few options in securing same-gender and same-race mentorships. The option for both women and ethnic minorities is cross-gender and cross-race mentorship. There were, however, concerns raised regarding cross-race and cross-gender matches because of potential mentors' unfamiliarity with ethnic and women's issues, while some mentors assumed similarity between their own experiences and those of their mentees (Tsui, Egan, & Reilly 1992).

Mentor's approaches to career development and support are largely based on their own training and personal work experiences, which may be vastly different from those encountered by their protégés from different racial and cultural backgrounds. An effective mentor must develop a working knowledge of the protégé's worldview, accepting the protégé's individuality and uniqueness (Brinson & Kottler, 1993), and should have appropriate competencies and attitudes that include genuine concern for the welfare of minority students, and appreciation of each protégé's uniqueness within her culture (Johnson, 2002).

ALTERNATIVE MENTORING MODELS

Alternative or nontraditional mentorships have been developed due to the shortage of ethnic minorities and women in academia and the business world. Also, the problems inherent in traditional mentoring—including the hierarchical relationship between the mentor and the protégé, which assumes that the mentor possesses knowledge that the mentee needs—necessitated the development of new mentoring models. The alternative model is presented by critics who claimed that relying on a single mentor carries the risk of becoming overly dependent on the one mentor, and the resultant weakening of the mentee's professional training due to lack of exposure to multiple viewpoints. The critics also argue that it is unrealistic to find an ideal mentor who can be all to a mentee (Kram, 1983; Noelinski, 1995; Swoboda & Millar, 1986). The most distinct change in these nontraditional models is the shift from a one-on-one dyadic model to one that acknowledges the role of multiple mentors (Hamilton, 2007).

Networking Mentoring

Networking mentoring is a departure from traditional mentoring. First, it is nonhierarchical. It is a multiple mentoring model with a group of mentors present at one point in time rather than sequentially. This model demonstrates a commitment from members to assist each other and to discuss shared interests. This model is perceived as empowering individuals to develop in unique professional ways. The protégés can choose a mentor who may provide only one aspect of mentoring. A protégé can also have various mentors who provide different aspects of the mentoring process. Indeed, it is a protégé-focused mentoring model (Kram, 1985). This model places more responsibility on the mentee in seeking out and maintaining the network of mentors (Noelinski, 1995; Swoboda & Millar, 1986). The benefits derived from this model include less intense relationships with any one mentor and shorter-term relationships. Moreover, the mentee can benefit from colleagueship with individuals from diverse backgrounds and viewpoints (Packard, 2003; Rice & Austria, 2007; Swoboda & Millar, 1986). Individuals, groups and organizations are potential mentoring resources.

Peer Mentoring Model

Peer mentoring serves primarily as information gathering. The relationship is relational and provides the protégé with information about career moves and networking information. It is nonhierarchical. Students transitioning into graduate schools with increased anxiety and feelings of insecurity are benefitted by this mentorship such as provided by campus support groups or buddy networks (Grant-Vallonme & Ensher, 2000).

Team Mentoring

Team mentoring is both dyadic and group focused, with varying ties between the team leader and each team member. Mentoring is a group effort with both individual and group-based outcomes, leaving the responsibility for mentoring to both the team members and the team leader (Hamilton & Scandura, 2003). Team members take advantage of the expertise of one individual and make it available to multiple learners at one time. This model is useful where the availability of mentors is limited. In team mentoring, the mentor does not always lead the members, but the members themselves provide mentoring to each other. There is lack of status difference between the mentor and the protégé (Hamilton, 2007).

Electronic Mentoring

Electronic mentoring increases access in terms of expanding the realm of who can mentor and who can be mentored, especially in light of the lack of women of color mentors. Web sites provide means to communicate long distance between mentors and protégés. Students can be connected to mentors in industry and academia through the Internet. Protégés and mentors are matched, taking into account the career goals of both the mentor and the protégé. One example of electronic mentoring is the American Psychological Association's Cyber Mentor Program, funded by the National Institute of Mental Health (NIMH), which utilizes state-of-the-art distance learning technologies, including Web casts and online classrooms. It is a two-year program designed to prepare doctoral-level behavioral and social scientists for careers as independent researchers in the area of HIV/AIDS in communities of color and establish a mutually supportive network of professional colleagues with common research interests (APA, Office on AIDS, 2009).

Another resourceful example has been the involvement of emeritus faculty members who have the knowledge and time available to mentor motivated students. The use of e-mail at the mentor's convenience makes the mentor's participation less of an intense time commitment. Electronic mentors have increased flexibility to establish contacts at times suitable for their schedules across geographic distances. As a result, alumni, emeriti faculty, and industry professionals can be recruited to support mentees. Personalized attention, feedback of projects, insight or advice on careers, and encouragement benefits of face-to face mentoring can be provided by electronic mentors (Hamilton, 2007; Packard, 2003).

Studies show that challenges in Internet mentoring include longer time to develop the relationship, concerns with privacy and confidentiality, and adequacy and functioning of computer systems (Hamilton, 2007). Strengths that have been identified in electronic mentoring include widening the pool of mentors and protégés and making available contacts with more diverse groups without the restriction of visual cues that are known to stifle relationship development (Hamilton & Scandura, 2003).

POSITIVE PSYCHOLOGY AND MENTORING

The underpinning of the strengths-based model of mentoring is positive psychology. The model believes that students and novices have the potential to achieve outstanding success given high expectations and the proper environmental support (Maton & Hrabowski, 2004). It follows the principles of positive psychology, which focuses and builds on the person's existing values and strengths—especially those pertaining to confidence, self-reliance, and initiative—rather than on their deficits. The mentor helps increase the mentee's self-esteem by a nonambivalent belief and respect in the capacity of the person to achieve (Seligman, 2002).

The mentor assists in the development of a social network, introduces the mentee to other professionals, and empowers the mentee by showcasing and giving public praise; the idea is to "let them shine" for their accomplishments and abilities (Austria, Briant, &Tarke-Karge, 2007; Peterson, 2006).

ON BEING MENTORED AND MENTORING
(ASUNCION MITERIA AUSTRIA)

The steadfast belief in my capacity to achieve was modeled by my late parents, Alberto Estrella Miteria and Maria Concepcion Miteria, as my first mentors. Although poor and without the benefit of higher education, they modeled and instilled in their children hard work, perseverance, integrity, honesty, and pursuit of excellence. I remember my father, who helped me rehearse day and night for my high school valedictorian address, or how both my parents would applaud my singing and oratorical abilities, skills I did not even know I had. They provided me with much love and encouragement to pursue psychology, notwithstanding the fact that many Filipinos had little understanding of what a psychology major could do at that time. They had an unswerving dedication to excellence. I honor their name by being the best that I can be as a person and as a professional. My husband, Roger, a retired professor and founding president of alumni associations in Chicago and Milwaukee, which have become the template for organized associations, has provided emotional, physical, and intellectual support and encouragement throughout my academic and professional career and a space to be what I am capable of becoming. Just as my parents have mentored me, so have I mentored my children. My children, Albert, with an MS in mechanical engineering and currently pursuing an MBA, is a senior vehicle evaluation engineer at Edmunds, Inc., and Marie, with a PhD in clinical child psychology and whose research interest is in Filipino ethnic identity, have now coached, provided support, and encouragement to others. They also are now our able professional consultants and coaches.

As a mentor, I have consistently been guided by the strengths-based model of positive psychology. This is my guiding principle in cross-racial and cross-gender mentoring and peer mentoring. I conscientiously provide assistance and encouragement in developing professional and social networks and have nominated students and peers to committees and other assignments to integrate them into academia or into the profession. I have invited mentees to participate in activities and events such as local, state, and national professional meetings, conventions, and receptions at conventions. I have invited students and colleagues as co-presenters in professional meetings, as I too have been invited to participate in various professional meetings by my colleagues. This provides the mentees the opportunity to learn the social expectations of psychologists in professional environments, meet others in the field, and gain recognition by colleagues and build their own networks.

ON BEING MENTORED (A. MARIE M. AUSTRIA)

Upon starting graduate school, I did not place a great deal of importance on the ethnicity of my supervisors, advisors, and mentors. My undergraduate university did not have a diverse faculty at the time; thus, most of my advisors and academic mentors were white men. My first year of graduate school changed my priorities and expectations when I discovered I could have mentors who shared my life and academic experiences. Consistent with the research cited in this chapter (Davidson & Foster-Johnson, 2001;

Evans & Cokley, 2008; Thomas, 2001), I deliberately sought the research and clinical supervision and mentorship of ethnic minority psychologists. For example, Dr. Roderick Watts was one of my research mentors and chaired my master's thesis. He was instrumental in guiding me in shaping ideas that resulted in my thesis and dissertation research on ethnic identity development. Dr. Watts was able to extrapolate some ideas and research findings with African American populations (e.g., factors that influence ethnic identity development, such as experiences of racism and racial socialization) to Asian American populations, and these ideas have gained some interest in the field among Asian American researchers and academicians.

I also sought mentorship from those who, if not ethnic minorities themselves, were culturally responsive and had research and/or clinical interests with ethnic minority populations. Dr. Gary Harper, who is not an ethnic minority, mentored me throughout my dissertation process as my dissertation chair. Dr. Harper had a collaborative style and challenged me to defend my ideas and make my research as sound as possible. He struck the perfect balance between encouraging me to think independently, while providing support and guidance when needed. I continued to seek mentorship from ethnic minority psychologists and women during my internship, postdoctoral, and early career experiences.

I am also one of the fortunate few to have followed the career path of my mother. My mother (the senior author of this chapter) is a clinical psychologist who has been the most instrumental in my choice of career and its progress. Little did I know that she was already mentoring me as a teenager when she introduced me to the Wechsler Intelligence Scale for Children and demonstrated how to administer some of the questions. Or when she brought my brother and me to APA conventions all over the country; not many can say that the annual convention of a large professional organization was their family's annual summer vacation. She introduced me to her colleagues, flagged some of the sessions in the convention program she thought I would find interesting, and attended sessions with me. I remember sitting next to her as we listened to the presentations of some of the big names—B. F. Skinner, Albert Ellis, Aaron Beck, David Barlow, and Donald Meichenbaum. As I pursued psychology as a graduate student, my mother encouraged me to participate in professional meetings and in the various divisions as a student representative and attend the breakfasts and social hours so I could network. She would send me announcements on professional meetings at the state and local levels as well. She showed me the workings of APA's governance and encouraged me to someday be involved on various boards. And as an early career psychologist, she has invited me to teach and guest lecture; she has invited me to participate on coauthoring opportunities; and has generally given constant encouragement and support to continue to progress and develop in our field.

Most importantly, however, my mother has been my lifelong mentor in my personal development. She (and my father) taught me how to be an empathic person; to be sensitive to the needs of others, especially those who are underserved; to be tolerant of others, appreciate others' differences, and celebrate the similarities; be a good listener; and serve the greater good. These are qualities that will serve me well in my profession. Good thing I learned these at an early age; and good thing I had the best mentor who was able to teach me these values and continues to do so to this day. I am forever grateful.

CONCLUSION

In conclusion, mentors must understand and appreciate the populations they serve as well as the impact of culture, family structure, language, racial and ethnic identity, stigma of status, and socioeconomic differences within the underrepresented groups (Grantham, 2004). To mentor well, it is important to focus on the strengths and values of the individual coupled with a non ambivalent belief in the individual's capacity to achieve. It is important to know oneself and one's strengths and weaknesses and to be ethically and culturally responsive to mentor women and ethnic minorities.

REFERENCES

American Psychological Association, Office on AIDS . (2009). *APA Cyber Mentor Program.* Washington, DC: Author.

American Psychological Association, Task Force on Women in Academe. (2000). *Women in academe: Two steps forward, one step back.* Washington, DC: Author.

Atkinson, D. R., Lowe, S. M., & Matthews, L. (1995). Asian American acculturation, gender, and willingness to seek counseling. *Journal of Multicultural Counseling and Development, 23,* 130–138.

Austria, A. M. (2003). People of Asian descent: Beyond myths and stereotypes. In J. D. Robinson, & L.C. James (Eds.), *Diversity in human interaction: The tapestry of America* (pp.63-75). New York: Oxford.

Austria, A. M., Briant, E., & Tarke, Karge, K. (2007, April). Advancing women and ethnic minorities in psychology. Invited symposium conducted at the Annual Convention of the Wisconsin Psychological Association, Madison, WI.

Berscheid, E. (1985). Interpersonal attraction. In G. Lindzey & E. Aronson (Eds.), *Handbook of social psychology* (Vol. 2, pp. 413–484). New York: Random House.

Blackwell, J. E. (1989). Mentoring: An action strategy for increasing minority faculty. *Academe, 75*(5), 8–14.

Brinson, J., & Kottler, J. (1993). Cross-cultural mentoring in counselor education: A strategy for retaining minority faculty. *Counselor Education and Supervision, 2,* 1–24.

Bruce, M. A. (1995). Mentoring women doctoral students: What counselor educators and supervisors can do. *Counselor Education & Supervision, 35*(2), 139–149.

Busch, J. W. (1985). Mentoring in graduate schools of education: Mentors' perceptions. *American Educational Research Journal, 22,* 257–265.

Carnevale, A. P., & Stone, S. C. (1985). *The American mosaic: An in-depth report on the future of diversity at work.* New York: McGraw-Hill.

Clark, R. A., Harden, S. L., & Johnson, W. B. (2000). Mentor relationships in clinical psychology doctoral training: Results of a national survey. *Teaching of Psychology, 27,* 262–268.

Cohen, L. M., Morgan, R. D., DiLillio, D., & Flores, L. Y. (2003). Why was my major professor so busy? Establishing an academic career while pursuing applied work. *Professional Psychology: Research and Practice, 34,* 88–94.

Crosby, F. J. (1999). The developing literature on developmental relationships. In A. Murrell, F. Crosby, & R. Ely (Eds.), *Mentoring dilemmas: Developmental relationships within multicultural organizations* (pp. 3–20). Mahwah, NJ: Erlbaum.

Davidson, M. N., & Foster-Johnson, L. (2001). Mentoring in the preparation of graduate researchers of color. *Review of Educational Research, 7*(4), 549–574.

Dreher, G. F., & Cox, Jr., T. H. (1996). Race, gender, and opportunity: A study of compensation attainment and the establishment of mentoring relationships. *Journal of Applied Psychology, 81*(3), 297–308.

Enomoto, E. K., Gardner, M. E., & Grogan, M. (2000). Notes to Athene: Mentoring relationships for women of color. *Urban Education, 35*(5), 567–583.

Erut, S., & Mokros, J. R. (1984). Professors as model and mentors for college students. *American Educational Research Journal, 21,* 399–417.

Evans, G. L., & Cokley, K. O. (2008). African American women and the academy: Using career mentoring to increase research productivity. *Training and Education in Professional Psychology, 2*(1), 50–57.

Gilbert, L. A. (1985). Dimensions of same-gender student-faculty role model relationships. *Sex Roles, 12,* 111–123.

Gilbert, L. A., & Rossman, K. M. (1992). Gender and the mentoring process for women: Implications for professional development: *Professional Psychology: Research and Practice, 23,* 233–238.

Girves, J. E., Zepeda, Y., & Gwathmey, J. K. (2005). Mentoring in a post-affirmative action world. *Journal of Social Issues, 61*(3), 449–479.

Gonzalez-Figueroa, E. G., & Young, A. M. (2005). Ethnic identity and mentoring among Latinas in professional roles. *Cultural Diversity and Ethnic Minority Psychology, 11,* (3), 213–226.

Grantham, T. C. (2004). Multicultural mentoring to increase black male representation in gifted programs. *Gifted Child Quarterly, 48*(3), 232–246.

Grant-Thompson, S., & Atkinson, D. (1987). Cross-cultural mentor effectiveness and African-American male students. *Journal of Black Psychology, 23,* 120–134.

Grant-Vallonme, E. J., & Ensher, E. A. (2000). Effects of peer mentoring on types of mentor support, program satisfaction and graduate student stress. A dyadic perspective. *Journal of College Student Development, 41,* 637–642.

Hamilton, B. A. (2007). Development of an electronic mentoring scale for the investigation of the effects of the Internet on mentoring practices. *Dissertation Abstracts International Section A: Humanities and Social Sciences, 67*(8-A), 3059.

Hamilton, B. A., & Scandura, T. A. (2003). E-mentoring: Implications for organizational learning and development in a wired world. *Organizational Dynamics, 31,* 388–402.

Haring, M. J. (1997). Networking mentoring as a preferred model for guiding pro-grams for underrepresented students. In H. T. Frierson, Jr. (Ed.), *Diversity in higher education:* Vol 1. *Mentoring and diversity in higher education* (pp. 63–76). Greenwich, CT: JAI Press.

Healy, C. C. (1997). An operational definition of mentoring. In H. T. Frierson, Jr. (Ed.), *Diversity in the higher education:* Vol 1. *Mentoring and diversity in higher education* (pp. 9–22). Greenwich, CT: JAI Press.

Hetherington, C., & Barcelo, R. (1985). Womentoring: A cross-cultural perspective. *Journal of the NAWDAC, 49*(1), 12–15.

Jacobi, M. (1991). Mentoring and undergraduate academic success: A literature re-view. *Review of Educational Research, 61,* 505–532.

Johnson, W. B. (2002). The intentional mentor: Strategies and guidelines for the prac-tice of mentoring: *Professional Psychology: Research and Practice, 33*(1), 88–96.

Jones, L., Castellanos, J., & Cole, D. (2002). Examining the ethnic minority student experience at predominantly white institutions: A case study. *Journal of His-panic Higher Education, 1*(1), 19–39.

Kitchener, K. S. (1992). Psychologist as teacher and mentor: Affirming ethical val-ues throughout the curriculum. *Professional Psychology: Research and Practice, 23,* 190–195.

Kram, K. E. (1983). Phases of the mentor relationship. *Academy of Management Jour-nal, 26*(4) 608–625.

Kram, K. E. (1985). *Mentoring at work: Developmental relationships in organizational life.* Glenview, IL: Scott Foresman.

Kram, K. (1988). *Mentoring relationships at work.* Lanham, MD. United Press of America.

Levinson, D. J., Darrow, C. N., Klein, E. B. Levinson, M. H., & McKee, B. (1978). *The seasons of a man's life.* New York: Ballantine.

Liang, B., Tracy, A, Kauh, T., Taylor, C., & Williams, L. (2006). Mentoring Asian and Euro-American college women. *Multicultural Counseling and Development, 34,* 143–154.

Maton, K. I., & Hrabowski, F. A. III. (2004). Increasing the number of African Amer-ican PhDs in the sciences and engineering: A strengths-based approach. *American Psychologist, 59,* 629–654.

Maton, K. I., Kahout, J. L., Wicherski, M., Leary, G. E., & Vinokurov, A. (2006). Mi-nority students of color and the psychology graduate pipeline: Disquieting and encouraging trends. *American Psychologist, 61*(2), 117–131.

Miller, J. B., & Stiver, I. P. (1997). *The healing connection: How women form relation-ships in therapy and in life.* Boston: Beacon Press.

Noe, R. A. (1988). Women and mentoring: A review and research agenda. *Academy of Management Review, 13*(1), 65–78.

Noelinski, T. (1995). Multiple mentoring relationships facilitate learning during fieldwork. *American Journal of Occupational Therapy, 49*(1), 39–43.

Oyserman, D., & Sakamoto, I. (1997). Being Asian American: Identity, cultural con-structs, and stereotype perception. *Journal of Applied Behavioral Science, 33*(4), 435–453.

Packard, B. W-A. (2003). Web-based mentoring: Challenging traditional models to increased women's access. *Mentoring & Tutoring, 11*(1), 53–65.

Park, S. M. (2000). Research, teaching and service: Why shouldn't women's work count? In B. Ropers-Huilman (Ed.), *Women in higher education: A feminist perspective* (2nd ed., pp 285–308). Boston: Pearson Custom Publishing.

Peterson, C. (2006). *A primer in positive psychology.* New York: Oxford University Press.

Powell, B. J. (1999). Mentoring: One of the master's tools. *Initiatives, 59,* 19–31.

Ragins, B. R., & Cotton, J. L. (1999). Mentor functions and outcomes: A comparison of men and women in formal and informal mentoring relationships. *Journal of Applied Psychology, 84,* 529–550.

Ragins, B. R., Cotton, J. L., & Miller, J. S. (2000). Marginal mentoring: The effects of mentor's quality of relationships program design on work and career attitudes. *Academy of Management Journal, 3,* 1117–1194.

Ragins, B. R., & Scandura, T. A. (1997). The way we were: Gender and the termination of mentoring relationships. *Journal of Applied Psychology, 82,* 945–953.

Rice, J. K., & Austria, A. M. (2007). Collaborative leadership and social advocacy among women organizations. In Chin, J. L., Lott, B., Rice, J. K., & Sanchez-Hucles, J. (Eds.), *Women and leadership: Transforming visions and diverse voices.* (pp.157-176), Malden, MA: Blackwell.

Santos, S. J., & Reigadas, E. T. (2005). Understanding the student faculty mentoring process: Its effects on at-risk university students. *Journal of College Student Retention: Research, Theory and Practice, 6,* 337–352.

Scandura, T. A., & Viator, R. (1994). Mentoring in public accounting firms: An analysis of mentor-protégé relationships, functions and protégé turnover intentions. *Accounting Organizations and Society, 19,* 713–734.

Seligman, M.E.P. (2002). *Authentic happiness.* New York: Free Press.

Smith, E. P., & Davidson, W. S. (1992). Mentoring and the development of African American graduate students. *Journal of College Student Development, 33*(6), 531–539.

Sullivan, A. M. (1996). From mentor to muse: Recasting the role of women in relationship with urban adolescent girls. In B. J. Ross Leadbeater & N. Way (Eds.), *Urban girls: Resisting stereotypes, creating identities* (pp. 226–249). New York: New York University Press.

Swoboda, D. T., & Millar, S. B. (1986). Networking-mentoring: Career strategy of women in academic administration. *Journal of the NAWDAC, 50,* 8–13.

Thayer, P. (2000, May). Retention of students from first generation and low income backgrounds. *Opportunity Outlook,* Washington, DC: Council for Opportunity in Education.

Thomas, D. A. (2001). The truth about mentoring minorities: Race matters. *Harvard Business Review, 79,* 99–107.

Tsui, A. S., Egan, T. D., & Reilly, C.A.I. (1992). Being different: Relational demography and organizational attachment. *Administrative Science Quarterly, 37*(4), 549–579.

Turner, C.S.V. (2002). Women of color in academe: Living with multiple marginality. *Journal of Higher Education, 73,* 74–93.

U.S. Census Bureau. (2002a). *Statistical abstract of the United States: 2002.* Table 15. Resident population by Hispanic origin status, p.17. Retrieved April 5, 2009, from www.census.gov/prod/2002pubs/01statab/pop/pdf

U.S. Census Bureau. (2002b). *Statistical abstract of the United States: 2004–2005.* Table 13. Resident population by sex, and Hispanic origin status, p. 14. Retrieved April 5, 2009, from www.census.gov/prod/2004pubs/04statab/pop/pdf

Wilde, J. B., & Schau, C. G. (1991). Mentoring in graduate schools of education: Mentees' perceptions. *Journal of Experimental Education, 59,* 165–179.

Young, R. W., & Cates, C. M. (2005). Playful communication in mentoring. *College Student Journal, 39*(4), 692–701.

Chapter 8

Mentoring Asian American Women

Reiko Homma-True

Overall, mentored individuals—both men and women—report having more satisfaction, career mobility and opportunity, recognition, and a higher promotion rate than nonmentored individuals (Fagenson, 1989).

It has been more than four decades since the passage of the Equal Pay Act of 1963 and the landmark Civil Rights Act of 1964, protecting women and men from employment discrimination based on race, color, religion sex, and country of origin. Yet nonwhites still experience more difficulties than whites in the workplace; racial barriers can limit minority access to the opportunity and development needed to advance at a particular stage of career (Thomas & Gabarro, 1999). Despite tremendous strides that have led to increasing numbers of women and minorities entering the workplace and achieving positions of power and influence, there is still much ground to be gained (Karsten, 2006). Although gender processes cannot be understood in isolation from class and race/ethnicity issues in the workplace, and women throughout the Unites States have not experienced a common oppression as women (Amott & Matthaei, 1996), they do share a complex legacy of disenfranchisement. Mentoring for women is needed at all levels and in all fields of employment.

Asian American women in the United States have unique historical, ethnic-cultural, and economic backgrounds that make advancement in the workplace challenging in specific ways. Mentoring has shown to be helpful; if these contexts are considered carefully, the mentoring of these women can be highly beneficial and assist in the recognition, advancement, and satisfaction of Asian American women in the workplace.

HISTORICAL BACKGROUND

Asian Americans are the fastest growing of all major racial/ethnic groups in the United States. According to the 2004 Census Bureau population estimate, there were approximately 13 million Asian Americans, and the proportion of women among them is about 51 percent (U.S. Census Bureau, 2006). Their ethnic-cultural backgrounds are diverse and include as many as 35 groups, such as Chinese, Filipinos, Japanese, Koreans, Southeast Asians, as well as South Asians. Asian American immigration to the United States began in the mid-1800s with the entry of Chinese men laborers and merchants, who needed to escape the famine in their home country and who sought their fortune in the fabled affluence of the Gold Rush. Although common laborers were unable to bring their wives with them, many merchants were able to bring their wives with them. In addition, other Chinese women were brought in as prostitutes (Kim & Otani, 1983).

Chinese immigration was blocked by increasingly violent anti-Chinese sentiment in the United States that led to exclusionary national legislation, specifically the Chinese Exclusion Act. This made way for the immigration of Japanese women, who were encouraged by their government to accompany their husbands, most of whom were laborers. However, Japanese immigration was also curtailed when anti-Japanese sentiment developed during World War II. Japanese were singled out for exclusion, removal, and detention, and immigration barriers were enacted against them. Although a small number of Korean and Filipino women were able to immigrate during that time, the influx of Asian women did not increase dramatically until the sweeping changes in immigration law in 1965, which included the liberalized entry of wives and families of Asian immigrants already in the United States (Espiritu, 1996). At this time, in addition to Chinese, Filipino, and Koran women, women from South Asian countries such as India, Pakistan, Nepal, and Bangladesh began to enter the country, and the trend is continuing. After the termination of World War II, another group of Asian women—mostly Japanese, Chinese, and Filipinas married to U.S. servicemen—were permitted to accompany their husbands into the United States (Hall, 2008). Since then, wives of U.S. servicemen from Korea and Vietnam entered as immigrants as the U.S. military's involvement shifted to other Asian countries. Another significant influx of Asian women occurred after the end of the Vietnam War in 1975, when a large number of Southeast Asian refugees sought refuge in the United States.

CURRENT STATUS OF ASIAN AMERICAN WOMEN

Because of the earlier restrictions for Asian women to enter the United States, the majority (62%) of the Asian women in the United States are foreign-born, many having arrived here since 1980 (U.S. Census Bureau, 2006). On the other hand, some groups, particularly Chinese and Japanese, now have women who are fifth-, sixth-, or seventh-generation Americans. Although many of the immigrant women have difficulty with English proficiency and limited educational background, Asian American women as a whole are well educated. The 2002 census data indicate that 43.8 percent of them have bachelor's degree or higher education, which is 16.5 percent higher than the 27.3 percent of white non-Hispanic American women of similar background. The traditional expectation for Asian women in their countries of origin has been that, once married, they should stay home to take care of their families. However, often pressed by economic necessity, many Asian American women in the United States are working. There is also a considerable subgroup variation among them: Filipino women had the highest rate of working, at 65 percent, while Pakistani women had the lowest rate, at 36.9 percent (U.S. Census Bureau, 2004).

Because of their difficulty with the English language, limited educational achievement, and job preparation, a number of immigrant Asian women are still working at low wages and under unhealthy conditions as garment sweatshop workers, restaurant workers, maids, and factory workers (Wong and Hayashi, 1989). However, Asian American women as a group have made considerable advancement in the labor market over the years. For example, while only a few Asian women were participants in management ranks and other leadership positions in the 1970s (Fong & Cabezas, 1976), the rate increased significantly by 2002, with 37.2 percent of them in the ranks of managerial and professional occupations (U.S. Census Bureau, 2004). Although that rate is slightly higher than the rate for the non-Hispanic white women, which was 36.9 percent, advocates for Asian American women believe it should be even greater, given that the educational achievement of Asian American women is higher than that of their white counterparts. According to a study conducted by Catalyst Inc. (2003), an organization dedicated to expanding opportunities for women in business, Asian American women—despite their high level of educational achievement—are the least likely to hold a position within three executive levels or have line or supervisory responsibilities. Among the Fortune 500 companies that responded to their survey, Asian American women made up less than 0.5 percent of the corporate officers.

This study also identified several factors that created problems for Asian American women to advance in their careers, including Asian cultural values that often work against them in their work as well as discriminatory stereotypes and misunderstandings held by their managers and decision makers, who are central in promoting them within organizations.

STEREOTYPING, SOCIALIZATION, AND DISCRIMINATION

Although Asian American women come from diverse social and cultural backgrounds, they often share similar experiences in that they face two horizons of difficulty in relation to professional advancement: prejudices in the workplace and sociocultural expectations at home. In the workplace, they are often perceived and treated with negative racist and sexist stereotypes. One such stereotype is the reflection of the Western portrayal of Asian women in movies and literature such as China dolls, Madame Butterfly, Suzy Wong, lotus blossom babies, and prostitutes. They are perceived as sex object playthings that can be easily exploited, taken advantage of, and not taken seriously. On the other hand, if they are assertive or aggressive, they are labeled as dragon ladies and derided for being cunning, overly ambitious, and manipulative. Another stereotype for Asian American women is that of efficient, loyal, hardworking handmaidens to bosses but not good enough to be given greater authority as bosses (Homma-True, 1990).

In addition to the stereotyped perceptions of the non-Asian community, Asian American women have had to deal with gender discrimination within their own communities, which hold onto the Old World tradition in which women are treated as second-class citizens to men. Most of their countries of origin in Asia and South Asia are governed by patriarchal social systems in which it is normative for women to sacrifice their own personal needs and be subservient to the demands of men. For example, Confucianism, which was the governing political and social foundation in China for centuries and later adopted by Korean and Japanese rulers, prescribed women to obey their fathers when young, their husbands when married, and their sons when old (Homma-True, 1990). An exception is Filipino culture, which recognizes maternal and paternal authority in a bilateral kinship system (Heras, 2007) and where many women are empowered to achieve positions of power more easily than in other Asian countries.

Many immigrant Asian families as well as U.S.-born Asian families still hold onto the Old World attitude about sex role and gender differences and teach their daughters to defer to the command of the men in their families. This expectation extends not only to how they should behave within their community but in the non-Asian community as well. Many Asian American women are thus socialized to be respectful, obedient, and subservient to authority and to place their own personal needs secondary to that of men and family members. When these beliefs and social roles are carried into the workplace, managers can take advantage of Asian women's compliant, hardworking performance and deference to authority and feel validation for stereotyping, ignoring women's professional needs, and depriving them of opportunities to fully realize their potential.

Speaking not only for Asian American women, but for men as well, Jane Hyun, a former human resources executive at J. P. Morgan Company, points out that Asians are socialized in such a way that reinforces the workplace stereotyping and development of career obstacles, which she labels the "bamboo ceiling" (Hyun, 2005). She quotes a study conducted by Kim, Atkinson, and Yang (1999), which identified traditional Asian values that endure even among second- and third-generation Asian Americans. They included emphasis on educational and occupational achievement; self-effacement; respect for elders; maintenance of interpersonal harmony; deference to authority figures; conformity to family and social norms; collectivism; and placing others' needs ahead of one's own. With the exception of emphasis placed on educational and occupational achievements, Hyun suggests other values emphasized by Asian parents are in stark contrast to the dominant U.S. cultural values emphasized in social, interpersonal situations, including qualities promoted in the working environment, which rewards individual initiative, assertiveness, self- promotion, and competitiveness. Although some may argue that Asian businessmen in Asia do not fit the stereotype, that they are perceived as very aggressive and competitive in international marketplaces, the majority of Asians in the United States, particularly women, are seen as less assertive and competitive in the non-Asian community. One explanation for the difference for Asian Americans in the United States could be the intersection of their cultural socialization and their persecution. When facing intense persecution and discrimination, they tried to protect themselves through the cultural skills they learned in the old country to adapt and to be accommodating, nonassertive, and compliant (Chan, 2003).

NEED FOR MENTORS AND ROLE MODELS

In order to break through the bamboo ceiling, Hyun (2005) advises Asian American workers to develop greater understanding about the cultural differences between their own and workplace values that create barriers for their career development and to develop strategies to make certain behavioral changes, such as learning to get their voices heard, saying no, and pushing back with diplomacy. She also points out the importance of the role that mentors can play for them in navigating through the organizational maze and suggests ways for finding and choosing mentors. Many Asian American women who responded to the survey by Catalyst Inc. (2003) agreed with Hyun's recommendation. When asked what they needed to advance their careers, 51 percent of the respondents indicated they needed mentors to nurture them in their professional development. They also identified the need for role models and informal networking, which would help them to develop better career strategies.

When exploring how to find mentors and what to ask from them, Asian American women can learn a great deal from the white American women, who struggled for many years to gain equal rights as men and abolish workplace discrimination. The white American women recognized that the American men leaders, whether in businesses, academia, or government, are primarily white and that there is a built-in formal or informal mentoring system, which begins early in their careers. Over the past several decades, they advocated to raise women's consciousness and actively develop mentoring strategies and networks of their own. Through their advocacy, white American women have made significant gains.

Based on the interviews with 106 protégés and mentors, both men and women, Jeruchim and Shapiro (1992) found it was helpful for women to have both men mentors as well as women mentors. They suggest that men mentors tend to offer more instrumental assistance and can sponsor greater advancement opportunities because of their position in the power hierarchy, while women mentors, often in less powerful positions, tend to provide more emotional support and personal advice. They also found it will take longer and require a more cautious approach for minority women to find mentors. Speaking specifically in reference to a black woman's situation, they recommend that, ideally, she should have two mentors: a white man who can help with advancement and a black woman with whom she can identify and get support from. Similar advice is applicable for Asian American women, who can benefit from multiple mentors: a white man mentor with access to opportunities and a wealth of professional, organizational knowledge; a white woman mentor, who can help with women- or gender-related issues; Asian American mentors, either men or women, who understand cultural issues; and minority mentors, either men or women, who can understand and help deal with shared minority-related concerns.

Speaking from her own experience of having always had at least two to three mentors at every stage of her career, Hyun (2005) advises that a worker should aim to find multiple mentors at any given point in time, because one mentor cannot fulfill all of her career knowledge and skills needs. She suggests that it is helpful to have an Asian mentor, who can serve as a role model and who can help the mentee deal with conflict over cultural issues. However, she also urges women to have non-Asian mentors as well, because they can identify and help the worker deal with cultural misperceptions that create barriers to their professional development. As an example, she cites the experience of Andrea Jung, chair and chief executive officer (CEO) of Avon Products and the only Asian American CEO of a Fortune 500 company, who was helped greatly by her white male mentor, Jim Preston.

Before seeking mentors, Jeruchim and Shapiro (1992) recommend individuals do a thorough self-assessment to determine what their needs are, where they are in the organizational hierarchy, and what their strengths and weaknesses are. These suggestions are applicable for Asian American women as well.

MENTORING AND CULTURAL ISSUES

Although it is important for both mentors and protégés to actively take initiatives to deepen the mentoring relationship after it is established, Hyun (2005) cites potential cultural problems for the Asian American protégé in this respect, particularly in relationship to hierarchy and authority. She cites a Chinese American mentor who was frustrated by two extreme types of protégés. One type was too distant and respectful, to the point of not being able to approach the mentor for help even when he was struggling with problems. The other type was too dependent, like a younger sibling, expecting to be taken care of in the company and not taking ownership of her own career development. Asian cultural dictates concerning the interpersonal relationship between a superior and subordinate is for the subordinate to be diffident to the person in authority and wait for the latter to make the first move. Yet the mentor is a very busy person, with a great deal of responsibility, and the protégé will need to remember this and be patient. The protégé also will need to recognize what her needs are, learn not to be overly deferential, and speak up to ask for help appropriately. Hyun also recommends that the protégé do her homework well and be accountable to the commitments made with the mentor. At the same time, it is important not to be too dependent on the mentor to fulfill every career need.

For mentors working with Asian American protégés, it is important to be attentive to some of the cultural issues, which often create problems for the protégé. Hyun (2005) urges the mentors to encourage the protégés to communicate openly and to practice active listening instead of dominating the conversation, to give the protégé a chance to speak. In addition, she makes other recommendations that are applicable to protégés of all races and genders: that mentors set firm guidelines and expectations from the beginning; provide clear performance measures; and take mentoring seriously. To correct the China doll image or stereotype of the Asian American woman protégé, women mentors can also role model how to act assertively without interjecting the dragon lady image in their behavior. All mentors can be advocates if they detect such prejudicial attitudes in their workplace. They can also help their protégés to increase their consciousness about the challenges they face as Asian American women and teach them how to assert and empower themselves despite the negative stereotypes. Another strategy to help Asian American women to recognize the issues they face is to begin the work before they enter the workforce. For example, some Asian American counselors in university counseling centers have conducted Asian American women's groups to explore experiences growing up, to understand the historical and cultural contexts of their treatment, and to ultimately develop stronger self-identities and become more empowered in dealing with challenges they will face in their futures (Liu, Tsong, & Hayashino, 2007).

MENTORING ACTIONS FOR ASIAN AMERICAN WOMEN

In the 1970s, a group of Asian American women in the San Francisco Bay Area were experiencing the same dilemma in their careers. Although they did not have the benefit of professional researchers, they recognized the problems as a universal issue for Asian American women as a group. They were inspired by the civil rights and women's movements during the 1970s and struggled on their own to distinguish themselves and achieve leadership positions in their fields—law, health, education, art, government, and business. However, they recognized the need to increase awareness and advocate for the difficulties faced by Asian American women. They felt the need to raise the consciousness of Asian American women and to advocate on their behalf not only within the Asian American community but in the larger communities as well. They incorporated in 1980 as the Pacific Asian American Women Bay Area Coalition (PAAWBAC) (www.PAAW BAC.org) with the mission to promote the personal, professional, and political development of Asian Pacific Islander (API) women. Specifically, they decided to focus on providing leadership opportunities for API young women, refugee and immigrant women, at-risk teens, and women in transition. As a vehicle for inspiring and empowering the API women, the group took inspiration from the legend of the Chinese woman warrior, Mu Lan, who successfully led a village's revolt against an oppressive emperor (Kingston, 1975). Beginning in 1983, they started annually to identify "women warriors"—contemporary Asian American women who distinguished themselves as leaders in their chosen field—and to make them visible as role models and inspirations to Asian American women.

Their next action was to recognize that these women warriors were serving as informal mentors to younger Asian American women and to create more systematic mentoring opportunities. They named it the Catalyst Fund Mentorship Program and created funding opportunities in 2002 through their own fundraising activities. Although the funding support is modest, it provides structure and visibility to what can be done to guide API women in PAAWBAC's target group through their careers and expands their horizons.

A case example is that of Sandy Ouye Mori, a 1983 woman warrior who was recognized for her leadership role as a founding member of the senior social service agency, Kimochi, Inc., in the Japanese American community.

She is the development director of Kimochi, which provides a variety of bilingual social services, including a meals program, residential program, transportation, translation, and other social services for Japanese and Asian elderly clients. She has mentored four Japanese American women through the Catalyst Fund. In the case of one young bilingual worker, she exposed her to many issues of aging faced by Asian elderly and taught her how to do multiple aspects of advocacy, program planning, funding and resource development, and community organizing. She often did this through personal modeling, taking her to meetings, helping her make public presentations, and introducing her to key decision makers. At the end of the project phase, the young protégé successfully coordinated and marketed the Health and Consumer Education lecture series at the agency and was able to expand her career opportunities.

Another group cited by Hyun (2005) that actively promotes mentoring for Asian American women is the Asian Network at Avon Products. The company has a strong career development program in its management practices as well as various internal employee networks, which encourage diversity initiatives. The Asian network has a senior management sponsor who supports and oversees their progress. One of their initiatives is to reach out actively to the Asian community to provide leadership opportunities for future leaders. They partner with the Organization for Chinese Americans and award 10 scholarships to college-bound Asian American women with demonstrated financial need, strong academics, and an interest in community service.

CONCLUSION

Asian American women, as a group, have had a long history of struggle not only within their own communities, but in non-Asian communities, to be accepted as equal to men and other non-Asian women and recognized for their competence as leaders. Despite the traditional, Old World expectation of women as housewives and homemakers who defer to the men of the household, the majority of them are working in the United States either as blue-collar workers, office workers, or professionals in a variety of occupations. Although many of them have significantly higher educational achievement than other American women, they have not been rewarded with greater recognition, leadership positions, or commensurate salaries. Some of the barriers to success are thought to be associated with prevalent cultural and workplace stereotypes about Asian American women: they are compliant but nonassertive workers with limited leadership potential recognized by their employers. Other barriers are internalized traditional Asian values, which discourage them from speaking up, breaking with traditional male-dominated social systems, and being competitive with their peers. There is increasing recognition of the need to develop culturally sensitive mentorship relationships and to raise awareness on the part of community leaders, managers, and Asian American women themselves. Increasing numbers of mentors and mentorship programs are needed to help Asian American women advance to positions in the workplace commensurate with their educational and competency levels.

REFERENCES

Amott, T. L., & Matthaei, J. A. (1996). *Race, gender, and work: A multi-cultural economic history of women in the United States* (Rev. ed.). Boston: South End Press.

Catalyst, Inc. (2003). Advancing Asian women in the workplace: What managers need to know. New York: Author.

Chan, C. S. (2003). Psychological issues of Asian Americans. In P. Bronstein & K. Quina (Eds.), *Teaching gender and multicultural awareness: Resources for the psychology classroom* (pp. 179–193). Washington, DC: American Psychological Association.

Espiritu, Y. L. (1996). *Asian American women and men.* Thousand Oaks, CA: Sage.

Fagenson, E. A. (1989). The mentor advantage: Perceived career/job experiences of protégé versus non-protégées. *Journal of Organizational Behavior, 10*(4), 309–320.

Fong, P. L. & Cabezas, A. Y. (1976). "Economic and Employment Status of Asian-American Women" Paper presented to The Conference on the Educational and Occupational Needs of Asian-Pacific Women, San Francisco, CA.

Hall, C. I. (2008). Asian American women: The nail that sticks out is hammered down. In N. Tewari & A. Alvarez, (Eds.). *Asian American psychology: Current perspectives.* New York: Psychology Press.

Heras, P. (2007). Psychotherapy with Filipinas. *Women & Therapy, 30*(3/4), 63–73.

Homma-True, R. (1990). Psychotherapeutic issues with Asian American women. *Sex Roles: A Journal of Research, 22*(7–8), 477–486.

Hyun, J. (2005). *Breaking the bamboo ceiling: Career strategies for Asians.* New York: Harper Business.

Jeruchim, J., & Shapiro, P. G. (1992). *Women, mentors, and success.* New York: Fawcett Columbine.

Karsten, M. F. (2006). *Gender, race, and ethnicity in the workplace: Issues and challenges for today's organizations.* Westport, CT: Praeger.

Kim, B.S.K., Atkinson, D. R., & Yang, P. H. (1999). The Asian Value Scale: Development factor analysis, validation, and reliability. *Journal of Counseling Psychology, 46*(7), 342–352.

Kim, E. H., & Otani, J. (1983). Asian women in America. In E. H. Kim (Ed.), *With silk wings: Asian American women at work* (pp. 120–135). San Francisco: Asian Women United.

Kingston, M. H. (1975). *The woman warrior: Memoirs of a girlhood among ghosts.* New York: Knopf.

Liu, Y., Tsong, Y., & Hayashino, D. (2007). Group counseling with Asian American women: Reflections and effective practices. In D. M. Kawahara & O. M. Espin (Eds.), *Feminist reflections on growth and transformation: Asian American women in therapy* (pp. 193–208). New York: Haworth Press.

Thomas, D. A., & Gabarro, J. J. (1999). *Breaking through: The making of minority executives in corporate America.* Boston: Harvard Business School Press.

U.S. Census Bureau. (2006). *Current population survey, annual social and economic supplements.* Washington, DC: U.S. Government Printing Office, .

Wong, D., & Hayashi, D. (1989). Behind unmarked doors: Developments in the garment industry. In Asian Women United of California, *Making waves: An anthology of writings by and about Asian American women* (pp. 159–171). Boston: Beacon Press.

Chapter 9

Madrinas, Comadres, and *Luminarias:* Latina Mentors in Action

Lillian Comas-Diaz

Esperanza and America were like psychological twins. Best friends since childhood, they wished to be the first in their families to graduate from college. While Esperanza hoped to become a school principal, America envisioned herself as a lawyer. Both girls promised to help each other achieve their dreams. Years later, America became a lawyer as Esperanza dropped out of college.

WHAT MADE THE DIFFERENCE?

Esperanza and America met in a Chicago barrio where they shared formative experiences. Esperanza, a Puerto Rican, was born and raised in Illinois. Her parents were born on the island and migrated to the mainland after they got married. They named her Esperanza—which means hope in Spanish—because she was their first-born child. Also a first child, America was born in Los Angeles and raised in Illinois. Her Mexican parents immigrated to the United States in search of the American dream. Esperanza and America shared similar socioeconomic backgrounds and family constellations. Besides being first-born children of (im)migrant parents, their parents were fervent proponents of educating their children. As a result, Esperanza and America performed at a high level in academic achievement. Moreover, a similar shade of brown skin color intensified their sisterly bond. Unfortunately, they received neither racial nor ethnic minority socialization, because their parents grew up as majority group members in Latin America. Consequently, Esperanza and America exchanged stories of racism and sexism and shared coping strategies. Both chose the same *luminaria*—a Latina luminary or role model—to identify with her power. They chose Linda (Cordova) Carter, the Mexican American actress who played Wonder Woman on television. "You have to be a wonder woman to overcome racism and sexism," Esperanza and America used to say.

Esperanza and America obtained full college scholarships. While Esperanza went to a state university in New England, America attended a California state college. However, their similarities seemed to end in college. Esperanza felt isolated and discriminated due to her ethnicity. America became a member of a growing number of Latino students. Moreover, Amparo Flores, a Latina psychology professor who mentored America, was the significant difference between Esperanza and America. Sadly, Esperanza did not encounter faculty of color during college.

Certainly, mentoring helped America to stay in college and achieve her professional dream. As a testament to her mentor, America acknowledged Dr. Flores during her graduation from law school. Regrettably, Esperanza did not receive mentoring during college. She identified such absence as the main reason for dropping out of the university. Esperanza's college educational experience seems consistent with Latino's achievement statistics. The fastest growing student college group, Latinos have a slow graduation rate (Bordes & Arredondo, 2005).

WHY DID ESPERANZA BECOME A STATISTIC?

The statistics on Latino education are bleak. Compared to 24.84 percent of the non-Hispanic white population, only 12.4 percent of the Latino population graduates from college (French & Romano, 2008). Scholars are researching the relevance of mentoring Latinos (Torres Campos et al., 2008). For instance, a study examining mentoring experiences found that Latino adolescents benefit from having mentors, regardless of specific personal and relational characteristics (Sanchez & Reyes, 2006). In other words, the significant factor for Latino achievement appears to be the presence of mentors.

The interaction of ethnicity and gender prompted the popular media to disseminate the importance of mentoring Latinas (Forestieri, 2008). Maria Ramirez, president of the Latina Leadership Network identifies the absence of mentors as the main reason for Latinas' low educational achievement (French & Romano, 2008). However, Latinas' gendered ethnicity frequently combines with other diversity variables to pose a significant challenge for mentoring. As culture places mentoring in a context (Darly, Bogat, Carvell, Murphy, & Sanches, 2007; Rivera-Goba & Nieto, 2007), many Latinas benefit from gender-specific and culturally congruent mentoring. To illustrate, Dr. Flores guided America in culturally sensitive ways. First, she took a personal interest in America. In fact, Flores became her academic *madrina.* In the Latino community, *madrina* (godmother) is a special relationship that involves parenting and mentoring. There is a Spanish *dicho* (saying) that describes the role of godparents in achieving success in life: *El que no tiene padrino (madrina) no se bautiza* (S/he who does not have a godfather or godmother does not get baptized). This saying implies that godparents will guide and instruct their godchildren in life. In other words, we need mentors to succeed in life. Indeed, a special function for *madrinas* and *padrinos* is to help godchildren achieve success. For this reason, many Latino parents ask influential members of the community to become their children's godparents.

As a *madrina,* Flores mentored America's professional socialization. She used collectivistic values to emphasize individual needs. A Cuban immigrant, Flores taught America cultural assertiveness. For instance, being assertive with Latino authority figures requires respect: One might say, "With all the respect you deserve, I need to express my needs to you" (Comas-Diaz & Duncan, 1985). The relevance of mentoring women resonates within the Latino community. Many Latinas have a cultural leadership mandate, since their communities assign them a central role. Latinas' heritage of leadership, resistance, and transformation promotes cultural evolution. Many mythistories relate the achievements of Latina leaders (Coll y Toste, 1977; Delacre, 1996). As an example, Latinas foster transculturation—the creation of a new culture out of the encounter of two different cultural sets (De Granda, 1968). Latinas embody transculturation through racial mixing in the form of *mestizaje* and *mulataje. Mestizaje* (mixing Native Americans with Europeans) and *mulataje* (mixing of Africans with Europeans and others) become subversive positions against the Eurocentric model (Buscaglia-Salgado, 2003). Transculturation advances progress as it encourages cultural flexibility—an ability to live with cultural ambiguities, contradictions, and paradoxes (Comas-Diaz, 2008). It affords a dialectical process whereby Latinas simultaneously affirm, challenge, and reformulate their cultural identities. Through these processes, Latinas foster resistance against colonization, cultural imperialism, and oppression. Such lineage endows Latinas with a gender-specific cultural resilience that enables them to survive, thrive, and evolve (Comas-Diaz, 2008). Latina psychocultural ancestry attributes to women the function of generativity. The nurturing of younger generations, generativity facilitates healing historical and contemporary trauma (Kay, 1998). In addition to nurturing, Latinas are responsible for educating their families. In other words, women nurture, heal, and mentor future generations.

Mentoring involves empowering Latinas to "remember" how to lead. *Madrinas* assist their goddaughters into awakening their dormant talents. Latinas' cultural background facilitates their leadership through their unique cultural gifts. Indeed, a significant foundation of Latinas' leadership style is their spirituality. Many Latinas adhere to transpersonality, a collectivistic value that promotes mentoring and transcendence. Transpersonality foments the transformation of individual self into an evolving collective identity (Comas-Diaz, 2006). Consequently, it enhances Latinas' leadership and mentoring qualities.

HOW CAN WE AWAKEN LATINA LEADERSHIP?

Mentoring Latinas involves the inclusion of several elements, such as cultural assertiveness, gendered ethnoracial socialization, and cultural consciousness, among others.

Cultural Assertiveness

Latinas raised with traditional gender roles face specific challenges in their need for achievement (Martinez Thorne, 1996). They have to adhere to a particular cultural worldview at home while functioning in a different culture. Straddling two cultures can be both a curse and a blessing. While some Latinas cope with mental health challenges, others redefine success beyond traditional and patriarchal areas. This contradiction is one of the many cultural paradoxes that inhabit Latinas' lives. As an illustration, to facilitate America's success, Flores taught her assertiveness within a cultural context. Assertiveness for Latinas is embedded in sociocentric values. Examples of cultural values that mediate assertiveness are respect to authority, *personalismo* (preference for personal relations over impersonal ones), and *verguenza* (a type of cultural shame). Effective assertiveness follows the cultural mores of these values. For instance, *familismo* is a Latino cultural mandate that designates as family members those individuals who have a significant role in the person's life. Thus, Latinos adhering to *familismo* often consider godparents, friends, mentors, teachers, close co-workers, and even neighbors as family members.

Similarly, the emphasis of *personalismo* on personal relations infuses the mentoring relationship with extracurricular activities. To illustrate, mentors often attend cultural, sport, and social events with their Latina mentees as a means of strengthening their bond (Forestieri, 2008). Moreover, being assertive demands adherence to the *personalismo* code, such as being diplomatic about conflictive topics, restraining self-expression, and monitoring of conversations, among other behaviors. A relational interpersonal style, *verguenza* is a type of socioemotional shame that denotes the presence or absence of pride elicited when individuals lose face (Comas-Diaz, in press). *Verguenza* is behind the instruction of being a credit (or a shame) to the Latino ethnicity. To avoid *veguenza,* Latinas need to behave within a cultural context. *Verguenza* transforms individual behavior into collective attribution. Consequently, individuals' public behaviors can become a reflection on the entire Latino community.

Gendered Ethnoracial Socialization

Mentoring Latinas requires socialization to cope with a combined ethnoracial and gender stress. Due to their ethnic minority status, many professionals of color contend with a special kind of stress. This minority stress involves being negatively stereotyped as a token (Comas-Diaz & Greene, 1994), being confused with another person of color (Dobbin, Kalev, & Kelly, 2007), being confused with the help (maid, secretary, nanny, etc.), and many other insults. As visible people of color, many Latinas are exposed to racial microaggressions—the assaults inflicted upon individuals on a regular and acute basis solely due to their race, color, or ethnicity (Pierce, 1995). Sometimes, even counseling exposes Latinas to racial microaggressions during the therapeutic encounter (Sue et al., 2007). Unfortunately, chronic exposure to microaggressions and racial sexism can result in low self-esteem, learned helplessness, depression, and anomie. Indeed, this kind of stress cost Esperanza her college degree. During her junior year, Esperanza had a negative interaction with a racist professor—a white middle-aged man. Esperanza obtained a deficient grade in an essay test and went to see the professor. When she inquired about her grade, he interrupted her: "I was in a bad mood when I corrected your exam." Without further explanation, he turned his back and walked away from Esperanza.

Individual racism interacts with institutional racism. There are organizational and systemic dynamics that require attention while mentoring Latinas. To succeed in predominantly white institutions, Latinas need to recognize, understand, and navigate sexist and racially excluding organizational dynamics. Furthermore, mentors need to acknowledge the effects of historical racism, sexism, and xenophobia on Latinas. Such historical events produce "soul wounds"—the result of sociohistorical oppression, trauma, ungrieved losses, internalized oppression, and learned helplessness among people of color (Duran & Ivey, 2006). Latinas need to recognize their soul wounds, because historical oppression tends to be replicated in hierarchical relationships. An example of a retraumatization of soul wounds was Esperanza's interaction with the professor around her test grade. As a result, Latinas' soul wounds can be addressed within the mentoring relationship.

Cultural Consciousness

Cultural consciousness fosters Latinas' coping with gendered racial stress. Mentors can aid Latinas to become culturally conscious. Cultural consciousness helps individuals to affirm and celebrate their ethnicity and culture (Comas-Diaz, 2007). Specifically, it entails a cultural journey whereby Latinas learn about their ancestry, history, and traditions in order to empower themselves. Indeed, Maria Ramirez, president of the Latina Leadership Network, stated that Latinas' success requires knowledge and appreciation of their cultural history (French & Romano, 2008). Cultural consciousness helps Latinas to rescue their cultural strengths and acknowledge their multiple intersecting identities. The cultural flexibility inherent in cultural consciousness helps Latinas to reformulate their evolving cultural identity. Moreover, cultural consciousness reconnects Latinas with their spiritual roots to enhance their resilience and power. Many Latinas use spirituality in their daily struggles. Spirituality validates Latinas' experience as a source of knowledge. This approach involves gaining wisdom through honoring, listening, respecting, accepting, revering, collaborating, teaching, and learning (Comas-Diaz, in press). A Latino spiritual worldview emphasizes family, community, and divinity oneness and harmony (Morones & Mikawa, 1992). Furthermore, spirituality fosters the development of meaning making out of adversity. It enhances Latinas' ability to speak in their words, voice their reality, and thus delineate their preferred future. As a result, cultural consciousness helps Latinas to address oppression (including internalized oppression) and to struggle for liberation. Because cultural consciousness advocates for global solidarity, Latinas can learn to liberate themselves by liberating others. Within this journey, mentoring entails a developmental process for Latinas.

WHAT ARE THE STAGES IN LATINA MENTORING?

Mentoring Latinas follows a cyclical developmental path. First, Latinas (like Esperanza and America) identify a *luminaria* (role model) to promote their achievement. Indeed, I use the term *luminarias* to describe Latinas who have achieved success and became a role model for other Latinas. *Luminarias* can be historical, spiritual, religious, literary, or political figures. They can also be contemporary Latinas. As mentioned earlier, Esperanza and America chose Mexican American Linda Carter's Wonder Woman as their role model.

After the identification with a *luminaria*, the next development sequence is to obtain mentoring from a *madrina*. Regardless of the mentor's gender, Latinas require attention to their gendered ethnicity. Once mentored, Latinas can be mentored again. Indeed, Latinas may have different mentors at different stages of their lives. To illustrate, America received mentoring from a Jewish male attorney when she was an associate in a law firm.

The next developmental sequence in mentoring Latinas is the selection of an appropriate mentor. Due to the limited number of Latino mentors, many Latinas engage in peer mentoring. I use the term *comadres* to designate those Latinas who mentor peer Latinas. Literally meaning co-mothers, the term denotes the relationship between a mother and her offspring's godmother. In this case, the offspring is Latina achievement. Thus, *comadres* help each other to increase self-esteem, well-being, agency, and effectiveness in life. *Las Comadres par las Americas* provides an illustration of how this system works. An informal Internet group that meets monthly, *Las Comadres* builds connections and fosters empowerment among Latinas (www.lascomadres.org/). One of its programs, *Reading with Las Comadres*, focuses on Latina authors (Jordan, 2007) to analyze the Latina experience in the United States. Particular emphasis is given to issues of immigration, acculturation, racism, sexism, oppression, cultural strengths, and many other relevant topics to Latinas.

The next developmental stage involves generativity or giving back to the community. *Comadres* can become *promotoras.* Community-based women who work to empower Latinos through education (Rios-Ellis et al., 2005; Vasquez & Comas-Diaz, 2007), *promotoras* embody generativity. They earn their community's respect and admiration. Moreover, *promotoras* are Latina mentors who promote consciousness and liberation through education and social action. Indeed, several *promotoras* use liberatory approaches such as Paulo Freire's (1973) education for critical consciousness. Within this context, Latinas' mentoring development resembles Tisdell's (2002) study of multicultural women's spiritual commitment. Her findings indicated that the women's adult development involved a spiral process of re-remembering spiritual and cultural values to promote social action.

HOW DO WE HELP LATINAS TO SEEK MENTORS?

Latinas seeking mentoring can reframe their concepts of mentor and mentee. To achieve this, Latinas need to recognize that mentoring is an active process. Thus, Latinas can invite potential individuals to mentor them. That is, Latinas have to seek and engage mentors. This process involves studying mentors' profiles (both personal and professional) and their mentoring styles. Afterward, Latinas can map their common areas of interest and match them with their findings on professors or supervisors. To illustrate, if there are no Latino or Latina faculty nor faculty of color, Latinas can explore the presence of supervisors with diversity variables who could relate to ethnic minority issues. For instance, Latinas can look for potential mentors who have cross-cultural experiences. When I was in graduate school, for example, I approached a white woman professor who had international experience. Having lived abroad, the professor encountered culture shock, learned a second language, and reexamined her

American identity when she returned to the United States. After my inquiry, I asked her to become one of my mentors. She agreed, and her help was invaluable to me.

In seeking mentors, however, Latinas have to consider the effects of gendered racism. Some potential mentors may be solely interested in the Latina stereotypes of exoticism, hypersexuality, virginity, and other objectified designations. Not only can this interest replicate soul wounds, but it can also re-create the colonizer's rape of the colonized woman. To prevent potential sexual harassment and abuse and blaming the victim, Latinas need to trust their instincts, use their cultural resilience, and rely on their support system for reality checks.

Cultural consciousness can help Latinas to identify who they are. This recognition enhances self-esteem, agency, and a projection into the future. A culturally conscious Latina is more likely to recognize, examine, and struggle against oppression. Latinas can rediscover the power of the collective. They can form alliances with other women, Latinos, and women of color. This approach leads to the development of solidarity. Becoming aware of divide-and-conquer dynamics promotes resilience. Moreover, solidarity enhances peer mentoring. Internet resources such as MySpace, Facebook, LinkedIn, Plaxo, and many others can help to create a cyberspace

Table 1
Recommendations for Latinas Seeking Mentoring

1. Remember who you are.
2. Become culturally conscious; learn about your culture, history, and ancestry.
3. Acknowledge multiple identities; be mindful of your gendered ethnicity.
4. Identify and use your cultural strengths.
5. Actively select your mentors; look for *madrinas* and *padrinos*.
6. Examine potential mentors' profiles for common areas (diversity variables, interests, etc.).
7. Check out their mentoring style (asking, direct observation, Internet information, etc.).
8. Learn to recognize conscious and unconscious bias, aversive racism and sexism, etc.
9. Identify systemic and organizational oppression.
10. Develop alliances and engage in support groups; use Internet resources (Facebook, etc.).
11. Become a *comadre* (peer mentor).
12. Nurture your cultural resilience.
13. Strategize what, when, and how to use coping mechanisms.
14. Support solidarity and avoid the divide-and-conquer dynamic.
15. Develop a global perspective; study international literature, geopolitical events.
16. Strategize what, when, and how to use coping mechanisms.
17. If spirituality provides support, use spiritual resources.
18. Become a *promotora*.
19. Engage in generativity and social action.
20. Acknowledge your own power; become a *luminaria*.

peer mentoring community. When Latinas are mindful of their gendered ethnicity, they promote a mentoring development in themselves and in others. Consequently, Latinas can be free to become *madrinas, comadres, promotoras,* and *luminarias.* Table 1 summarizes some recommendations for Latinas seeking mentoring.

CONCLUSION: ON THE RISE

After several years of silence, America made contact with Esperanza in a Latina Internet group. She invited Esperanza to visit and meet her newborn daughter.

"This is my daughter, Esperanzita," America said.

"You named her Esperanza!"

"Yes, because you will be her *madrina,*" America said.

Esperanza and America renewed their childhood promise. They helped each other achieve their dreams. They became *comadres* and peer mentored each other again. Esperanza regained hope and returned to college. She joined a health education *promotoras* group. Her work with the Latino community landed Esperanza an elected political office—she became a member of the city council. Afterward, Esperanza graduated from college and enrolled in a master's in public health program. America and little Esperanzita attended her graduation. Currently, America and Esperanza nurture a *luminaria* on the rise.

REFERENCES

Bordes V., & Arredondo, P. (2005). Mentoring and 1st year Latina/o college students. *Journal of Hispanic Higher Education, 4*(2), 114–133.

Buscaglia-Salgado, José F. (2003). *Undoing empire: Race and nation in the mulatto Caribbean.* Minneapolis: University of Minnesota Press.

Coll y Toste, C. (1977). *Puerto Rican tales: Legends of Spanish colonial times.* San Juan, PR: Ediciones Libero.

Las Comadres para las Americas. Retrieved on July 18, 2007, from http://www.lascomadres.org/

Comas-Diaz, L. (2006). Latino healing: The integration of ethnic psychology into psychotherapy. *Psychotherapy. Theory, Research, Practice & Training, 43*(4), 436–453.

Comas-Diaz, L. (2007). Ethnopolitical psychology: Healing and transformation. In E. Aldarondo (Ed.), *Promoting social justice in mental health practice* (pp.91–118). [Mahwah, NJ: Erlbaum.

Comas-Diaz, L. (2008). *Spirita:* Reclaiming womanist sacredness in feminism. *Psychology of Women Quarterly, 32,* 13–21.

Comas-Diaz, L. (in press). Interventions with culturally diverse populations. In D. Barlow (Ed.), *Handbook of clinical psychology.* Oxford.

Comas-Díaz, L., & Duncan, J. W. (1985). The cultural context: A factor in assertiveness training with mainland Puerto Rican women. *Psychology of Women Quarterly, 9*(4), 463–475.

Comas-Díaz, L., & Greene, B. (1994). Women of color with professional status. In L. Comas-Díaz & B. Greene (Eds.), *Women of color: Integrating ethnic and gender identities in psychotherapy* (pp. 347–388). New York: Guilford Press.

Darly, N., Bogat, G. A., Carvell, T. A., Murphy, S. E, & Sanchez, B. ((2007). Gender, ethnicity, development and risk: Mentoring and the coordination of individual differences. *Journal of Community Psychology, 34*(6), 765–780.

De Granda, G. (1968). *Transculturación e interferencia lingüística en el Puerto Rico contemporáneo* [Transculturation and linguistic interference in contemporary Puerto Rico]. Bogotá, Colombia: Ediciones Bogotá.

Delacre, L. (1996). *Golden tales: Myths legends, and folktales from Latin America.* New York: Scholastic Press.

Dobbin, F., Kalev, A., & Kelly, E. (2007). Diversity management in corporate America. *Contexts, 6*(4), 21–28.

Duran, E., & Ivey, A. E. (2006). *Healing the soul wound: Counseling with American Indians and other native people.* New York: Teachers College Press.

Forestieri, C. (2008). Nurturing through mentoring. *Latina Style, 4*(5), 12–13.

Freire, P. (1973*). Education for critical consciousness.* New York: Seabury.

French, E., & Romano, G. (2008). Creating scholars and leaders, Rising through the ranks! *Latina Style, 14*(6), 19–20.

Jordan, T (2007). *Reading with Las Comadres will highlight Latinas authors.* Retrieved October 2, 2007, from www.publishers.org/main/PressCenter/LasComadres Release.htm

Kay, A. (1998). Generativity in the shadow of genocide: The Holocaust experience and generativity. In D. P. McAdams & E. de St. Aubin (Eds.), *Generativity and adult development: How and why we care for the next generation* (pp. 335–359). Washington, DC: American Psychological Association.

Martinez Thorne, Y. (1996, January 19). The importance of mentoring Latinas. *Hispanic Outlook in Higher Education,* 1–2.

Morones, P. A., & Mikawa, J. K. (1992). The traditional mestizo view: Implications for modern psychotherapeutic interventions. *Psychotherapy, 29*(3), 458–466.

Pierce, C. M. (1995). Stress analogs of racism and sexism: Terrorism, torture and disaster. In C. V. Willie, P. P. Reiker, & B. S. Brown (Eds.), *Mental health, racism and sexism* (pp. 277–293). Pittsburgh, PA: University of Pittsburgh Press.

Rios-Ellis, B., Aguilar-Gaxiola, S., Cabassa, L., Caetano, R., Comas-Diaz, L., Flores, Y., et al. (2005). *Critical disparities in Latino Mental Health: Transforming research into action.* (White paper). Institute for Hispanic Health, National Council of La Raza.

Rivera-Goba, M. V., & Nieto, S. (2007). Mentoring Latina nurses: A multicultural perspective. *Journal of Latinos and Education, 6*(1), 35–53.

Sanchez. B., & Reyes, O. (2006). Descriptive profile of the mentorship relations of Latino adolescents. *Journal of Community Psychology, 27*(3), 299–302.

Sue, D., Capodilupo, C. M., Torino, G. C., Bucceri, J. M., Holder, A. M., Nadal, K. L., & Esquilin, M. (2007). Racial micoragressions in everyday life: Implications for clinical practice. *American Psychologist, 62*(4), 271–286.

Tisdell, E. J. (2002). Spiritual development and cultural context in the lives of women adult educators for social change. *Journal of Adult Development, 9*(2), 127–140.

Torres Campos, C. M., Phinney, J. S., Perez-Brena, N., Kim, S., Ornelas, B., Nemanim, L., et al. (2008). A mentor-based targeted intervention for high-risk Latino college freshmen: A pilot study. *Journal of Hispanic Higher Education, 8,* 158–164.

Vasquez, M., & Comas-Diaz, L. (2007). Feminist leadership among Latinas. In J. L. Chin, B. Lott, J. Rice, & J. Sanchez-Hucles (Eds.), *Transforming leadership: Diverse visions and women's voices* (pp. 264–280). Malden, MA: Blackwell.

Chapter 10

Women of Color as Mentors

Melba J. T. Vasquez and Jessica Henderson Daniel

Mentoring has been identified as a key factor in success, and much has been written about the challenges for women to obtain mentoring. We will focus on the experience of women of color as mentors. Typically, people tend to mentor people who remind them of themselves, including along the variables of gender and ethnicity/race (Rhode & Williams, 2007). In a society where race is often salient, women of color are likely to have different life experiences from those of white women. As a consequence, attending to the unique experiences and effects of mentoring or lack of mentoring for women of color as well as mentoring by women of color is important.

In one study (Giscombe, 2008), women of color reported having more in common with men of color than with white women in their attitudes regarding exclusivity of the work environment and their perceptions that practices intended to support inclusion were not as effective as they could be. Such a finding suggests that race/ethnicity can trump gender in the lives of women of color in the workplace. It is noteworthy that women of color and white women did report similar experiences and perceptions, including level of social exclusion from the old boys' network and a lack of support from firms for their family responsibilities.

The definition of mentoring, especially since the relatively recent popularity of personal and professional coaching, has varied. Traditionally, mentoring might have been described as the activities conducted by a person (the mentor) for another person (the mentee) in order to help the other person perform a job more effectively and to progress in their career. A mentor is an experienced and trusted advisor; an experienced person in a context in which the mentee benefits from direction and guidance. A mentor might use a variety of approaches, such as coaching, training, discussion, counseling, and role modeling. Today, there is much discussion and debate about the definitions and differences regarding coaching and mentoring. In this chapter, mentoring will consist of two primary functions: career related (with the content on knowledge and advice to support both development and performance) and psychosocial (with a focus on being a role model and the provision of affective support). The lessons can be conveyed both explicitly and implicitly (American Psychological Association, Centering on Mentoring Task Force, 2006).

Mentoring is an important responsibility for those who have accomplished positions of seniority and leadership in the context of the workplace or organizational environment. Although the goals of mentoring by women of color are similar to those of other mentors, some may be unique. Particularly important strategies for women of color include: to prevent or mediate sex and racial/ethnic discrimination in the workplace (Wetchler, 2007); to suggest possible pathways for the development of a healthy identity (Josselson, 1987; Torres, 2006); to promote self-efficacy and confidence in a particular arena (Rosales, 2006); to recapitulate the loving, comforting, and warm sense of family in a challenging context (Segura-Herrera, 2006); to warn of potential pitfalls and reveal opportunities (Garcia, 2006); to help transform commitments to social justice to applications in research, practice, and theory (Quijada, 2006); and to offer an alternative vision of what women of color could be as leaders (Astin & Leland, 1991). Daniel (2009) describes a mentoring program focused on increasing the number of black women psychologist researchers.

STATUS OF WOMEN AS LEADERS

Women comprise 60 percent of the workforce, yet fewer than 16 percent hold corporate positions, and even fewer women of color do so (Catalyst, 2008). In 2008, women held 15.7 percent of corporate officer positions at Fortune 500 companies; in 2007, this number was 15.4percent. Women held 6.2 percent of top earner positions, and in 2007 the number was 6.7 percent. The number of companies with no women corporate officers increased from 74 to 75 in 2008.

Mentoring as a way to address the barriers in academia in general and in particular for women in science, technology, engineering, and math (STEM) fields and the business world is discussed in part 2 of this volume. Mentoring undergraduate women is critical for ensuring the inclusion of women across various sectors in U.S. society

Research findings indicate that women of color experience more barriers on the road to achievement than do white women or men of color. Giscombe (2008) reported the results of women of color in accounting for Catalyst (a nonprofit organization working globally with businesses and professions to build inclusive workplaces and expand opportunities for women and business). Key findings were that women of color in a client-based environment faced the following barriers: lack of similar role models, stereotyping, greater level of exclusion from networks, and difficulty in accessing high-visibility assignments and business development opportunities.

MENTORING AS A MEANS OF LEADERSHIP DEVELOPMENT

Mentoring is considered a tool for the development of women as leaders; thus, it is critical to address barriers in accessing and developing mentoring relationships (Jeffcoat, 2008). Mentoring is also important for women who have made their careers an important anchor point (as opposed to primary family, husband, children, friends, or some combination). Anchoring in work seems not to take place unless an important other takes a personal interest in a woman's career (Josselson, 1987). If people tend to mentor people similar to them, what does that mean for women of color who have few role models and potential mentors? Women of color who have achieved have had fewer options to have mentors similar to themselves but have likely received some mentoring from a variety of people.

Catalyst conducted an examination of women of color in U.S. securities firms (Bagati, 2008). Their findings and descriptions provide a particularly poignant description of the experience of U.S.-born women of color:

> women of color risk experiencing a deceleration in their career trajectories as a result of the combined effects of race/ethnicity, gender and birth country. Women of color face disadvantages that white women, men of color, and white men do not. These start with an exclusionary workplace, lead to difficulties forging connections with others—including managers, mentors, and in informal relationships—and result in fewer business development opportunities. With fewer connections and chances to shine, women of color advance at a slower rate than others, and, ultimately, many are faced with a "concrete" ceiling.

> In particular, U.S.-born women of color perceived a greater level of exclusion, especially when it came to relationships with other

employees, than foreign-born women of color did. They also perceived diversity efforts at their firms to be ineffective in addressing subtle racial biases and providing adequate manager training. These women were more likely to have lower organizational commitment and to be disadvantaged by inequitable distribution of important client engagements. (Bagati, 2008, paragraphs 4 and 5)

What are the experiences of women of color in the various arenas in which they are leadership pioneers? What are the effects of these experiences? What are the effects on identity? What are the challenges? What are the obstacles? What are the unique strategies and contributions that women of color make as we contribute to the increased presence of women's leadership in general? How do women of color transform experiences in ways to provide mentoring to others?

IDENTITY DEVELOPMENT AND MENTORING FOR WOMEN OF COLOR

What happens to the identities of women of color in this society? The way society constructs gender and race/ethnicity has major influence on the development of identity for us. Specific experiences in family and community affect identity, as do the expectations in society. In early development, girls and adolescents of color have to deal with several difficult issues not faced by majority adolescent girls, such as racist prejudicial attitudes, conflict between the values of our groups and those of larger society, and a scarcity of high-achieving women of color to serve as role models (Eccles, Wigfield, & Byrnes, 2003). Such difficulties can impede identity formation, leading to identity diffusion or inadequate exploration of different possible identities.

Cross (1991) argues that one must consider the development of both personal identities and racial group identity. For example, a woman of color may have a positive personal identity but be less positive of her ethnic group as a whole, or she may have negative personal identities but have positive orientations toward her group. Ideally, we have both positive personal identities and positive group identities. In U.S. society, it is a challenge to be positive about oneself and one's group unless we have messages within our families and communities about the positive nature of our ethnic groups. This kind of inoculation against the negative messages in society about our groups is critical to forming positive group identities.

Women of color in the United States are generally identified as being black, Latina/Hispanic, Asian American, and Native American/Alaskan Native. Within these categories are a range of ethnic groups with particular values and traditions. Women of color are diverse and vary in their level of identification with their group memberships.

Several authors have addressed the challenges of managing group memberships in a multicultural society: Gil and Vazquez (1996) in *The Maria Paradox: How Latinas Can Merge Old World Traditions with New World Self-Esteem*; Chow (1999) in *Leaving Deep Waters: Asian American Women at the Crossroads of Two Cultures*; and Bell and Nkomo (2001) in *Our Separate Ways: Black and White Women in the Struggle for Professional Identity.*

CHALLENGES TO POSITIVE IDENTITY FOR WOMEN OF COLOR

Several areas of social psychological research inform us of the current experiences of women of color that present challenges to a positive identity and, in effect, leadership roles (Vasquez & Comas-Diaz, 2007). When a woman of color has achieved and is perceived as a role model and potential mentor, she has to continue to deal with these experiences, as well as consider them for the mentees with whom she works.

Women's Performance May Be Devalued

Most people remain unaware of the different interpretations they place on identical behavior by women and men, including gendered assumptions about competence (Rhode & Williams, 2007). In a review of various studies, Heilman (2001) concluded that, because of gender stereotypes, ambiguity in evaluation criteria, lack of structure in evaluation processes, and denial of credit for successes to women, women's performance is systematically negatively biased and devalued. Even successful women may be penalized if they are violating gender expectations, or their successes may be attributed to special help or manipulations on the part of the women. Rhode and Williams (2007) suggested that women in predominantly male environments tend to experience polarized evaluations. A few women superstars might attract special attention and receive higher evaluations than their men colleagues, but women just below that level tend to receive disproportionately lower evaluations. Yet the presence of a few highly regarded women at the top creates the illusion that the glass ceiling has been shattered for everyone else. They also point out how women of color are often doubly disadvantaged because of negative assumptions about competence associated with race as well as gender. The small numbers place women of color under unique observation. The achievements of women of color are particularly likely to be attributed to affirmative action rather than competence and merit.

Subtle Racism and Exclusion

Contemporary racism and discrimination are subtle. Although people of color are aware of racism and discrimination, whites who perpetrate it generally are not aware of their behaviors. Social psychologist John Dovidio and his colleagues (1996) have conducted research that indicates that, although expressions of open hostility and clear dislike are not as evident on a daily basis as they were in the past, European Americans experience anxiety and uneasiness around people of color. In general, European Americans consciously endorse egalitarian values and deny their negative feelings about people of color, and so will not discriminate directly and openly. However, because of feelings of anxiety and uneasiness, they will discriminate, often unintentionally, when their behavior can be justified on the basis of some factor other than race or ethnicity (e.g., "questionable qualifications"). Dovidio and his colleagues (1996), who termed this phenomenon *aversive racism,* indicated that, while most have a nonprejudiced self-image, they also engage in discrimination. When one is anxious and uneasy because of discomfort around people who are perceived to be different, distancing behaviors are communicated. One may not be conscious of it, but the receiver usually is.

Successful women of color often have the experience of being on the "outer edge of the inner circle," a phrase coined by one of our clients. Although a woman of color officially may have the prestige, status, and even the salary of an executive, she may often feel that she is not really accorded the respect, value, and inclusion that her peers experience. Specific behaviors experienced may include failure to make eye contact, failure to initiate interaction at key events, as well as constantly being questioned with the inference that she has not completed a task well or that she lacks the skills and knowledge to perform her duties. On the other hand, she may be called upon constantly by others—including women and men of color, white women, and even white men seeking support from her as a role model and mentor. The emotional toll associated with receiving mixed messages—valued and devalued as well as competent and incompetent—can be high.

Writer Gwendolyn Parker (1997) talked about these kinds of experiences in the halls of privilege, from Harvard College, to New York University Law School, to a prestigious law firm, and to a prestigious corporation. She described her loneliness and the feeling that she was "trespassing," the title of her 1997 book. The steady stream of messages in those places was that her presence, and that of others of color, was counterfeit. These experiences occurred despite the fact that she and other persons of color had credentials and achievements that were often superior to those of their peers.

Rhodes and Williams (2007) describe a well-documented process, in-group favoritism, which also impedes gender equality in the workplace. This dynamic is apparent in the informal networks of mentoring, contacts, and support critical for workplace rewards. Because employees generally feel most comfortable with those who are like them, women (and women of color, in particular) remain out of the loop for advice, favorable assignments, and professional development opportunities. People tend to accord preferences to members of their own identity groups.

Role Restrictions for Women of Color

Societal expectations and role restrictions are also barriers for women of color. Ability has very little to do with what happens to the identities of women and people of color. All too often, highly competent women of color move toward more traditional pathways once they are in college (see chapter 4). Is it that they discover they are not able after all? This is apparently not the case. Arnold (1995) conducted a longitudinal study of high school valedictorians who graduated in 1981. Female high school valedictorians, in their second year of college, changed their aspirations for demanding careers and also began to think of themselves as not as smart as their male peers, despite continuing to perform as well.

The college and career paths of the Latina and African American women in Arnold's study of valedictorians seemed to be even more affected by negative societal expectations. For example, Arnold described a Mexican American female valedictorian who worked during college, married, had a son, and at the last follow-up, when participants were in their early 30s, had not completed college. One African American female valedictorian reported a life-threatening example of her university experiences. A university medical doctor told her the abdominal pains she was experiencing resulted from the stress from her major (which was engineering) being too difficult and that she should change to an easier major. She was later rushed to surgery because of acute appendicitis. This particular student persisted through the completion of her degree, but her experiences were difficult and she believed she received her engineering degree only because of the support network of African American engineers. A Mexican American valedictorian in the study reported similar support networks among Hispanics and African American and Chinese friends. This student reported that she never had a white friend throughout college (Arnold, 1995).

Mentors should be aware of other major problems that Arnold (1995) discovered among these talented women and men of color who were valedictorians. The lack of money along with no knowledge about the process of pursuing college and careers were major barriers that countered their valedictorian status. These students took longer to complete college, averaging almost six years for their undergraduate degrees, while the white valedictorians tended to complete college in four continuous years. The African American and Mexican American valedictorians were more likely than whites to change institutions during their college careers. One of the implications of this information is the vital need for mentoring for talented students of color.

Stereotype Threat

Steel (1997) identified a phenomenon that happens when people believe that there are certain negative stereotypes about their abilities: They tend to feel threatened and anxious, which in turn leads to underperformance. Stereotype threat is a term coined by Steele (1997) to describe the experience by members of a group when they are evaluated in a domain in which they are regarded, on the basis of stereotype, as inferior. In the face of threat to self-esteem, derived from this identification with the area in which they are both aspiring and at the same time expecting to be negatively regarded, they undergo "choking under pressure" (Baumeister & Showers, 1984), and, as a result, they commonly underperform. A person from the stereotyped group tends to become highly anxious, try harder (Steele, 1997), and obtain significantly lower scores than they would under nonthreatening conditions (Steele & Aronson, 1995). This phenomenon has been observed in a number of different situations and contexts, including the hypothesis that the negative stereotyping of women as inferior in math and science would lead to the effect of stereotype threat on women's performance in mathematics (Spencer, Steele, & Quinn, 1999). The researchers tested a group of math-identified women compared to math-identified men, both groups equally qualified according to their grade point averages and SAT scores (women and men who saw themselves as good in math). In one condition they told participants that, in the past, the test had shown gender differences in order to evoke the negative stereotype of women's ability in math. In the second condition, the investigators told the participants that, in the past, the test had not shown gender differences. In the stereotype-threatening condition, the women obtained significantly lower scores than the men. In the second condition, there was no difference between the women and men in test performance.

STRATEGIES TO IMPROVE IDENTITY AND OPPORTUNITY FOR LEADERSHIP

What can women of color who have achieved a reasonable amount of power, status, and position do to encourage organizations to counteract these challenges to the identities—and thus positively affect the sense of capability, motivations, and leadership goals—of women of color?

Claude Steele (1997) suggested that people who have been negatively stereotyped require positive, optimistic mentor/supervisor–employee relationships. A critical factor in overcoming negative stereotyping is that supervisors and mentors must have optimism about women of color's potential and that they communicate this fundamental, nonambivalent belief in their employee's ability. Constructive criticism accompanied by the expectation of high standards are essential, along with an expression of confidence in the person's ability to achieve excellence (Vasquez & Comas-Diaz, 2007).

Mentors must understand or reconceptualize intelligence and related abilities to be expandable or incremental (Dweck, 2002) qualities that are increased by training and experience. Aronson (2002) found that students who were taught to consider intelligence expandable and who then changed how they thought about intelligence in response to training were able to increase their engagement in their education and thus be more academically successful.

Aronson (2002) suggests creating environments with an emphasis on cooperation instead of competition. An emphasis on cooperation has been noted to be helpful for stereotyped college students renegotiating their identification with academia, and it should be equally helpful to women of color in a process of overcoming anxiety about nontraditional roles created in the wake of earlier stereotype threat experiences in grade school, high school, or college classes. Ideally, women of color are provided with the opportunity to work collaboratively and collectively.

Create an environment where diversity feels natural. Cultural differences should not only be tolerated, but respected and celebrated. Related to this concept is that those who own privilege, those who are the power brokers and decision makers, must become comfortable with those different from them. Their actions and reactions when interacting with persons of color need to be consistent with their stated nondiscriminatory stance.

Mentors must be open to varied models of women's leadership. Decision makers tend to assume that those who are promoted to positions of leadership and responsibility should look and act like those who have been successful before them (usually white men). Women of color are bypassed for higher roles, because their styles sometimes are perceived to be different than those who have held those roles. It is important that both those women and the decision makers realize that different styles may be just as effective, and perhaps valuable in different ways. Joyce Fletcher (2001) described women's roles as potentially adding feminine wisdom and experience to organizational knowledge.

PERSONAL RECOMMENDATIONS FROM
TWO WOMEN OF COLOR MENTORS

What are the strategies recommended for individual women of color who wish to develop skills and abilities to further develop leadership qualities and abilities? We have experienced a variety of forms of mentoring, including from other women of color elders, men of color elders, white men, white women, and from peers in all categories. We would like to share information that we have learned to incorporate over the years. Some of the recommendations are based on work by Vasquez and Comas-Diaz (2007) and Daniel (2009).

Evaluate your fit in regard to values, skills, and capacity for challenge, both in terms of the job requirements and the degree of friendly versus nonfriendly environment for women of color. For example, we each have varying capacities to tolerate and cope with rejection and pain versus the ability to feel energized by being pioneers in nontraditional settings and roles.

Remember that no one is perfect and that mistakes are a part of life. Everyone makesmistakes. Learn from them, and move on. Do not allow them to be a part of your identity. Learn to revise yourself as part of the recovery process.

Do acknowledge painful feelings and reactions to hurtful events. Transform hurt and rejection into anger, and use that anger in constructive ways. Anger, and even rage, are normal reactions to experiences of discrimination. Use your rage and anger to empower your lives. We can transform those feelings into healthy, assertive expressions that say, "We count." "I am to be respected." "You may not mistreat me." "I am deserving." Anger is a healthy signal that tells us as well as those around us where our boundaries are, what we instinctively feel is tolerable or intolerable, and can signal when those limits have been trespassed. Choose your battles carefully; not all issues are worth the time and energy expenditure.

Women of color's group membership may determine the degree to which the expression of anger is tolerated. A black woman may be experienced as being more angry than she really is because of the stereotype of the angry black woman. Expressions of anger across groups are not perceived the same. Women of color need to be aware of the differences as they express themselves. Beginning with a statement about one's affective state, rather than assuming that the listener will be able to accurately label the state, may prevent misunderstandings.

Do not forget to immerse yourself into the positive aspects of your culture from time to time. Honor your multicultural identity; you are able to operate in several different contexts, which evoke different parts of yourself. Work on the delicate balance of knowing how and when various aspects of yourself will be most effective in what contexts. People of color are often multicultural and are able to develop skills of flexibility and adaptability to adjust to environments that are diverse and complex. Ramirez (1998) has long suggested that the complex immigration, international, intercultural and multicultural experiences of persons of color lead to the development of complex interpersonal skills and abilities. Mentoring across those differences can be both challenging and rewarding (Alvarez, Blume, Cervantes, & Thomas, 2009; Wedding, McCartney, & Currey, 2009).

Surrounding oneself with people who belong to one's cultural groups may provide models about how and when to express one's cultural identity in the workplace. Generational differences can provide important historical information and explain differences in perceptions rather than generate disrespect and dismissive responses in response to one's elders. Mentors can be peers as well as elders. All contributions can be valuable (Daniel, 2009).

Persistence is the most important variable that determines whether someone may complete graduate school and accomplish a variety of other achievements. Tenacious goal pursuit with a *balance* of flexible adjustment maintains one's sense of well-being and prevents depression. Knowing when to persist and when to adjust goals and expectancies becomes adaptive. It is difficult, because only those who are tenacious with their goals and pursuits make progress; on the other hand, tenacious goal pursuits in the face of unattainable goals may lead to depression and despair.

Thomas (2001) observed that whites tend to be placed on a fast track based on perceived potential, while persons of color need to establish a "proven and sustained record of solid performance" before they will be mentored by those in power. Such a pattern can result in demotivating persons of color and can generate feelings of being deskilled. Women of color's awareness of this mentoring pattern can inform their decision making when they are at a point of continuing or redirecting their efforts.

Take risks. Allow curiosity and energy to give direction to areas in which you wish to explore your power and salience. Risk takers often find that true fearlessness is not the elimination of fear, but the transcendence of fear; the movement through it and not against it. Fearlessness means the willingness to lean into the anxiety and fear. Risk taking builds positive aspects of one's identity. Taking risks does not mean moving forward without seeking the advice of trusted persons. Sometimes the risk level may be inflated due to a lack of information and planning. Play to win—to succeed. Learn as you go through the process, and seek allies along the way.

Remember that people are complex individuals. A difficult or painful disagreement or interaction with someone does not necessarily mean that the person should be written off. Rather, we are all in a position of learning about ourselves and others, and change is possible, and we may share perspectives and goals with that person on other key issues.

Observe role models and mentors. Mentors are scarce. Use situational mentors and mentors at a distance at times. We have received much mentoring and guidance from peers and sometimes have learned from watching younger students and early career professionals. Observe skills and strengths of others and decide whether you wish to cultivate those as well.

Mentors can be intentional and unintentional as well as known and unknown. Announcements are not always necessary. Mentoring entails a relationship. Relationships can vary in intensity and duration. Flexibility is critical.

Be willing to mentor, support, and empower others. Empowering others can be the same as empowering ourselves. The precious and powerful standing up for each other is one of the most exquisite gifts to give and to receive. Be particularly sensitive toward those who make errors or experience failures.

Engage in self-care and balance, because the overlay of expectations and challenging experiences can be overwhelming at times. Failure to take care of ourselves can result in the experience of depletion, discouragement, and burnout, with negative consequences to ourselves, our families, and our work.

CONCLUSION

Our commitment to provide mentoring to others is informed by our identities as womanists, feminists, and multiculturalists. The values related to those identities include encouraging the voices of those who are vulnerable; promoting skills needed to effectively question inequity and unfairness and to promote social justice; promoting empowerment, which includes helping those who have been oppressed learn to know their strengths; and encouraging broad participation, engagement, and involvement.

Workplace experts have said for years that creativity is enhanced by plurality and diversity. If a goal is to achieve a status equivalent to that of white men, we will have to participate equally in those contexts where the most important and far-reaching decisions are made. We must be present in sizeable numbers in these settings and must perform effectively in order to achieve a balance between men's and women's power.

We are grateful for the opportunities and experiences that we have had and the support and mentoring we have received, and we are determined to continue to promote leadership for all groups traditionally oppressed. We have been provided with opportunities on the shoulders of others and will continue to lend our shoulders likewise. *Si se puede!* Yes we can!

REFERENCES

Alvarez, A. N., Blume, A. W., Cervantes, J. M., & Thomas, L. R. (2009). Tapping the wisdom tradition, essential elements to mentoring students of color. *Professional, Psychology, Research and Practice, 40,* 181–188.

American Psychological Association Centering on Mentoring Task Force. (2006). *Introduction to mentoring: A guide for mentors and mentees.* Retrieved June 14, 2009, from http://mentoring.apa.org/intromentoring.pdf

Arnold, K. (1995). *Lives of promise: What becomes of high school valedictorians: A fourteen year study of achievement and life choices.* San Francisco: Jossey-Bass.

Aronson, J. (Ed.). (2002). *Improving academic achievement.* New York: Academic Press.

Astin, H. S., & Leland, C. (1991). *Women of influence, women of vision: A cross-generational study of leaders and social change.* San Francisco: Jossey-Bass.

Bagati, D. (2008, October). *Women of color in securities firms: Women of color in professional services series.* Retrieved June 7, 2009, from http://www.catalyst.org/publication/280/women-of-color-in-us-securities-firmswomen-of-color-in-professional-services-series

Baumeister, R. F., & Showers, C. J. (1984). A review of paradoxical performance effects: Choking under pressure in sports and mental tests. *European Journal of Social Psychology, 16,* 361–383.

Bell, E.L.J.E., & Nkomo, S. M. (2001) *Our separate ways: Black and white women and the struggle for professional identity.* Boston: Harvard Business School Press.

Catalyst. (2008, December). *2008 Catalyst census of women corporate officers and top earners of the Fortune 500.* Retrieved June 7, 2009, from http://www.catalyst.org/publication/283/2008-catalyst-census-of-women-corporate-officers-and-top-earners-of-the-fortune-500

Chow, A. S. (1999). *Leaving deep waters: Asian American women at the crossroads of two cultures*. New York: Plume.

Cross, W. E. Jr. (1991). *Shades of black: Diversity in African American identity*. Philadelphia: Temple University Press.

Daniel, J. H. (2009). Next generation: A mentoring program for black female psychologists. *Professional Psychology: Research and Practice, 40*(3), 299–306.

Dovidio, J. F., Gaertner, S. L., Kawakami, K., & Hodson, G. (2002). Why can't we just get along? Interpersonal biases and interracial distrust. Cultural Diversity & Ethnic Minority Psychology, 8, 88–102.

Dweck, C. S. (2002). Messages that motivate: How praise molds students' beliefs, motivation, and performance (in surprising ways). In J. Aronson (Ed.), *Improving academic achievement* (pp. 38–61). New York: Academic Press.

Eccles, J. S., Wigfield, A., & Byrnes, J. (2003). Cognitive development in adolescence. In R. M. Lerner, M. A. Easterbrooks, & J. Mistry (Eds.), *Handbook of psychology: Vol. 6. Developmental psychology* (pp. 325–350). Hoboken, NJ: Wiley.

Fletcher, J. K. (2001). *Disappearing acts: Gender, power and relational practice at work*. Cambridge, MA: MIT Press.

Garcia, M. (2006). The brown diamond: A Latina in the sciences. In J. Castellanos, A. M. Gloria, & M. Kamimura (Eds.), *The Latina/o pathway to the Ph.D: Abriendo caminos* (pp. 243–253). Sterling, VA: Stylus.

Gil, R. M., & Vazquez, C. I. (1996). *The Maria paradox: How Latinas can merge Old World traditions with New World self-esteem*. New York: Perigee.

Giscombe, K. (2008, May). *Women of color in accounting: Women of color in professional services series*. Retrieved June 5, 2009, from http://www.catalyst.org/publication/254/women-of-color-in-accountingwomen-of-color-in-professional-services-series

Heilman, M. E. (2001). Description and prescription: How gender stereotypes prevent women's ascent up the organizational ladder. *Journal of Social Issues, 57*, 657–674.

Jeffcoat, S. Y. (2008, May). *Mentoring women of color for leadership: Do barriers exist?* Dissertation retrieved June 7, 2009, from http://www.ohiolink.edu/etd/send-pdf.cgi/Jeffcoat%20Sandra%20Yvonne.pdf?acc_num=antioch1220894689

Josselson, R. (1987). *Finding herself: Pathways to identity development in women*. San Francisco: Jossey-Bass.

Parker, G. M. (1997). *Trespassing: My sojourn in the halls of privilege*. Boston: Houghton Mifflin.

Quijada, D. A. (2006). Collegial alliances? Exploring one Chican's perspective on mentoring in research and academia. In J. Castellanos, A. M. Gloria, & M. Kamimura (Eds.), *The Latina/o pathway to the Ph.D.: Abriendo caminos* (pp. 255–266). Sterling, VA: Stylus.

Ramirez, M., III., (1998). *Multicultural/Multiracial psychology: Mestizo perspectives in personality and mental health*. Northvale, NJ: Jason Aronson.

Rhode, D. L., & Williams, J. C. (2007). Legal perspectives on employment discrimination. In F. J. Crosby, M. S. Stockdale, & S. A. Ropp (Eds.), *Sex discrimination in the workplace* (pp. 235–270). Malden, MA: Blackwell.

Rosales, R. (2006). Manteniendo nuestra cultura (Sustaining our culture): Cultural and social adjustments of Latina/os in doctoral programs. In J. Castellanos, A. M. Gloria, & M. Kamimura (Eds.), *The Latina/o pathway to the Ph.D.: Abriendo caminos* (pp. 201–220). Sterling, VA: Stylus.

Segura-Herrera, T. A. (2006). Querer es poder: Maintaining and creating *familia* as a doctoral student. In J. Castellanos, A. M. Gloria, & M. Kamimura (Eds.), *The Latina/o pathway to the Ph.D.: Abriendo caminos* (pp. 221–231). Sterling, VA: Stylus.

Spencer, S. J., Steele, C. M., & Quinn, D. (1999). Stereotype threat and women's math performance. *Journal of Experimental Social Psychology, 35,* 4–28.

Steele, C. M. (1997). A threat in the air: How stereotypes shape intellectual identity and performance. *American Psychologist, 52,* 613–629.

Steele, C. M., & Aronson, J. (1995). Stereotype threat and the intellectual test performance of African Americans. *Journal of Personality and Social Psychology, 69,* 797–811.

Thomas, D. A. (2001). The truth about mentoring minorities, race matters. *Harvard Business Review, 79,* 99–107.

Torres, V. (2006). Bridging two worlds: Academia and Latina/o identity. In J. Castellanos, A. M. Gloria, & M. Kamimura (Eds.), *The Latina/o pathway to the Ph.D.: Abriendo caminos* (pp. 135–147). Sterling, VA: Stylus.

Vasquez, M., & Comas-Diaz, L. (2007). Feminist leadership among Latinas. In J. L. Chin, B. Lott, J. K. Rice, & J. Sanchez-Hucles (Eds.), *Women and leadership: Transforming visions and diverse voices* (pp. 264–280). Malden, MA: Blackwell.

Wedding, D., McCartney, J. L., & Currey, D. E. (2009). Lessons relevant to psychologists who serve as mentors for international students. *Professional Psychology: Research and Practice, 40,* 201–205.

Wetchler, J. D. (2007). Avoiding sex discrimination litigation and defending sex discrimination suits. In F. J. Crosby, M. S. Stockdale, S. A. & Ropp (Eds.), *Sex discrimination in the workplace* (pp. 7–18). Malden, MA: Blackwell.

Part IV

Mentoring for All Women

Chapter 11

A Mentor—A Friend in Deed

Mary E. Reuder

The dictionary defines a mentor as a "trusted adviser." So, presumably, mentoring would consist of giving "trusted advice." But in everyday life, this is a very constricted conception of what it is to mentor. In this chapter, mentoring is viewed more broadly, as the looking out for and taking care of the needs of others. Within this framework, there is no formal hierarchy of mentor–mentee so much as a straightforward sensitivity to the needs of others, be they colleagues, students, superiors, or subordinates.

Sometimes mentoring is a simple appreciation of another person's achievement—a friendly note or telephone call. Or it might consist of passing on information concerning a job opportunity or providing special help in preparing a vita. The modus operandi will depend upon the relative status of the mentor and mentee, but the actions are invariably acts of thoughtfulness for other persons and their needs. To this end, the following paragraphs describe various kinds of mentoring depending upon the status of the mentor—fellow student, teacher or professor, department chair, supervisor, or colleague—with illustrative examples of each and a particular emphasis on how such mentoring can prepare persons for leadership in organized psychology.

There is a very simple kind of mentoring that, if started very early in one's development, leads to a mindset or habit that often expands to much more complex and interactive mentoring later on. Basically, this consists of not only appreciating the work of others, but also of letting them know that you appreciate it. At one point, I was reading the book review section of a newsletter. The reviews were not only informative, but also extremely interesting. It suddenly dawned on me that most of these reviews were by a single reviewer, issue after issue; a truly thankless job. So I wrote a brief note to this person whom I knew only by name, telling her how much I appreciated the work and effort. Several years later, this person spotted me at an American Psychological Association (APA) meeting and was effusive with appreciation. Although she was an established and well-known scientist and I was a neophyte, that brief note had been important. Many years later, this same scientist nominated both me and my husband to fellow status in the New York Academy of Sciences. I was truly stunned by this out-of-the-blue mentorship on her part. It also planted the idea of nominating others for similar appointments when a future appropriate situation rolled around. Needless to say, fellow status in the academy for an experimental psychologist was and is deeply valued on my part. That mentor was truly a friend in deed.

Another, often overlooked, kind of mentoring consists of the sharing of special information based on experience. When I was a graduate student, the required doctoral French examination was my albatross. I had memorized over 2,000 words, taken the test, and failed it. Only three tries were allowed, or no PhD! So I memorized another 2,000 words, ready to try again. Then a fellow student sought me out to tell me that, on the examination he had just taken, there was a passage from an article in the current French version of the *Reader's Digest*. He suggested that it would not hurt to look it up—just in case. Needless to say, I carefully reviewed both the French and English versions—and headed for the test with trepidation. Luck! There was the passage which, by then, I was able to translate with fluency. And I passed. It is highly likely that one reason I have a PhD today is a direct consequence of the thoughtfulness of that fellow student who shared his experiences.

A similar experience has given me tremendous personal pleasure. A number of years ago, I served as the fellows chair of an APA division. During my seven or eight years in that position, I learned that, often, whether a candidate became a fellow depended upon the way in which her credentials were presented. Many otherwise apparently qualified persons were rejected, because they failed to present their accomplishments in a manner that reflected the APA criterion of "outstanding and/or unusual." Once I was no longer on any fellows committees, I found it both fun and rewarding to share this knowledge with others. One cannot, of course, create relevant data. However, one can arrange relevant data in such a manner as to make it clearly stand out as meeting the criteria. And so, across the years, one or two at a time, I have been able to help others by assisting them in reworking resumes that had been found wanting by various fellows committees and the APA Membership Committee. I know that these colleagues were delighted to be elected, but I am the one who had the rewarding experience of watching the effects of re-creating the resume emerge with such positive results. Mentoring is truly fun.

Sometimes mentoring takes the form of simply helping out another person. At a time when my husband and I were young assistant professors just getting started, a colleague, friend, and former student phoned in a panic state. Although she had successfully passed advanced graduate statistics courses (with As), she was absolutely frantic over the analysis of her dissertation data. It was clearly not a situation to be resolved over the telephone, and she lived in another state. So we invited her to visit us for a couple of weeks. We set up a table in the living room (right beside a sofa bed), placed the Friden calculator thereon, and conducted a one-on-one statistics interpretation course every evening while she pursued her analysis each day. Basically, it was the reassurance and not the instruction that enabled her to calm down and prepare her dissertation write-up. Again, the mentoring was basically just being a friend when needed.

There was a time at my institution when a budget crisis had the whole place in turmoil. This was also a time, it turned out, when very few persons outside of top administration were aware that the *Chronicle of Higher Education* was a source of help-wanted ads. One senior colleague, however, took it upon himself to carefully scan all of the ads, trying to match them with the qualifications of various persons, both faculty and staff, whose jobs were threatened. Then he wrote an initiating letter of recommendation for that person. It did help some people. And it also led to some amusing side effects. At least one recipient of his letters wanted to know "what was in it for him?" that made the letter writer take such initiative. My colleague tried to explain that it was fun. Matching the advertisement requirements with the talents of his various friends (who often were unaware of his activity) and writing letters to tie them together was a constructive enterprise during the time of turmoil. Further, the pleasure he derived when one or another successfully landed a new opportunity was intensely gratifying.

Mentoring sometimes takes place without either the mentor or the mentee being aware that mentoring is actually happening. I would probably not have had a PhD and academic career today had it not been for the impulsive actions of a friend. Being the first college graduate in my family, I was very unsophisticated and totally uninformed about higher education beyond a bachelor's degree. My friend was not. She had just arranged to go east to New York City for a master's degree. She corralled me and said,

"Why don't you come to graduate school, too? That way I'll have some-one to go with and talk to." So we combed the bulletin boards for adver-tisements of graduate schools located reasonably near the one she was to attend. Being Midwesterners, our perception of distances on maps of the East Coast was highly distorted. Everything on the East Coast looks close together on a map! We figured that both Providence, Rhode Island, and Washington, DC, were right next to New York City—and sent for forms within that geographic span. When Brown University actually sent forms in reply, I was overwhelmed. With two weeks until the application dead-line, my friend marched me to the registrar's office to get my records sent out and then made sure that I filled out the application and mailed it in. Some weeks later, an acceptance came and my career began.

In retrospect, much of my mentoring experience stemmed from the ba-sic philosophy of the small Catholic women's college we attended. From the day that we entered as freshmen, we were imbued with the dictum that, to the degree one was given ability and opportunity, one owed it to society to seize an opportunity and to give back to society—both directly and indi-rectly. And our professors truly served as role models in that regard, even after we had graduated. Once, when I was still a beginning graduate stu-dent, one of my undergraduate professors found me at an APA meeting and insisted that I accompany her to a meeting that was being held away from the convention location. This turned out to be the formal organizational founding of the American Catholic Psychological Association—a forerun-ner with many metamorphoses of Division 36 of APA. It was a consequence of charter membership in this organization that other career opportunities unfolded across the years. Participation in an invited symposium led to a much-needed publication. Active attendance at the annual business meet-ings led to being elected to executive committees and ultimately to division president and later to council representative.

Many years later, I was able to reciprocate by mentoring for that profes-sor. She had obtained her PhD from a university that was not overenthu-siastic about professional women. She and another woman were the two top students in her graduating class. However, she was a nun and the other woman was not. So that chapter of Sigma Xi decided the other woman needed it more for her career. And, of course, they wouldn't elect more than one woman. Such was the social climate of the times. Well along in my ca-reer, I was fortunate enough to be on the board of directors of Sigma Xi and learned how to get persons elected to its chapter-at-large. The pleasure I re-ceived from being able to get my mentor elected was a truly intense expe-rience. And there was a fun side effect. I had an excuse to telephone the famous B. F. Skinner at his home to ask him to serve as cosponsor. I was in awe, and he was delighted.

When one is in a relatively high-status relationship position, the pos-sibilities for mentoring increase proportionately. One often has the chance to aid not only colleagues but students as well. Back in the 1960s, I taught a course in experimental psychology in which each student was required to design and execute an original experiment. It took quite a bit of shepherding to get the students to formulate their ideas, design their studies, analyze their data, and write their reports. But the ideas the students came up with were usually from their own experiences, were exciting to test, and often led to significant outcomes. So I spent my summers rechecking all of the calculations and sending special-delivery letters to many of the students telling them that I wanted to sponsor them to read their papers at the Eastern Psychological Association meetings. These, incidentally, were nontraditional students in the School of General Studies from whom no one expected such things. Often the most interesting and creative papers were from a C-level student with low academic expectations. Watching their faces when they gave their papers at the professional meeting right along with professors and graduate students was pure pleasure. And this mentoring provided an additional bonus for me. I wrote up many of these papers and published them with the students as senior authors. This gave them an extra credential upon graduation and helped my vita in the publish-or-perish world. Even more gratifying, of course, has been the pleasure of watching several of these students progress to become colleagues in the field. In consequence, although I have never written a book, I have had many vicarious tomes to savor.

Colleagues sometimes share students' fears of inadequacy with statistics and data analysis. Not all training programs effectively reach all of their graduates in this regard. And once one has a PhD in hand, it is taken for granted that one is competent in statistics. I routinely taught statistics, measurement, and research courses, and I discovered that if I listened closely, some colleagues were very indirectly asking for help—usually in the form of "I don't quite know what's wrong. Would you look at it?" Because the real problem was fear, it didn't take long to review the papers and critiques and suggest an appropriate approach. It was from one such extensive conference that a colleague in a different department became as solid in research productivity as she was excellent in counseling. And it was flattering for me, because it is always fun to be able to play "expert."

Not everybody has the initiative to carry out good ideas. Yet the 1995 APA program on "Mentoring Women and Persons of Color to Participate in APA" stemmed from Carole Rayburn's awareness of problems in this area. Not only was her program a success, it also had an unforeseen side effect for one participant. This person returned home to find a letter inviting her to apply for a full professor opening at a major, prestigious institution. The letter stated clearly that it came as a direct consequence of her participation in that mentoring program. The flattered participant was not in a position to apply to the offer, but instead wrote a strong letter recommending a former student whose credentials matched the job description to a remarkable degree.

Finally, hidden mentoring can help both the individual and the profession. For many years, I was on the Sigma Xi National Lectureship Committee. The group collectively tended to think of chemists, engineers, mathematicians, physicists, and biologists (and especially Nobel Prize winners) as potential speakers. Having personally sat through many tedious presentations by otherwise famous and gifted people, I insisted that members of the committee had to personally know that a recommended candidate was a good speaker. Then I made it a point at every regional and national meeting that I attended to go to all of the invited addresses. From these, I culled the most effective speakers and was able to get most of them onto the list of national lecturers. To this day, most of them have no idea how they were selected. And the number of outstanding psychology speakers helped to change the perspective of the committee with respect to our discipline.

One might summarize all of this as "need a mentor, be a mentor." Develop the habit. Become a friend in deed.

All of the above examples represent a type of mentoring that may not be what the average person thinks about upon hearing the term. However, like many positive behaviors, informal mentoring and its effects were ultimately noted by business, industry, academe, and other organizations. Naturally, for these purposes, mentoring had to be formalized into a structured arrangement.

Customarily, a mentor is assigned to a mentee—usually a new employee or member of a department. It is assumed that the mentor will be something of a "big brother" to the mentee. In order for such an arbitrary relationship to be effective, certain precautions are critical. The mentor cannot be a person in either a competitive or supervisory position with regard to the mentee. In addition, however, is necessary for the two persons to have compatible personalities. When this relationship proves successful, it reportedly aids in reducing turnover and increases morale.

The manner in which the relationship evolves is very difficult to formalize. Allen (2005) pointed out that it is often easier to define what a mentor isn't than to clearly define the specific characteristics. Thus, a mentor is not a formal teacher but rather helps a mentee solve a problem and may incidentally "teach" by supplying relevant information. It could be something as small as supplying the name and location of the nearest bank or providing information on the characteristics of various housing locations, and rental costs.

Although not a guidance counselor, a good mentor often serves as a guide through the social learning of the office network and power structure. It can be especially important for the mentor to clarify the procedures for advancement or promotion by explaining which of the publication criteria or other qualifications are most likely to be weighted. The mentor also might provide a sensitive listening ear to personal problems and provide helpful information—but does not serve as a therapist or guidance counselor.

A mentor is not a supervisor but may inadvertently provide supervisory guidance in solving a problem. For example, a mentor may provide a sympathetic yet carefully evaluative review of a proposed research article or office project. Although I did not realize it at the time, one dean took it upon himself to shape my administrative skills very subtly. Whenever I submitted a memo or budget request, I would frequently get back a suggestion about how to improve something, a better product to purchase, or information on products that might make things better. It took me years to realize it, but it had a major effect on my career.

There is one area where assigned mentorship appears to be severely limited. Several organizations call for persons to serve as a pool of mentors for new members. Usually an enthusiastic number of persons volunteer. Then they wait. The new members usually do not know what to ask, and the pool members rarely learn who the new members are. All too often, it ends in a standstill. Yet, even here, much depends upon personalities. On occasion, long-time friendships have arisen from such mentoring pools.

REFERENCE

Allen, R. (2005). Mentoring: A skill professional statisticians can develop. *Amstat News, 1335,* 9–12.

Chapter 12

Mentoring Needs of EVERYWOMAN: The Accidental Mentor and Beyond

Carole A. Rayburn

My mother, Mary Helen Milkie Miller, was my first and most persistent mentor. From the time that I was four, she convinced me that college was the very next place I would go after high school. Terrible things happened, she warned, to those who did not continue their education beyond high school. She so convinced me in her serious and active honing of my potential that I had visions of being a truant and going to a juvenile delinquency center if I dropped out of high school and failed to attend college. She had graduated from a very good university with a degree in economics when few women were earning college degrees. From a good home with two successful brothers, she nonetheless was one of three daughters who did not get any encouragement or incentive to go beyond high school. Perhaps that was what motivated her to ensure that her daughter would receive all of the faith, guidance, counsel, and encouragement to seek the highest levels of education possible. In any event, though I did not always appreciate meeting her high expectations, she did get me off to a fine start.

Schools and teachers in general were experienced by me as extremely happy and rewarding places and people. One of the rewards of having high grades in junior high school was being asked to work in the office of the school counselor, Katherine Bliss. Ms. Bliss, a warm, caring, wise counselor, was quick to encourage students and to bring out the best in them. Seeing how she handled very difficult problems with the students, lessening their fear of punishment, accepting them as basically good persons, and helping them to improve their behavior no doubt was a strong reason that I wanted to emulate such a wonderful person. Part of my wanting to help others in counseling and psychotherapeutic relationships, then, was my identity with this kind, knowledgeable, and skilled woman. She was indeed mentoring me by the example of her work and personality.

Although the high school teachers who served as good mentors to me are too numerous to mention all of them, my homeroom teacher, Ida Lou Holmes, stands out. The student council had representatives from every homeroom, and Mrs. Holmes decided to draw a student's name from the pieces of papers placed in a big box. I will never know whether Mrs. Holmes truly drew my name or if she just decided on her own that I would make the best student council representative for my class when she pulled a piece of paper from the box and called out my name as the winner. She mentored me every day by her encouragement and praise that I, a rather shy adolescent at times, badly needed. She certainly piqued my interest in governance, politics, and serving others.

Teachers at the four universities that I attended performed various degrees of mentoring in the sense of guiding, counseling, and encouraging me. The most helpful ones were patient, kind, skillful, and insightful. They could see the best in me that I often failed to envision within myself. Their enthusiasm was contagious and soothed the depths of my being, enabling me to gain a greater sense of self-worth for whatever project I was completing.

From the time that I was a young child, I had always been attracted to rocks and stones that I dug out of the dirt in a park near my home. I would bring these dirt-covered, treasured finds home, wash them, clean them with a toothbrush, polish them, and discover their internal facets once I broke them in two with my hammer. In that way, I was able to gaze upon their inner core and to see their luster and beauty shining through. I think of mentoring in that way: The mentor has the vision to look beyond the surface of another person and to imagine the finished product after the outer, unpolished exterior is primed and the true innermost or potential part is encouraged to come to fruition in shining glory.

At my universities, my peers were often quite good at mentoring me, and I mutually mentored them. Many times, good, trusted classmates are invaluable in being honest but not cruel in sharing their assessment of your skills and progress. One such treasured friend and mentor was Elaine N. Miller. We toiled in many psychology classes together, cheering each other on to survival in the most difficult classes and with the most critical professors. We remained friends throughout our lives, and when she died a few years ago, I felt a very deep loss. Mentors can become so much a part of you that their deaths leave a large hole in your life, but the memories of their friendship and comradeship are so dear that what is most remembered are the happy times.

As a lifelong feminist, one really negative incident stands out in my memory concerning a psychologist whom I first met during my practicum and externship at a local general hospital and who shortly afterward became the chair of the psychology department at my university. I thought quite highly of him and his clinical skills. However, his woman assistant overhead him say to a potential applicant to the clinical master's program, "Let's see . . . You're male and young, and if you are rich too, you are in!" His deep bow to male chauvinism in its ugliest form left an indelible stain on the way that I perceived this person whom I had so esteemed and admired as a mentor.

During my master's degree study, I married Ronald Allen Rayburn, a most affirming mentor as well as a beloved husband. The youngest son of a mother who was an extremely intelligent and skilled writer, he was used to strong and talented women and was very motivated to help a woman to find the best within herself en route to self-actualization. He was an electrical-electronic engineer who was brilliant at analysis of not only physical instruments and environments but people as well. He could have been a psychologist as well as an engineer. Ronnie observed what I could do and extrapolated much beyond that to what I could do in the future. One of the mentoring skills he had was lessening my fear of math, statistics, and computers. Sharing his skills and knowledge was his forte, and he truly wanted to have the very best develop in those whom he loved. Shortly before he died at a very early age, he left me with the most poignant and affirming words that anyone could ever give another person. He was working on his doctorate in engineering and knew that he would never live to complete it. He said, "I guess, after all, you are my major accomplishment." In every way, I am grateful that he was—and still is in my memory—my most treasured soul mate and mentor.

Another man who was vital in mentoring me while I was externing at the general hospital during my master's program was William R. Reevy. Whenever something was presented in rounds or seminars that did not make sense to me, Dr. Reevy said to look up all the presenting symptoms in the hospital library until I found an explanation for the matter that perplexed me. Intuitively, I knew that I was right, but Dr. Reevy persuaded me to produce the hard evidence to prove my doubts had been warranted. This tremendous mentor and I have kept in touch for many decades, and I have met his wife Carolyn and his three children and their families. Again, this mentor and my other mentors have become an integral part of my life, never to be forgotten.

Two of the most unforgettable professors during my doctorate years were Rita Buddeke and Calvin Burnett. On the day that I registered for classes at the university, Dr. Buddeke saw that I was standing in line for an advisor whom she knew was notorious in needlessly demanding students to redo their dissertation over so much that they spent years more before graduating—if they were able to overcome their frustration and depression enough to focus on graduating at all. Dr. Buddeke yanked me out of that line and said that she would be my advisor. Thanks to this wonderful nun and psychologist who became not only my advisor but my esteemed mentor as well, I graduated with my PhD after only slightly more than two years in the doctoral program.

Dr. Calvin Burnett had been my professor for a course, and he so impressed me that I asked him if he would sit on my oral defense of my dissertation. His presence was also important because my study, "Socioeconomic and Ethnic Variables in Concept Formation of Late Childhood," involved white and African American children, and Dr. Burnett, an African-American, could be most discerning of that aspect of my study. He was always encouraging and affirming, wanting to bring out the highest potential within me. Dr. Burnett became the president of Coppin State College in Baltimore, Maryland. My doctoral experience was definitely richer and more meaningful with the presence of and mentoring by these two professors in my life.

A friend and coworker in the psychology department of a juvenile delinquency center, Suzanne B. Sobel—who had considerable political and networking acumen—was instrumental in guiding me onto a new path in my life when I was sensing a call to the gospel ministry. This would mean a real separation from my work at the center and from my private practice and consulting in psychology. After listening to me for countless hours about the pros and cons of such a decision, Suzanne said, "Why don't you?" I trusted her wisdom and that she had known me for years as a friend and colleague, and so I decided to leave everything to go off to a theological seminary. Although the environment in ministry at that time (and even now in my denomination) was far short of being conducive to women clergy, I gained a special knowledge and insight into the stresses of clergy and especially of women seminarians and clergy. I was able, trusting my strong intuitive powers and motivated to question what was happening in this field, to develop several inventories in religion (Rayburn, 1997), clergy stress (Birk, Rayburn, & Richmond, 2001; Rayburn & Richmond, 1986), spirituality (Rayburn & Richmond, 1996), and state-trait morality (Rayburn, 1987; Rayburn, Birk, & Richmond, 1994; Rayburn & Richmond, 1994). I was also able to publish after graduation from seminary all but one seminary class paper. With the quarter system, I had to double the class papers that would have been expected in the semester system, so there were many potentially publishable papers to submit. The number of journal articles and book chapters that resulted from this newly cultivated field, which led directly from Dr. Sobel's carefully thought through recommendation, contributed to my being appointed a fellow in the American Psychological Association (APA) Division on the Psychology of Religion (as well as being elected as the president in this division and receiving its mentoring and research awards) and in many other APA divisions.

A lifetime fervent feminist, I was not fully prepared for the extreme chauvinism that was to face me as one of four women in an essentially male bastion of 350 seminarians (Rayburn, 1981a, 1981b, 2008; Rayburn, Natale, & Linzer, 1982; Rayburn & Richmond, 2002). Not only was I thrust into a new city and state, a new field of study, and into the fast-paced quarter system, but I was thrown into a climate not as friendly and accepting of women's leadership and accomplishment—at least within the seminary setting—as the one in which I had spent most of my life. Being greeted by the professor as part of the almost totally male classes twice a day with "Good morning, gentlemen!" was not my idea of welcoming nor inclusion. The professor in one class often called upon me to elucidate concepts in Philip Zimbardo's book that we were using as our class textbook. However, this class experience was rendered uncomfortable by his continued reference to the class as "brothers" and "brethren." Being the only woman in the class, I was no longer willing to tolerate such a putdown. Not wanting to start a world war, I waited until the end of one of the classes, after the other students had left the room. I approached him about my not feeling comfortable or included when I was labeled with the male identity of "brother" and "brethren." As he screamed and almost foamed at the mouth, causing all of the students to return to the room, he wrote on the blackboard in huge letters, "BRETHREN = SISTERS." I replied, "All right, then, if they are the same, tomorrow I will call YOU SISTER!" I thought he would fall over in shock. However, the next day, he referred to "Brethren and SISTER Rayburn!" So, in a very real sense, I ended up mentoring many of my seminary professors and coseminarians as well, bringing them up to date in more gender-fair balance.

To maintain any semblance of equilibrium in such a setting, I had to call home to Maryland several times a week to touch bases with feminist friends and colleagues. For the first time in my life, I joined the local chapter of the National Organization for Women, whose president, Joan Walker, became a mentor in how to traverse the paths of feminism in a severe patriarchal establishment. One of my coseminarians, a man of color, Michael Meyers, was also of great help in mentoring me through such an environment, encouraging and even praising me for having the courage to be at seminary.

Decades later, Reverend Meyers and his family are still very good friends. He invited me on several occasions to provide a special program at his churches in Texas and Louisiana, in which I did frontline counseling and therapy, consulting, and even the pastoral services of preaching. He had prepared these churches, African American congregants, for me—a white woman—and mentored me in how to best serve them.

Spanning several years before and after I applied to seminary, I was very active in the APA Division of Clinical Psychology's Committee on Equal Opportunity and Affirmative Action (EOAA). There I met Dr. Bonnie Strickland and Dr. Diane Willis, both warm, affirming, and very wise mentors who counseled me and nominated me for various APA governance positions. The EOAA committee developed a talent bank for women, ethnic minorities, lesbians, gay men, persons with disabilities, and other diverse populations. The Division of Clinical Psychology's Section on the Clinical Psychology of Women and the Section on Ethnic Minority Affairs evolved from the EOAA committee (Rayburn, 1984, 1993; Strickland, 2008).

Dr. Strickland became a president of APA and was a founder of the American Psychological Society. She was always generous with her counsel in leadership and governance within professional organizations. When I was president of the Maryland Psychological Association (MPA), I was able to offer a bit of mentoring to her when she came to the MPA conference at Johns Hopkins University in Maryland while she was running for APA president. Also president of the American Association of Applied and Preventive Psychology (AAAPP; the clinical arm of the American Psychological Society), Dr. Strickland was instrumental in serving as a mentor to me and recruiting me for membership chair and fellows chair for AAAPP.

Dr. Willis was very active in the Division of Clinical Psychology's Section on the Clinical Psychology of Women, and we turned to each other as mentors in this section and for other APA governance matters. Dr. Willis was elected as president of the APA Divisions of Clinical Psychology and of Psychotherapy, and I was elected president of the Division of Clinical Psychology's Section on the Clinical Psychology of Women.

Dr. Asuncion Miteria Austria—Professor of Psychology, Chair and Director of Clinical Training for the Graduate Program at Cardinal Stritch University, former EOAA member, former president of the Section on the Clinical Psychology of Women and of the Section on Ethnic Minority Affairs, APA Council Representative, and recipient of numerous honors and awards from APA—has been a mentor for me, and I have reciprocally been a mentor for her. I have asked her to present and to serve as a discussant on numerous APA conference symposia. We have intensely worked together on issues concerning women and ethnic minorities and have nominated each other for division offices to serve in these matters. On the basis of my having served as adjunct advisor, having been a fellow in several APA divisions, and having studied in many diverse psychology fields, Dr. Austria invited me to serve as a reader and advisor to her graduate psychology students at Cardinal Stritch University. Working with her students has added another delightful dimension to my professional experiences. A Filipino American, Dr. Austria has taught me much about her birth culture and about Asian Americans. This ethnicity knowledge that she shared has served me quite well, as when I presented research studies at a conference in the Philippines and was even able to coordinate studies using one of my psychological inventories with a Filipina professor in the Philippines. Having been mentored by Dr. Austria and learning about Filipinos, I truly appreciated the beauty, friendliness, and resilience of these people (Austria, 2008; Rayburn & Osman, 2005). Another role that I deeply appreciate is serving as fellows chair (my second term) for the Division of Clinical Psychology; Dr. Austria recommended me for this position. She has been a wonderful and joyful mentor, bringing out the best in me and all others who are fortunate enough to be mentored by her.

Dr. Violet Franks, a former president of the Division of Clinical Psychology's Section on the Clinical Psychology of Women, has also been a lifelong friend and colleague. I mentored her with regard to section matters, and she mentored me on the Springer Focus on Women series, for which she was an editor for Springer Publications, asking me to co-edit the series with her. Her suggestions have always been invaluable, particularly regarding publishing and editing. Recounting her experiences with mentors, Dr. Violet Franks related that she has had "a few good mentors and many tormentors—those who put you down instead of acknowledging the good that you do!" Learning to recognize the difference between good mentors and tormentors is vital, she emphasized. Attending to your own stress and strain in working with a tormentor in a mentoring situation is all important. This was the case of Sr. Rita Buddeke pulling me out of the line to a more tormenting than mentoring faculty member in the previously mentioned situation in graduate school.

Dr. Cyril Franks, incomparable editor of the journal *Child and Family Behavior Therapy*, a founder of Behavior Therapy, and founder and first president of the Association for the Advancement of Behavior Therapy, has constantly given me the very sagest of advice and publishing and editing guidance. He has been extremely gracious in honoring me on several occasions by inviting me to co-chair symposia on behavior therapy at APA conventions and with such leaders and extraordinary proponents in this field as himself and his colleagues. Dr. Franks combines gentleness, firmness, and a fine sense of humor in his mentoring. He knows everybody and is generous in sharing his considerable skills and vast knowledge, as well as his networking abilities, with those whom he mentors.

Although women have been prized in general as good role models and fine mentors—and indeed they are that—some men have bridged the gap between the genders and thus have become models themselves of fine feminists and wonderful trainers of women mentees. Gilbert and Rossman (1992) have noted this advantage of having a man mentor in terms of potentially giving the mentee much visibility, recognition, and networking. Getting back into a more active role within APA divisions, I was in a rather unique position of being the liaison between the Divisions on the Psychology of Religion and the Psychology of Women, trying desperately to bring about a rapprochement between these two seemingly different worlds. When the best of my efforts nonetheless failed, I resigned from this role. The Division of Psychology of Religion did not seem inviting to a staunch feminist involved in religious and spiritual matters; nor at that time did the Division of the Psychology of Women appear to be tolerant of women who valued religion and spirituality. To his day, there is less of an understanding between the two value systems than a religious and spiritual woman would desire. Easing my transition into greater involvement in the Division of Psychology of Religion was a gentle, wise Sister Eileen A. Gavin, a psychology department chair at the College of St. Catherine and president of the Division of the Psychology of Religion. Through Dr. Gavin's mentoring, I was able to better navigate in the division. Years later, when Dr. Violet Franks and I co-edited the Springer Focus on Women series, I was pleased to invite Dr. Gavin to co-edit a book with two other colleagues for this series, and I wrote a chapter about one of my all-time favorite Americans, Dr. Alice Paul, author of the Equal Rights Amendment, who was instrumental in getting the l9th Amendment to the U.S. Constitution passed, giving women the right to vote (Rayburn, 2007). All of this I owe to good networking and mentoring!

Another nun, feisty and devoutly feminist Margaret Gorman, saw me as a sister feminist in religious endeavors and mentored me and greased the wheels to get me elected as president of the Psychology of Religion Division. Much of this Dr. Gorman did behind the scenes without my knowing the extent to which she was responsible for my successful election.

Dr. Mary Reuder is an experimental psychologist, professor emerita of psychology at Queens College at the City University of New York, a former president of the APA Divisions of General Psychology and simultaneously of the Psychology of Religion, and continually elected council representative from the Division of the Psychology of Religion to APA. Years ago, she gave a paper on creative teaching at the Eastern Psychological Association, which so inspired me and a colleague that we wished that we had been taught by this teacher par excellence in our undergraduate years. In her presentation, Dr. Reuder spoke of drawing the most and the best out of her students, impressing upon them the need to give their best to any projects that they undertook. Dr. Reuder has mentored me in governance as well as by reviewing my curriculum vita in preparation for applying for fellow status in APA divisions. Dr. Reuder is peerless in her ability to organize and shape a vita to maximize election to fellow status in almost any APA division. Her skill in this ability and her prowess in keen psychopolitical understanding are legendary. Analytical in her approach to all things, she seems to use the Socratic method for pulling ideas out of her mentees by asking questions and getting them to delve into their minds to pull out better-than-adequate answers. Forever seeking the truth in what is supposed to be a rational world, she elicits clear thinking and deliberation from others. She does this usually in a nonjudgmental fashion, but she is not lax in redirecting any serious straying from reason by interjecting the appropriate questions and patiently waiting for the best and most accurate answers. When she was not able to attend council one year, she honored me by allowing me to act as her substitute. Her mentoring in this regard gave me additional insights into top-level APA governance.

Dr. Ralph Hood, whom I also met in the Division of the Psychology of Religion, has been another tremendous mentor. Dr. Hood has helped me with publications in the psychology of religion, inviting me to write chapters for some books that he was editing (Rayburn, 1995d). He is a truly egalitarian and open-minded man in the field of the psychology of religion.

Dr. Samuel M. Natale—psychologist, Jesuit priest, journal editor, conference convener at Oxford University, and university professor—has in all ways been a fine mentor and esteemed colleague and friend through many decades. Dr. Natale invited me to be an associate and guest editor for the *Journal of Pastoral Counseling* for which he was the editor at Iona College. Convening bi-yearly conferences at his alma mater, Oxford University in England, he continued to invite my presentations throughout the years. He also has invited me to be a reviewer for journals that he edits. Dr. Natale mentors both women and men, and he does so with such a delightful sense of humor as to relax and affirm those with whom he works. A highly creative person, he engenders creativity in mentees and has always been open to new ideas of others. Dr. Natale is pleased by the success of those whom he teaches and mentors, inviting the challenges and innovations of others. As with most good mentors, he is goal oriented as well as keenly observant and appreciative of the personal skills and talents of mentees.

Dr. Lee J. Richmond—past president of the American Counseling Association and of the National Career Development Association, professor formerly at Johns Hopkins University and currently at Loyola College in Maryland, coauthor and co-editor (Eanes & Richmond, 2001) of several books, contributor to journals, researcher, recipient of teaching awards and honors—has been a long-time mentor to me as well as an esteemed friend and colleague. We have developed and copyrighted 17 psychological inventories and presented and published studies involving them nationally and internationally. We have been a research team for several decades, mentoring each other through the instrument design, statistical analyses, presentations, and publications. We also developed, presented, and published the theory, field, and discipline of theobiology—the interface of theology, religion, and spirituality with biology and the other sciences

(Rayburn, 2001; Rayburn & Richmond, 1998, 2002). We comentor, bouncing ideas off of each other and guiding the thread of these weaves to a completed garment.

Dr. Janice Birk, professor, past president of the APA Division of Counseling Psychology, and a former nun, has been a perfect fit for working with Dr. Richmond and me on clergy stress (Birk et al., 2001; Rayburn, Richmond, & Rogers, 1982, 1983, 1994) and state-trait morality (Rayburn, 1987; Rayburn & Richmond, 1994; Rayburn, Richmond, & Birk, 1994). Her careful, scholarly approach served as a fine model in our mentoring team of three. She has been an esteemed friend and colleague for decades.

From Drs. Richmond and Birk, I developed better presentation and publication skills. Besides their confidence in and affirmation of me as a co-researcher, both of them are highly skilled and talented teachers and counselors who helped to draw from me my best efforts in our joint research, presentations, and publications (Birk et al., 2001; Rayburn, Birk, & Richmond, 1994; Rayburn, Richmond, & Rogers, 1986).

For years as a member of the APA Division of the Psychology of Women, I had read with interest the sage and insightful Aunt Academe column in the division newsletter by Harriet Aronson. Dr. Aronson is a professor at the University of North Texas in Denton, past president of the Division of Clinical Psychology's Section on the Clinical Psychology of Women, and a clinical psychologist who began her career in medical school research, making a name for herself for her study that established the efficacy of tricyclics for the treatment of depression. Taking more of a nature (biological) approach to learning theory rather than the more popular nurture (environmental) one, she chaired a funded APA task force to study the effects of changing gender roles on the clinical profession and academic programs. Dr. Aronson's psychopharmacology background may be what has made her a provocative and challenging mentor and one who is a very good listener and who reflects with constructive criticism on the ideas and thoughts of those whom she mentors. I have been fortunate through the years to receive helpful suggestions from her at crucial points in my research. She knows the field well, is good at networking, and strives to bring out the best in others. She mentors well. It is important for mentees to realize that some mentors may initially seem intimidating by being at all critical and not 100 percent flattering. It is essential to not turn away from such mentoring, however, but to learn that mentoring is, above all, a growth experience and that one Dr. Aronson is worth far more than a galaxy of empty praise-bearing advisors or counselors.

Dr. Florence Denmark—a past president of APA, the International Council of Psychologists, and many divisions of APA; an APA Council Representative; editor and chapter author of several books and journals; and the recipient of multitudes of honors and awards, including election to fellow of the New York Academy of Sciences—received the 2004 APA Gold Medal for Lifetime Achievement and the 2007 Raymond Fowler Award for

Outstanding Service to APA. Dr. Denmark, Robert Scott Pace Distinguished Research Professor of Psychology at Pace University, is an internationally recognized policymaker, scholar, and researcher who has maintained a long-time interest in mentoring and has been a caring and laudatory mentor of many individuals. I consider myself fortunate for being one of her mentees and that her social skills, wisdom, and networking abilities have been made available to me to help me over the humps in my career. In fact, it was her strong interest in mentoring and her caring to share her knowledge that led her to propose that this handbook for women mentors be written. Many professional women owe much to Dr. Denmark for her generously sharing her vast talents, skills, and considerable political acumen and networking.

It certainly is no coincidence that almost all of the mentors in my life participated in a series of workshops on mentoring given at the APA Convention, August 11–13, 1995. I had proposed such workshops, and APA was so committed to mentoring that I was allowed, as chair, to put together a 12-hour series of six workshops of 2 hours each (Rayburn, 1995a, 1995b, 1995c). The workshop series was called Mentoring Women and People of Color for Leadership in Organized Psychology, Workshops 1 and 2 were about identifying barriers. Workshops 3and 4 discussed solutions and strategies. Workshops 5 and 6 were about building leadership skills. Presenters were quite diverse, with women and men, lesbians, gay men, and persons with disabilities being represented. In fact, APA even helped to pay for a reception after the final workshop, being committed to the social networking and long-lasting effects that such an experience had brought about. All reports indicated that the mentoring workshops were a success and that attendees and presenters alike profited from the outreach. Women who participated in these workshops and who have been comentors for me include Harriet Aronson, Asuncion Miteria Austria, Joan Chrisler, Lillian Comas-Diaz, Florence Denmark, Cyril and Violet Franks, Gwendolyn Puryear Keita, Mary Reuder, Nancy Felipe Russo, Bonnie Strickland, and Diane Willis. Joan Chrisler, past president of the APA Society for the Psychology of Women and the Division of General Psychology, has invited me to write chapters for books that she has edited and to co-chair and be a member of an APA division committee especially concerning women and international psychology. I have invited Dr. Chrisler to be part of several symposia that I have organized for APA annual conventions and have repeatedly supported her bid for APA divisional offices and for an international psychology association.

THE ACCIDENTAL MENTOR

Most of my life, others have credited me with having been their mentor, but at the time I did not realize that I was playing this role in their lives. They credited me for encouraging them to take a certain job, starting a specific academic program, or even writing a book. Possibly this was related to my enthusiasm, intuitive prowess, creative thinking, and caring for people. I have usually been one to come up with several ideas, which like, Winston Churchill's reputed brainstorms, proved to have at least 3 out of 10 that were usable. Too, I most likely caught people just at the juncture of their deciding to make some decision, to conclude some action. Perhaps all they needed was someone who would listen to them and analytically critique their idea or action and then to enthusiastically give them the go-ahead. My recipe for good mentoring, formal or—as in the case of acci-dental mentoring—informal, is one part strong belief in the individual's potential, skills, and talents to creatively design and produce some unique work one very large part enthusiasm, and another generous helping of encouragement. Enthusiasm is contagious and spurs mentees on to higher reaches of their productivity and satisfaction with a job well done. Much of a good mentoring relationship is sensible and sensitive caring toward the other person.

EVERYWOMAN NEEDS A MENTOR

Whether she is entering the halls of academe; beginning on the path to a new job or career track; or learning to cook, sew, or keep house beautiful, EVERYWOMAN can benefit from having a mentor—preferably a woman mentor who has been there and done that and can show her how it is done. This cuts down on needless trial and error and saves precious time, trouble, and painful frustration. Of course, some hands-on performance, even the wringing-of-the-hands variety, is necessary to the learning pro-cess, but this does not need to be drawn out forever. When we do things without the advice, teaching, and guidance of more experienced women, we may fear failure and give up the project before we can have the satis-faction of seeing a job successfully completed. There is no special reward or door prize for roughing it by not having a mentor and doing all of the hard work void of constructive objective listening and feedback that a mentor can provide. Besides, the modeling of a close interpersonal pro-fessional mentoring relationship is one that can prove beneficial to both mentors and mentees throughout their lives.

THE IMPORTANCE OF HAVING A MENTOR

Throughout an individual's life span, the way is made lighter and the goals are illuminated more clearly by having a mentor. Mentors come in all genders, races, and ethnicities and contribute to mentees in unique and priceless ways. Sometimes the mentor reaches out to the mentee, as in the case of Dr. Buddeke rescuing me from sure frustration and mentoring doom. More often, however, the potential mentee needs to do the searching and reaching. Sometimes this search by the mentee starts with a feeling of discomfort in not readily seeing the next step on the road to achievement, a sense that something is missing, not well enough defined, or simply in need of reflecting upon with a trusted teacher, guide, inspiring tutor, coach, or counselor. Nor are mentors to be limited in number, time, or place. The very important person or persons in one's life may come along at various times in life and at diverse places in one's career. Each mentor may share the mentoring role with others and for many different and specific matters. The common thread is drawn around meaningful caring and sharing, hand holding, anticipatory planning, fear reduction, trusting, and enthusiastic honing of the mentee's innermost potential skills, talents, and knowledge. Vital to the best mentoring relationship is the mentor's belief in the mentee's promising future, the confidence that the mentee will be a success.

Benefits to those who have mentors include receiving more information (Ragins, Cotton, & Miller, 2000; Ragins & Kram, 2007), generally having more career satisfaction (Fagenson, 1988), more positive job experience and employment options (Baugh, Lankan, & Scandura, 1996), and higher incomes (Dreher & Ash, 1990; Whitely, Dougherty, & Dreher, 1991). Heisted (1999) reported that mentoring provides improved employee motivation, commitment, performance, and retention and may serve to identify talent, accelerate leadership development, and provide on-the-job-training.

IMPORTANCE OF HAVING WOMEN MENTORS FOR WOMEN MENTEES

While men as well as women may provide excellent mentoring to mentees, women mentors often seem to be the most approachable for women mentees. They also serve as wonderful role models—women who have made it and who are willing to share with others from a position of success and power emit the sweet and enticing scent of success that beckons others to follow their lead. Women mentors benefit in the mentoring relationship by gaining a loyal base of support, organizational recognition and status, improved job performance, and career reinvigoration (Kram, 1985). Concerning the accessibility of mentors, women perceive that mentoring relationships are less available to them than to men (Ibarra, 1993; Ragins & Cotton, 1991), and, because of the dearth of women as role models and mentors, women seeking women mentors have often been more frustrated and anxious in this goal. Acclimating to a new and challenging or threatening graduate program and environment may seem frightening, overwhelming, even a culture shock in terms of the mores of the setting (Ellis, 2001; Wilson, 2003). This most certainly was the case for me when I entered the ministerial program at a seminary (Rayburn, 1981a, 1981b).

While I was getting my ministerial training at a seminary, in which men students clearly dominated the program, it would have helped immensely if there had been more than one woman professor to serve as a role model and mentor to guide me through this experience. There was only one woman on the faculty, the biblical languages professor, and although she was a bona fides feminist, she did very little for me that would have been considered coaching or mentoring. Her lack of reaching out to the four women seminarians might have been due to her own insecurity in being seen as bucking the patriarchal system of ecclesia. Or she might have fallen into the trap of relishing her special place as the only woman professor in an otherwise all-male enclave. Or she might have mistakenly thought that, since I already had my PhD in psychology, I did not need additional mentoring. I, on the other hand, was almost overwhelmed with the male chauvinism of seminary existence; during this period of my life, I was more conscious of the pitfalls for women in seminary and who were intent on becoming clergypersons. I concentrated daily on just how to survive to get through with my master's of divinity program and to make as few waves as possible. Of course, for a devout religious and spiritual feminist in such a setting, an occasional tidal wave was inevitable. Even a tsunami might erupt on a rare occasion. For both calmer and unnerving times en route to completing my seminary training, I would have benefitted tremendously from the sensitive caring and sharing of a trusted guide. Such a mentor would have reduced my frustrations, anxieties, fears, and anger. I did have a man mentor assigned to me when I began my seminary program, but a woman's insights and guidance in addition to or instead of his might have benefitted me more. Furthermore, although there were several men advisors and teachers who were helpful at times in my seminary training, usually they seemed unable to overcome the pervasive basic men's bias that prevented them and the seminary body as a whole to be more welcoming and accepting of women in seminary. One of my professors had even related in class that "theology just isn't a woman's 'cup of tea.'" This not only seemed to be taken out of rational context, but also was despite the fact that I was getting an A in his theology class and graduating magna cum laude! Besides the unaddressed sexist attitudes toward women, power games, and gender politics might have factored into such a setting as seminary. Though the one woman on the faculty was a feminist and outspoken, she might well have been restricted by these political power games and thus limited in her ability to initiate the opportunity to initiate a mentoring relationship with the very few women in seminary.

The fact that very few women had gone through the ministerial track at this seminary meant that there were no real role models for me or the other women in ministry. For women who choose to enter traditionally men-dominated fields, this scarcity of women role models and mentors is a handicap and a disadvantage that men students do not experience. In a very real way, the many feminists whom I called several times a week from back home were mentoring me in helping me keep my head about me and overcome the putdowns in a discriminatory setting. In the seminary and in other male-dominated fields, women are at best novelties to marvel about or at worst ill-fitting pieces in the ecclesial picture-puzzle of holiness.

At the very least, a woman mentor could have provided the support, attention, and understanding by listening to the mentee's ideas and strategy planning. Bouncing off ideas with a mentor and getting some objective and constructive feedback goes a long way to lessening feelings of isolation and wandering too far off the path on the road to optimal career development. Just knowing that someone truly cares about one's progress in the program and personal development and having the opportunity to network with a mentor and to continue the relationship can result in higher productivity, greater satisfaction, earlier promotion, and even the possibility of higher salaries (Castro, Caldwell, & Salazar, 2005; Ragins & Cotton, 1999; Wilson, 2001).

Access to within-profession and within-department mentors to enable women to maneuver and clarify implied regulations and rules of the academic and business environments are often not sufficiently available to women. This hampers their advancement (Cawyer, Simonds, & Davis, 2002), although women and ethnic minorities may achieve through mentoring relationships advantages like those usually given to junior members of ethnic majority individuals (Wilson, 2001). Women mentors working with women mentees enables women of all ranks to come together, supporting professional women and their field of concentration as well (Wilson, 2003).

It is particularly vital for women mentees, especially those in traditionally male-dominated fields, to know that their mentors will patiently listen to what they say and offer objective critical feedback. This lessens women mentees' sense of isolation, fright, and fear of failure and loss of self-esteem and self-confidence. Women mentors can provide guidance without gender bias.

COMPARISON BETWEEN WOMEN AND MEN MENTORS OF WOMEN MENTEES

Men mentors often need to overcome their gender biases, power compulsions, and gender politics before they can be good mentors for women. From potential women mentees' part of the relationship, they have been socialized to function as subservient, obedient students and women with assertive men, and such double-bind roles may interfere with cross-gender mentoring (Olson & Ashton-Jones, 1992). Men mentors have somewhat of an advantage, due to the power differential, to promote and sponsor women mentees, giving the mentees more visibility, recognition, and networking opportunities (Gilbert & Rossman, 1992). On the other hand, women mentors usually provide their women mentees more social support and networking, focusing less on the power differential within the mentoring relationship than men mentors do. Thus, women mentees who choose women mentors usually do so on the basis of purposefulness, while those who choose men mentors do so for the power and influence possibilities.

While men who mentor women often focus more on the power differentials within the mentoring relationship and may turn out mentees who strongly identify with them (see the case of the psychology department chair previously mentioned who would award admission to graduate school based on the applicant being "male, young, and rich"), women who mentor women are more likely than their men counterparts to emphasize networking and social supports. Further, women mentors may more often target women mentees' abilities and potential especially to satisfy the women mentors' needs for successful mentees who will enable the women mentors to get validation and status advancement (Allen, Poteet, & Russell, 2000). As more women enter men-dominated fields, the playing field will be leveled more and the situation for both women mentors and women mentees will reflect equality and more evidence the benefits of having women mentors (Castro et al., 2005).

Concerning executive mentors, women were as likely as men to be mentors and to report outcomes and intentions for future mentoring similar to what was found for the men (Ragins & Scandura, 1994). In regard to termination of the mentoring relationship, when gender differences in tenure, rank, and other organizational and demographic variables were controlled, women and men mentors (ranked by a matched group of former mentees) evidenced no differences in reasons for termination of the relationship nor in the duration or number of prior relationships (Ragins & Scandura, 1997).

COMPARISONS OF CROSS-CULTURAL AND CROSS-ETHNIC MENTORING RELATIONSHIPS

I have been fortunate to have not only women and men mentors but also mentors from cultures different from my own North American white one. Calvin Burnett and Reverend Michael Meyers, as well as Francis Terrell of the University of North Texas in Denton, are African American men who have been and continue to be my mentors. I met Dr. Terrell through the networking skills of another fine mentor, Dr. Harriet Aronson, professor emerita from the University of North Texas. Dr. Terrell has helped me tremendously in several research projects, getting me student populations to assess for my studies in inventory development. A very modest, scholarly, spiritual researcher and professor, he has done notable research on African Americans and their health issues as social identity.

Women mentors from other ethnic and cultural backgrounds who have been and still are mentors and comentors for me include Asuncion Miteria Austria, an Asian American originally from the Philippines, and in a co-mentoring and copublishing sense, Lillian Comas-Diaz, a Latina American originally from Puerto Rico. Dr. Comas-Diaz is the executive director of the Transcultural Mental Health Institute, a clinical professor at George Washington University, a private practitioner, former director of the APA Office of Ethnic Minority Affairs, and recipient of numerous professional awards. Dr. Comas-Diaz had approached me and asked me to co-edit a book with her, *WomanSoul: The Inner Life of Women's Spirituality* (Rayburn & Comas-Diaz, 2008). This joint effort proudly includes spiritual women across many racial, ethnic, and cultural backgrounds, and it has been a thrilling inspiration to learn of their journeys through life and their connection with the spirituality that sustained them. Such cross-cultural mentoring has proved to be a priceless learning and enriching experience, the spiritual feast for a lifetime of meaningful and blessed existence.

There has been continual underrepresentation of people of color in faculties and in professions, leading to limited cultural mentors available to potential mentees of the same or different cultural background (Castro et al., 2005; Dinsmore & England, 1996). Sensitivity to differences in power dynamics and cross-cultural communication is needed, especially between North American whites and people of color (Brinson & Kottler, 1993). The many Asian and Latino/Latina mentees and the relatively few mentors of these backgrounds may be a handicap in the mentoring relationship that North American whites do not seem to have (Thomas, 1993). However, it is essential to note that ethnic and racial groups cannot be legitimately piled into four or more large groups of Africans, Asians, Hispanics, and Europeans, since many intra- and intergroup differences usually exist. So in the Asian group, it is vital to understand that Chinese does not equal Korean nor Japanese nor Filipino nor Cambodian nor Laosian nor Vietnamese; likewise, in African American does not equal West Indian nor South African nor Haitian nor Kenyan nor South African nor Jamaican. Hispanic does not equal Mexican nor Brazilian nor Argentine nor Columbian nor Cuban nor Guatemalan nor Peruvian. In the European American or European descent group, North American does not equal British nor Swedish nor Polish nor Irish nor German nor Russian nor Spanish nor Italian nor Norwegian. Each group has its own cultural identification and mores. If ever there was a case for one size does *not* fit all" this is it!

CRITICAL THINKING VERSUS ONE SIZE FITS ALL

While much can be said for fitting into the academic community with its rules, regulations, politics, communication pipelines, philosophies, and values, there will come a critical point in the life of the mentee when critical thinking—popular or not, politically correct or not—will be necessary to truly develop into a skillful, analytical professional who can think outside the box. Throughout life, we are most often taught the concept that one size fits all, no matter how otherwise diverse the environment may be perceived. In networking, for instance, women may have ideas or beliefs thrust upon them in a one-size-fits-all approach. Women's professional and social organizations may, largely for the sake of the cohesiveness of the organization than for the stability or independent thinking of its members, attempt to bring about groupthink. Forcing consensus socially or intellectually to give the appearance of unity in a common cause can be deadly to critical thinking. Underlying such imposed "agreement" of proposed ideas is often the attempt to cover up dissenting vices or thoughts, justifying groupthink. Thus, all individuals in a group will appear to undoubtedly think and act alike, or at least the group or organization believes that they *should* be clones for the common good. Such actions are far more likely to develop perpetual followers rather than leaders.

In terms of ethnicity, the one-size-fits-all approach may lead people of diverse backgrounds to deny or hide their ethnic individuality. For instance, while North Americans usually desire to use English as their common language and to demonstrate loyalty to the United States, no requirement or understanding should rule out racial/ethnical and cultural pride and identity in the countries of their ancestors as well. Strivings for any unity in the population pools of people need to have a culminative undertone of all parts of the individual for an ideal blending of color, culture, and ethnicity. Should groupthink win out over the successful blending of these component parts, anger, anxiety, guilt, and shame may result.

In religious denominations, religious or spiritual identity may push groupthink for every tenet of the denomination rather than allowing the subtle, diverse differences to emerge. Many persons may deeply espouse some of the faith traditions and concepts of holy books but be more ecumenical on other points. To the extent that they are not allowed to think for themselves and chance censure for thinking outside the group, they may well become uncomfortable, feel threatened and unworthy, and clash within themselves rather than to be at war with the religious establishment. For instance, religious and spiritual feminists may be miserable in a seminary that preaches gender fairness but holds to traditions of gender bias and discriminates against women clergy.

When groupthink becomes the desirable goal, critical thinking as well as creative thinking is threatened almost to extinction. Therefore, mentors do a service to mentees by alerting them to balance their social need to fit in and gain acceptance by others with their personal needs of being true and authentic with themselves and others.

Special caution needs to be taken in communicating genuine caring for the whole person; not just their educational and professional development but their personal identity and development as well. The tremendous learning possibilities in the two-way street of acquiring knowledge about and appreciation of another culture are extremely beneficial to both mentor and mentee. Both mentors and mentees of color may sense isolation within their faculties, careers, or jobs and understandably may fear and resent any perception that they must deny or relinquish facets of their cultural identity in order to be more acceptable and accepted (Brinson & Kottler, 1993; Williams & Schwiebert, 2000).

Davis and Thakur (1999) studied the impact of subculture differences in mentoring relationship perceptions and needs. African Americans were found to place higher value on same-race mentors, especially those who had similar life experiences. For Latino/Latina Americans, mentor commitment of time to develop a personal relationship with them, for both psychological and social support, was essential. Asian Pacific Islanders valued mentors with proven accomplishments and the respect of their community.

By broadening the circle of connections both within and outside the college and work setting, mentors can lessen the sense of isolation and increase the opportunities for success of mentees of color. Introducing mentees of color to successful mentors and professional women of color can provide them with more diverse and meaningful role models and widen their horizons (Ellis, 2001). In selecting a mentor, Latinas and Latinos differed significantly in regard to mentor age, preference for a close personal relationship with the mentor, and mentor support of self-esteem, and these variations were thought to be related to gender differences of mentees within each ethnicity (Thakur, 2008). Compared to Latinos, Latinas considered mentor age less important and the desire for a closer personal relationship and support of their self-esteem more important (Thakur, 2008).

The influence of the power differential in mentoring relationships must be taken into account. It is likely, according to Thakur (2008), that individuals may seek mentors who have power over them. Latinos (traditionally raised to be more macho, authoritarian, demanding, and controlling) have a higher power base in their culture than Latinas (who have traditionally been reared to be obedient, submissive, and respectful to their parents, especially to their fathers and other men). Thus, Latinos may more often choose to work with a Latino mentor and to view mentor age as an important element in the power differential between their mentors and themselves. Gender differences per se infer a power differential in the mentoring relationship, with Latinas feeling more comfortable in working with cross-gender mentors of various ages. The greater need of Latinas for closer personal relationships with and psychological and social support from their mentors was compared to Latinos' greater need for more career support from their mentors. The power differential was seen as the explanation for these cultural gender differences.

GUIDELINES FOR WOMEN MENTORS

Mentors function to guide, teach, coach, advise, model, protect, supervise, train, and challenge mentees (Kram, 1985, 1988). There are many facets to the role of the potential mentor. Mentors can enhance mentees' careers by smoothing the transition from the academic to the professional or business world, by sponsoring, exposing to new challenges, giving visibility through networking, coaching in new roles, and protecting from adverse situations and persons (Kram, 1985). Through role modeling, counsel, friendship, acceptance, affirmation, and confirmation, mentors can foster professional identity and competence (Kram, 1985). Mentors can facilitate mentees' development or redefine their professional identity through providing a balance of challenge and support (Castro et al., 2005).

Mentors choose from the multifaceted functions of a mentor which specific role(s) they should assume. If the mentee chooses more than one mentoring relationship within the same academic or work setting, the mentor may want to coordinate the efforts of the multiple mentors or at least encourage the mentee to organize schedules and goals with multiple mentors in mind.

With time constraints to be considered, mentors need to strike a balance between their own professional development and mentoring activities. Be accessible, accountable, intentional, and focused in the mentoring relationship. Quantity as well as quality of time commitments are highly important (Castro et al. 2005).

Maintain clear and flexible boundaries, with open communication and constructive feedback. In such an intensely personal as well as professional relationship, imbued by the power differential between mentor and mentee, mentors must focus on the growth and development of the mentee. While aspects of the mentoring relationship may include friendship, with sharing of experiences and concerns, mentorship is primarily a professional and structured enterprise targeting the mentee's learning and professional development. Mentors need to expect the dynamic of power shifts over time when mentees grow into colleagues (Castro et al. 2005).

Mentors would do well to be on watch for the unassimilated, isolated, shy, or quiet students in the academic culture and to get them involved as soon as possible. Such mentor actions can save the professional lives, as well as change the lives, of students who might otherwise slip through the academic cracks (Castro et al. 2005).

By patiently and gradually giving up control in the mentoring relationship, the mentor imbues mentoring with goodness, value, and intrinsic meaning.

Affirm, affirm, and affirm—and with a good sense of humor, enthusiasm, encouragement, and flexibility. Set boundaries and have reasonable goals that are always challenging and inspiring. Be sure to maintain open communication lines. Mentors draw out the potential skills within mentees. By believing in the potential and skills, talents, and commitment of mentees, mentors can better see and correctly identify their unique qualities, consolidate them, and communicate these perceptions to the mentees. Mentors need to be aware of and also communicate to mentees that humans are the most complex creations in the universe, no less than the moon or the stars. Humans are more complex than even rocket science. What makes people so much more difficult to study and to deal with is the fact that people are both subject and object.

Knowing the mentees' strengths and weaknesses, passions, spirit, and potentials, mentors are more able to help mentees to enliven their desire for learning and development. Mentors' awareness and appreciation of the importance of creativity and intuitive prowess in mentee success in leadership, as well as the possibility of helping mentees to develop these attributes, will greatly enhance the mentoring process and relationship (Rayburn, 2006).While going at the mentee's pace, mentors do well to expect more of the mentee than she expects of herself. By lessening mentees' fears in starting a new project, expressing their ideas, meeting new challenges, and networking with new people, mentors can model through their personal experiences that confronting their fears is necessary for progress. Avoidance of fear is nonproductive. Fear reduction is the aim in learning to do research, write, publish, and present studies.

By affirming and confirming mentees' worthiness to be in a graduate program and to receive mentoring, mentors validate mentees and lessen their fear of being invalidated by themselves and others. Mentors do well to inform and encourage mentees to maximize their efforts and output: rather than doing anything for a simple purpose, write a paper that can be presented at a professional meeting, then be prepared with the mentor's help for publication, and perhaps be the basis for applying for a grant.

In explaining expectations to mentees, mentors model the expected performance, provide chances for practice of the involved skills, and explain how performance will be evaluated. In this way, trust is built and performance success rates will be raised.

GUIDELINES FOR WOMEN MENTEES

Mentees, the less experienced individuals in mentoring relationships who are nurtured and trained by mentors for their career/job growth and development (Allen et al., 2000), are the main beneficiaries of mentoring. Mentees usually must take the initiative in establishing mentoring relationships (Fallow & Johnson, 2000). In seeking a mentor, mentees first need to analyze themselves concerning their own strengths and weaknesses; the strength of their motivation to succeed and commit to a professional program; their way of reacting to frustration; their method of dealing with keeping time commitments and scheduled meetings; their personalities with regard to extraversion or introversion; their present and future goals; their career concerns; and their physical, social, and intellectual attributes. Knowing themselves will go a long way to helping their mentor to understand them and most effectively work with them in the mentoring relationship.

An optimal way for a mentee to begin seeking and committing to a mentoring relationship is to have a courageous, curious, inquiring mind; to ask questions; and seek somebody to help answer them. Curious minds and creative thinking, with as much trust in intuitive thinking as possible—or playing one's hunches—will serve mentees well in their research and growth and development, in getting and sustaining the mentoring relationship, and in entering the career or work force after graduation.

While women may have both formal (assignment with a faculty advisor for a specified period of time) or informal (developed on its own with no specific longevity) mentoring relationships, the former often provides less coaching, counseling, social interaction, role modeling, and friendship for women than does informal mentoring (Ragins & Cotton, 1999).

Especially in historically men-dominated fields with underrepresentation of women role models and mentors, women mentees often need to be instructed in the rules, social mores, and history of the professional culture. Without such preparation by especially women mentors, the novice would most likely dwell for too long in an atmosphere of marginalization, isolation, and loneliness (Cawyer et al., 2002).

Mentors often have several needs for various problem-solving situations and may need to initiate mentoring relationships with more than one mentor, within the academic or job setting and in both formal and informal arrangements.

In assessing their skills, mentees should neither underrate nor put down themselves. It is important for them to remember that, in dealing with humans, their task is complex—humans are both the subject and object of this enterprise. Mentees need to polish all of their attributes to make themselves as attractive to potential mentors as possible: They need to become a more visible presence and to show commitment by getting more involved in coursework, research projects, professional meetings and conferences, professional associations and by paying close attention to and feedback on the mentor's advice and critiques.

In seeking a mentor, mentees first need to clarify their expectations, goals, and commitment for the mentoring relationship. Dialogue with others about the prospective mentor(s) is necessary to establish common professional philosophies and values and methods of teaching, coaching, tutoring, training, guidance, networking, and research practices. Given the scarcity of women mentors in most academic and career settings, potential mentees may need to sell themselves to mentors as committed and promising mentees. Individuals seeking a mentor need to know what they want, including a mentoring relationship, and to state this clearly and initiate the relationship as soon as possible.

Mentoring relationships need to be given much loving care. Patience, professional respect, and courtesy are a two-way street. Mentees and mentors alike may find it an advantage to maintain the mentoring relationship for many years. Mentees may share their success and glory by coauthoring or copresenting research for which the mentor has played a significant role. An appreciation lunch, a presentation at a professional-social event, or a presentation of a certificate of recognition of the mentor by the mentee will go a long way to cement a fine and lasting mentoring arrangement. Positive reinforcement is a good learning tool for everyone concerned.

CONCLUSION

Everywoman can benefit from mentoring, deriving more information, tutoring, teaching, counseling, guidance, social support, networking, and protection as the mentored woman progresses in her development. Women mentors benefit, too, in getting more experience in teaching, counseling, and guiding the mentee to greater success and satisfaction with work well done. Women have been less available as role models and mentors in academic and work settings due to gender discrimination that still puts women at a decided disadvantage. There are some indications that that may be improving and that the invaluable flesh-and-blood successful women mentors will be more available for the many potential women mentees who seek their services.

REFERENCES

Allen, T. D., Poteet, M. L., & Russell, J. E. (2000). Protégé selection by mentors: What makes the difference? *Journal of Organizational Behavior, 21,* 271–282.

Austria, A. M. (2008). Spirituality and resilience of Filipinos. In C. A. Rayburn & L. Comas-Diaz (Eds.), *WomanSoul: The Inner Life of Women's Spirituality* (pp. 119–126). Westport, CT: Praeger.

Baugh, S. G., Lankua, J., & Scandura, T. A. (1996). An investigation of the effects of protégé gender on responses to mentoring. *Journal of Vocational Behavior, 49,* 309–323.

Birk, J., Rayburn, C. A., & Richmond, L. J. (2001). Religious Occupations and Stress questionnaire (ROS): Instrument development. *Counseling and Values, 45,* 136–144.

Brinson, J., & Kottler, J. (1993). Cross-cultural mentoring in counselor education: A strategy for retaining minority faculty. *Counselor Education and Supervision, 32,* 241–253.

Castro, C., Caldwell, C., & Salazar, C. F. (2005). Creating mentoring relationships between female faculty and students in counselor education: Guidelines for potential mentees and mentors. *Journal of Counseling & Development, 83,* 331–336.

Cawyer, C., Simonds, C., & Davis, S. (2002). Mentoring to facilitate socialization: The case of the new faculty member. *International Journal of Qualitative Studies in Education, 15,* 225–242.

Davis, S. K., & Thakur, R. P. (1999, August). *Implications of ethnic variations in the design and management of mentoring systems.* Paper presented at the International Conference of the Academy of Business Administration, London.

Dinsmore, J. A., & England, J. T. (1996). A study of multicultural counseling training at CACREP accredited counselor education programs. *Counselor Education and Supervision, 36,* 58–77.

Dreher, G. E., & Ash, R. A. (1990). A comparative study of mentoring among men and women in managerial, professional, and technical positions. *Journal of Applied Psychology, 75,* 539–540.

Eanes, B. E., & Richmond, L. J. (2001). *What brings you to life?* Mahwah, NJ: Paulist Press.

Ellis, E. M. (2001). The impact of race and gender on graduate school socialization, satisfaction with doctoral study, and commitment to degree completion. *Western World of Black Studies, 25,* 30–45.

Fagenson, E. A. (1988). The power of a mentor: Protégés' and non-proteges' perceptions of their own power in organizations. *Group and Organizational Studies, 13,* 182–192.

Fallow, G. O., & Johnson, W. B. (2000). Mentor relationships in secular and religious professional psychology programs. *Journal of Psychology and Christianity, 19,* 363–376.

Gilbert, L. A., & Rossman, K. M. (1992). Gender and the mentoring process for women: Implications for professional development. *Professional Psychology Research and Practice, 23,* 233–238.

Hegstad, C. D. (1999). Formal mentoring as a strategy for human resource development: A review of research. *Human Resource Development Quarterly, 10,* 383–390.

Ibarra, H. (1993). Personal networks of women and minorities in management: A conceptual framework. *Academy of Management Review, 18,* 56–87.

Kram, K. E. (1985). *Mentoring at work: Developmental relationships in organizational life.* Glenview, IL: Scott, Foresman.

Kram, K. E. (1988). *Mentoring at work: Developmental relationships in organizational life.* New York: University Press of America.

Olson, G. A., & Ashton-Jones, E. (1992). Doing gender: (En)gendering academic mentoring. *Journal of Education, 174,* 114–127.

Ragins, B. R., & Cotton, J. L. (1991). Easier said than done: Gender differences in perceived barriers to gaining a mentor. *Academy of Management Journal, 34,* 939–951.

Ragins, B. R., & Cotton, J. L. (1999). Mentor functions and outcomes: A comparison of men and women in formal and informal mentoring relationships. *Journal of Applied Psychology, 84,* 529–550.

Ragins, B. R., Cotton, J. L., & Miller, J. S. (2000). Marginal mentoring: The effects of type of mentor, quality of relationship, and program design on work and career attitudes. *Academy of Management Journal, 43,* 1177–1194.

Ragins, B. R., & Kram, K. E. (2007). *Handbook of mentoring at work.* Thousand Oaks, CA: Sage.

Ragins, B. R., & Scandura, T. A. (1994). Gender differences in expected outcomes of mentoring relationships. *Academy of Management Journal, 37,* 957–971.

Ragins, B. R., & Scandura, T. A. (1997). The way we were: Gender and the termination of mentoring relationships. *Journal of Applied Psychology, 82,* 945–953.

Rayburn, C. A. (1981a). Some reflections of a female seminarian: Woman, whither goest thou? *Journal of Pastoral Counseling, 16,* 61–65.

Rayburn, C. A. (1981b). Wilderness wanderings. In E. M. Stern (Ed.), *The other side of the couch: Faith of the psychotherapist* (pp. 153–164). New York: Pilgrim Press.

Rayburn, C. A. (1984). EOAA inroads and the Division of Clinical Psychology. *Clinical Psychologist, 37*(1), 13–14.

Rayburn, C. A. (1987). *State-Trait Morality Inventory.* Washington, DC: U.S. Copyright Office.

Rayburn, C. A. (1993). Section IV, The Clinical Psychology of Women: The first twelve years (1980–1992). *Clinical Psychologist, 46*(1), 33–37.

Rayburn, C. A. (1995a, August). *Workshops 1 and 2: Mentoring women and people of color for leadership in organized psychology—Identifying barriers.* Presented at the American Psychological Association Annual Convention, New York.

Rayburn, C. A. (1995b, August). *Workshops 3 and 4: Mentoring women and people of color for leadership in organized psychology—Solutions and strategies.* Presented at the American Psychological Association Annual Convention, New York.

Rayburn, C. A. (1995c, August). *Workshops 5 and 6: Mentoring women and people of color for leadership in organized psychology—Building leadership skills.* Presented at the American Psychological Association annual convention, New York.

Rayburn, C. A. (1995d). The body in religious experience. In R. W. Hood, Jr. (Ed.), *Handbook of religious experience* (pp. 476–494). Birmingham, AL: Religious Education Press.

Rayburn, C. A. (1997). *Inventory on religiousness.* Washington, DC: U.S. Copyright Office.

Rayburn, C. A. (2001). Theobiology, spirituality, religiousness, and the Wizard of Oz (William C. Bier Award Address). *Psychology of Religion Newsletter, 26*(1), 1–11.

Rayburn, C. A. (2006). Development of the Creative Personality Inventory and the Intuition Inventory. In S. M. Natale (Ed.), *Conflict and the "sleep of reason"* (pp. 105–112). New York: Global Scholarly Publications.

Rayburn, C. A. (2007). Alice Paul: Constitutional amendment maker an ERA author. In E. A. Gavin, A. Clamar, & M. A. Siderits (Eds.), *Women of vision: Their psychology, circumstances, and success* (pp. 61–78). New York: Springer.

Rayburn, C. A. (2008). Implications of creativity and intuition springing forth from spirituality. In S. M. Natale (Ed.), *Beatitude past utterance: Balancing life, career, values, ethics* (pp. 143–152). New York: Global Scholarly Publications.

Rayburn, C. A., Birk, J., & Richmond. L. J. (1994). *State-Trait Morality Inventory (STMI).* Washington, DC: U.S. Copyright Office.

Rayburn, C. A., & Comas-Diaz, L. (Eds.). (2008). *WomanSoul: The Inner life of women's spirituality.* Westport, CT: Praeger.

Rayburn, C. A., Natale, S., & Linzer, J. (1982). Feminism and religion: What price holding membership in both camps? *Counseling and Values, 26,* 154–164.

Rayburn, C. A., & Osman, S. (2005). Spirituality, morality, life choices, and peacefulness in North American women. In A. D. Thomas, N. Dayan, A. B. Bernado, & R. Roth (Eds.), *Helping others grow (proceedings of the 60th annual convention of the International Council of Psychologists, Manila, the Philippines* (pp. 151–155). Aachen, Germany: Shaker-Verlag.

Rayburn, C. A., & Richmond, L. J. (1986). *Religious Occupations and Stress questionnaire.* Washington, DC: U.S. Copyright Office.

Rayburn, C. A., & Richmond, L. J. (1994). *State-Trait Morality Inventory (STMI).* Washington, DC: U.S. Copyright Office.

Rayburn, C. A., & Richmond, L. J. (1996). *Inventory on Spirituality (IS).* Washington, DC: U.S. Copyright Office.

Rayburn, C. A., Richmond, L. J., & Birk, J. (1994). *Religious Occupations and Stress questionnaire.* Washington, DC: U.S. Copyright Office.

Rayburn, C. A., Richmond, L. J., & Rogers, L. (1982). Women, men, and religion: Stress within sanctuary walls. *Journal of Pastoral Counseling, 17,* 75–83.

Rayburn, C. A., Richmond, L. J., & Rogers, L. (1983). Stress in religious leaders, *Thought: Fordham University Quarterly Review, 58*(230), 329–344,

Rayburn, C. A., Richmond, L., & Rogers, L. (1986). Priests, brothers, and the Religion and Stress Questionnaire. ERIC/CAPS #ED-273-865.

Rayburn, C. A., Richmond, L. J., & Rogers, L. (1994). Women religious professionals and stress. In L. B. Brown & H. N. Maloney (Eds.), *Religion, personality, and mental health* (pp. 167–173). New York: Springer-Verlag.

Rayburn, C. A., & Richmond, L. J. (1998). "Theobiology": Attempting to understand God and ourselves. *Journal of Health and Religion, 37,* 345–356.

Rayburn, C. A., & Richmond, L. J. (2002). Theobiology: Interfacing theology and science [in special issue "Theobiology: Interfacing theology, biology, and other sciences for deeper understanding"]. In C. A. Rayburn & L. J. Richmond (Eds.), *American Behavioral Scientist, 45,* 1793–1811.

Strickland, B. R. (2008). Early outreach: The EOAA Committee. *The Clinical Psychologist, 61*(3), 7–8.

Thakur, R. P. (2008). *Role of mentoring in development of leaders: Is there a difference between Latina and Latino in mentor selection criteria?* Retrieved March 18, 2009, from www.g-casa.com/PDF/Kakow%202008/krakow%papers%20 pdf/papesr%20database%20krakow/Thakur.pdf

Thomas, D. A. (1993). Racial dynamics in cross-race developmental relationships. *Administrative Science Quarterly, 38,* 169–191.

Whitely, W., Doughterty, T. W., & Dreher, G. E. (1991). Relationships of career mentoring and socioeconomic origin to manager's and professional's early career progress. *Academy of Management Journal, 34,* 331–351.

Williams, J., & Schweibert, V. L. (2000). Multicultural aspects of the mentoring process. In V. L. Schweibert, *Mentoring: Creating connected, empowered relationships* (pp. 57–70). Alexandria, VA: American Counseling Association.

Wilson, P. F. (2001). Core virtues for the practice of mentoring. *Journal of Psychology and Theology, 29,* 121–130.

Wilson, R. (2003). Strength in numbers: A summer program gives a boost to women for Ph.D.s in mathematics. *Chronicle of Higher Education, 49,* 45.

Chapter 13

Perspectives from a Nontraditional Mentor

Helen D. Pratt

Mentoring is one of the oldest means of passing the acquired knowledge of one person on to others. Historically, tradesmen and professionals taught junior apprentices through the practice of mentoring. Academic learning is an essential part of teaching individuals a knowledge set and how to apply that knowledge. The addition of a mentor to this process can enhance the learning of the student and facilitate transfer of special skills (political, survival, networking) and expertise to the new learner.

Women and minorities, in particular, are frequently faced with the challenges of not having access to mentors who look like them, share their gender, or value their research interests. Access to mentors who can facilitate their overall development and enhance their research skills, publication records, and teaching skills is very limited for this group. Even well-intentioned mentors often do not understand the struggles that mentees who do not look or behave like the majority group face. Appropriate mentors can provide much added value to the mentee. I found it difficult to find African American women professors, and those that I did find were often overwhelmed, not at the full professor level, did not conduct research, nor did

Table I
Some Commonly Shared Negative Experiences of Minorities and Women

- Being treated as though invisible
- Having views and statements ignored or severely criticized
- Statements by colleagues or supervisors that minorities are inferior or not qualified for admission to the program or the job
- Feeling like the scapegoat
- Feelings that the rules of the game changed when the minority's or woman's turn came to play or be evaluated
- Feelings of isolation
- Feelings of exclusion
- Feelings of marginalization
- Feeling as though one's credentials are in question
- Feeling the need to constantly prove oneself
- Feeling tired and exhausted because of the excess energy it takes to survive the environment on a daily basis
- Never knowing who to trust
- Having to always be hypervigilant in order to be prepared to overcome the next obstacle or fight the next fight

they have a publication history. However, one assistant professor who was an African American woman nominated me for several prestigious awards and wrote effective letters that resulted in my receiving those honors. Most of my mentors were white men. Although they were wonderful in helping to develop my research and publication interests, they were often limited in their understanding of my personal, cultural, and ethnic needs. Because I was aware of this problem, I sought mentoring for the later issues from other sources.

Unfortunately, many women and minorities share a set of emotions that result from their experiences with teachers, professors, trainers, and supervisors who belong to the majority culture and do not value them (See Table 1). The ability to overcome these negative emotions is best accomplished through the mentoring process (Vasquez et al., 2006; Waitzkin, Yager, Parker, & Duran, 2006; Walcott & Pratt, 2000). This chapter focuses on defining mentoring, briefly describes the author's experiences with mentoring, and offers specific suggestions for developing effective mentoring skills.

WHAT IS A MENTOR?

The Office of Educational Research and Improvement of the U.S. Department of Education (1993) states:

Mentoring—from the Greek word meaning enduring—is defined as a sustained relationship between a youth and an adult. Through continued involvement, the adult offers support, guidance, and assistance as the younger person goes through a difficult period, faces new challenges, or works to correct earlier problems.

Gibson (2005) points out that, in academia, mentors and advisors are usually thought of as being the same. However, not all faculty advisors are mentors, and not all mentors are faculty advisors. While advisors do give direction and advice, mentors generally will address more than one area of the mentee's life and will vary her level of involvement and advice depending on the needs of the mentee. An effective mentor will tailor the degree, type, frequency, and intensity of the attention, support, information, and encouragement provided to a mentee based on the situation and needs of the mentee. I hold that mentoring also should include culturally sensitive counseling (Castro, Caldwell, & Salazar 2005; Gibson, 2005; Griffin & Ayers, 2005).

There are two types of mentoring: informal and formal. Informal mentoring or natural mentoring generally involves friendship, collegiality, teaching, coaching, and counseling. In contrast, formal or planned mentoring occurs through structured programs in which mentors and participants are selected and matched through formal processes. This process could also result in friendships and also involves teaching, coaching, and counseling (Castro et al., 2005; Gibson, 2005; Griffin & Ayers, 2005; Walcott & Pratt, 2000).

EXPERIENCES THAT SHAPED MY MENTORING STYLE

Although I was a so-called nontraditional mentee throughout college and my early professional years, I was always fortunate to find mentors. This was most likely because my views of what constituted a mentor were shaped very early. Being mentored started for me as a young girl at home, in Sunday school and church, as well as in elementary school. My mother taught me to help care for my siblings, to protect them, and to teach them. She was my guide, counselor, and friend. My mother was my first mentor, the first person to teach me how to read the behavior and affect of other people, how to detect and avoid danger, how to negotiate and compromise, how to resolve conflict, how to follow good and effective leaders, and how to be an effective leader. Subsequent mentors simply expanded on my mother's early teaching. My current style of mentoring has some elements of mothering woven into it.

I have had the honor of having advisors, mentors, and supervisors who were self-proclaimed mentors. I am fortunate that each of the mentors I sought out generously gave of their time and expertise to help me reach my goals. I am blessed to have had two individuals seek me out and offer their mentoring services. I had the good sense to accept their offers. Even with all this support, I was never the favorite or the protégé of any mentor. However, I maximized every experience and found the take-home lessons from each mentor.

When I was in college, I observed that my professors often had identified students who they mentored. What I saw was that "real" mentees received special privileges: They usually had (a) access to funding to pay for their education, (b) help developing research ideas, (c) opportunities to work on research projects with experienced researchers, (d) opportunities to have their names included on publications, and (e) they were inducted into honor societies. These privileged people seemed to matriculate faster than their peers through the program of study; they seemed to get published earlier; and appeared to land good jobs and fellowships after graduation.

I decided I wanted those privileges and set out to find ways to provide myself with similar experiences. I knew I would have to design experiences that gave me credentials that equaled or rivaled my peers. I sought out exemplars who had the ability to help me and worked to get them to mentor my efforts. My success at accomplishing these goals has served as a foundation for my mentoring strategies and techniques. My primary guides for developing how I wanted to mentor others came from my personal experiences with mentors and by observing the support given to my young, white, men colleagues. As I began to mentor, I struggled with whether to expend my limited resources to the privileged (primarily white men) or reserve my efforts for the underprivileged (people of color, women, and older persons). I vowed that I would provide mentoring that was supportive, nurturing, empowering, and that would facilitate long-lasting collegial relationships for those I chose to mentor. I decided to cast a wide *inclusionary* net for those I would mentor to serve as an example for diversity. I do not deny anyone access to my mentoring; I allow mentees to self-select. I provide them with a written list of expectations and requirements for paying me back for my services. Potential mentees can then make an informed decision about whether they want to access my mentoring services.

ON BEING A MENTOR

The most frequent type of mentoring I provide is informal. Doctoral and master's-level students from several universities have often approached me to help them as they matriculate through their programs. Some ask for my help because (a) I am African American, (b) I am married and have a family, (c) I was an older student (nontraditional), (d) I am a psychologist, (d) they were referred by some of my colleagues, or (e) for all of these reasons. In each case, the potential mentee usually has an academic advisor, a training advisor, and sometimes other mentors. Therefore, I must help them integrate my advice with that of the other key people in their careers. In my present position, I am often asked to mentor women and minorities who are (a) struggling with the demands of medical residency training, (b) struggling with the demands of their psychology training programs, or (c) are trying to decide the next stage of their careers.

I soon realized that the opportunities to mentor individuals who looked like me would be rare. I found that minority students were reluctant to work with me because they could not see my "power"; they did not trust my generosity and offers to help them with research, clinical experiences, and presentations. They did not trust receiving something that was free when they all have been taught that nothing in life is free. Consequently, most of my psychology mentees were men, and primarily white men. Because I worked in a medical setting, many of my mentees represented a different discipline, were also white, and primarily men. Mentees of color were foreign medical graduates (African, Asian, Asian Indian, Arab) but still primarily men.

To increase the numbers of mentees who were women and minorities from the United States, I had to make my commitment to helping women and people of color known throughout the organization in which I am employed. I volunteered to sit on disciplinary panels to have access to helping those who fit within my target groups. I also had to call the universities I worked with and ask for women and people of color to be recruited for the psychology programs and to be sent to me when possible. I knew that I had to be proactive and call and request mentees who looked like me. But I took all comers. I believe that mentors must have a commitment to promoting opportunities for women and minorities regardless of their discipline or professional affiliation.

As I gained experience as a professional and as a mentor, I realized that I needed to accomplish several things to be attractive to women and minority psychologists. And I had to institute some criteria for potential mentees to receive my time and efforts; this seemed to help overcome some of their distrust. I had also established a strong positive reputation as an effective mentor. I completed a comprehensive self-assessment (see Table 2), established my criteria for a mentor–mentee relationship (see Table 3), and prepared a written set of guidelines for my mentees (see Table 4). I decided that some initial self-disclosure was necessary to helping establish the tone of our relationship, so I decided to tell them (a) what motivated me to become a mentor; (b) why I would mentor them in particular, and (c) and what I wanted in return by asking them to pay a price for my time (see Table 5). I also required them to sign a contract affirming that they understood what it took to meet my expectations and to meet weekly goals (as one of my mentors had done with me). If they did not meet those goals, mentees were told I would not give them my time. Additionally, I gave each mentee a written set of guidelines designed to help them be effective mentees (see Table 6).

Table 2
Essentials for Becoming an Effective Mentor, Part I

Prior to establishing any mentoring relationships, conduct a thorough self-assessment:

- Determine your prejudices and biases. Do not work with individuals who you basically do not like, hate, or do not want to be around.
    - What are your views on the "isms"
        - Do you have bias toward or against any gender?
        - What are your views on sexual orientation?
            - Are you homophobic?
        - What are your views on religion?
            - Are you for or against any specific belief?
        - What are your views on race?
            - What are your stereotypes? And you do have some!
        - What are your views on social class?
        - What are your views on where a person obtained his or her education?
        - What are your views on weight and body type?
        - What do you view as beautiful in human features?
        - What are your views on people from other countries?
        - What are your views on students or colleagues who do not speak English fluently?
- Why are you mentoring?
- If you are being forced to mentor because it is a part of your job, how will you make the necessary adaptations to do your job well?
- How will you assess the needs, wishes, and talents of your mentee so your help is directed and facilitating versus making him or her in your own image?
- How will you know when to shift the mentoring role to a peer relationship?
- How will you handle conflict?
    - What is your conflict management style?
        - How will you adjust it to be an effective mentor?
        - Do you hold grudges?
            - How will you learn that this is not a professional skill to teach a mentee?
- When will you know to get help or support to work through your issues that are interfering with the mentoring relationship?
- What do you want in return for giving a particular mentee the gift of your time and experience?

Table 3
Essentials for Becoming an Effective Mentor, Part II

The following should occur prior to establishing mentoring relationships:

1. Establish and clarify the reasons why you want to mentor.
2. Determine whether you are secure and comfortable with who you are.
3. Determine what essential characteristics the mentee must possess.

4. Determine your selection criteria for a mentee.
5. Determine expectations for the mentor–mentee relationship.
6. Determine personal expectations for the mentee's behavior.
7. Determine the mentee's obligation for your help.
8. Determine what situations, factors, and events would cause you to terminate the mentor–mentee relationship.
9. Determine whether you know how to effectively communicate with others.
10. Determine how mentoring will help you reach your goals.
11. Determine whether you really like and enjoy mentoring.
12. Determine whether you really have the time, energy, and desire necessary to make a commitment to the mentoring relationship.
13. Devote a specific amount of time to work with the mentee.
14. Clarify your personal beliefs, values, and morals to determine your "isms."
15. Determine whether you know what a mentor is and if you are prepared to play each of those roles.

Table 4
Essentials for Becoming an Effective Mentor, Part III

Provide each mentee with specific information about the mentoring relationship.

- Clearly specify your expertise.
    - Require the mentee to review you vita, read some of your work, and conduct an Internet search using your name.
    - Give the mentee a copy of your vita and names of previous mentees as references.
- Specify in writing the nature of the relationship.
- Clarify what the two of you will accomplish during your work together.
- Set aside a specific amount of time to work with the mentee.
- Consistently be available during scheduled meeting times.
- Provide several methods of contact and use all of them if you change the schedule. Be sure to reschedule.
- Clearly establish expectations for the mentoring relationship.
    - Attend all scheduled meetings.
    - Complete all homework assignments.
    - Come to all meetings with pen and paper to take notes.
- Cleary communicate the criteria for terminating the relationship.
    - For example, inconsistent attendance at scheduled meetings
    - Incomplete homework assignments
    - Specify bounds of confidentiality; with whom will you share information about the mentee, when, and how.

Table 5
Examples of Contractual Expectations for Mentees

Once the established time period for the formal mentoring relationship has ended, each mentee agrees that he will:

- Reach out and help one African American woman who is struggling to become a psychologist.
- Reach out and help one nontraditional student or intern who is struggling to become a psychologist.
- Promote tolerance and understanding.
- Treat each person who comes into her reach (professionally or clinically) with dignity and respect and positive regard.
- Call or write me and tell me when each of these tasks has been completed, and have the affected individual contact me verifying the same.

Table 6
How to Enhance Mentor–Mentee Relationships: Suggestions for Mentees

When you chose a mentor:

- Research his qualifications.
- Read the works of the mentor, ask questions about that work.
- Read the vita of the mentor; ask questions about her life.
- Determine whether this person is someone who warrants your respect.
- Determine whether you like the person.
- Determine whether the person treats you with respect and as though he or she likes you.
- Determine what value you will derive from the relationship.
- Be prepared
  - When meeting with a mentor, always
    - Arrive on time If you must cancel, leave messages at all contact numbers, e-mails, and a personal note on the mentor's office door. Then be sure to reschedule.
    - Have an agenda with your goals for the session.
    - Bring writing implements.
    - Take notes and summarize each meeting.
    - Bring copies of notes from previous sessions (one for the mentor).
    - Complete all assignments.
    - Provide the mentor with monthly progress reports.
- Set expectations
  - Tell the mentor what you expect from the relationship.
  - Tell the mentor your dreams, goals, and hopes for your career.
  - Provide the mentor with your vita and accomplishments.
  - Look for multiple mentors.
  - Find mentors in several different settings.

- Find mentors who can mentor different aspects of your life
  - Personal
  - Professional
  - Emotional
  - Social
  - Relationship coaching

Feedback from my former mentees (now colleagues) consistently tell me that my mentoring support helped them to matriculate through programs faster, obtain preferred internships, get published, manage intimate relationships more effectively, and develop a strong sense of confidence in their abilities. I am fortunate to have continued relationships with most of the individuals I have mentored.

RESOURCES THAT GUIDED MY EFFORTS

Two of the most important resources that helped with remaining goal oriented and focused were a joint publication of the Committee on Women in Psychology and the American Psychological Association Commission on Ethnic Minority Recruitment, Retention, and Training in Psychology (1998) titled *Surviving and Thriving in Academia* and the "Ask Aunt Academe" columns that appear in the *Feminist Psychologist,* currently being written by Phyllis Bronstein. The advice from both of these resources has been invaluable, and each resource offers essential advice for anyone who is entering academia as a student or professor.

CONCLUSION

Mentoring is an effective means of helping women and minorities successfully gain access to knowledge and skills to help them become effective professionals. Mentoring is an important means of developing networks for psychologists that can help them stay strong and effective professionally and personally.

REFERENCES

Castro, C., Caldwell, C., & Salazar, C. F. (2005). Creating mentoring relationships between female faculty and students in counselor education: Guidelines for potential mentees and mentors. *Journal of Counseling & Development, 83*(3), 331–336.

Committee on Women in Psychology and Commission on Ethnic Minority Recruitment, Retention, and Training in Psychology. (1998). *Surviving and thriving in academia: A guide for women and ethnic minorities.* Washington, DC: American Psychological Association.

Gibson, S. K. (2005). Whose best interests are served? The distinction between mentoring and support. *Advances in Developing Human Resources, 7*(4), 470–488.

Griffin, L. L. & Ayers, S. F. (2005). The roles and process of mentoring. *Journal of Teaching in Physical Education, 24*(4), 297–301.

U.S. Department of Education, Office of Research, Office of Educational Research and Improvement. (1993). *Education Research Consumer Guide: Mentoring.* OR 93-3059, ED/OERI 92-38. http://www.ed.gov/pubs/OR/ConsumerGuides/mentor.html

Vasquez, M.J.T., Lott, B., García-Vázquez, E., Grant, S. K., Iwamasa, G. Y., Molina, L. E., Ragsdale, B. L. & Vestal-Dowdy, E. (2006). Personal reflections: Barriers and strategies in increasing diversity in psychology. *American Psychologist, 61*(2), 157–172.

Waitzkin, H., Yager, J., Parker, T., & Duran, B. (2006). Mentoring partnerships for minority faculty and graduate students in mental health services research. *Academic Psychiatry, 30*(3), 205–217.

Walcott, D., & Pratt, H. D. (2000). *Surviving the politics of academia.* Kalamazoo, MI: Western Michigan University (Grant funded).

Chapter 14

Beyond Mentoring: Opening Doors and Systems

Shari E. Miles-Cohen, Gwendolyn Puryear Keita, Gabriel H. J. Twose, and Susan J. Houston

Mentoring, as it has been traditionally defined, occurs when a relationship is formed and nurtured between two individuals in which one member uses her considerable knowledge and expertise in a specific area to provide guidance and counseling to the other, who is less experienced and lacking in much of the knowledge and skills necessary to perform successfully in a particular area or field. A traditional definition of mentoring involves a senior faculty member or other professional guiding the career advancement of a student or junior colleague (Johnson, 2002). Mentoring has been characterized more comprehensively as "an interpersonal relationship that changes over time and includes the intentional process of nurturing, support, protection, guidance, instruction, and challenge within mutually agreed-upon and ethical parameters that include integration of personal and professional aspects of an individual's life" (Williams-Nickelsen, 2007, p. 2). More broad definitions go beyond the model of interpersonal relationships to include self-mentoring (Moss et al., 1999; U.S. Department of the Army, Office of the Quartermaster General, 2002) and other alternative models

(Knouse, 2001; Luckhaupt et al., 2005; Mayer, Files, Ko, & Blair, 2008; Rosser, 2007; Spencer, 2006).

This chapter explores five categories of mentoring activities identified by the American Psychological Association (APA) Committee on Women in Psychology (CWP) as effective for empowering women at individual and structural levels. These include: (a) CWP's macro-mentoring initiatives that, over the past three decades, have helped to establish organizational structures and policies that support, advance, and address barriers for women in psychology; (b) CWP's activities related to mentoring by committee; (c) resources developed by CWP in conjunction with the APA Women's Programs Office (WPO) designed to provide women with information they need to self-mentor in the absence of (or in addition to) critical advice and support from a senior professional; (d) CWP's virtual mentoring activities; and (e) CWP's newest initiative: the Leadership Institute for Women in Psychology (LIWP).

Discussions include highlights of each of the five categories, which are explored further through references to best practices. The authors have also included recommendations derived from the National Leadership Workshop on Mentoring Women in Biomedical Careers Meeting Proceedings (Office of Research on Women's Health, National Institutes of Health [ORWH], 2008).

THE APA COMMITTEE ON WOMEN IN PSYCHOLOGY

The American Psychological Association established the Committee on Women in Psychology as a continuing committee in 1973. From the beginning, the committee's mission has focused on "ensuring that women in all their diversity achieve equality within the psychological community and in the larger society, nationally and globally" (Association Rules 2008). Efforts are geared toward raising the visibility of issues pertaining to women in psychology, recommending changes in existing structures and policies that will benefit women, and actively advocating these changes. More information about the events leading up to the founding of CWP can be found in *CWP: Two Decades of Change, 1973–1993* (American Psychological Association, 1993).

The APA CWP has proven its capability to empower current and future women psychologists, which is directly related to its success initiating universal change and developing tools to help women to self-mentor. Effective mentoring for all professionals, men and women alike, benefits career development, psychosocial development, and quality of professional life (Williams-Nickelson, 2007, 2009). Unfortunately, many women report difficulties in establishing effectual mentoring relationships (Gilbert & Rossman, 1992; Kite et al., 2001; Noe, 1988; Packard, Walsh, & Seidenberg, 2004; Sambunjak, Straus, & Marusic, 2006). Professional women who do not have mentors experience difficulty in learning unspoken rules, earn lower salaries, and experience less overall career achievement and success (Jackson et al., 2003; Ragins & Cotton, 1999). The committee saw this as a significant barrier to women psychologists' chances of success and so began to create relevant resources and establish mechanisms through which access to information, advice, and support, similar to that which mentors can provide, would be ensured.

MACRO-MENTORING: CREATING OVERARCHING INITIATIVES

Throughout 1969 and 1970, the Association for Women in Psychology formally protested sexist practices within psychology. Members were outraged that the discriminatory actions of recruiters during APA conventions had been allowed to continue. In response, APA's chief executive officer at the time, Kenneth Little, took the unprecedented step of removing employers with sex discriminatory advertisements. The impact of this refusal to accept prejudice as the status quo continued to resonate throughout CWP's early history and expanded to affect responses to the unique needs of ethnic minority women, aging women, women with disabilities, poor women, and lesbians.

As a result of AWP's "demands," the APA Council of Representatives established a Task Force on the Status of Women in Psychology, which was charged with collecting data on how women were faring in the field of psychology and the general public and developing recommendations for action based on what these data confirmed. To this day, CWP continues to collect and monitor data on women's status and considers this, along with using the results to craft reports and recommendations for the association leadership, to be among its highest priorities.

Preparing women to function in the extant system is important, but even more critical is finding ways to positively impact the environment, processes, and systems within academia and psychology in general that maintain discriminatory practices. CWP has been and continues to be in a position to mobilize the resources and influence of APA to encourage positive change on a large scale. Research shows that structural and systemic transformations are an effective means to alter situations that impact many. Therefore, CWP has given particular attention to the pursuit of programs and initiatives that work to the advantage of women psychologists and consumers of psychological services on an expansive and enduring scale. (Caso et al., 2002).

REACHING BEYOND APA

CWP recognized that, in order to create and sustain systemic and structural change, work had to be carried out within a broader community of women and men committed to women's issues, galvanizing psychologists to engage in positive social change. *Models for Organizing Psychologists* (American Psychological Association Committee on Women in Psychology, 1990) is a step-by-step guide on how to organize women psychologists as an official cohort within their professional organizations. While the guide offers tools for women to organize all varieties of organizations, its impact within APA in particular has been marked. A review of the 52 APA division Web sites on October 13, 2009 found that 19 APA divisions have established committees, subcommittees, or sections on women's issues. In addition, 22 APA divisions have appointed official representatives to the Committee on Women in Psychology Network (American Psychological Association, Women's Programs Office, 2009). The Network serves as a coalition of women's committees within psychology, including representatives from divisions, state, and regional associations without formally-organized committees on women. The committee has collaborated with other organizations to identify short- and long-term priorities and cultivate responsive courses of action. Making use of the best thinking and scholarship available, of committee members' expertise and interests, and of the support of like-minded entities, CWP continues to develop an agenda geared toward the future.

Best Practice #1—Considering Women's Needs: Structural and Systemic Change within APA

CWP realized one of its first victories in 1973, when, in direct response to its recommendation and influence, the Division of the Psychology of Women (Division 35), now the Society for the Psychology of Women, was formed. In 1977, APA established the Women's Programs Office to support the expanding scope and volume of the committee's endeavors. The Task Force on the Status of Women in Psychology and CWP worked diligently and achieved numerous successes throughout these early years. Successes included:

- The Board of Professional Affairs established a Task Force on Sex Bias and Sex-Role Stereotyping in Psychotherapeutic Practice.
- The Education and Training Board (now Board of Education Affairs) established a Study Panel on Sexism and Racism in Graduate Education.
- CWP organized training workshops on sex discrimination in education and employment at every regional psychological association meeting.

In 1982, in response to a request from CWP, the Publications and Communications Board joined with the committee to establish a joint ad hoc Committee on Underrepresented Groups in the Publications Process. The group was to identify strategies for increasing the participation of women and minorities in the publications process. This committee presented sessions at the annual APA convention for women to encourage women to become journal reviewers, to make the publication process more open and understandable, and to teach strategies to increase the changes of journal acceptance.

Best Practice #2—Serving as a Sponsor and Mentoring by Committee: Not Your Mother's Traditional Dyadic Model

Mentors recommend their mentees for positions that can potentially advance their careers, visibility, and positioning in the profession. CWP works on behalf of individual women to raise the visibility of their contributions. In many ways, this serves a mentor's role in promoting an individual's capabilities. CWP is actively committed to the practice of nominating women for positions in APA governance, leadership programs, and awards.

Committee Positions. Serving on an APA board or committee offers exceptional opportunities for exposure, networking, and impacting the development of APA policies and procedures. CWP has always been one of the groups that enthusiastically participates in the APA nominations process. The committee makes use of its network, comprised of representatives throughout state associations and APA divisions, to identify and nominate appropriate, well-qualified candidates to leadership positions. Additional professional and personal networks provide links to APA members who distinguish themselves through their scholarship, practice, and public work in the area of public interest policy. CWP, Division 35, and the Women's Caucus of Council join together each year to submit and support individuals they know will work to further their goals. CWP Network members of divisions and state psychological associations also nominate individuals for APA positions as well as positions in their own organizations.

Fellow Status. Divisions are encouraged to nominate qualified women and men who work in support of women's issues for fellow status within the association. Fellow status is bestowed upon members who have shown evidence of extraordinary contribution and/or outstanding performance to the field. This distinction not only serves as a way of recognizing professional achievement and accomplishments but also categorizes each recipient as a member of an elite group and thus well admired by their peers.

Leadership Awards. For approximately 20 years, CWP has acknowledged psychologists who have made outstanding contributions to women's issues with annual CWP Leadership Awards. These awards are presented to emerging and distinguished leaders in the field. Certainly, such recognition early in one's career influences career advancement. Likewise, an honor later in someone's career may influence the strength or weakness of the ever-present glass ceiling, well known for precluding women from the uppermost reaches of the career ladder. The committee appreciates the various challenges that women face at all stages of their careers and incorporates appropriate distinctions wherever they are called for.

SELF-MENTORING: RESOURCES FOR
INDIVIDUAL EMPOWERMENT

An individual who self-mentors cultivates her own career development through reflection, self-tutoring, and resource-finding techniques (Moss et al., 1999; U.S. Department of the Army, Office of the Quartermaster General, 2002). CWP develops and disseminates resources to address the needs of those who must self-mentor by providing user-friendly materials to psychologists and future psychologists, supplying authoritative information, moral support, opportunities to develop skills, and possibilities for networking.

Best Practices #3 and #4—Mentors Provide
Authoritative Information and Moral Support

Early Career Psychologists. Chrisler (1998) and Sandler (1991) suggest that early career academic psychologists benefit from mentoring relationships. For those who do not have a mentor and for those who would like additional information, CWP published *Survival Guide to Academia for Women and Minorities* in 1992 (American Psychological Association, Committee for Women in Psychology & Women's Programs Office, 1992). This guide was revised through a collaboration between CWP and the APA Commission on Ethnic Minority Recruitment, Retention, and Training in Psychology; the updated guide (APA CWP, 1998) *Surviving & Thriving in Academia: A Guide for Women and Ethnic Minorities,* is divided into four parts. Part I, "Deciding on Academia: What Are Your Options?" addresses untenured or early career women and ethnic minorities seeking and selecting faculty appointments in academic psychology departments, focusing primarily on the recruitment process. Part II addresses "Strategies for Maximizing Your Chances for Promotion and Tenure." By making the rules of the system more explicit, women and ethnic minorities can examine their own personal standards in the context of the external demands of the tenure and promotion processes. Part III focuses on strategies for coping with the emotional trauma of an adverse decision regarding promotion and tenure in ways that can help the new academician avert a negative career shift. Part IV, "Facing Adversity Functionally," is designed to help those who experience tenure denial learn functional strategies for challenging negative decisions. Although these strategies apply to many individuals, they are not prescriptive and are intended as suggestions only.

Women and Minorities in Governance. One of the committee's strategic goals is to enhance women's leadership within and outside of APA. Increasing the number of women and ethnic minorities in APA governance is an ongoing priority. At the 1998 APA annual convention, CWP and the Committee on Ethnic Minority Affairs cosponsored a training luncheon designed to share the knowledge and experience of senior professionals with women and ethnic minorities interested in becoming involved in APA governance—an example of large group mentoring. In 1999, CWP sponsored a symposium entitled "Women and Minorities in APA Governance: Making a Difference," an open session with the goal of providing information about processes and strategies for success. Similar symposia were offered at the 2000 and 2001 APA annual conventions.

APA now collects data on women, ethnic minorities, gay men, lesbians, bisexuals, and individuals with disabilities serving on and running for office in APA governance—the level at which APA policy is proposed, discussed, and approved. In this way, APA can track the progress of efforts to ensure a broad diversity in representation throughout the APA governance structure, including the governance pipeline, to determine where diversity issues may need to be most vigorously addressed. Ensuring diverse representation at the governance level is integral to APA's vibrant future.

Publications Pipeline. Increasing the proportion of women and ethnic minorities who serve as editors of journals, especially APA journals, has likewise been a long-standing high priority. Journal editors play a critical role, influencing the careers of individuals as well as the field as a whole. The number and effect of publications and quality of a publication outlet are key in promotion and tenure decisions for psychologists in academia and academic medicine, and in determining fellow status in APA and other societies (APA CWP & Commission on Ethnic Minority Recruitment, Retention and Training in Psychology, 1998).

Journal editors also function as gatekeepers for the scientific record (American Psychological Association Committee on Women in Psychology, 2004). CWP has delivered information on the publications process, beginning with *Understanding the Manuscript Review Process: Increasing the Participation of Women* (American Psychological Association, Committee on Women in Psychology and Women's Programs Office, 1982, 1983, 1988) authored by a panel of knowledgeable contributors, all of whom had served as an editor, reviewer, editorial board member, or member of APA's Publications and Communication Board. This accessible guide flows directly from CWP's efforts to "eliminate inequities in the publication process" (Keita, 1988, p. 1). The committee saw this as a priority in 1982 and continues to view increasing the participation of women in the publication process as central to its mission. As stated in the first edition,

[i]n order that the process leading to publication be equitable, all professionals must understand the process of why and how decisions are made to publish or not publish a manuscript. Psychologists must understand how editors and reviewers look at manuscripts. In addition, they must understand how the author's own attitudes and skills may enhance or impede the acceptance of manuscripts. (Loeffler, 1983, p. 1)

All of the articles offer positive suggestions for authors to increase the probability of their manuscripts being published.

CWP recognized that eliminating sexist language in APA publications was a key step toward positive change (Kelley, 1996). An APA policy requiring authors of articles published in APA publications to use nonsexist language was adopted as a result. This policy is reflected in the Publication Manual (American Psychological Association, 1974, 2001). Later, the guidelines were expanded to include other areas where bias existed, and these are documented in "Guidelines to Reduce Bias in Language," including gender, sexual orientation, racial and ethnic identity, disabilities, and age. CWP continues to monitor the implementation of the nonsexist language guidelines and their application in APA publications, reports, correspondence, and other printed material (American Psychological Association Committee on Women in Psychology, 1993).

CWP also provides or collaborates with others to offer a variety of resources for those who must self-mentor or who need additional information regarding the publishing pipeline. To reach the largest audience possible, CWP sponsors or cosponsors programming at the annual APA convention. Notable 2009 convention programming regarding the publishing pipeline included practical sessions such as "How to Publish Your Manuscript"; "Join the Publication Pipeline—How to Review a Manuscript"; "How We Did It—Discussions with Women APA Journal Editors"; and "Research & Training Funding—Discussions with Representatives from Federal Agencies."

Best Practice #5—Mentors Impart Skills

To support women's advancement in their careers, CWP has sponsored programs on "Negotiation Skills for Women in Psychology" at the 2005 and 2006 APA conventions, "Negotiation Skills Facilitate Career Advancement for Women in Psychology" in 2007, and "Speed Mentoring for Women in Academic Positions: Bring Your Questions" in 2008. These symposia were open to interested women and men who attended convention. Presenters have included distinguished women of diverse backgrounds from academic, academic medicine, and clinical settings, all of whom have served in leadership roles (e.g., section heads, deans, and provosts) and have been outstanding role models.

Best Practice #6—Mentors Assist Mentees with Building Their Professional and Social Networks by Providing Networking Opportunities

In collaboration with Division 35, CWP developed directories of Hispanic and black women in psychology to raise the visibility of ethnically diverse women's contributions and to highlight the work of individual women psychologists. These directories also served the individual empowerment goal of building a network among women psychologists of color. Often, an ethnic minority woman psychologist is the only one in her department. By using this directory, she has a ready-made community to access when she needs support, guidance, or information. Each directory, containing approximately 200 biographical sketches, fosters communication within and between the two groups of women and serves as a resource for individuals and institutions seeking the psychological expertise of black and Hispanic women. With the publication of this directory, CWP established a de facto network of qualified black and Hispanic women psychologists and debunked the myth regarding their nonexistence.

Best Practice #7—Develop Alternate Delivery Methods: Web-based Resources

Although very successful in terms of their immediate audiences, the governance and negotiation skills symposia offered at APA conventions reach a fraction of the universe of women who can benefit from CWP resources. A type of self-mentoring that warrants specific mention is Internet-based programs, increasing access of those in need of information and resources (Packard et al., 2004). Many CWP documents and publications are also Web based to reach as many women as possible, including databases focused on practicum placements, financial aid, and graduate faculty interested in women's issues.

Three Web-based databases maintained and regularly updated by the Women's Programs Office help to achieve this goal are:

Graduate Faculty Interested in the Psychology of Women. In response to regular requests for information concerning women faculty and graduate programs with a focus on women's issues, WPO maintains and updates this database, which is drawn from a survey of graduate psychology departments' activities relevant to women and women's issues in psychology. Posted on the APA Web site, users with an interest in studying the psychology of women can search the database by state and region, alphabetically, and by departments to locate relevant graduate programs across the country.

Directory of Selected Scholarships, Fellowships, and Other Financial Aid Opportunities for Women and Ethnic Minorities in Psychology and Related Fields. For those women who must secure their own funding for graduate school, the Women's Programs Office maintains and regularly updates this financial aid directory to assist students and professionals in identifying avenues of funding. The directory serves as a valuable online resource for many future psychologists who might otherwise be unable to fund their endeavors.

Internship Opportunities in the Psychology of Women. The literature suggests that women clinical psychology students may have a difficult time identifying and sustaining a positive mentoring relationship (Williams-Nickelsen, 2009). The clinical internship is a crucial stage of a future practitioner's preparation. WPO responds to requests from students seeking information on internship opportunities by periodically surveying internship programs to inquire about faculty, training and emphasis, research related to women's issues, expertise in the assessment and treatment of women, activities related to women, and on-site options for interns (i.e., day care, flexible hours, etc.). The results are presented in this internship directory and posted on the APA Web site.

LOOKING TO THE FUTURE: THE LEADERSHIP INSTITUTE FOR WOMEN IN PSYCHOLOGY

We do not want psychology to become a profession in which women predominate in the rank and file but men predominate in the leadership, as has been the case with other occupations (American Psychological Association Task Force on the Changing Gender Composition of Psychology, 1995, p. 12; Pion et al., 1996)). The absence of women in leadership positions undermines the empowerment of all women (United Nations Economic and Social Council, 2006). CWP, recognizing that APA lacked a flagship to promote women's advancement to leadership roles in academia, business, government, and at the community level, saw the importance of creating a formal, ongoing, and comprehensive program to promote women's advancement to senior leadership roles within and outside psychology and in APA. The committee responded to the call of member Helen Coons and began developing what would become the Leadership Institute for Women in Psychology.

CWP seated a planning committee that generated the LIWP mission statement: *The mission of the CWP Leadership Institute for Women in Psychology is to prepare, support, and empower women psychologists as leaders to promote positive changes in institutional and organizational life and increase the diversity, number, and effectiveness of women psychologists as leaders.* With this overarching mission in mind, the CWP Leadership Institute for Women in Psychology has several objectives: (a) ensure that midcareer and senior women in psychology have the knowledge and skills necessary to compete for leadership/management positions in academic and other professional settings; (b) enhance the number and effectiveness of women psychologists holding institutional leadership positions in academic and other professional settings; (c) increase the diversity of women psychologists in institutional leadership positions; and (d) create networks of women psychologists in senior management/leadership positions in varied professional settings.

The Institute planning committee was unable to identify quantitative or qualitative research that assessed the leadership training needs of women in psychology or the extent to which women in psychology identify as "leaders" (A. Eagly, personal communication, January 24, 2007). The absence of such data underscored the need to evaluate leadership training needs among women psychologists in diverse professional settings.

The inaugural CWP LIWP focused on the leadership training needs of 30 midcareer women psychologists, selected through a competitive process, who are APA members in good standing; at least 10 years post-PhD, -EdD, or -PsyD, and hold the rank of associate professor or above in academic or academic medical settings. (Future LIWPs will focus on midcareer women psychologists who work in other professional settings and senior women psychologists.) The program agenda included five modules of lectures and skills-focused, highly interactive, case-based workshops encompassing leadership styles, negotiation skills, research, funding and publication strategies, mentoring, and career development and goal setting. Participants left with clearly defined professional goals and the opportunity to join a monthly mentoring forum designed specifically for them. They were then invited to return to Washington, DC, for an in-person, day-long, follow-up about six months later. The second LIWP class began in August 2009.

In designing the program, the planning committee followed many of the National Leadership Workshop recommendations, a few of which are highlighted below: employ nontraditional mentoring, , use novel approaches to develop and disseminate programming, don't re-create the wheel, and consider the needs of minority women.

Recommendations Employ Nontraditional Mentoring Models and Use Novel Approaches to Develop and Disseminate Programming

LIWP employs traditional and alternative means to mentor program participants, including traditional dyadic models, multiple mentors, peer mentoring, virtual mentoring, speed mentoring, and self-mentoring. Group and peer mentoring were successfully demonstrated during the program—participants had access to a distinguished faculty member and to the other participants. One of the program outcomes was to foster an ongoing peer mentoring relationship with class members, especially the members of the small groups that formed during the meeting. Staff provided the participants with their group rosters and encouraged them to meet via conference call and staff assisted individuals who were interested in organizing small group meetings.

Virtual Network and Web Meetings. LIWP used electronic resources to reinforce the cutting-edge nature of the program for psychology. The LIWP program established an online professional networking site and an online meeting application tool for the 2008 inaugural class and faculty members through NING and WebEx.

Networking Site: NING. NING is similar to Facebook and MySpace with a less cluttered, more professional presentation, greater security, and the opportunity to opt out of advertisements. It comes with extensive management features such as a message forum, private messaging, blogging, photo and video sharing, and a feature ensuring the network's privacy. Participants and the planning committee have posted LIWP-specific information such as meeting agendas, PowerPoint presentations, evaluation forms, photos, job announcements, and requests for proposals.

WebEx: Web Meetings and Conferencing. WebEx is the leading software for holding online meetings (Web conferencing). Designed for geographically dispersed group members to conduct meetings in real time, WebEx allows users to concurrently view on their desktops PowerPoint presentations or Word documents, to hold breakout sessions, and to engage in a question-and-answer (polling) area. WebEx also allows for group editing of documents in real time and offers a recording option allowing users to view the session at a later date or time. As part of LIWP's ongoing programming, Web conferencing presentations include "Getting in the Game: How to Influence Policy" and "How to Say No: Setting Professional Boundaries and Priorities." Virtual networks and Web meetings also fall under Recommendation 2—Use Novel Approaches to Develop and Disseminate Programming).

Recommendation #3—Don't Re-create the Wheel

To design a mentoring program, it is a good idea to explore existing programs and resources. Many mentoring programs exist, and at least six have been endorsed by the National Leadership Workshop (ORWH, 2008) as programs to emulate. Rather than creating the LIWP from scratch, the LIWP Planning Committee used the good works of these already existing to inform their discussions when developing the LIWP programming and curriculum.

Recommendation #4—Consider the Needs of Minority Women

The LIWP Planning Committee is a diverse group of distinguished women psychologists who have agreed to serve as mentors to the LIWP participants. One of the LIWP priorities is to ensure that leadership issues and training opportunities are available to midcareer and senior women in psychology in all of their diversities and the planning committee has been successful in recruiting women of color, lesbian and bisexual women, and women with disabilities.

The highlights above only skim the surface of the LIWP mentoring activities. This newest addition to CWP programming toward empowering women in psychology is still in its early stages, but the LIWP is well on its way to becoming an APA institution.

CONCLUSION

The Committee on Women in Psychology strives to empower women through a host of mechanisms that work at the individual and systemic levels. CWP recognized early on that empowering women individually and collectively, ensuring equity within the psychological community, hinged on its ability to document women's status, develop recommendations and implementation guidelines, develop mechanisms to increase women's participation, and network with other groups interested in women's equality. CWP has worked independently and in collaboration with other groups as a catalyst for structural and systemic change that in effect removed hurdles for women generally, to enable as many women as possible to advance and succeed.

To this end, the CWP continues to develop and provide information and resources to psychologists and future psychologists that enable women to self-mentor. Mentors provide critical information and support to individual women to help them address barriers to their own advancement. Not all women have ready access to effective mentors or mentoring throughout their careers, however. For women who have a positive and effective mentor, the information and resources that CWP provides complement that mutually rewarding relationship. For women who do not have a mentor, this approach allows CWP to reach a broader audience, empowering women with information and resources so that they can facilitate their own career advancement. With the development of its Web-based resources and the launch of its Leadership Institute for Women in Psychology, CWP continues to work to empower women within APA and the broader psychological community.

REFERENCES

American Psychological Association. (1974). *Publication manual of the American Psychological Association* (2nd ed.). Washington, DC: Author.

American Psychological Association. (2001). *Publication manual of the American Psychological Association* (5th ed.). Washington, DC: Author.

American Psychological Association Committee on Women in Psychology. (1990). *Models for organizing psychologists.* Washington, DC: American Psychological Association.

American Psychological Association Committee on Women in Psychology. (1993). *CWP two decades of change, 1973–1993.* Washington, DC: American Psychological Association.

American Psychological Association Committee on Women in Psychology. (1992). *Survival guide to academia for women and ethnic minorities.* Washington, DC: American Psychological Association.

American Psychological Association Committee on Women in Psychology & Commission on Ethnic Minority Recruitment, Retention and Training in

Psychology. (1998). *Surviving & thriving in academia: A guide for women and ethnic minorities.* Washington, DC: American Psychological Association.

American Psychological Association Committee on Women in Psychology & Women's Programs Office. (1982). *Understanding the manuscript review process.* Washington, DC: American Psychological Association.

American Psychological Association Committee on Women in Psychology & Women's Programs Office. (1983). *Understanding the manuscript review process* (2nd ed.).Washington, DC: American Psychological Association.

American Psychological Association Committee on Women in Psychology & Women's Programs Office, Public Interest Directorate. (1988). *Understanding the manuscript review process: Increasing the participation of women* (3rd ed.). Washington, DC: American Psychological Association.

American Psychological Association Women's Programs Office. (2009). *CWP Division Representatives 2009 Appointments.* Retrieved from http:www.apa.org/pi/wpo.

American Psychological Association Task Force on the Changing Gender Composition of Psychology. (1995). *Report of the Task Force on the Changing Gender Composition of Psychology.* Washington, DC: American Psychological Association.

Caso, R., Clark, C., Froyd, J., Inam, A., Kenimer, A., Morgan, J., & Rinehart, J. (2002). A systemic change model in engineering education and its relevance for women. Proceedings of the 2002 American Society for Engineering Education Annual Conference & Exposition. Session 2553. Montreal, Quebec.

Chrisler, J. (1998). Teacher versus scholar: Role conflict for women. In L. H. Collins, J. C. Chrisler, & K. Quina (Eds.), *Career strategies for women in academe: Arming Athena* (pp. 107–134). Thousand Oaks, CA: Sage Publications.

Gilbert, L., & Rossman, K. M. (1992). Gender and the mentoring process for women: Implications for professional development. *Professional Psychology: Research and Practice, 23,* 233–238.

Jackson, V., Palepu, A., Szalacha, L., Caswell, C., Carr, P., & Inui, T. (2003). Having the right chemistry: A qualitative study of mentoring in academic medicine. *Academic Medicine, 78*(3), 328–334.

Johnson, B. (2002). The intentional mentor: Strategies and guidelines for the practice of mentoring. *Professional Psychology: Research and Practice, 33*(1), 88–96.

Keita, G. (1988). Introduction. In American Psychological Association Committee on Women in Psychology & Women's Programs Office, Public Interest Directorate, *Understanding the manuscript review process: Increasing the participation of women* (3rd ed., pp. 1–2). Washington, DC: American Psychological Association.

Kelley, P. C. (1996). Can feminist language lead change organizational behavior? *Business & Society, 35,* 84–88.

Kite, M. E., Russo, N. F., Brehm, S. S., Fouad, N. A., Hall, C.C.I., Hyde, J. S., & Keita, G. P. (2001). Women psychologists in academe: Mixed progress, unwarranted complacency. *American Psychologist, 56,* 1080–1098.

Knouse, S. B. (2001). Virtual mentors: Mentoring on the Internet. *Journal of Employment Counseling, 38,* 162-169.

Loeffler, D. (1983). Introduction. In American Psychological Association Committee on Women in Psychology & Women's Programs Office, Public Interest Directorate, *Understanding the manuscript review process: Increasing the par-*

ticipation of women (2nd ed., pp. 1–4). Washington, DC: American Psychological Association.

Luckhaupt, S. E., Chin, M. H., Mangione, C. M., Phillips, R. S., Bell, D., Leonard, A. C., & Tsevat, J. (2005). Mentorship in academic general internal medicine. *Journal of General Internal Medicine, 20,* 1014–1018.

Mayer, A., Files, J., Ko, M., & Blair, J. (2008). Academic advancement of women in medicine: Do socialized gender differences have a role in mentoring? *Mayo Clinic Proceedings, 83*(2), 204–207.

Moss, P., De Bres, K. J., Cravey, A., Hyndman, J., Hirschboek, K. K., & Masucci, M. (1999). Mentoring as feminist praxis: Strategies for ourselves and others. *Journal of Geography in Higher Education, 23,* 413–427.

Noe, R. A. (1988). Women and mentoring: A review and research agenda. *Academy of Management Review, 13,* 65–78.

Office of Research on Women's Health, National Institutes of Health. (2008). *National Leadership Workshop on Mentoring Women in Biomedical Careers.* Bethesda, MD: National Institutes of Health.

Packard, B. W., Walsh, L., & Seidenberg, S. (2004). Will that be one mentor or two? A cross-sectional study of women's mentoring during college. *Mentoring and Tutoring, 12,* 71–85.

Pion, G. M., Mednick, M. T., Astin, H. S., Hall, C.C.I., Kenkel, M. B., Keita, G. P., Kohout, J. L., & Kelleher, J. C. (1996). The shifting gender composition of psychology: Trends and implications for the discipline. *American Psychologist, 51,* 509–528.

Ragins, B. R., & Cotton, J. (1999). Mentor functions and outcomes: A comparison of men and women in formal and informal mentoring relationships. *Journal of Applied Psychology, 84*(4), 529–550.

Rosser, S. (2007, November). *Mentoring though ADVANCE: Speed mentoring and ADEPT.* Paper presented at the Office for Research on Women's Health Workshop in Mentoring Women n Biomedical Careers, National Institutes of Health, Bethesda, MD.

Sambunjak, D., Straus, S. E., & Marusic, A. (2006). Mentoring in academic medicine: A systematic review. *Journal of the American Medical Association, 296,* 1103–1115.

Sandler, B. (1991). Women faculty at work in the classroom: Or why it still hurts to be a woman in labor. *Communication Education, 40,* 6–15.

Spencer, K. G. (2006). A feminist path to finding LGBT mentoring: A student perspective. *Feminist Psychologist, 33*(2), 19.

Turner, C., Gonzalez, J., & Wood, J. L. (2008). Faculty of color in academe: What 20 years of literature tells us. *Journal of Diversity in Higher Education, 1*(3), 139–168.

United Nations Economic and Social Council. (2006). *Absence of women from leadership positions undermines democracy, Commission on status of women told.* Retrieved June 8, 2009, from http://www.un.org/News/Press/docs/2006/wom 1541.doc.htm

U.S. Department of the Army, Office of the Quartermaster General. (2002). *Quartermaster warrant officer mentorship guide.* Retrieved August 31, 2007, from http://www.quartermaster.army.mil/oqmg/warrant_officer_proponency/ Mentorship_Program/GUIDE/Chapter_VII.htm

Williams-Nickelsen, C. (2007). *Women mentoring women: A model for psychology.* Washington, DC: American Psychological Association of Graduate Students.

Williams-Nickelsen, C. (2009). Graduate student mentoring: A model for professional psychology. *Professional Psychology: Research and Practice, 40,* 284–291.

Part V

Mentoring from the Perspective of Mental Health

Chapter 15

The Road to Leadership Roles

Jean Lau Chin

LEADERSHIP STATUS: CHOICE OR ASCRIPTION

Who is a leader? While we typically admire good leaders, individuals typically do not declare, "I want to be a leader" or "I am a leader." Such a declaration is likely to be viewed as self-promotion or arrogance. It is also likely to be viewed as a quest for power, which is typically socially taboo. The attainment of leadership status is better when it is ascribed as opposed to self-declared. The risks of such self-declarations include having one's motives questioned, being viewed as overrating oneself, or being viewed as having an inflated sense of self-importance. Consequently, men and women will often deny their aspirations to leadership or be less likely to self-identify as leaders. If being ascribed the status of leader is preferred over one's self-designation, and if the choice to be a leader is so frequently denied, how then do we mentor women to be leaders?

It is a fact that the ratio of women leaders compared to men is disproportionately low, even in fields dominated by women. If we add dimensions of race and ethnicity, women of color show even higher levels of discrepancies in the ranks of leadership (Chin, Lott, Rice, & Sanchez-Hucles, 2007). Most leaders are men, whether in government, corporations, or most other formal positions of leadership globally. In Western countries, the majority of men leaders are typically white despite the growing diversity within the population of these countries. The relative absence of white women and women of color in positions of leadership creates yet another challenge for how to mentor women for leadership positions. Who is there to mentor younger women into leadership positions?

What Is Leadership?

What is leadership? Northouse (2004, p. 3) defines leadership as "a process whereby an individual influences a group of individuals to achieve a common goal." Early definitions of leadership tended to emphasize power, command, and control aspects of leadership. Early definitions also focused on leadership as a status rather than leadership as a process. Contemporary definitions of leadership are more likely to emphasize transformational styles of leadership in which the leader offers a vision and direction to inspire and motivate followers (e.g., Hogan & Kaiser, 2005; Rost, 1991; Vroom & Jago, 2007; Yukl, 2006). Contemporary definitions are also likely to minimize the holding of power as characteristic of leadership, probably in reaction to the dictators ascending to power following World War I such as Mussolini and Hitler; hence, it is the abuse of power by leaders that has been subject to criticism rather than leadership itself. As a result, contemporary definitions often refer to shared power or servant leadership as characteristics of the modern and effective leader (Greenleaf, 2003).

Using Northouse's definition of leadership, we need to move away from paradigms of leadership that imply the abuse of power and the exploitation of others. These are simply instances of bad leadership. While leadership theories have been criticized for their North American bias, the expansion of leadership theories to include an attention to gender, race, and culture is just beginning. The literature on gender, race, and ethnicity will have much to offer to the conversation about the exercise of good leadership, but the question of integrating the these bodies of literature has been limited, with some exceptions (e.g., Eagly & Carli, 2007).

Research on leadership suggests that transformational styles of leadership and authenticity are desirable for today's leader in a global and diverse society. This includes leadership vision, embracing the values and concerns of diversity, and promoting social justice goals. The growing interdependence, cultures of collaboration, and shared accountabilities among different groups highlight the importance of team approaches over individual solutions to leadership. With a growing emphasis on multiculturalism, global citizenry, diversity, and multiple perspectives, effective leadership is increasingly viewed as inclusive, empowering, collaborative, and authentic.

The multinational, multicultural dimensionality of today's organizations requires leaders to be global in focus and sensitive to respecting people from around the world and from very diverse backgrounds, beliefs, and mores. This means becoming culturally literate and transculturally competent in a global world, with a growing focus on complexity and multidimensionality in today's world (Chin, 2009).

DIVERSE WOMEN LEADERS: DOUBTS ABOUT COMPETENCE

Transformational leadership styles and the concept of shared power are consistent with feminist values and principles as we now evolve models of feminist leadership (Chin et al., 2007; Eagly & Carli, 2007). Feminist women leaders tend to seek leadership positions to achieve social justice goals and to effect social change compared to men, who tend to seek leadership positions for power and status. The introduction of race and culture enriches the discussion further; values that are central to diverse cultures can expand the scope of leadership theories that have evolved from a more narrow North American perspective. For example, the discussion of leadership in non-Western cultures introduces concepts of collectivistic leadership and benevolent leaders that suggest a different view of power and authority in the leader–follower relationship. Racism and immigration also shape the experiences of diverse leaders and influence their exercise of leadership.

The literature on leadership suggests that different situations and contexts warrant different types of leaders and leadership styles (i.e., contingency theories). Moreover, a group's identity is likely to influence what its members expect and want from the leader (i.e., leader–member exchange theories, which center on the interactions between leaders and followers—the dyadic relationship is the focal point). Developing transformational leaders within a feminist and multicultural framework is syntonic with feminist principles and fundamental to mentoring women to be leaders for 21st-century corporate, civic, educational, and philanthropic institutions. Porter and Daniel (2006) point out that feminism is, by definition, a transformational ideology, with the aim of improving the social conditions for all members of society such that effective feminist leadership requires the conscious incorporation of four components of transformational leadership as described by Kark, Shamir, and Chen (2003):

a. Inspirational motivation—stirring others to action by communicating one's vision vividly, with optimism and enthusiasm
b. Idealized influence—modeling behaviors that place the group's good over one's personal needs and reflect high ethical standards
c. Individualized consideration—supporting, coaching, and encouraging constituents

    d. Intellectual stimulation—problem solving with constituents in collaborative and innovative ways

In attempting to be effective leaders, diverse women face unique and complex challenges as they negotiate their paths to leadership (Chin et al., 2007). They face added stressors of being expected to behave according to stereotypic norms based on gender, race, and ethnicity. They can be primary caretakers for family members, including elder parents or young children; balancing work and family falls more heavily on the shoulders of women. There are fewer successful role models who can serve as mentors. Moreover, the appraisals of women as leaders are often obscured by mixed messages or negative appraisals that question their competence because they may not behave in predictable ways. Although slight gender differences have been demonstrated between men and women leaders, how men and women behave as leaders typically tends to be quite similar; yet women are more likely to receive more negative appraisals for the same behaviors (Eagly & Karau, 2002).

In 2000, 1.3 percent of corporate officers in 400 of the Fortune 500 companies were women of color. Personal resilience, mentors, and a knack for creating opportunity were among the tools used by women of color executives to break down the "concrete ceiling." Senior-level women of color described exclusionary and risk-averse organizational cultures as key barriers to career advancement (Catalyst, 2001); that is, the old boys' network and unwillingness to take risks with those who appear different disadvantage women from accessing positions of leadership.

Stereotypes of women being communal (nurturing) and men being agentic (task oriented) often work to disadvantage women in the typical double bind. It is a known that most leaders are men; consequently, characteristics associated with leaders tend to be masculine. As a result, both men and women often expect or desire their leaders to be men. When women enact or ascend to these roles, they need to overcome the perceptions and expectations of them which often translate into doubts about their competence as leaders. If too agentic or task oriented, they are viewed as harsh, unemotional, and cold. Witness the criticisms of Hillary Rodham Clinton in her decisive and assertive approach. If too communal or collaborative, women are viewed as weak and indecisive.

Perceptions of women intersect with those of race and ethnicity to compound the barriers women of color face in leadership positions. Asian American women, for example, are often viewed as quiet, soft-spoken, acquiescent, and servile—traits that are incongruent with leadership roles that demand assertiveness and decisiveness. Yet African American women are often viewed as angry, intimidating, and hostile—traits that may preclude them from consideration for positions of leadership. These examples suggest how perceptions unwittingly use white male norms against which women and women of color are measured. As people hold images in their mind about who is a leader and what is leadership, they often resort to images of those already in such roles of leadership; these perceptions and expectations generally operate outside of consciousness. In the United States, where white men have traditionally dominated such positions, white women and women of color must grapple with the fact that they do not look like or act like the typical leader.

Women of color have different experiences based on their unique cultures, backgrounds, and lifestyles, which often results in their experience of exclusion from key workplace relationships. In a report by Catalyst (Bagati, 2008), they were more likely to be dissatisfied with overall managerial interaction and support, distribution of key client engagements, access to influential mentors, and access to business development opportunities.

Mentoring women to be leaders, then, means helping them to realistically identify their strengths and weaknesses and how these will be related to effective leadership. It means helping to distinguish between biases and perceptions that are unrelated to the exercise of effective leadership.

PRIVILEGE: ACCESS AND OPPORTUNITY

For white men or those in leadership positions, the privilege of not needing to face challenges of gender and race often goes unnoticed. For women and diverse leaders, access may be limited or denied. They simply do not have the opportunities for meeting with those who could facilitate access to positions of leadership. Opportunities for modeling behaviors are often absent. Personal, gender, and cultural identities may serve to disadvantage women from learning the behaviors associated with effective leaders; at the same time, they may be faced with doubts about their having the potential for being leaders. Men may use their larger physical size to be aggressive or challenge the authority of women leaders when they feel threatened. For example, they may talk over women because their voices will carry; they may physically block more petite women from view. When challenged, they may justify these behaviors as speaking one's mind or suggesting that women just need to jump in.

FEMINIST LEADERSHIP: UPHOLDING CORE VALUES AND A COMMITMENT TO CHANGE

Feminist leadership is transformational in nature, seeking to empower and enhance the effectiveness of one's team members while striving to improve the lives and social conditions of all stakeholders, including those indirectly affected, such as consumers and other members of society. This definition by Porter and Daniel (2007) contains the elements central to educating feminist, culturally competent leaders. They suggest that *values* make up the heart of feminist leadership and create a mnemonic for other elements, which include:

- *V*ision that is transforming, effectively communicated, and courageously executed
- *A*ction that is collaborative, community focused, and respectful
- *L*earning that is empowering, reflexive, and lifelong
- *U*nderstanding of power and boundaries issues that strive to empower
- *E*thical practices that promote inclusiveness, integrity, and responsibility
- *S*ocial constructivism that informs one's practice of leadership

Using this definition, our role as mentors of women for potential leadership roles is to support them in identifying and upholding their core values, and to encourage them to identify their passion and commitment—what drives them in what they choose to do and where they want to go. Within a feminist leadership model, social justice goals, achieving equity, and promoting diversity are essential values and goals toward validating self-esteem, promoting equal opportunity, and effecting social change.

PATH TO LEADERSHIP: LADDER OR MAZE?

Typically, we talk of career ladders and climbing the ladder of success when we teach about advancement. However, if aspirations for leadership are to be hidden, if quest for power is viewed as negative, if perceptions and appraisals of diverse women are biased and stereotypic, if the privilege held by white men makes them blind to the denial of access and opportunity, and if women are less likely to be in leadership roles, then what is the path to leadership roles for women, and how do we mentor them?

Eagly and Carli (2007) capture these phenomena using their metaphor of the labyrinth—the challenges that women face as they navigate indirect, complex, and often discontinuous paths toward leadership. In fact, the path to leadership positions is often unclear or hidden; *it is a maze*. Overt paths may be hidden, intentionally or unintentionally. Rules of engagement may change by virtue of race and gender; this has been termed aversive racism in which unintended consequences of systemic bias serve to disadvantage those not already in these positions (Dovidio & Gaertner, 2004).

As a result, diverse women often are challenged to be twice as good to counter the biases, perceptions, and expectations. They tend to go overboard. Instead, they need to learn to strike the balance; how and when to be tough and aggressive versus warm and compassionate. They need to create access and opportunities where there are none. As trailblazers, they are likely to meet resistance as the first nonwhite man to be in a leadership position.

They need to recognize that masculine environments are ingrained and that men may try to overpower when they feel threatened by a woman's authority. Women may also be unable to accept another woman's authority because they expect or want a man to be in charge, and themselves are inculcated to such environments.

The double standard is another dimension of the maze. Women will be condemned for crying and viewed as not tough enough; yet when they are aggressive like men, they are condemned for behaving in an overbearing way. Women are expected to be nice; cultural values of Asian women, in particular, prescribe modesty. As a result, self-promotion is more characteristic and accepted of men.

Access and opportunity are often central to people obtaining positions of leadership. It is a matter of being in the right place at the right time. It is the politics of knowing the right people. It is in the opportunity to perform those tasks which bring recognition and provide access to leadership roles. Often women and racial and ethnic minorities are excluded from these opportunities. Women face the challenge of work-family balance more so than men. Racial and ethnic minority women often find they must choose between their participation in multiple social contexts—those that meet their affiliation needs for race and ethnicity and those that are useful for ascending to positions of leadership.

MENTORING WOMEN TO BE LEADERS

What is a mentor? Mentors are more experienced individuals who help those who are less experienced to advance their careers, enhance their education, and build their networks. To mentor women into leadership roles, we must first focus on values that guide women's careers and paths. This guidance is important if we identify the path to leadership as a maze. For mentors, the task is one of identifying promising protégés and urging them in their career paths and role choices. A mentor, then, is someone who believes in you. For mentors, the responsibility is to reach down and pay back when you've ascended to higher levels of authority and leadership. For mentees, it is to seek those to whom you aspire and admire based on core values and career choices.

Women as mentors often have the advantage of sharing in the experiences of bias and barriers that are different from men. Work-family balance, pregnancy, caretaking of family members, and child care are some of the challenges faced by women as they ascend the career ladder. The balancing of work and family is different for women than it is for men. Today, social expectations still prescribe roles according to gender. Although men are increasing playing greater roles of co-parenting and sharing in the housework, women still bear the burden. Mentors can offer role modeling on how to do something and lead the way. Modeling how to juggle living with difference in two cultures is something mentors can do for women of color. How does one return to one's culture of origin and community, retain one's identity, and still participate actively in multiple contexts where the tolerance for difference may be lacking? While the emphasis is on women mentoring women, men can be good mentors, especially when they are able to create access in ways that women may not. Given the barriers we still face today, some women have been too competitive to allow themselves to reach down and help those behind them.

A mentor is empowering and offers a mutuality in a give-and-take relationship. Mentors can help mentees to identify personal and professional goals and to promote self-esteem, self-awareness, self-motivation, and self-efficacy. In the event that this focus on self is too self-absorbing, mentors can help mentees recognize their humility. Mentors can help women into leadership roles by encouraging them to be there, speak up, work hard, have a vision for where we want to be, and come together for a common cause.

REFERENCES

Bagati, D. (2008). Women of color in U.S. securities firms—Women of Color in Professional Services Series. New York: Catalyst Research Reports.

Catalyst. (2001). *Women of color executives: Their voices, their journeys.* New York: Catalyst Research Reports.

Chin, J. L. (2009). The dynamics of gender, race, and leadership. In R. H. Klein, C. A. Rice, & V. L. Schermer (Eds.), *Leadership in a changing world: Dynamic perspectives on groups and their leaders* (pp. 73–92). Lanham, MD: Lexington Books.

Chin, J. L., Lott, B., Rice, J. K., & Sanchez-Hucles, J. (Eds.). (2007). *Women and leadership: Transforming visions and diverse voices.* Malden, MA: Blackwell.

Dovidio, J. F., & Gaertner, S. L. (2004). Aversive racism. In M. P. Zanna (Ed), *Advances in experimental social psychology* (Vol. 36, pp. 1–52). San Diego, CA: Elsevier Academic Press.

Eagly, A. H., & Carli, L. L. (2007). *Through the labyrinth: The truth about how women become leaders.* Boston: Harvard Business School Press.

Eagly, A., and Karau, S. J. (2002). Role congruity theory of prejudice toward female leaders. *Psychological Review, 109*(3), 573–598.

Greenleaf, R. K. (2003). *The servant-leader within: A transformative path.* New York: Paulist Press.

Hogan, R., & Kaiser, R. B. (2005). What we know about leadership. *Review of General Psychology, 9,* 169–180.

Kark, R., Shamir, B., & Chen, G. (2003). The two faces of transformational leadership: Empowerment and dependency. *Journal of Applied Psychology, 88,* 246-255

Northouse, P. G. (2004). Introduction. In Northouse, P. G. (Ed.), *Leadership: Theory and practice* (3rd ed., pp.1–15). Thousand Oaks, CA: Sage.

Porter, N. & Daniel, J. H. (2007). Developing transformational leaders: Theory to practice. In J. L. Chin, B. Lott, J. K. Rice, and J. Sanchez-Hucles (Eds.),

Women and leadership: Transforming visions and diverse voices, (pp. 245–263). Malden, MA: Blackwell Publishing.

Rost, J. (1991). *Leadership for the 21st century.* New York: Praeger.

Vroom, V. H., & Jago, A. G. (2007). The role of the situation in leadership. *American Psychologist, 62*(1), 17–24.

Yukl, G. (2006). *Leadership in organizations* (6th ed.). Upper Saddle River, NJ: Prentice Hall.

Chapter 16

A Social Psychological Approach to Mentoring

Janet Sigal and Katharine L. Loeb

Social psychology is an ideal framework through which to examine the process of mentoring. It is defined as the effect or influence of other people on the behavior of individuals (Aronson, 2008). Therefore, a mentoring relationship can easily be analyzed utilizing social psychological models or theories.

This chapter describes some models that can be adapted to the mentoring relationship. Following this brief introduction to social psychological explanatory mechanisms, we outline three prototypes of new faculty members who might benefit from a mentoring experience. These prototypes were developed from a series of interviews conducted with faculty members at various universities. We explore the mentoring process in terms of the needs of individuals at varying stages of their academic careers. We also present some issues related to mentoring new faculty members, as well as propose a model designed to develop effective mentoring relationships. Finally, we extend our analysis to mentoring doctoral students involved in research relationships and the mentoring of American Psychological Association interns at the United Nations.

SOCIAL PSYCHOLOGICAL MODELS

Several areas of social psychology seem particularly relevant to the mentoring setting. For example, communicator credibility, a major research topic in social psychology (Aronson, 2008), is composed of two components. Expertness is defined in terms of the knowledge an individual possesses based on education, years of experience, and credentials. From this perspective, it seems clear that a primary mentor for a new faculty individual should be a senior faculty member in the department. This senior person should be familiar not only with intradepartmental processes, but also should be knowledgeable about university issues and procedures. The second component of communication credibility is trustworthiness, which is essential in a mentoring relationship. Issues related to trust include confidentiality, the mentor's motivation to be truthful and honest in characterizing the department's climate, and the mentor's connections to other departmental and university faculty members. As will be discussed in a subsequent section, this relationship can be complicated if the senior faculty member has a dual role with the mentored new assistant professor in the form of contributing to the latter's recommendation for tenure.

Interpersonal perception is another social psychological area that can be applied to the mentoring relationship. The mentor will communicate an impression to the new faculty member that may crystallize that individual's perception of the department as a whole. In interpersonal perception, first impressions are crucial and can help determine how the new faculty person reacts to the department in the first year. Therefore, it is important that the mentor possess many positive qualities, including warmth and concern for the welfare of the person being mentored. If the new faculty person responds positively to the mentor, he will, by extension, develop a positive impression of the department. In addition, the mentor's own view of the department could be conveyed to the new faculty member and can have a direct influence on that individual's perception of the whole department. Finally for this theory, a department that establishes a mentoring program may be perceived as a caring faculty.

Leadership is a third social psychological research area that can be applied to the mentoring situation. The mentor can be characterized as the leader of the mentoring dyad. One of the current issues in the field is the distinction between transformational and transactional leaders (Chrisler & Clapp, 2008). A transformational leader views the process as collaborative, fosters participation by all individuals in the process, and emphasizes encouragement rather than criticisms of followers. A transactional leader, however, focuses on the task and emphasizes critical guidance rather than encouragement of followers. Men leaders traditionally have been more transactional in style, whereas women leaders more often have been characterized as transformational leaders, although there are many examples that do not reinforce gender stereotypes. A mentor should be perceived more positively when exemplifying a transformational as opposed to a transactional style.

Another aspect of a leadership analysis of mentoring involves the precise nature of the mentoring relationship. In clinical psychology, it is clear that a faculty member in a psychology department should not play dual roles with students. In other words, if the faculty member teaches a doctoral student, that person should not also be the student's therapist. Similarly, a faculty mentor ideally should only be in a supportive role and not in an evaluative role with respect to the new faculty member. As discussed later in this chapter, this distinction between the two roles may be difficult to adopt if a senior faculty member is the mentor.

A related social psychological explanatory mechanism is the concept of group dynamics, which is defined as the study of groups and also as the forces in a group (Forsyth, 1990). These forces include communication between the mentor and the faculty member being mentored as well as cooperation and participation levels in the department as a whole. One aspect of the group process, or interactions among members of the department, involves the formal and informal departmental group structure. The manner in which the leaders of the department are chosen, whether formally or informally, democratically, or imposed on the department by administration, may affect the mentoring relationship. It is very important for the new faculty member to understand the structure, particularly as it applies to a new faculty member's requirements. Departmental norms also must be communicated to the new individual. For example, in many departments "face time" is quite important, both within the department and at university events and meetings. In particular, for the first few years of a faculty member's adjustment to the new demands, the mentor should emphasize that attendance at and participation in all departmental meetings is essential. Attendance at university meetings should be mandatory, because one of the goals of a mentor would be to introduce the person being mentored to the administration and faculty in other departments. In addition, the mentor should stress the importance of being reasonably available to students, both in the office setting and via e-mail. However, excessive student demands for 24/7 access should not be expected. Another norm for new faculty members is to become aware of the dynamics in the department and to "earn idiosyncrasy credits" by conforming to norms and volunteering for tasks and committees within and outside the department before attempting to innovate. Once the faculty member is accepted as a valued professor, it is more likely that suggested changes will be viewed positively. Another concept associated with departmental norms is the idea of fostering mentoring relationships. If the department is the type to establish a norm of interdependence (dependence of faculty upon each other to achieve group goals) and helping, it is more likely to set in place an official and effective mentoring process for new faculty.

Another important social psychological concept is cohesiveness. Although this concept generally is applied to larger groups, it also can be used to examine mentoring relationships. Cohesiveness implies positive bonds that develop among group members. In an effective mentoring relationship, these bonds should develop rather quickly once the relationship is established. If the two people in the mentoring relationship share the same goal of easing the new faculty member's transition into the department and the university, then cohesiveness should develop. Once again, the motivation of the mentor is very important. Ideally, the mentor's only concern should be the adaptation of the new faculty person into the department. If the mentor has any other hidden motivation for volunteering to be in this relationship, that factor may negatively affect the individual being mentored. Another aspect of the setting involves the cohesiveness of the department. In an analysis similar to families, departments may be cohesive, enmeshed, detached, or hostile and divided into factions. In a cohesive department, all members share the same goals and visions and are collectively concerned about the welfare of the department, the students, and the university. In an enmeshed department, faculty members interfere with each other and try to impose their views onto new faculty. A detached department climate contains several individuals who work well independently but establish few connections with other faculty in the department. In a hostile department, several factions oppose each other. In the last case, the mentor may try to either protect the new faculty member from becoming embroiled in factional disputes or recruit the person being mentored into one or another faction. Clearly, the latter approach is inappropriate. In the best type of mentoring relationship, the mentor should present a fair, balanced, and realistic view of the departmental climate. The mentor also may facilitate social climate interactions of the new faculty person. In some departments, support groups such as women's groups, or groups based on the discipline to which the new individual belongs may enhance the person's involvement and comfort in the new environment.

Another social psychological research area that provides a further analysis of the mentoring relationship is prosocial or helping behavior. There is a distinction between egoistic and altruistic helping that may be applied to this setting (Baumeister and Bushman, 2008). Egoistic helping is exemplified by a situation in which the helper has motivations other than just selfless aid. The mentor, for example, may offer to help the new person to gain some stature in the department or to gain service credits within the department. Mentors who volunteer simply because they want to ease the transition of the faculty member into the department without accruing any rewards for this action would be seen as altruistic helpers. In that sense, senior faculty mentors often will be characterized as altruistic in nature.

PROTOTYPES

There are at least three different types of new faculty hires. The first, which is the most common, is the person who is an early career professional.

These individuals traditionally arrive at the university directly after either completing the doctoral degree or after a postdoctoral position. This type of individual is the most basic type and requires the most significant amount of mentorship. The second prototype is a midcareer individual who has arrived at the university after several years at another university. This individual requires less mentoring than the early career professional. The third type of new faculty member is a senior-level career individual who has amassed credentials in the field as a practitioner and now is a full-time faculty member. The amount of mentoring required for this individual depends on whether the person has had teaching experience. In particular, if that person has been in an adjunct position in the department, less mentoring may be required.

These following discussions of the mentoring needs of the three different types of new faculty members in a department are based on a small number of semistructured interviews conducted with men and women early career professionals, middle, and senior new hires. The interviewees represented a number of different universities in the Northeast and were all from psychology departments. Following the analysis of responses to specific semistructured questions, we will summarize some of the issues that were raised and some recommendations stemming from responses to our interviews.

Early Career Professionals

Most of the interviews were conducted with early career professional faculty members who ranged in age from 27 to 35 years. Most of these individuals had been at their universities for two years or less. Clearly, generalization from such a small volunteer sample is difficult, but we did note many similarities among the responses of our participants. The interviews were conducted either in a face-to-face setting or on the telephone.

Individuals were asked what issues were raised in terms of role expectations when they were interviewed for the assistant professor position. In general, all respondents indicated that teaching requirements and research responsibilities were discussed in some detail, but more general information was given rather than specifics.

In terms of whether they were assigned a formal mentor or had voluntary mentors once they were hired, most of the respondents had an assigned formal mentor but mentioned that they also were mentored spontaneously by other faculty members in the department. In the beginning when they first arrived at the university, they generally met often with the officially assigned mentor, but as they became more integrated into the department, the meetings became more infrequent. The meetings might have been weekly or monthly at first and then occurred when needed. One individual stated that he now seeks people out to help with issues, and another said that almost all the faculty in her department have stopped by and said that their door was always open. Both men and women faculty members acted as mentors.

The next questions in our interview dealt with academic mentoring. In general, the department chair or director of the specific program consulted with the new faculty member concerning courses assigned and the schedules for class times. For most of our respondents, there was a discussion of the level of students in different programs as well as student expectations. In doctoral programs, the importance of high-level teaching and adhering to strict professional standards was emphasized. For new faculty teaching graduate students, the distinction was made between master's-level courses and in doctoral-level courses. Particular emphasis was placed on distinctions between the level of undergraduate and graduate students for some of our early career professional participants. For some respondents, grading was discussed by the mentor and the departmental chair. One respondent suggested that the difficulty of determining the appropriate difficulty level of examinations was a concern for her. If students did not do well on an examination, she consulted with her mentor. All individuals had been observed several times since arriving at the university. The observations were seen as universally helpful to the recipients of the feedback in terms of boosting their confidence; in most cases, it was validation of the excellence of their teaching. However, some of the interviewees said that their mentors made valuable suggestions about how to motivate students and get them more involved in the class. All respondents felt that the academic mentoring was very effective.

Almost all of the early career professionals were mentored in terms of university service requirements. They were nominated for effective committees either by their mentor, other faculty, or the chair. In two cases, the faculty hire was protected for the first year or two by waiving the requirement for university service in order to permit the respondent to develop a research program or become more adjusted to the position.

One of the questions raised the issue of mentoring toward tenure and promotion. Many of the interviewees felt that there were clear expectations communicated either by a mentor or the chair. In most cases, excellence in teaching was emphasized along with publishing good-quality research. One respondent felt that other junior faculty members were more helpful about specific details such as developing a faculty portfolio. In another case, the participant thought that the university-based workshop on new faculty orientation was very effective.

We asked several questions related to research issues. Some of the new faculty hires had research fellows assigned to them, some had lab space, and others had good technological support. In one case, the faculty member was encouraged to apply for research release time, but it was a competitive process. One individual had a reduced teaching load and could send drafts of articles to her mentor. Another individual could have been assigned a research fellow, but she was so new that she wanted to establish her teaching credentials before beginning a strong research program.

In terms of departmental climate, the majority of respondents indicated that the climate in the department was positive, cohesive, and very supportive. Faculty members got along and also approached the person and asked what they could do to ease the transition into full-time teaching. In one case, there had been some minor personality conflicts, but the department was a "family" and generally got along. One individual said that she was informed about issues in the department by both men and women, but that women were more direct and men spoke in more general terms.

Middle Career Professionals

Midcareer professionals have either transferred to a new university or entered the university world after another career, possibly as a practitioner. The people we interviewed in this category were men and women in their 40s. On average, the respondents had taught at the university for three years.

In terms of expectations when they were hired, more advanced issues were addressed, such as the numbers of dissertations the faculty member was supposed to chair and the requirements of working with doctoral students. In one case, the person had already been an adjunct at the university and was aware of expectations. Half of those interviewed had a mentor, and the other half did not have a mentor and were asked to choose one. They met regularly with their mentor but felt free to approach the mentor at other times when they had questions. Many senior faculty members, both men and women, were available as mentors.

In terms of academic mentoring, they consulted with the departmental chair or the director of their program about their assigned courses and schedule. In one case, the difference between master's and doctoral students was discussed officially with a mentor, and in one other case, the different levels of students emerged as a result of informal comments. In all cases, there was no mentoring in relation to grading procedures, but in one case the complexities of grade inflation were discussed. All individuals felt that the feedback from observations of teaching done by various faculty members was a validation that they were doing a good job and was encouraging and helpful.

The chair in all cases nominated the individual for university service and discussed the required steps toward tenure and promotion. In terms of developing their portfolios for faculty review, other more junior faculty mentors were helpful. All of the middle career individuals were assigned graduate assistants, and some had release time for research. Some collaboration occurred with other faculty members in the department, and, for one individual, there was collaboration with people in other departments on grant applications. In one case, the individual felt that grant support was not very available. In terms of climate issues, respondents felt that the climate was spontaneously and informally discussed.

Senior Career Change Participants

There were very few respondents in the senior-level career category, but it seemed clear that the hands-on field experience of these applicants was a primary reason for hiring this senior person. In one case, there were two mentors who met with the individual about once a month. One dealt more with procedural administrative departmental details and the other with university processes. One of our respondents felt that, because he had been an adjunct at the university, academic mentoring was unnecessary. In fact, he felt that there were too many observations and that the feedback was pleasant but not helpful. Research fellows were assigned, and the individuals felt that their colleagues were collegial and supportive.

ISSUES AND RECOMMENDATIONS

As can be seen from our small interview study, there is a much greater need for consistent, constant mentoring for early career professionals, but even middle career academics require some mentoring to adjust to a new environment. In this section, we discuss some of the issues that were raised throughout our interviews and in earlier parts of this chapter. We also describe recommendations for more effective academic mentoring of new faculty and propose a model for departments that do not have a mentoring program in place. Some of these recommendations stem from our interview with the director of graduate programs at one institution.

One of the issues is whether there should be formal or informal mentors and whether there should be an assigned mentor or spontaneous mentors. Many respondents suggested that there should be an assigned formal mentor, particularly for early career professionals since it is difficult to make the transition from graduate student status to assistant professor. The recommended level was a senior faculty member. However, some of those interviewed suggested that there also should be a junior faculty member who can assist the new person with issues such as faculty portfolios. Participants also agreed that it would be easier to assign a mentor for teaching than for research. If a research mentor was assigned, it should be someone in the same discipline as the new faculty hire.

The clear downside of an assigned faculty member is possible personality clashes. Also, another researcher suggested that sometimes volunteer faculty mentors are marginal individuals in the department or those who have a biased view of their colleagues. There should be someone overseeing the mentorship program who can be approached if a new faculty person has difficulty with an assigned faculty mentor. In addition, the department chair should support the mentorship program. Mentors should be positive people who are warm and caring and have good relationships with other departmental colleagues. Interestingly, early career professionals felt that assigned formal mentors were preferable, but middle career individuals thought that informal mentors would be more effective. In addition, informal mentors should seek out new faculty members who are not assertive to determine whether there are issues that require a mentor. One middle career individual felt that mentoring in more informal settings such as group lunches might be preferable to always meeting in the department. In general, it seems that multiple mentors for various aspects of adjusting to the new position would be helpful, especially for early career professionals but also for middle career individuals. One other difference between the two types of faculty hires is that the middle and senior career individuals, not surprisingly, found the multiple and constant observations of teaching to be unnecessary and annoying.

A second issue is confidentiality, which also leads to another possible recommendation. There definitely are limits to confidentiality. Clearly, if student welfare is at risk, the mentor would be required to share the offered information with the administrators in the department. However, there is another related issue. A mentor generally is seen as a supporter and encourager of the new faculty member. This person should have a positive attitude toward the new individual, with the expectation that the person will succeed and remain in the department. However, it is possible, especially in the case of a senior faculty mentor, that this individual also may be an evaluator. Because the new faculty person will be aware of this dual role, that person might be reluctant to disclose any difficulties that she is having in terms of teaching, research, university connections, departmental climate, or with a particular faculty member. In addition, although the mentor might be a senior faculty member, it might not be possible for the mentor to protect the new person if the senior person is not part of the administration of the department. Ideally, the senior faculty mentor might offer to observe the early career professional in a teaching setting without delivering a written evaluation to the department. By keeping the observation confidential, the mentor may encourage the new person to request help when necessary. This process would be easier in larger departments. One other suggestion has been made that research mentoring might be a role for senior professionals who are in the early career professional's field, but at other universities. However, although additional outside research mentors may be helpful, some government-issued career development awards require an on-site research mentor who is responsible for ensuring protected research time and sufficient resources to help the junior faculty members develop into effective independent investigators.

A third problem occurs when there are factions in a department. In this case, the mentor must remain a consistent, practical, and fair advocate for the new individual without biasing that person in one direction or another.

The mentor also should protect the person being mentored from becoming embroiled in departmental politics.

MENTORING MODEL

Based on the above information and social psychological considerations, we have developed an overall model for departments that currently do not have a mentoring program for new faculty members. We recommend that there should be a pool of volunteer mentors (at least five or six people) who are senior, tenured faculty members. One person should be assigned to be the director of the program. The potential members should determine the content of the mentoring process. Issues include whether there will be formal assigned or spontaneous mentors and whether each new person will have one senior mentor or one senior and one more junior mentor. The mentors should decide on how often the mentoring dyad should meet and what areas should be covered. In addition, a positive, advocacy-oriented, protective attitude should be assumed to be characteristic of mentors. There should be a specific effort to avoid dual roles of advocate and evaluator, and confidentiality and the limits of confidentiality should be determined once the program is in place. These policies should be transparent to the mentored individual. All aspects of the academic experience should be covered by individual mentors. In addition, the mentors should meet periodically to determine how the process is going. Possibly at the end of one year, new faculty hires should fill out a confidential evaluation of the mentor and the program which will be used by the director to increase the effectiveness of the mentoring program.

MENTORING OF DOCTORAL STUDENTS

Research mentoring of doctoral students is another area in which a social psychological approach may be applied to increase the effectiveness of the process. The senior author utilizes a team approach for her examination of cross-cultural perceptions of domestic violence as well as other research projects. Once a doctoral student indicates an interest in her research and joins the team, the first year, the new doctoral student is an apprentice, both to the faculty member and to the senior doctoral student on the team. During the first semester, the new research team member becomes involved in completing projects that must be prepared for conference submissions. By the first or second semester, the new student has developed an idea for his required second-year research project. All members of the research team participate in the planning and completion of each project. At this point, the new team member will be given the responsibility to coordinate her project, beginning with developing the materials, organizing the research participants, and inputting the data. Under the direction of the faculty mentor, the student learns by participating in the project from beginning to end. After the faculty member has analyzed the data, the student is responsible for writing a first draft proposal for a conference presentation. If the proposal is accepted, then the doctoral student attends the conference as the first author of the research project.

Throughout this project, the faculty member and the doctoral student team leader act as mentors to the new research team member. This individual learns how to do research by full participation on the team and is guided and mentored by the faculty member and the doctoral team leader. By the second year, doctoral student team members become full-fledged researchers who participate as colleagues in the research process.

MENTORING AT THE UNITED NATIONS

In 2006, the senior author was selected as a representative on the American Psychological Association's (APA) nongovernmental organization team at the United Nations (UN). In a sense, although it is a volunteer position for individuals of senior stature in their field, when you begin at the UN, you are a neophyte once again. The UN system is incredibly complex and highly structured, and it takes a long time to become knowledgeable about the process of interaction within the system.

I was fortunate to have Dr. Florence Denmark, the main representative for APA at the UN, as my mentor. When I arrived with another new representative, she first took us on a tour of the United Nations building. It was very exciting to go behind the scenes where the public is not permitted. However, it took us a long time before we became familiar with the UN main Secretariat Building.

At first, everything was confusing to us. However, Dr. Denmark introduced us to many UN and NGO people and was the major reason that I now feel comfortable in that setting. As a mentor, she was able to assign me to a major NGO project at the beginning of my second year. I was named as co-chair of the International Day of Older Persons (IDOP). The entire process was overwhelming at first, but under Dr. Denmark's guidance and mentorship, I organized our planning committee and we had a very successful IDOP. The event attracted close to 300 people to the morning session, 100 people to the afternoon session, and 80 people to a fundraising lunch. There were representatives from the United Nations' five regions of the world who spoke about human rights for older persons. It was exciting to see the event grow from the initial sessions, where the mission statement and theme was developed, to a well-attended event that produced excellent feedback from the audience. In addition to assigning me this enormous task, which gave me tremendous experience in dealing with UN staff people and handling crises, my mentor helped me to become well known through the NGO committee and gave me confidence to become more assertive at the UN.

In 2008, the APA NGO UN team selected three APA interns from a pool of 20 or more qualified student applicants. These three graduate students were from very diverse backgrounds—from Hong Kong, Japan, and India—and have made significant contributions to the team's efforts throughout the year. Once they were selected and accepted the position, I took them on a tour of the UN building and discussed our expectations for the graduate students during their internship year. It has been a pleasure to mentor these students in a manner similar to how I was mentored by Dr. Denmark.

CONCLUSIONS

Many of the social psychological theories and models described in the early section of this chapter have been useful in analyzing the mentoring process for junior faculty, doctoral students in research teams, and APA team representatives and graduate student interns at the UN. From all of our interviews and analyses, it seems clear that all university departments should develop mentoring programs for new faculty members. These programs can help the department develop a good relationship with junior faculty members as well as create a positive impression of the department if the mentor is perceived as a credible communicator, a warm and trustworthy person with no hidden agendas, and an advocate and protector of the junior faculty member. In this case, the junior faculty person will feel wanted and respected and will be helped in the significant transition from graduate student to junior faculty member.

REFERENCES

Aronson, E. (2008). *The social animal* (10th ed.). New York: Worth.

Baumeister, R. F., & Bushman, B. J. (2008). *Social psychology: Human nature.* Belmont, CA: Thomson Wadsworth.

Chrisler, J., & Clapp, S. K. (2008). In M.A. Paludi (Ed.), *The psychology of women at work,* (pp. 39–65). Westport, CT: Praeger.

Forsyth, D. (1990). *Group dynamics* (2nd ed.). Pacific Groves, CA: Brooks/Cole.

Part VI

Conclusion

Chapter 17

Conclusion

Carole A. Rayburn, Florence L. Denmark, Mary E.
Reuder, and Asuncion Miteria Austria

We, the co-editors and contributors, and you, our readers, have been on
a journey, traveling on a path to greater satisfaction, fulfillment, and success in life, profession, and career. This examination of the various functions of mentoring—particularly women mentoring and diverse women
mentoring—has included discussions of meaningful and sensitive caring,
sharing, hand holding, anticipatory planning, fear and need reduction,
advising, counseling, guiding, protecting, networking, teaching, coaching,
advocating for, being role models for, sponsoring, challenging, critical thinking and critiqueing, and accepting and confirming mentors; building mentees' self-esteem and self-confidence; and being aware of, sensitive to, and
instructing mentees in terms of gender, race, and ethnic issues that have
hindered achievement and progress and how to overcome these barriers.
As trusted advisors, mentors need to be positive, enthusiastic, and encouraging and emphasize mentees' strengths, core values, potentials, and self-
awareness.

We have discussed informal and formal mentoring and their and advantages and disadvantages, as well as good mentoring and bad mentoring

(or "tormenting"). The most empowering mentoring stresses the need to develop sensitivity to gender, cultural, racial, and ethnic differences in mentees and others, in the world of academe, and the world beyond the campus and office. Mentors need to take into account the effects of family, community, religious and/or spiritual background, school, culture, racial and ethnic identity, and socioeconomic status on protégés and mentors. One size definitely does not fit all: Critical thinking and creative planning are urgently called for in beneficial mentoring relationships. Mentoring increases knowledge, experience, and confidence and lessens fears, shyness, self-blaming, and poor self-image. When the mentoring relationship is good, it bridges the gap between academe and the environment beyond to make interpersonal interactions more realistic, meaningful, and flexible. Hopefully this handbook has given you some tools with which to better build your house of confidence, self-worth, authenticity, and sensitivity to diversity in accomplishing your professional, social, and personal goals.

While we have stressed women and diverse women mentors working with mentees to advance them to their highest goals, in a most meaningful sense, *all* women benefit from mentoring. *Every* woman—whether her goal is to be a good homemaker, artist, contractor, administrator, teacher, or successful in any other line of endeavor—can benefit from being given a helping hand by a caring and sensitive trusted advisor, teacher, guide, and role model. Otherwise, she might be lost for quite some time in the morass of trial and error.

Good mentoring is a win–win situation for both the mentor and mentee. Good mentors derive pleasure and delight from the challenge and fun in seeing the mentee traverse the road to deeper understanding and more success. The mentor also develops skills in teaching, guiding, advising, networking, and role modeling.

There is, unfortunately, a serious dearth of women and women of diverse race, culture, and ethnic background to serve as role models and mentors to the many protégés and mentees who seek mentoring relationships. This scarcity is due, in part, to the siphoning away of women's time and energy into assigning them to service tasks at their work sites. Further, women often are wives and parents, managing somehow homes, family responsibilities, and jobs and careers. As long as women are viewed by faculty and students as less powerful—though often more purposeful—men will be chosen more often as mentors than women are. Women and diverse women may be especially left out of the crucial informal networks that often define career advancement. In terms of both diverse women and men mentors, students need to reach out to multiple mentors and mentors of multicultural backgrounds to meet their personal and professional needs.

Not only are there too few diverse women mentors and role models, but diverse women students are seriously underrepresented at most levels of graduate education. Besides problems and barriers of tokenism, diverse women are often subjected to professional isolation, exclusion from vital networking and collaboration opportunities, unfair criticism and devaluation of research interests, and sexualization of their racial, ethnic, and cultural images. Through good mentoring, especially with fine role models of successful women and diverse women, women mentees can learn to reject the sexism, racism, and elitism in academe and society at large; to bury as nonviable corpses of a moribund past such barriers; to build up their self-esteem and self-worth; to speak up and initiate dialogue with potential mentors to make known what they want and need; and to continue to reach out for mentors when needed throughout their lives, professions, and careers. Women protégés and mentees need to overcome their tendencies toward reticence and their tendencies to be self-deprecating and unnecessarily perfectionistic, with all-or-none thinking.

The vital and viable feminist model of mentoring places emphasis on sharing power, collaboration, relational sharing or offering of mutuality, and commitment to diversity. Changing the system of the university, workplace, and home as they now present barriers to the advancement of women and of diverse women is also a serious goal. As needs of students change, more advanced means of communication and mentoring come into play, including blogs; distance teaching; and the academic faculty, organization, or system as a whole becoming the mentor. Three types of faculty hire were also discussed: early career professionals, midcareer persons, and senior-level career individuals.

Earlier models of mentoring were more transactional (task oriented and stressing critical guidance); current mentoring is more transformational (collaborative, encouraging, inspiring, committed to change and a multicultural framework, and holding onto core values). Contributors, in addition to giving the history and guidelines for mentors and mentees, shared their personal and professional experiences with mentoring relationships—the good, the bad, the ugly, and the wonderful. They walked us through their experiences with mentoring, delving step by step into the waters of learning by doing, planning, interacting, networking, and coming out into the warmth and blue skies of professional and career fulfillment. Share in our mentoring experiences, and then share these—and yours—with others!

Index

Academia, mentoring in, 6, 40
American Catholic Psychological Association, 192–93
Asian American women: discrimination against, 152–53; and leadership, 151; stereotyping of, 152–53; and their need for mentors, 153–55
Aunt Academe's Harriet Aronson, 206
"Aversive racism," 178

"Bamboo ceiling," 225–26
Barriers to effective mentoring: cultural variables, 137–38, 254–55; egoistic helping, 264; race and gender, 133–36, 224
Becoming a good mentor, 73–76
Benefits of mentors, 5–12, 15
Business, mentoring in, 6

Career advancement, 87
Characteristics of a mentoring relationship, 26–28
Chronicle of Higher Education, 191
Comadres, 167
Committee for Women in Psychology (CWP), 234–37
Community in Action for Community Level Change, 113

Community in Action Neighborhood and Opportunity Bill, 186
Creativity, 205; creative teaching, 204; creativity and intuition, 217, 276
Critical thinking, 213–15, 276; vs. "one-size-fits-all," 213–15
Cross-cultural and cross-ethnic mentoring, 212–13
Cultural assertiveness, 164–65, familismo, 164; personalismo, 164; verguenza, 164–65
Cultural consciousness, 166, 168
C-Webb, 118

Devaluation of women's performance, 177
Difficulties in finding mentors, 10–11, 15
Divide-and-conquer dynamics, 168

Eastern Psychological Association, 193, 204
Effective mentoring in STEM, 52–55
Engineering, mentoring in. See STEM
Equal Opportunity and Affirmative Action Committee (EOAA), 202; talent bank, 202

Ethnic minorities: in psychology, 130; university enrollment, 129–30; U.S. population of, 129

Female praxis, 94–96
First National Community Action Youth Summit, 110, 113, 116–17, 122–24

Gendered ethnoracial socialization, 165
Generativity, 167

Information for mentors, 52–55, 56–59
Information for protégés, 55–56
In-group favoritism, 55
Imposter phenomenon, 67
Institutions as mentors, 28
Intersectionality, 89–92

Latina mentoring, strategies in, 166–67
Life-work integration, 86
Luminaria, 161–69

Madrina, 163–64, 169
Mathematics, mentoring in. *See* STEM
Mentor: "accidental," 191, 207–8; characteristics, 8–10; characteristics of an effective, 132–33, 138–39, 228–30; cohesiveness, 263–64; communicator credibility, 262; defined, 81, 189, 195; functions of, 131, 226–28, 257–58; gender politics, 84–85; Greek mythology, 81–82; hidden, 194; identity development and women of color, 176–77; importance of having, 208–9; importance of having women mentors, 209–11; and leadership and identity development, 175; mentors vs. tormentors, 203; parents as mentors, 141–44; social psychological models, 262–64; Telemachus, 81; women and men mentors of women mentees, 211–12; women mentors, risks for, 83–84
Mentoring: benefits of, 133, 231; best practices, 236–42, defined, 80, 110,

174; feminist restructuring, 92–94; for everywoman, 208; functions of, 275; good mentoring, 276–77; history of, 130; leadership, 253; negative incidents, 83, 177, 182, 199, 202; multiple with multicultural backgrounds, 276; network mentoring, 96–97; peer, 97–98; recipe for good mentoring, 208; responsibilities, 75–76; Socratic, 205; styles of alternative mentoring, 139–41; transactional versus transformational, 277; undergraduate women, 44, 46, 68–71; web-based, 99–100
"Mentoring Women and Persons of Color to Participate in APA," 193
Mentoring Women and People of Color for Leadership in Organized Psychology, 207
Mestizaje and *mulataje,* 163
Multiple mentors, 154
Multiple mentorship model, 49–50
Mythistories, 163

National policy initiatives, 45–48

The Odyssey, 46
Ozziddi Project, 112–15, 116, 118, 124

Pacific Asian American Women Bay Area Coalition (PAAWBAC), 156
Paul, Alice, 204
Personal reflections, 15–17, 73–76
Professional networks, 71
Promotoras, 167, 169
Psychocultural ancestry, 163
Psychology departments, mentoring in, 6–9

Racism and exclusion, subtle, 177–78; "outer edge of the inner circle," 178
Reaching Out to Others Together (ROOT), 113–14, 115, 124
Recommendations for Latinas seeking mentors, 168–69
Relationship between mentor and protégé, 55–56

Sciences, mentoring in. *See* STEM
Service learning: academic, 111; defined, 110–11, 113, 119; Venn model, 111
Sexual harassment, contrapower, 88–89
Skinner, B. F., 192
Social capital, 109
Social learning theory, 7
"Soul wounds," 165
Status of women as leaders, 174–75
STEM (Science, Technology, Engineering, Math), 175; mentoring in, 60–84
Stereotype threat, 179–80; patriarchal threats, 179–80
Strategic collaboration, 98–99; to improve women's identity and leadership opportunity, 180–81
Strategic promotion to institutionalize mentoring, 100–103
Styles of alternative mentoring: electronic, 140–41, 241–42; leadership institutes, 242–44, 255, 262; networking, 139–40, 240–41; peer mentoring, 140; positive

psychology, 141–43; self-mentoring, 238; speed mentoring, 240; team, 140

Technology, mentoring in. *See* STEM
Theobiology, 205
Title IX of the Education Amendments of 1972, 57
Traditional mentoring, 47–50
Transculturation, 163
Transformative mentoring, 56
Transpersonality, 164

Undergraduate mentoring: benefits of, 65–68; methods of, 68–71
Undergraduate mentors: availability of, 67–68; responsibilities of, 68

Women mentees, guidelines for; returning students and older women, 86
Women mentors, guidelines for, 216–17
Women of color, restrictions for, 89–92, 179
Womentoring and group mentoring, 96

About the Volume Editors and Series Editor

Note. All of the co-editors and the series editor are also chapter contributors.

CAROLE A. RAYBURN, PhD, M Div, is a clinical, research, and consulting psychologist in Silver Spring, Maryland. A graduate of American and George Washington universities, The Catholic University of America, and Andrews University Theological Seminary, Dr. Rayburn has presented her work in multifaceted areas of research nationally and internationally. She has 19 copyrighted inventories on clergy stress, state-trait morality, religiousness, spirituality, the relationship between work and religiousness/spirituality, peacefulness, traumatic experiences and health, well-being, body image and intimacy comfort, leadership, mentoring, life style choices, attitudes towards children, the creative personality, and intuition. She has proposed, with Dr. Lee Richmond, a theory and discipline — theobiology — the interface of theology, religion, and spirituality with all sciences. She was associate editor of the *Journal of Pastoral Counseling* and co-editor of the Series on Women, with Dr. Violet Franks, for Springer Publications. Dr. Rayburn has taught at Strayer College, the Johns Hopkins University, and Loyola College in Maryland. She has worked with adjudicated juvenile delinquents and also young children at several Montessori schools, serving also as forensic psychologist and expert witness in courts. Dr. Rayburn has done groundbreaking research in clergy and religious occupations stress, particularly regarding women in seminary and ecclesia. She is past president of the Baltimore (Maryland) Association of Consulting Psychologists, the Association of Practicing Psychologists of Montgomery and Prince Georges Counties (Maryland), the Maryland Psychological Association, the American Psychological

Association Division of the Psychology of Religion, and the Montgomery County (Maryland) National Organization for Women.

FLORENCE L. DENMARK, PhD, is an internationally recognized scholar, researcher, and policymaker and the Robert Scott Pace Distinguished Research Professor of Psychology at Pace University. She has received many awards, including the American Psychological Foundation Gold Medal for Lifetime Achievement in the Public Interest, the Ernest Hilgard Award for Career Contribution to General Psychology, the Raymond Fowler Award for Outstanding Service to APA, and the Elder Award from the 2009 Multicultural Conference. She wrote *Psychology of Women: Handbook of Issues and Theories, Engendering Psychology, and Women and Gender Revisited.*

MARY E. REUDER, PhD, is professor emerita of the City University of New York, Queens College, APA fellow of five divisions, past president simultaneously of the APA Division of the Psychology of Religion and of the APA Society for the Teaching of Psychology. She is the recipient of several mentoring awards. She has represented the APA Division of the Psychology of Religion on the APA Council of Representatives for over 20 years and has received numerous awards from that division and from the Divisions on General Psychology and International Psychology.

ASUNCION MITERIA AUSTRIA, PhD, is professor of psychology, chair and director of clinical training of the Graduate Program in Clinical Psychology at Cardinal Stritch University. As a fellow of the APA, she has served as president for the APA Division on Clinical Psychology's sections on the Clinical Psychology of Women and the Clinical Psychology of Ethnic Minorities. She has received numerous awards for mentoring, education, and outstanding contributions to the clinical psychology of women, including the 2006 award for Distinguished Leadership for Women in Psychology, the 2007 award for Distinguished Elder Psychologist, and the 2008 Charles and Shirley Thomas Award for student mentoring and development. She currently serves on the APA Council of Representatives and the Board for the Advancement of Psychology in Public Interest.

MICHELE A. PALUDI, PhD, is the series editor for women's psychology for Praeger. She is the author or editor of 33 college textbooks and more than 160 scholarly articles and conference presentations on sexual harassment, campus violence, psychology of women, gender, and sexual harassment and victimization. Her 1990 book, *Ivory Power: Sexual Harassment on Campus,* received the 1992 Myers Center Award for Outstanding Book on Human Rights in the United States. Paludi chaired the U.S. Department of

Education's Subpanel on the Prevention of Violence, Sexual Harassment, and Alcohol and Other Drug Problems in Higher Education. She was one of six scholars in the United States to be selected for this subpanel. She also was a consultant to and a member of former New York State Governor Mario Cuomo's Task Force on Sexual Harassment. Paludi serves as an expert witness for court proceedings and administrative hearings on sexual harassment. She has had extensive experience in conducting training programs and investigations of sexual harassment and other equal employment opportunity issues for businesses and educational institutions. In addition, Paludi has held faculty positions at Franklin & Marshall College, Kent State University, Hunter College, Union College, and Union Graduate College, where she directs the human resource management certificate program. She teaches in the School of Management.

About the Contributors

A. MARIE M. AUSTRIA, PhD, received both her master of arts and doctoral degrees in clinical child psychology from DePaul University in Chicago, where she was a Patricia Roberts Harris Fellow. She completed her clinical internship at the University of New Mexico School of Medicine, Department of Psychiatry, Division of Child and Adolescent Psychiatry in Albuquerque. She has recently relocated to the St. Louis area but had previously provided school-based psychological services that included assessment and consultation. She has taught courses in multicultural counseling, family therapy, and psychopathology at DePaul, the University of Wisconsin-Milwaukee, and Cardinal Stritch University in Milwaukee. She has made numerous presentations at the annual conventions of the American Psychological Association (APA) from her research involving the ethnic identity development of Filipinos and Filipino Americans. Her clinical interests include psychotherapy and assessment with traditionally underserved populations, including racially and ethnically diverse children, adolescents, and families from low-income backgrounds. She is also committed to community interventions and outreach.

BIANCA L. BERNSTEIN, PhD, is a professor of counseling psychology, educational leadership, and policy studies, and women and gender studies at Arizona State University (ASU) in Tempe. Her psychology degrees are from the University of California at Berkeley and the University of California at Santa Barbara. She has served as Director of the Division of Graduate Education at the National Science Foundation and Dean of the Graduate College at ASU and teaches courses on counseling women, clinical supervision, and grant strategy. Her over 200 publications and scholarly presentations have focused on the advancement of women and underrepresented minorities, graduate education reform, and clinical supervision. She has won a number of awards for her work on equity and inclusiveness. Dr. Bernstein's CareerWISE research program for building personal resilience and improving persistence among women in science and engineering PhD programs, is supported by the National Science Foundation.

JEAN LAU CHIN, EdD, ABPP, is professor and dean of the Derner Institute for Advanced Psychological Studies at Adelphi University in New York. Prior to her current position, she held executive management positions as Systemwide Dean of California School of Professional Psychology at Alliant International University, President, CEO Services; executive director, South Cove Community Health Center; and co-director, Thom Child Guidance Clinic. Dr. Chin is an educator, administrator, clinician, and scholar, and is licensed as a clinical psychologist. She has published extensively including 12 books and over 200 professional presentations in the areas of diversity and cultural competence, clinical training, Asian American and women's issues, health and mental health, and leadership. Her most recent books are *Diversity in Mind and in Action* and *Women and Leadership: Transforming Visions and Diverse Voices.* She has served in many leadership positions including many national and local boards. Current memberships include advisory committee for Women Services and Eliminating Mental Health Disparities Committee for Substance Abuse Mental Health Services Administration, U.S. Dept of Health and Human Services; president-elect of Division of Ethnic Minority Issues for the American Psychological Association; president of the National Council of Schools and Programs of Professional Psychology; advisory board of ERASE Racism; and board member of Nassau County Mental Health Association. She has received many awards and is a recent recipient of the Nassau County Executive's 2009 Women of Distinction Award.

JOAN CHRISLER, PhD, is professor of psychology at Connecticut College. She has published extensively on issues related to women's health and embodiment, especially on attitudes toward menstruation, premenstrual syndrome, body image, and weight. She has a long-standing interest in promoting women's professional development, and she has won the Florence Denmark Award for Distinguished Mentoring from the Association for Women in Psychology and the Distinguished Leader for Women in Psychology Award from the Committee on Women in Psychology of the American Psychological Association for her efforts in this regard. Her most recent books are *Women over 50: Psychological Perspectives* (2007), *From Menarche to Menopause: The Female Body in Feminist Therapy* (2004), and *Lectures on the Psychology of Women* (4th ed., 2008). She recently served as president of the

Society for the Psychology of Women and as editor of *Sex Roles: A Journal of Research.*

LILLIAN COMAS-DIAZ, PhD, is the executive director of the Transcultural Mental Health Institute, a clinical psychologist in private practice in Washington, DC, and a clinical professor at George Washington University School of Medicine. The former director of the American Psychological Association's Office of Ethnic Minority Affairs, Comas-Diaz also directed the Yale University Department of Psychiatry Hispanic Clinic. The author of over 100 publications, Comas-Diaz's writings focus on women's issues, culture, spirituality, ethnicity, social class, and creativity. She is the co-editor of the textbooks *Clinical Guidelines in Cross Cultural Mental Health; Women of Color: Integrating Ethnic and Gender Identities in Psychotherapy;* and *Woman-Soul: The Inner Life of Women's Spirituality.* She currently serves as an associate editor of *American Psychologist.*

JESSICA HENDERSON DANIEL, PhD, ABPP, is director of training in psychology in the Department of Psychiatry at Children's Hospital Boston. She is an associate professor in the Department of Psychiatry at Harvard Medical School. She is a past president of the Society for the Psychology of Women (Division 35), first African American woman to serve on the APA Board of Directors (2005–2007), and chaired the APA Centering on Mentoring Task Force (2006). She is the recipient of numerous mentoring awards. She is an APA fellow and holds the Diplomate of the American Board of Professional Psychology.

DARLENE DEFOUR, PhD, is a social psychologist/community psychologist. She is a graduate of Fisk University and received her doctorate from the University of Illinois at Urbana-Champaign. She is currently an associate professor of psychology at Hunter College of the City University of New York, where she teaches classes on social psychology, personal adjustment, psychology of women, theories of ethnic identity development, and issues in black psychology. DeFour has served on the Board of Directors of the National Association of Black Psychologists. She is also active in several divisions of the American Psychological Association.

AJEENAH HAYNES, PhD, is a senior survey analyst at Child Trends. She is a recent graduate of Howard University, where her concentration area was medical sociology. Her research interests are the psychosocial determinants of health outcomes. Her dissertation work examined time discounting, market, and sociocultural factors associated with obesity among four U.S. Hispanic populations. Haynes is currently assisting with several projects at

Child Trends, including research examining relationships and birth control use among community college students; barriers and motivators to family planning service use among teen and young adult Latinas; and knowledge and understanding of natural family planning among young adult Latina and African American women. Haynes has administered health behavior–based studies using experiment-control research design methods and has assisted with the African American Women as We Age project, where her research efforts and findings were used toward the final manuscript, "African American Women as We Age," published by the National Council of Negro Women. She is a member of the American Sociological Association and the Association for Institutional Researchers.

SUSAN J. HOUSTON has had a long career in association administration. For over 25 years, she has managed programs in continuing professional education, women's programs, public interest issues, and association governance initiatives. From 1987 to 1996 she worked in the American Psychological Association's (APA) Continuing Education Program (CE), initially coordinating the development and implementation of CE offerings, moving on to direct the Sponsor Approval System, through which organizations offering CE credit for psychologists become approved by APA. She also worked as the director of Program Implementation in the continuing education program of the American Society of Health System Pharmacists. Seeking to broaden her experience and pursue her interest in working to address issues affecting underserved populations, Ms. Houston served as APA Women's Programs Officer then as staff liaison to the APA Board for the Advancement of Psychology in the Public Interest and Director of Governance for the Public Interest Directorate.

RYAN P. JACOBSON, MA, is a graduate student in the social psychology program at Arizona State University, Tempe. His dissertation research focuses on the role of culture in normative social influence.

GWENDOLYN PURYEAR KEITA, PhD, is the executive director of the Public Interest Directorate of the American Psychological Association. She oversees the achievement and implementation of the public interest mission to apply the science and practice of psychology to the fundamental problems of health, human welfare, and social justice and the promotion of equitable and just treatment of all segments of society through education, training, public policy, and public information. She directs and oversees public interest initiatives to address critical issues affecting human welfare such as HIV/AIDS; end-of-life issues; socioeconomic status; violence prevention; and work, health, and stress-related issues. She directs and oversees initiatives to address discrimination and other inequities for children;

women; ethnic minorities; lesbian, gay, bisexual, and transgender people; older adults; persons with disabilities; and members of other underrepresented and underserved groups. She has coauthored several books and journal articles and has presented extensively on women's issues (women's health in particular) and work, stress, and health. She has convened three conferences on psychosocial and behavioral factors in women's health and is co-editor of *Health Care and Women: Psychosocial, Social, and Behavioral Influences* (1997). Keita is also co-editor of *Women and Depression: Risk Factors and Treatment Issues* (1990) and *Understanding Depression in Women: Applying Empirical Research to Practice and Policy* (2006), a publication resulting from the 2000 Summit on Women and Depression. Keita was instrumental in developing the new field of occupational health psychology, has convened seven international conferences on occupational stress and health, and co-authored several books and journal articles on the subject. Keita has presented before Congress on depression, violence, and other issues.

MARIA D. KLARA, PhD, is completing her doctoral degree at Pace University. She served as a graduate assistant to Florence Denmark. Before coming to Pace, she received a BA from Boston College and an MS degree in counseling psychology from Northeastern University. After receiving her MS and before coming to Pace, she worked for two years in a short-term residential facility with children and their families.

KATHARINE LOEB, PhD, is an associate professor of Psychology at Fairleigh Dickinson University. She is also the director of research at the Mount Sinai Eating and Weight Disorders Program, and adjunct associate professor of Psychiatry at the Mount Sinai School of Medicine. Dr. Loeb received her PhD from Rutgers University and completed her internship at the University of Medicine and Dentistry of New Jersey. She was awarded an National Institute of Mental Health (NIMH) Research Fellowship at Columbia University's College of Physicians and Surgeons. Dr. Loeb has conducted extensive research in the areas of treatment for anorexia nervosa, bulimia nervosa, and binge eating, in addition to her work on pediatric overweight, cognitive-behavioral therapy and family-based interventions. Dr. Loeb has co-authored many publications and presentations on eating disorders, has received several grants for her research, and has served as the co-chair of the *Eating Disorders Workgroup for the Diagnostic and Statistical Manual of Mental Disorders, Fourth Edition, Text Revision (DSM-IV-TR).*

JENNIFER MARTIN, PhD, is the department head of English at a public alternative high school for at-risk students in Michigan and holds a PhD in education. She created an intervention strategy to reduce the high rate of peer sexual harassment that was occurring within the school; this became her dissertation research. Currently she is the Title IX Education Task Force Chair for the Michigan National Organization for Women. Martin serves as a mentor to adolescent girls in the alternative high school, and she has started a successful women's studies program, where students are involved in service learning projects and have partnered with a domestic violence and sexual assault nonprofit organization. She is also an advocate for at-risk students in general. In addition to high school teaching, Martin is a lecturer at Oakland University, where she teaches courses in graduate research methods in education and feminist methods and introduction to women and gender studies in the Department of Women and Gender Studies. Her research interests include peer sexual harassment, feminist identification, teaching for social justice, service learning, and the at-risk student.

SHARI E. MILES-COHEN, PhD, is the senior director of the Women's Programs Office (WPO) at the American Psychological Association. The WPO works to improve the status, health, and well-being of women psychologists and consumers of psychological services. In her role as senior director, Miles-Cohen staffs the Committee on Women in Psychology and related task forces and working groups; serves as an information and referral resource on women's issues; and develops and disseminates reports, pamphlets, and other materials addressing research, practice, and consumer concerns relevant to women's lives. Prior to her service at WPO, Miles-Cohen was executive director for the Society for the Psychological Study of Social Issues, an international group of behavioral and social scientists with a historic legacy. It was the "arranger and stimulator" of *The effects of segregation and the consequences of desegregation: A social science statement,* which was appended to *Brown v. Board of Education.* This statement marked the first time that psychological research was cited in a Supreme Court decision, because the data were seen as paramount to the Court's decision to end school segregation. Miles-Cohen has also served as director of the Union Institute Center for Women, the African American Women's Institute at Howard University, and the Women's Research & Education Institute (WREI). Her work has taken her throughout the United States, to China, South Africa, Europe, the newly independent states of the former Soviet Union, East Europe, and the Caribbean to promote the interface between research and policy related to women's issues. As a community activist, she directed a crisis intervention service for women and assisted homeless women transition to independent living. She served as a WREI Congressional Fellow for U.S. Representative Ronald V. Dellums, where she worked on women's issues, health care, and education. She has maintained her commitment to leadership development by serving as a mentor to girls and women from various cultural, academic, and professional backgrounds. She is a member of the boards of the National

Council for Research on Women and the African American Women's Resource Center and serves as an advisor to the mayor of Washington, DC, as a member of the DC Commission for Women. In addition, she is a member of the American Psychological Association; the Society for the Psychology of Women and its sections on Black Women, Latinas/Hispanic Women, and Lesbian and Bisexual Women's Issues; the Society for Ethnic Minority and Cultural Psychology; the Association of Black Psychologists; the Society for Psychologists in Management; and the Washington Area Women's Foundation Washington 100.

GERMON MILLER, PhD, has served as a crisis educator and a juvenile crew arbitrator for 30 years, beginning in Philadelphia, Pennsylvania. Despite being a domestic survivor, she was able to complete her academic degrees to include a BS in biology from the University of Pennsylvania, a BA/MA from Antioch University, and a doctorate in behavioral sciences from the University International Studies (Frankfurt, Germany) while teaching for Department of Defense Dependent Schools. On her return to the United States in 1991, she increased her participation in youth antiviolence programs by establishing the AKERU Discipline Sciences Program to assist juveniles whose lifestyles were beyond the scope of standard classrooms. Her "sidewalk university" concept was designed to eliminate the stigma associated with teens from poverty environments. She then established an intern program where human/social service students could personally interact with active youth gang/crew members and glean knowledge that is not documented in periodicals. Her pseudonym is Mama G (Mama Gangsta), and she is recognizable for her "edutainment" motivational presentations and her personal achievement of becoming a 10th-degree grandmaster in the martial arts, having accumulated over 1,900 trophies, 2 gold medals, and 4 world titles after the age of 25. Her belief is based on the Afrikan tradition of *gyneme* (fear nothing except the Creator) and her motto from comedienne Moms Mabley, "If you always do what you always done, you always get what you always got!" To date, the AKERU has been presented to over 40,000 youth on the topics of antiviolence, HIV awareness, domestic abuse, incarceration, homelessness, and single parenting. She has organized youth summits internationally and has served as a Student Pledge against Gun Violence representative for six years. Her journals were published in November 2008 under the title of *A Journey of Self-Preservation — The Legacy of Akeru!*

ARVILLA PAYNE-JACKSON, PhD, is a professor at Howard University. She received her doctorate from the University of Pennsylvania. Her primary areas of research are in the fields of medical anthropology, sociolinguistics, ethnographic evaluation, and service learning. She has conducted fieldwork in the United States, the Caribbean, Latin America, and Africa. Payne-Jackson has published several books and monographs on ethnomedicine and numerous articles on service learning. Among them are "Fostering Social Capital and Community Capacity for Change: Strategies and Impacts of Two Service Learning Teams" (with Linda Camino) in *The Bridge* (2005); "Evaluation as a Form of Experiential Learning at Howard University" (with Rodney Green) in *Community Works Journal: A Resource Journal of Learning Experiences that Build Community* (2005); "A Model of Service Learning" (with Ajeenah Haynes) in *Proceedings of the Twelfth International Literacy Conference on Learning* (2005); and "Graffiti as a Sense of Place: Lorton Prison, Virginia" (with Jonathan Hayden) in *Reflections* (2004). She has also done ethnographic evaluation and consulting for federal agencies, community, and nonprofit organizations, including the White House Office of National Drug Control Policy; the Center for Substance Abuse; the U.S. Department of Health and Human Services RARE HIV/AIDS Crises Response Team, Early Head Start, Washington, DC; Innovation Center/4H — Youth-Adult Service Learning Projects; Marshall Heights Community Development Organization, Fighting Back Initiative; the Center for Social Responsibility and Community, State University of New York at Oneonta; the Academy for Educational Development; and the Jamaica Blue Cross.

HELEN D. PRATT, PhD, is the director of behavioral and developmental pediatrics in the pediatrics program at Michigan State University/Kalamazoo Center for Medical Studies. She holds two academic appointments: professor of pediatrics and human development at Michigan State University (Kalamazoo campus) and adjunct professor of psychology at Western Michigan University in Kalamazoo. Pratt has published 43 articles in peer-reviewed journals (authored 7 and coauthored 36 articles). She has authored 5 and coauthored 10 book chapters and has co-edited 6 books and 5 special journal issues. Her research interests include research and management of human aggression as related to children, adolescents, and women. Helen chose to implement a systematic approach to entering and thriving in academia. She and her colleagues formed a support group where they developed strategies for becoming tenured full professors and shared their expertise. Helen remains active clinically and in her community while mentoring others to help them attain their doctoral degrees, licensure, academic appointments, and matriculate through the professorate while developing professionally.

JENNIFER GORMAN ROSE, MA, has had a full-time teaching position as a senior lecturer in psychology at Connecticut College since 1999. She teaches applied research methods and the laboratories for introductory psychology courses. She is currently a faculty co-advisor of the Connecticut College chapter of Psi Chi, the national honor society in psychology;

she is a co-chair of the researchers' caucus in the Association for Women In Psychology (AWP); she is a member of the Society for Menstrual Cycle Research; and she recently completed a term as the professional affiliate representative for division 35 in the American Psychological Association. She also co-facilitates a feminist psychology research group with Joan C. Chrisler in which they meet with undergraduate and graduate students on a weekly basis to discuss individual and group research projects. Her areas of expertise include research on women's reproductive health, attitudes toward women, gender roles, and eating disorders.

NANCY FELIPE RUSSO, PhD, is a Regents Professor of Psychology and Women and Gender Studies at Arizona State University, Tempe, where she has served as the leader of the HerStories component of the National Science Foundation-funded CareerWISE research program designed to improve persistence among women in science and engineering PhD programs. Russo is author or editor of more than 200 publications related to the psychology of women and women's issues. She is a Fellow of the New York Academy of Sciences, the American Psychological Association, and the American Psychological Society. Most recently she was awarded the Denmark-Gunvald Award for significant contributions to the psychology of women and gender by the International Council of Psychologists. She has also received the American Psychological Association's Award for Distinguished Contributions to Psychology in the Public Interest.

KATHLEEN SCOTT, BSc, is a graduate student in the Department of Sociology and Anthropology at Howard University. She completed her undergraduate studies in social work at the University of Guyana. She was coco-ordinator with Arvilla Payne-Jackson of the First National Community in Action Youth Summit held in November 2007 at Howard University. Her area of expertise is women and children who live in difficult circumstances. Her current research focus is on women who are victims of the criminal justice system. The title of her research thesis is *Women and Crime: The Relationship between Selected Social and Demographic Factors and Female Crime in the United States from 1985 to 1997.*

JANET SIGAL, PhD, is a professor of psychology at Fairleigh Dickinson University. She received her PhD in social psychology from Northwestern University. She teaches courses in social and experimental psychology, and social and cultural issues in clinical psychology. Dr. Sigal has numerous presentations at national and regional conferences and has several publications and chapters in many books. Her research interests include cross-cultural perceptions of sexual harassment and domestic violence. Dr. Sigal is a fellow of divisions 35 and 52 of the American Psychological Association (APA). She is the chair of the Membership Committee of Division 52, and is currently the co-chair of the Program Committee for 52 for the APA 2010 Convention. In 2006, Dr. Sigal was selected as a member of the APA UN NGO team. She is the co-chair of the NGO Committee on the Family, and the Vice Chair of the NGO UNICEF Committee Working Group on Violence Against Children.

TINA STERN, PhD, grew up in Cleveland, Ohio, and has lived in Atlanta, Georgia, since 1987. She earned her undergraduate degree from Boston University, her master's degree from Cleveland State University, and her PhD from the University of Georgia. She is a professor of psychology at Georgia Perimeter College, where for many years she has taught courses on the psychology of women. In addition, as a licensed psychologist, Stern maintains a clinical practice specializing in women's issues. Since her days at Boston University, she has been interested in and has written about issues related to women and, in particular, the psychology of women.

BONNIE R. STRICKLAND, PhD, is professor emeritus of psychology at the University of Massachusetts. She received her PhD from The Ohio State University in 1962. She has been a professor for all of her professional career and is the editor or author of over a hundred books, book chapters, and research articles. A Diplomate in Psychology, she has also maintained a small, independent practice. She has held a number of offices in the American Psychological Association, including being president in 1987.

REIKO HOMMA-TRUE, PhD, has mentored many Asian American women throughout her career as a teacher, clinician, and community advocate. During 1997–1999, she served as president of Asian American Psychological Association, where she created mentoring initiatives to assist Asian American women students, academicians, and professionals. She was the first woman and a minority to be appointed as the deputy director of public health in San Francisco, overseeing a large mental health, substance abuse, and forensic medical and psychiatric service system from 1985 through 1996. She pioneered the development of culturally and linguistically responsive services to diverse populations in California and other regions. At the time of the 1989 Loma Prieta Earthquake in the San Francisco region, she organized a citywide disaster mental health assistance initiative. After the Kobe region in Japan was devastated in 1995 by a large-scale earthquake, she obtained a Fulbright Senior Fellowship to help train mental health professionals and organize disaster mental health assistance in Japan. She now oversees a clinical psychology master's program in Tokyo for California School of

Professional Psychology, Alliant International University, and maintains a private consulting practice in San Francisco and in Japan.

GABRIEL H. J. TWOSE is a former employee of and current intern at the American Psychological Association's Women's Programs Office, where he has worked on topics such as mentoring, the sexualization of girls, and post-partum depression. Additionally, he is a graduate student at Clark University, currently pursuing his doctorate in social psychology. His research interests revolve around the psychological aspects of postconflict reconciliation, particularly as related to the efficacy of truth-telling mechanisms.

MELBA J. T. VASQUEZ, PhD, ABPP, is a psychologist in independent practice in Austin, Texas. She publishes widely about ethics, multicultural ethics in psychotherapy, psychology of women, and supervision. She is the first Latina to serve on the APA Board of Directors (2007–2009) and is a past president of the Texas Psychological Association and of APA Divisions 35 (Society of Psychology of Women) and 17 (Society of Counseling Psychology). She is coauthor with Ken Pope of *Ethics in Psychotherapy & Counseling: A Practical Guide* (2007, 3rd edition). She is a Fellow of APA, holds the Diplomate of the American Board of Professional Psychology, and has received numerous awards, including for mentoring service.

JUDITH WATERS, PhD, LPC, is professor and acting director of the master of arts program in counseling at Fairleigh Dickinson University in Madison, New Jersey. Her current research focuses on the issues of occupational stress (e.g., law enforcement) and substance abuse and addictions. Two of her mentors are major contributors to this book: Florence L. Denmark and Mary Reuder. Waters attended City College and completed her undergraduate education at Queens College, where she was fortunate enough to have Mary Reuder for experimental psychology. Reuder guided her undergraduate career until she won a National Institute of Mental Health Predoctoral Fellowship and a New York State Regents Predoctoral Fellowship that enabled her to earn a doctoral degree in social/personality psychology at the Graduate Center of the City University of New York. Among her mentors at the Graduate Center were the late Stanley Milgram, the late Harold M. Proshansky, the late Bernard Seidenberg, and the late Barbara Dohrenwend. Her dissertation sponsor was Florence L. Denmark. Her first teaching experience was at Brooklyn College, once home to Abraham Maslow and Philip Zimbardo. At Fairleigh Dickinson University, she publishes with her students, an important tradition that was handed down to her by Reuder and Denmark.